SATURDAY AM

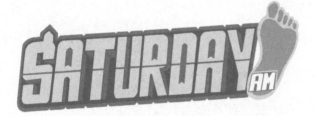

PRESENTS...

SAIGAMI

VOLUME 1

(RE)BIRTH BY FLAME

STORY AND ART BY Seny

ROCKPORT

CONTENTS

SAIGAMI

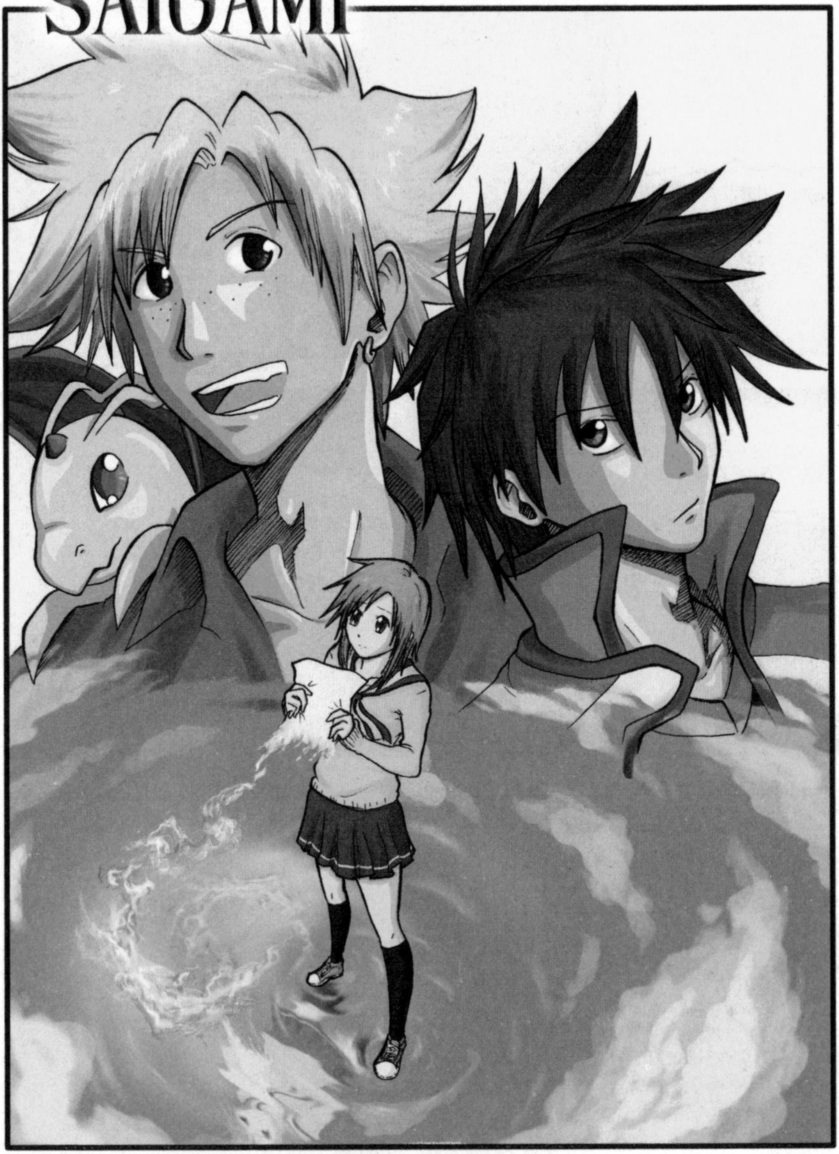

Chapter 1: It All Began with a Letter

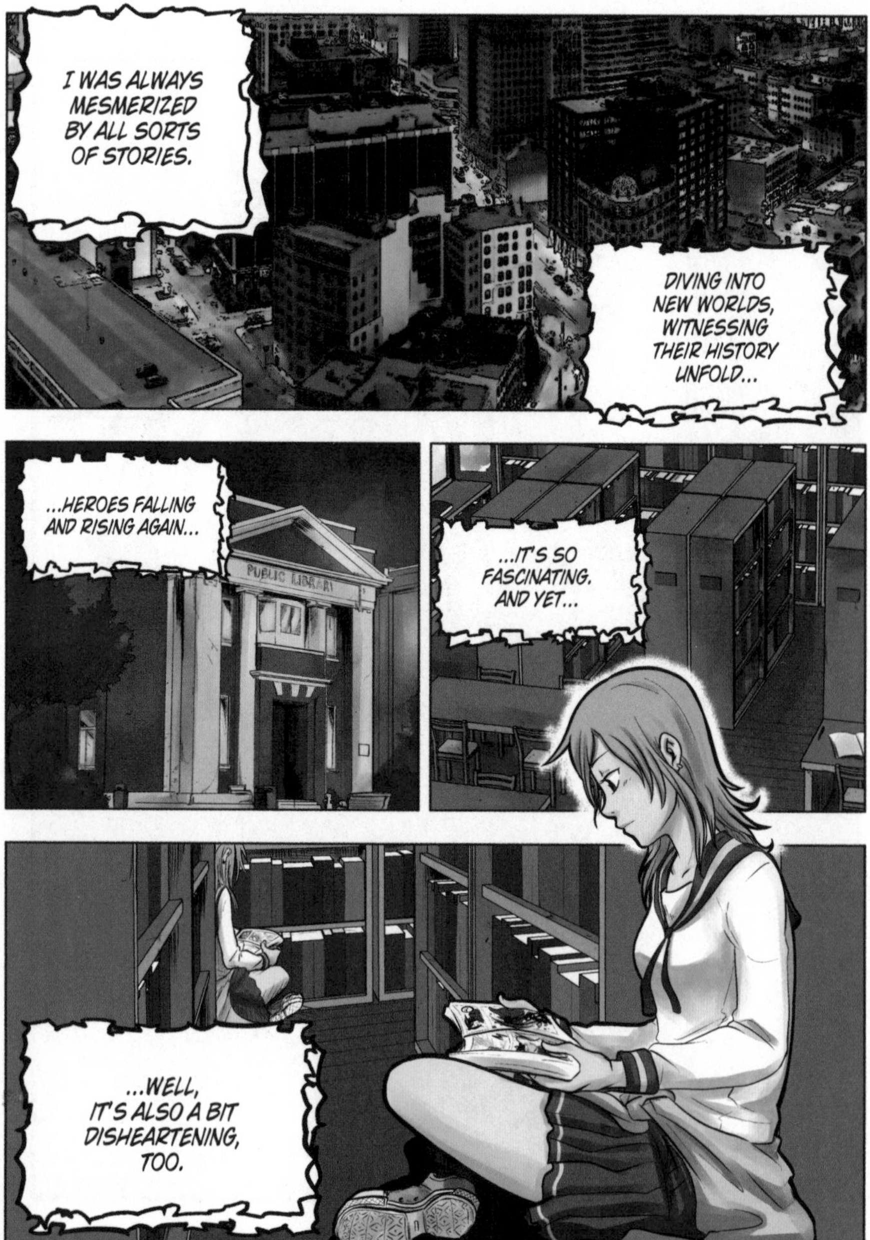
I WAS ALWAYS MESMERIZED BY ALL SORTS OF STORIES.
DIVING INTO NEW WORLDS, WITNESSING THEIR HISTORY UNFOLD...
...HEROES FALLING AND RISING AGAIN...
PUBLIC LIBRARY
...IT'S SO FASCINATING. AND YET...
...WELL, IT'S ALSO A BIT DISHEARTENING, TOO.

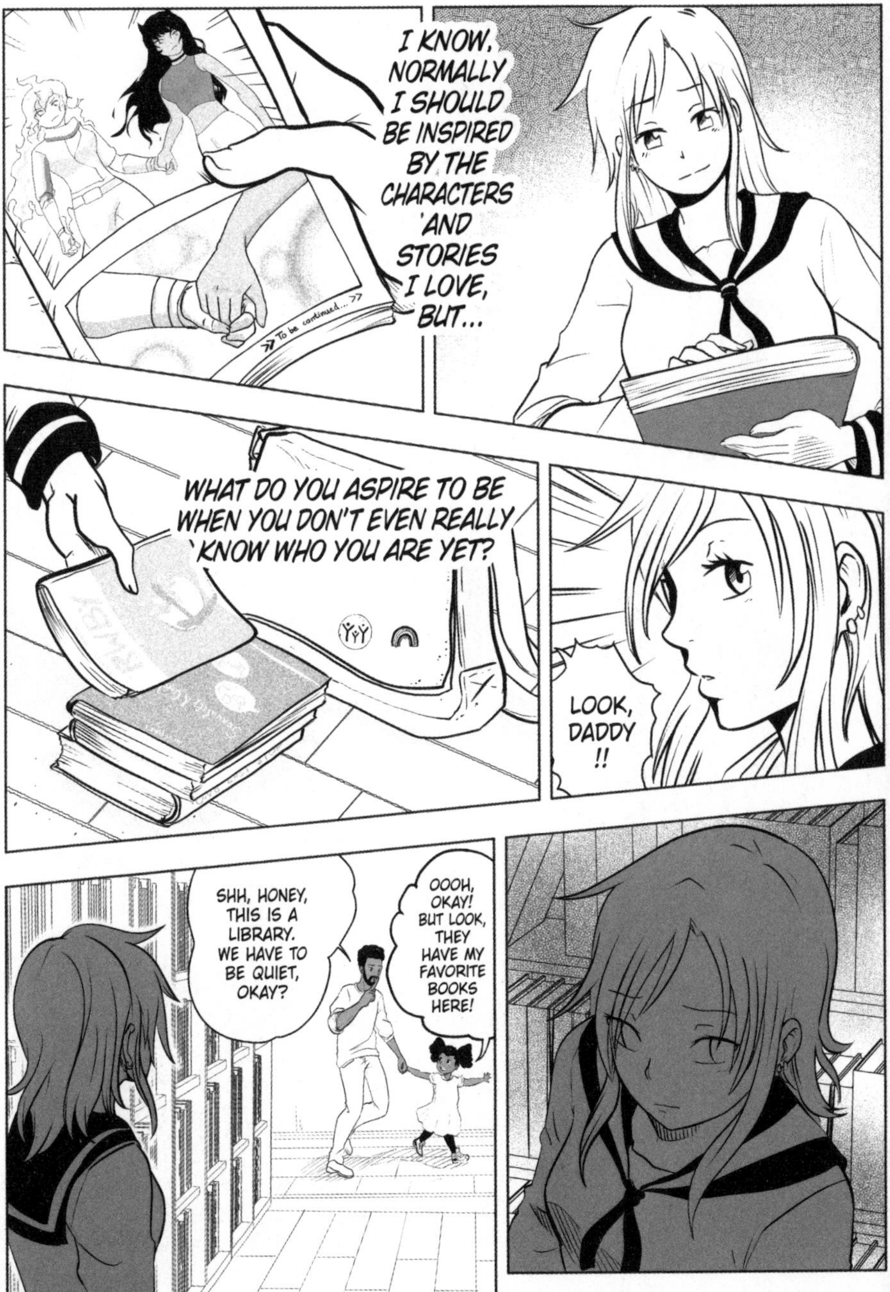
To be continued...
I KNOW, NORMALLY I SHOULD BE INSPIRED BY THE CHARACTERS AND STORIES I LOVE, BUT...
WHAT DO YOU ASPIRE TO BE WHEN YOU DON'T EVEN REALLY KNOW WHO YOU ARE YET?
LOOK, DADDY !!
SHH, HONEY, THIS IS A LIBRARY. WE HAVE TO BE QUIET, OKAY?
OOOH, OKAY! BUT LOOK, THEY HAVE MY FAVORITE BOOKS HERE!

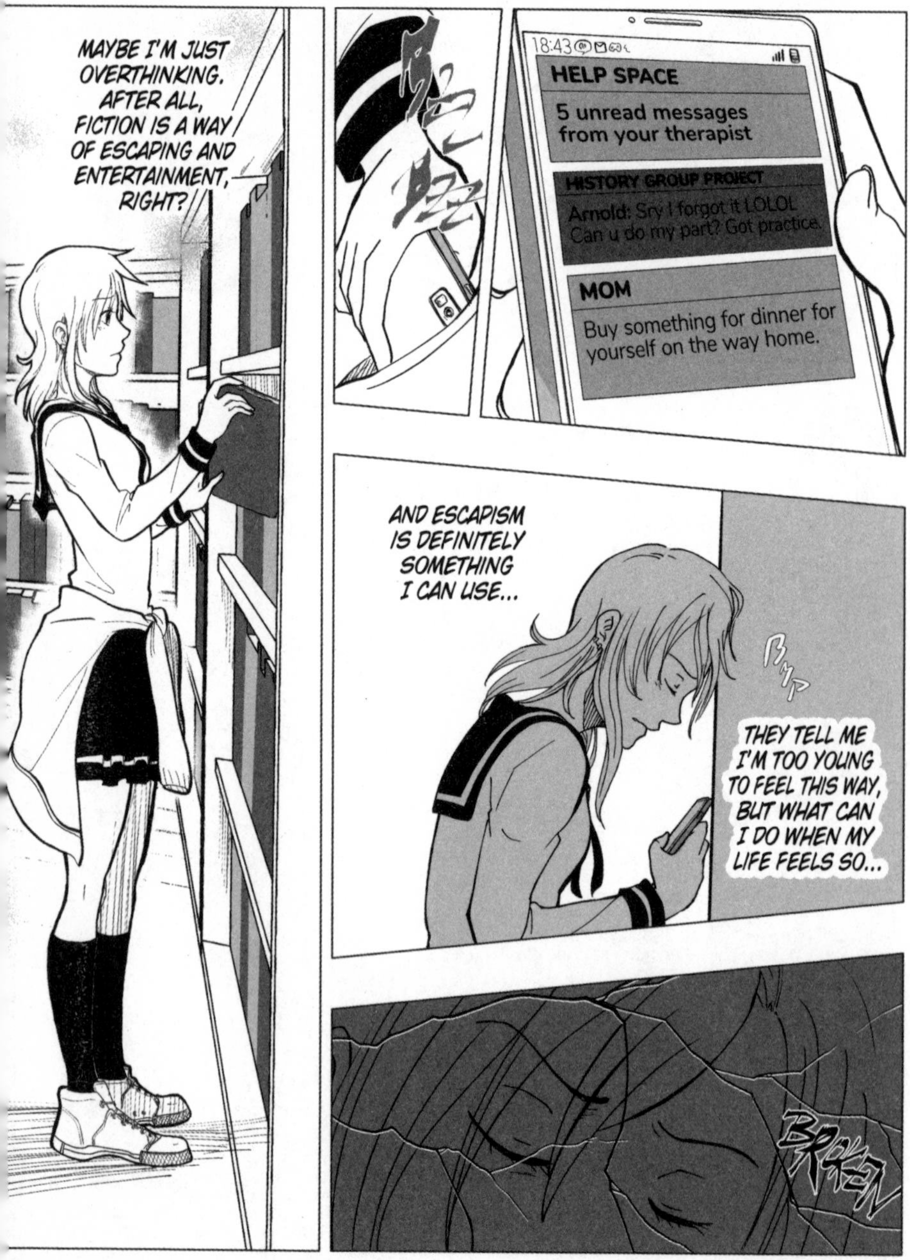
MAYBE I'M JUST OVERTHINKING. AFTER ALL, FICTION IS A WAY OF ESCAPING AND ENTERTAINMENT, RIGHT?
18:43
HELP SPACE
5 unread messages from your therapist
HISTORY GROUP PROJECT
Arnold: Sry I forgot it LOLOL Can u do my part? Got practice.
MOM
Buy something for dinner for yourself on the way home.
AND ESCAPISM IS DEFINITELY SOMETHING I CAN USE...
THEY TELL ME I'M TOO YOUNG TO FEEL THIS WAY, BUT WHAT CAN I DO WHEN MY LIFE FEELS SO...
BROKEN

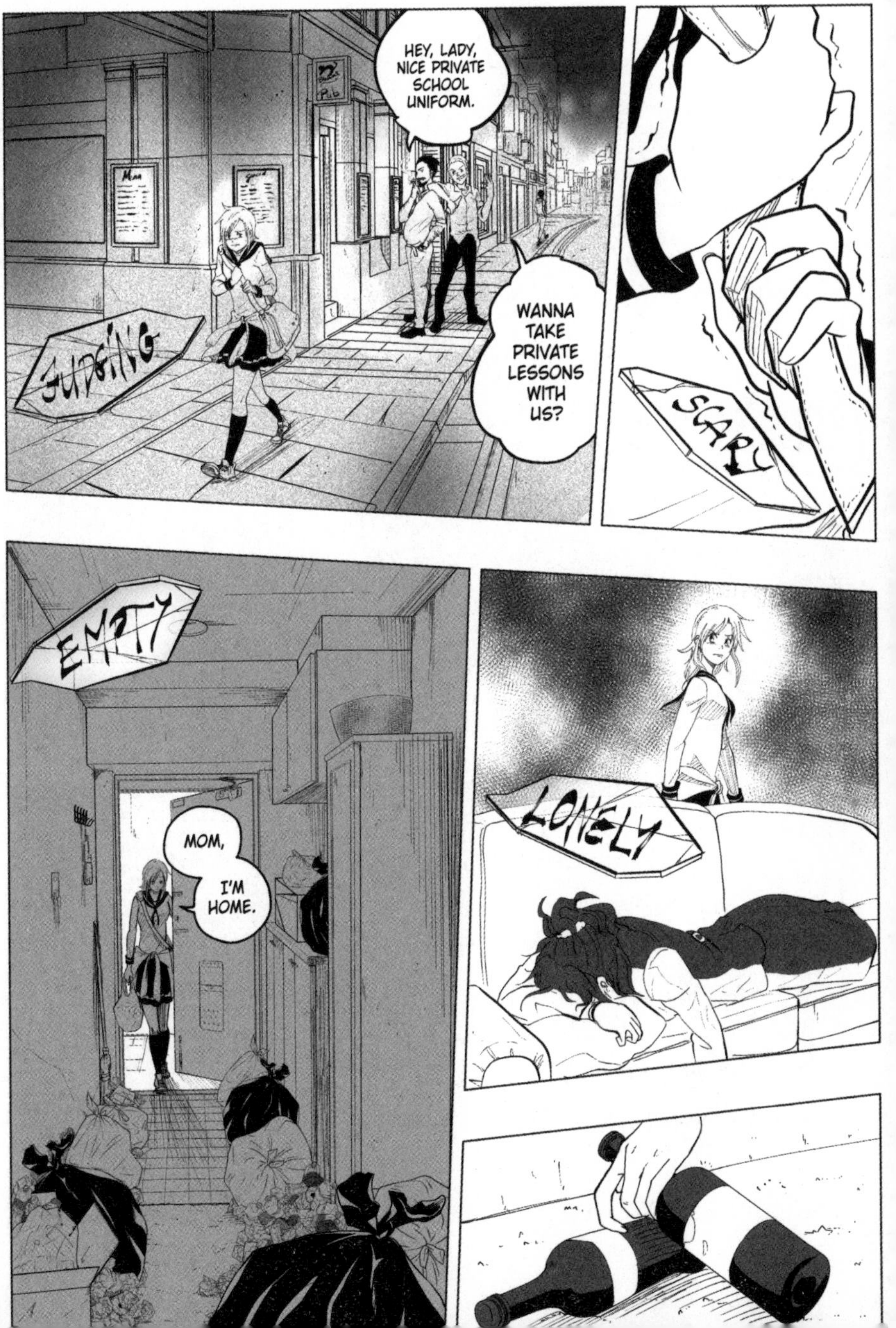
HEY, LADY, NICE PRIVATE SCHOOL UNIFORM.
WANNA TAKE PRIVATE LESSONS WITH US?
JUDGING
SCARY
EMPTY
MOM,
I'M HOME.
LONELY

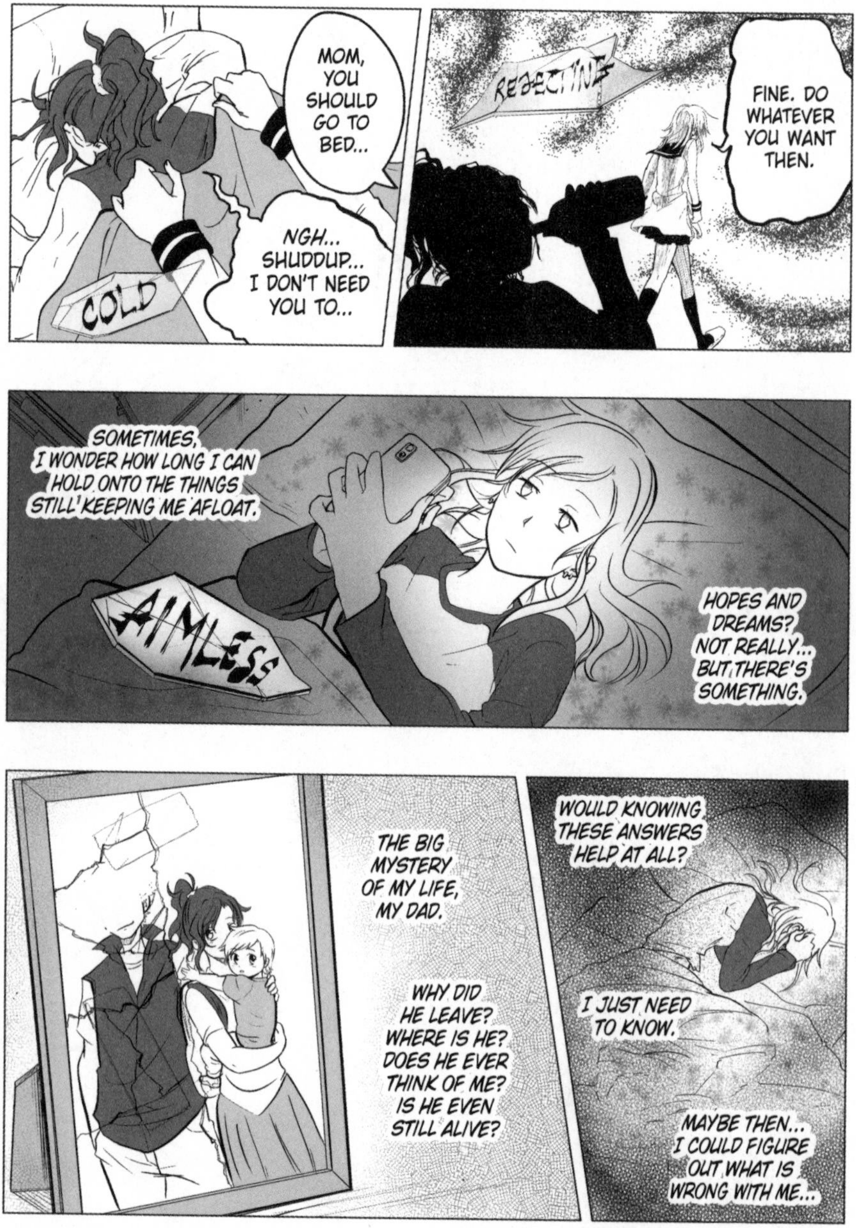
MOM, YOU SHOULD GO TO BED...
NGH... SHUDDUP... I DON'T NEED YOU TO...
COLD
REJECTING
FINE. DO WHATEVER YOU WANT THEN.
SOMETIMES, I WONDER HOW LONG I CAN HOLD ONTO THE THINGS STILL KEEPING ME AFLOAT.
AIMLESS
HOPES AND DREAMS? NOT REALLY... BUT THERE'S SOMETHING.
THE BIG MYSTERY OF MY LIFE, MY DAD.
WHY DID HE LEAVE? WHERE IS HE? DOES HE EVER THINK OF ME? IS HE EVEN STILL ALIVE?
WOULD KNOWING THESE ANSWERS HELP AT ALL?
I JUST NEED TO KNOW.
MAYBE THEN... I COULD FIGURE OUT WHAT IS WRONG WITH ME...

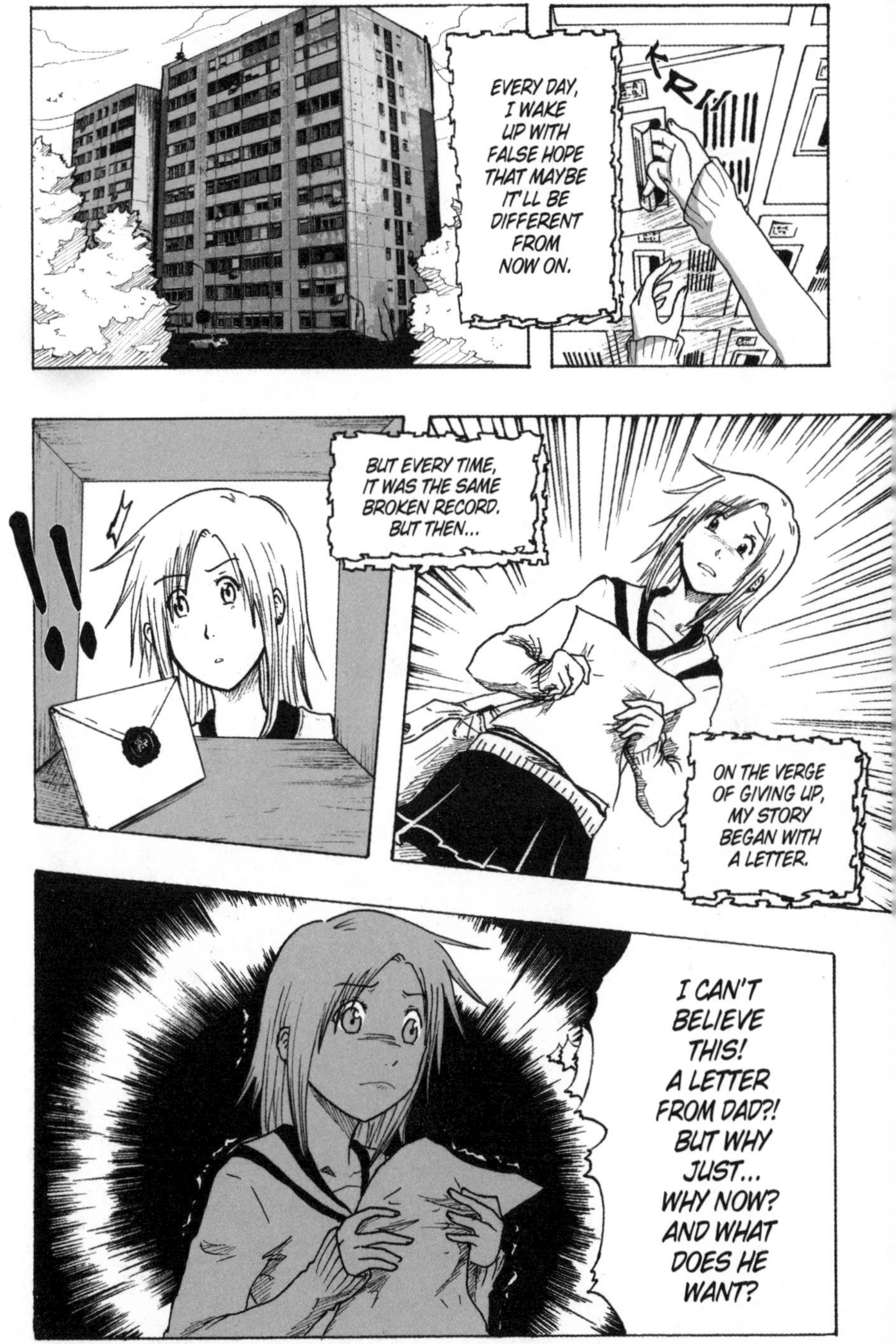
EVERY DAY, I WAKE UP WITH FALSE HOPE THAT MAYBE IT'LL BE DIFFERENT FROM NOW ON.
!!
BUT EVERY TIME, IT WAS THE SAME BROKEN RECORD. BUT THEN...
ON THE VERGE OF GIVING UP, MY STORY BEGAN WITH A LETTER.
I CAN'T BELIEVE THIS! A LETTER FROM DAD?! BUT WHY JUST... WHY NOW? AND WHAT DOES HE WANT?

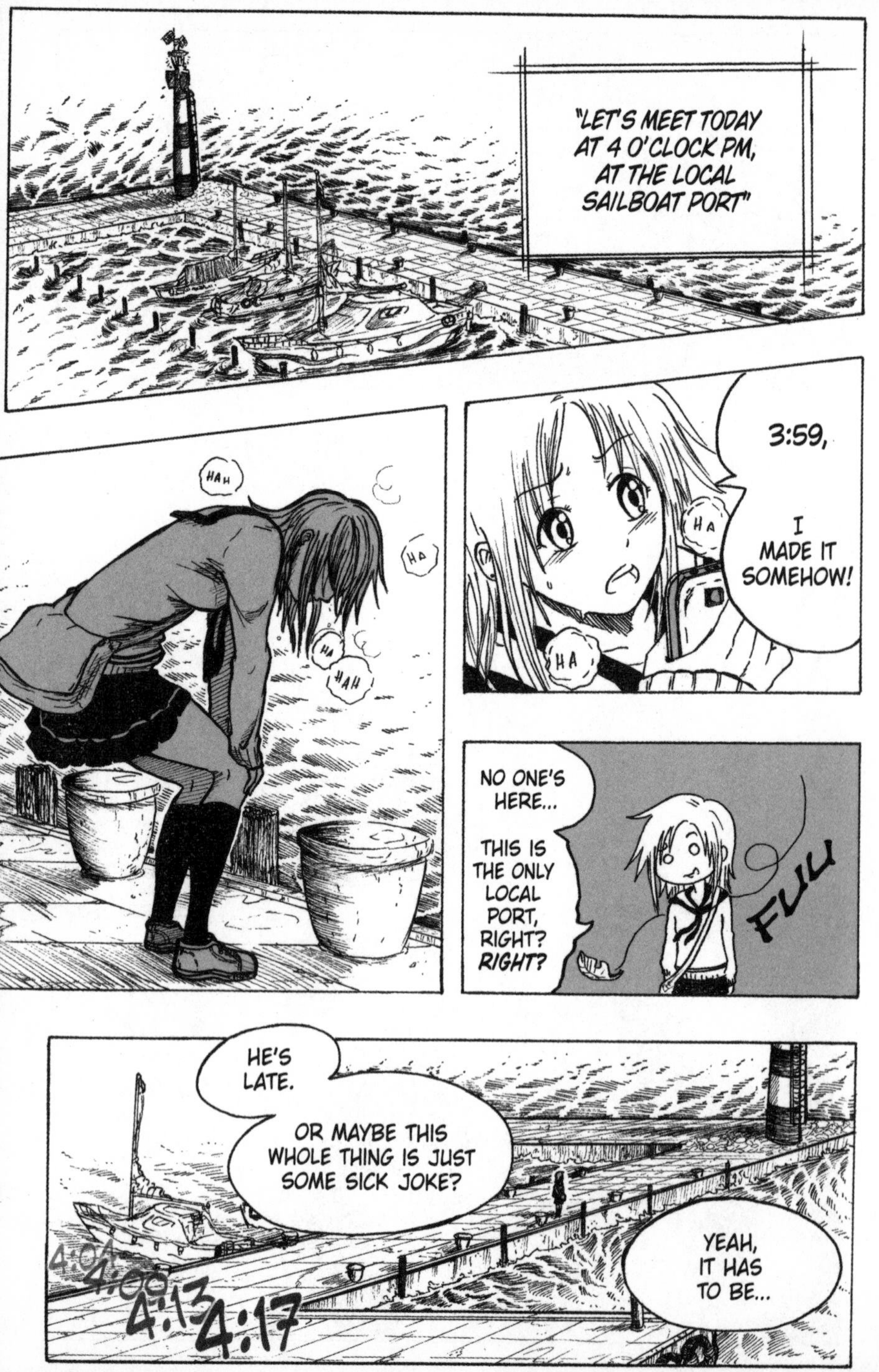

"LET'S MEET TODAY AT 4 O'CLOCK PM, AT THE LOCAL SAILBOAT PORT"
HAH
HA
HA
HAH
3:59,
I MADE IT SOMEHOW!
HA
HA
NO ONE'S HERE...
THIS IS THE ONLY LOCAL PORT, RIGHT? *RIGHT?*
FUU
HE'S LATE.
OR MAYBE THIS WHOLE THING IS JUST SOME SICK JOKE?
4:04
4:09
4:13
4:17
YEAH, IT HAS TO BE...

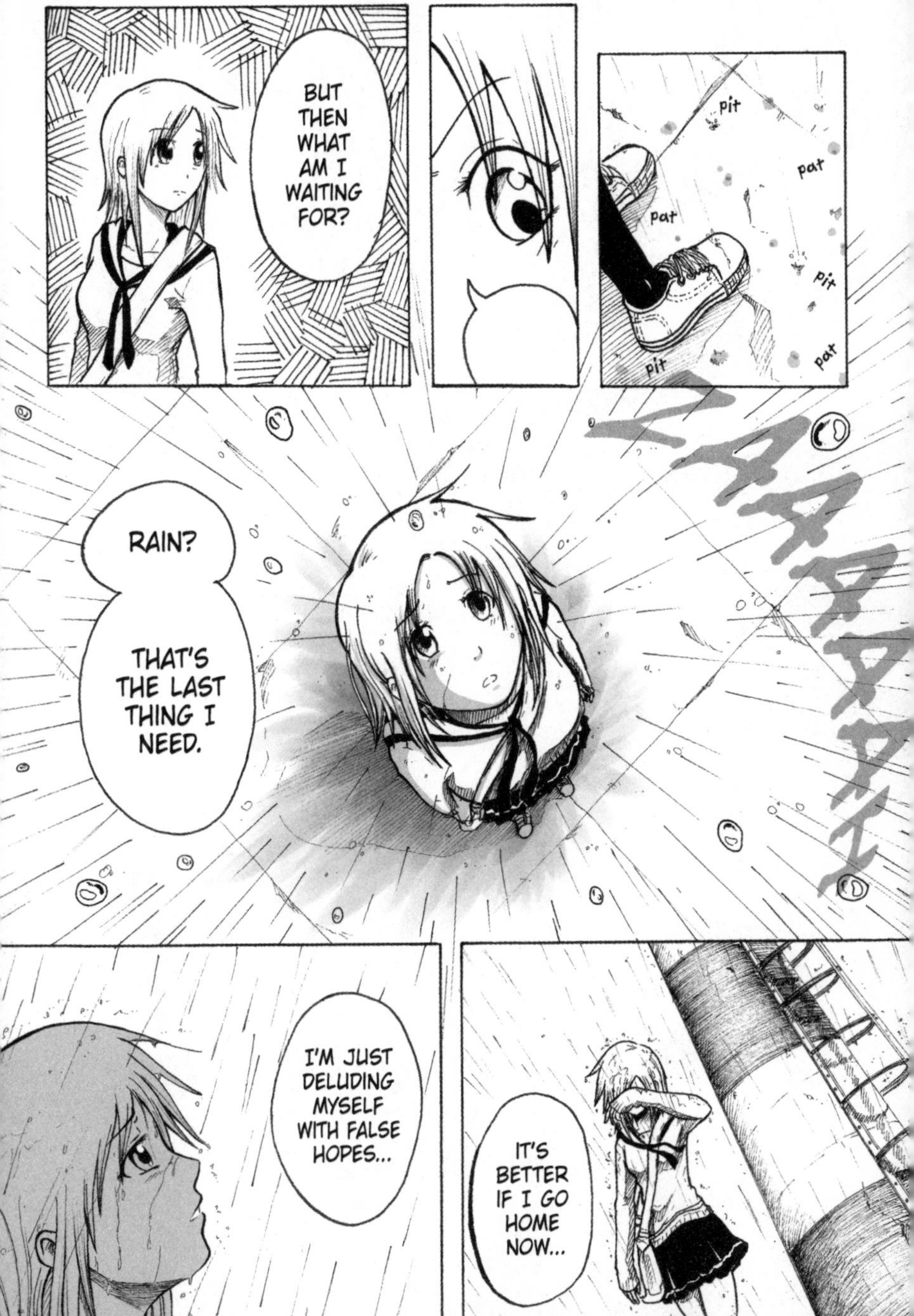
BUT THEN WHAT AM I WAITING FOR?
pit
pat
pat
pit
pit
pat
RAIN?
THAT'S THE LAST THING I NEED.
ZAAAAA
I'M JUST DELUDING MYSELF WITH FALSE HOPES...
IT'S BETTER IF I GO HOME NOW...

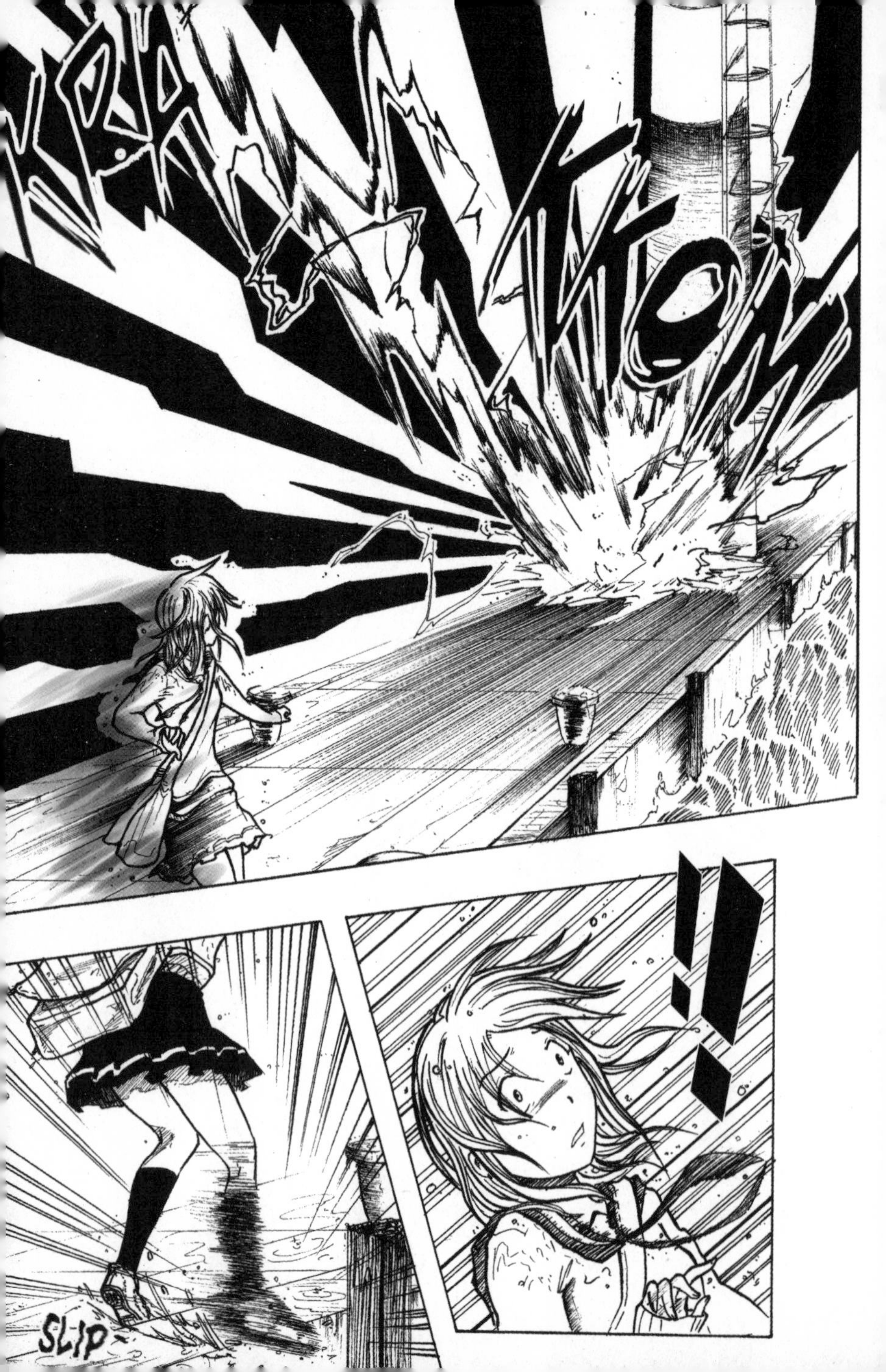
KRAAKATOOM
SLIP
!!

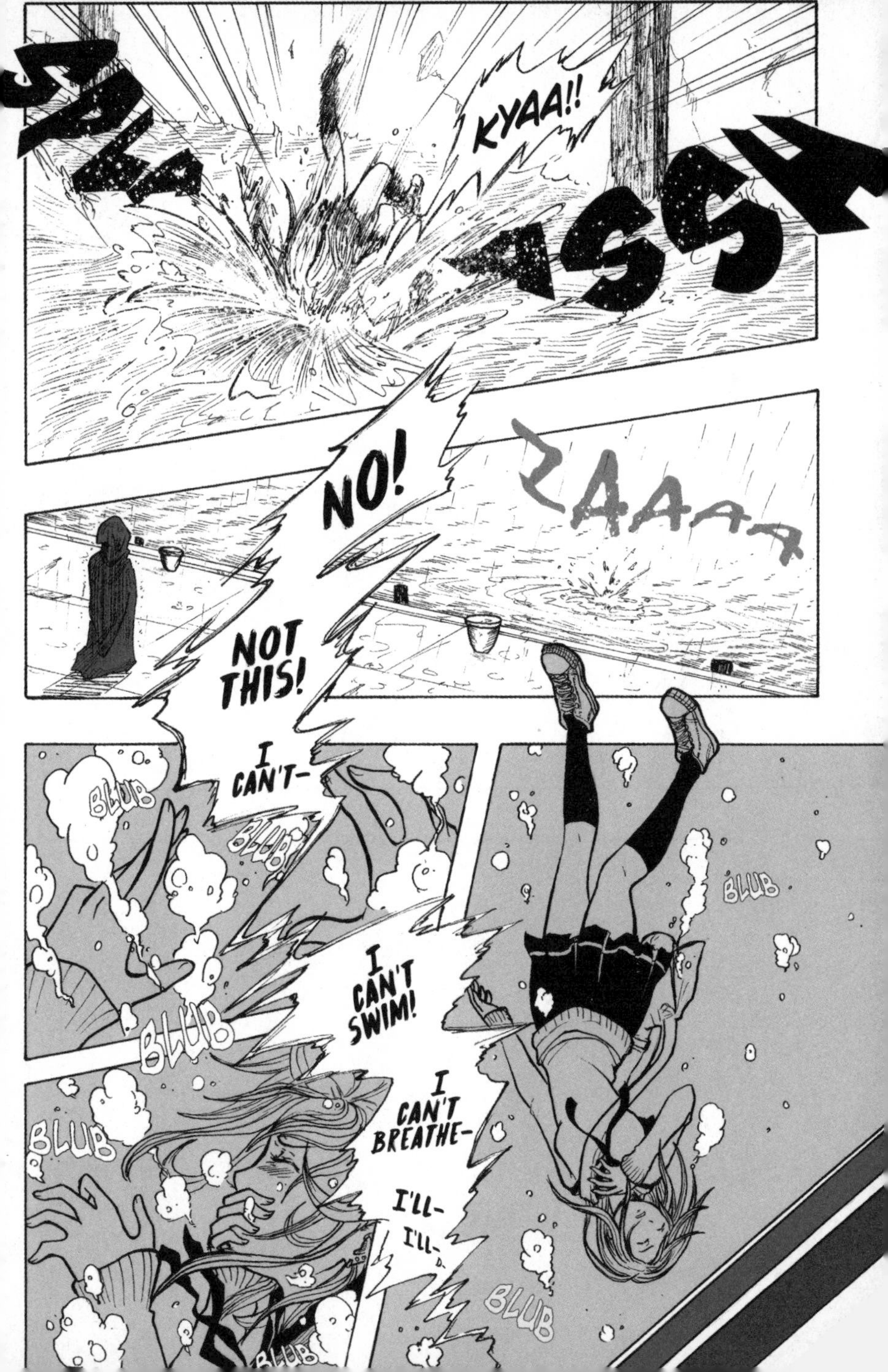

SPLAASSH
KYAA!!
NO!
ZAAAA
NOT THIS!
I CAN'T-
BLUB
BLUB
BLUB
I CAN'T SWIM!
I CAN'T BREATHE-
I'LL-
I'LL-
BLUB
BLUB
BLUB
BLUB

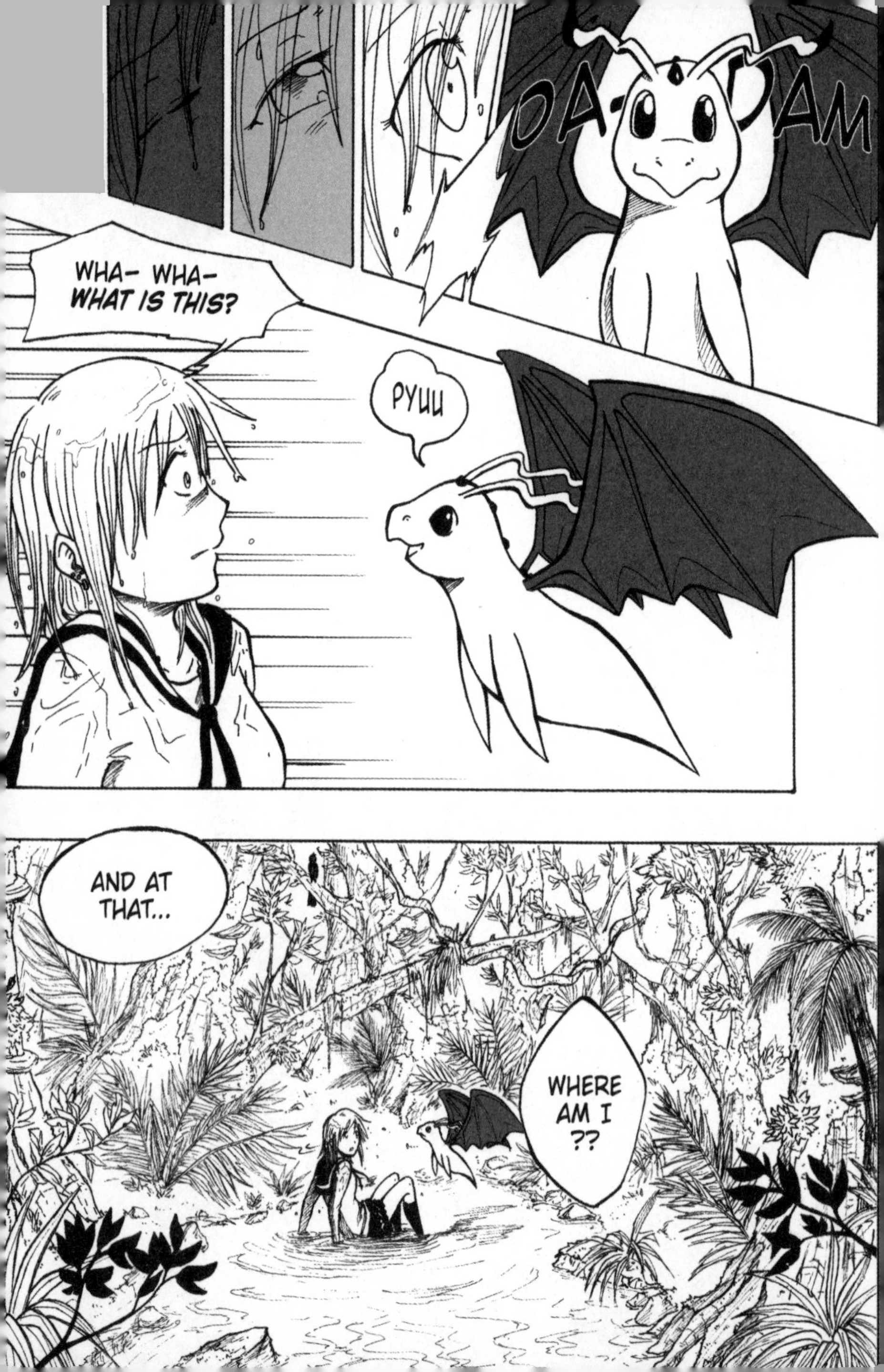
DA-DAM
WHA- WHA- WHAT IS THIS?
PYUU
AND AT THAT...
WHERE AM I ??

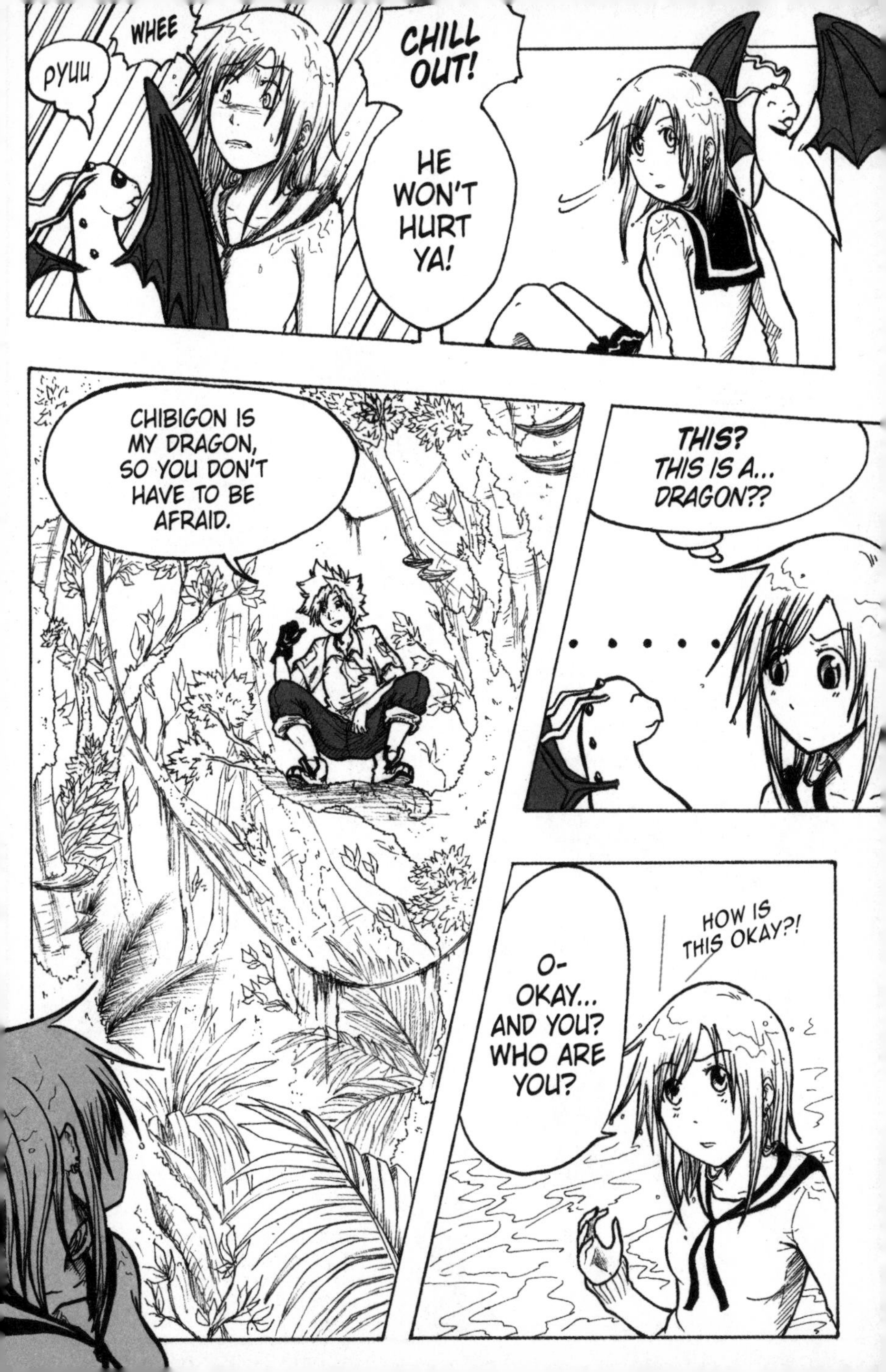
PYUU
WHEE
CHILL OUT!
HE WON'T HURT YA!
CHIBIGON IS MY DRAGON, SO YOU DON'T HAVE TO BE AFRAID.
THIS? THIS IS A... DRAGON??
O-OKAY... AND YOU? WHO ARE YOU?
HOW IS THIS OKAY?!

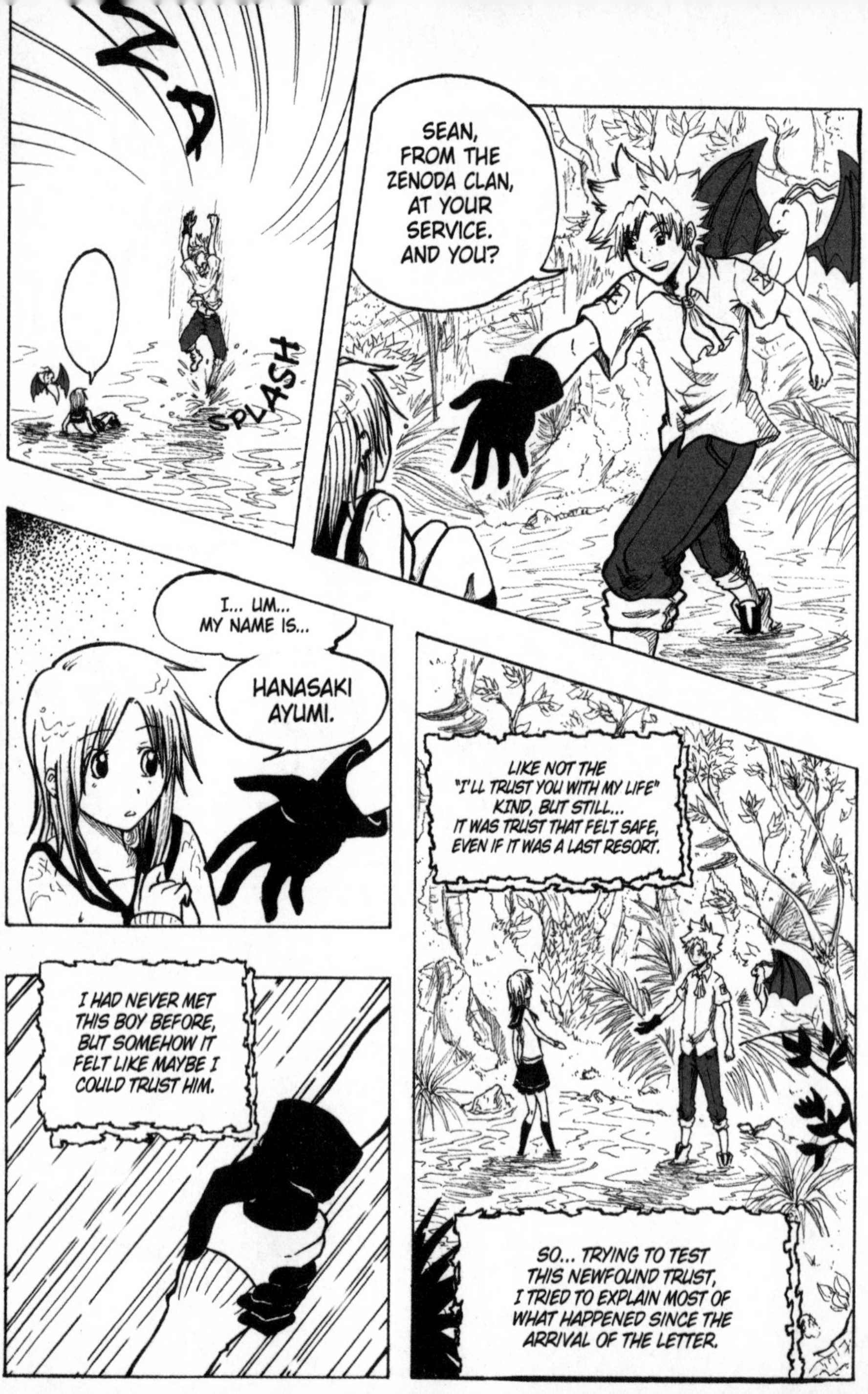

ZA
SPLASH
SEAN, FROM THE ZENODA CLAN, AT YOUR SERVICE. AND YOU?
I... UM... MY NAME IS...
HANASAKI AYUMI.
I HAD NEVER MET THIS BOY BEFORE, BUT SOMEHOW IT FELT LIKE MAYBE I COULD TRUST HIM.
LIKE NOT THE "I'LL TRUST YOU WITH MY LIFE" KIND, BUT STILL... IT WAS TRUST THAT FELT SAFE, EVEN IF IT WAS A LAST RESORT.
SO... TRYING TO TEST THIS NEWFOUND TRUST, I TRIED TO EXPLAIN MOST OF WHAT HAPPENED SINCE THE ARRIVAL OF THE LETTER.

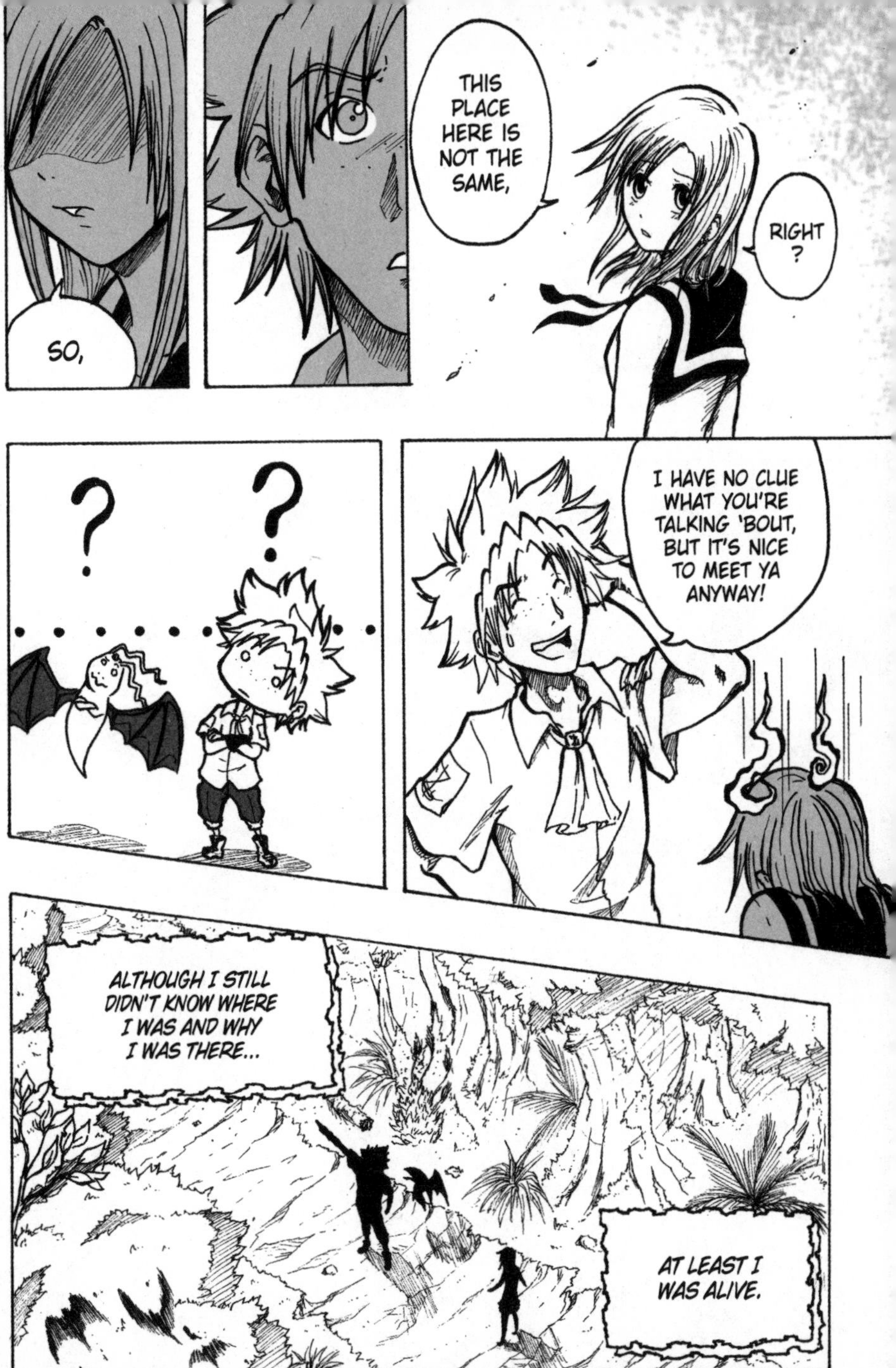
SO,
THIS PLACE HERE IS NOT THE SAME,
RIGHT?
I HAVE NO CLUE WHAT YOU'RE TALKING 'BOUT, BUT IT'S NICE TO MEET YA ANYWAY!
ALTHOUGH I STILL DIDN'T KNOW WHERE I WAS AND WHY I WAS THERE...
AT LEAST I WAS ALIVE.

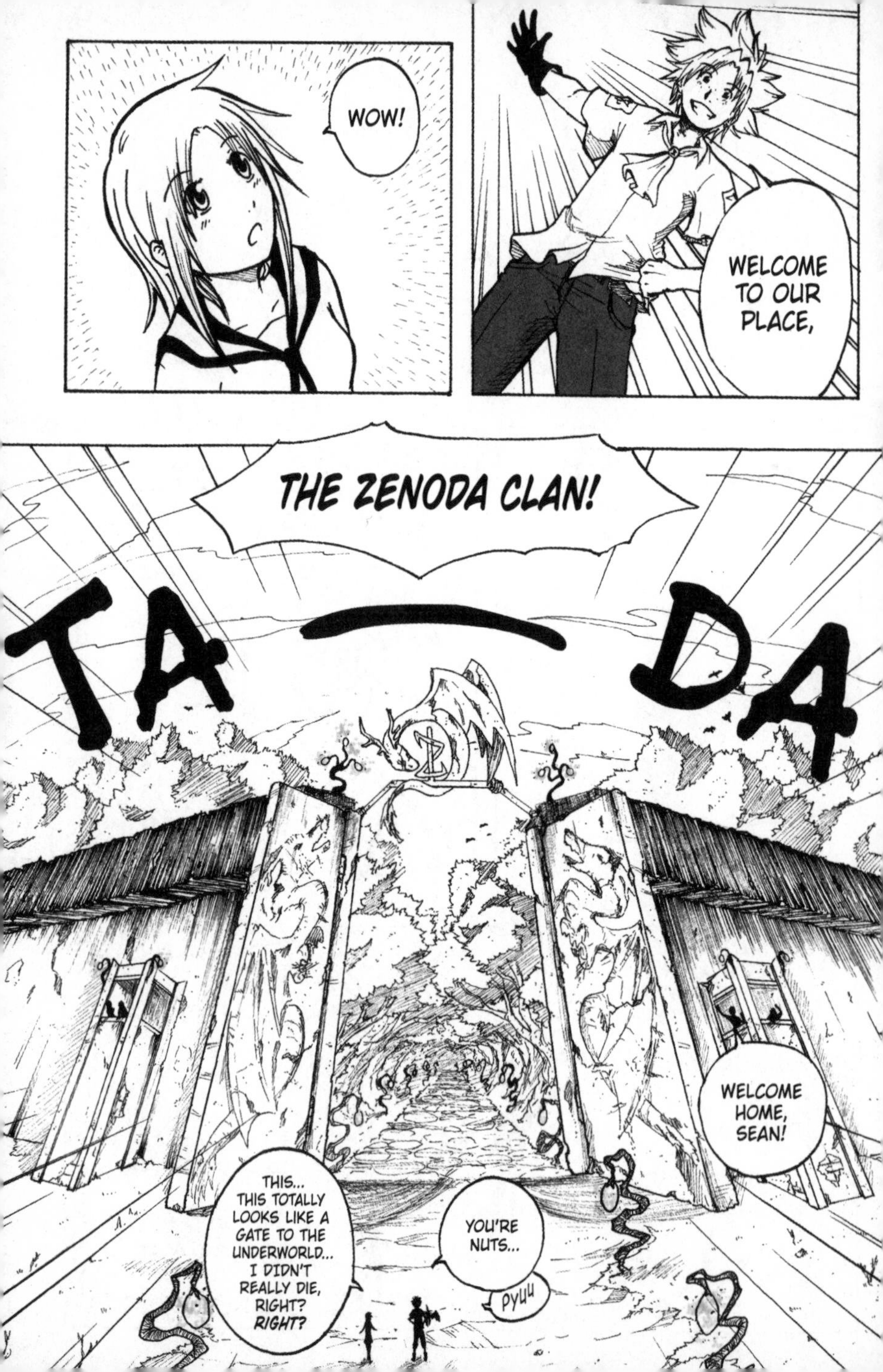
WOW!
WELCOME TO OUR PLACE,
THE ZENODA CLAN!
TA—DA
WELCOME HOME, SEAN!
THIS... THIS TOTALLY LOOKS LIKE A GATE TO THE UNDERWORLD... I DIDN'T REALLY DIE, RIGHT? *RIGHT?*
YOU'RE NUTS...
pyuu

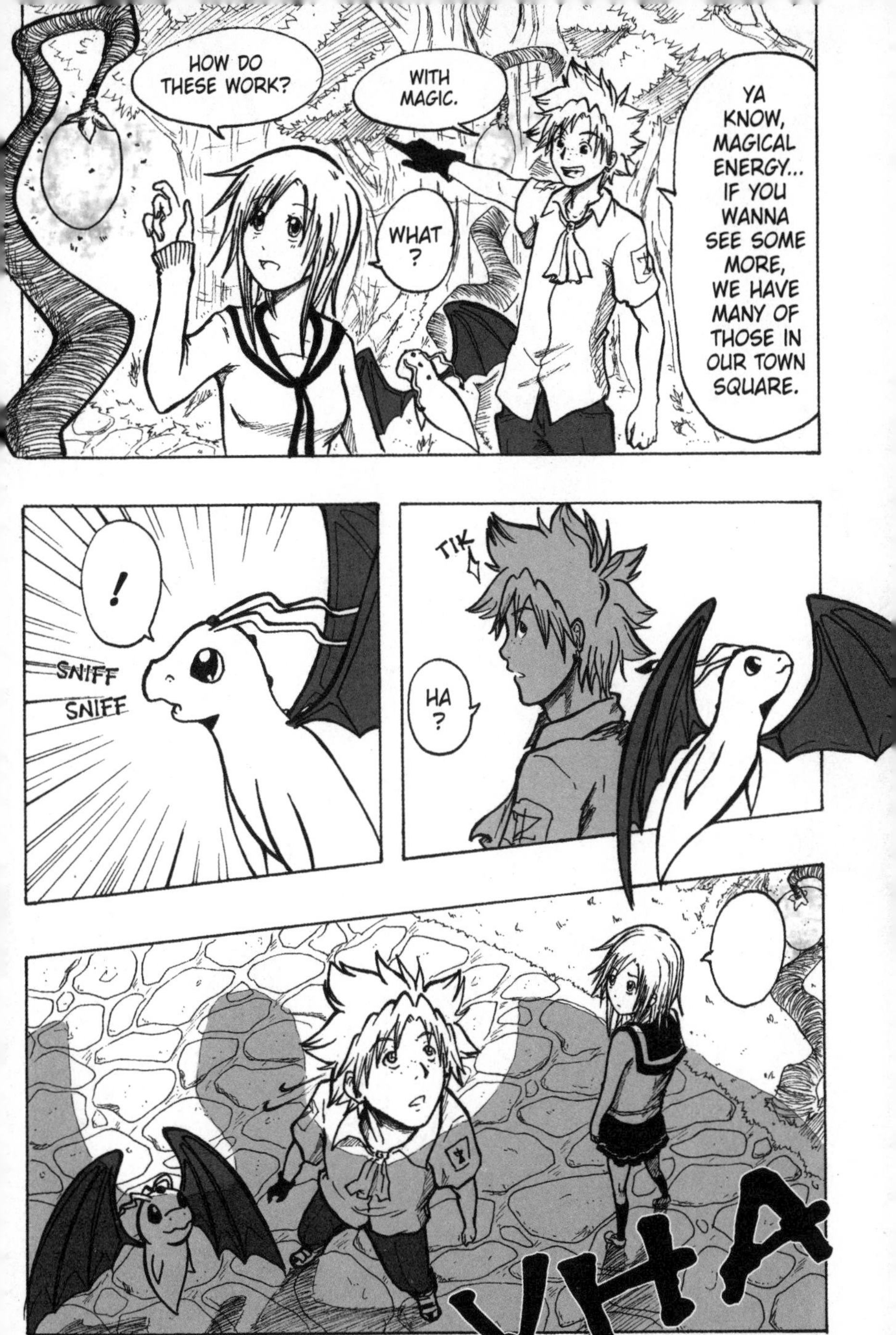
HOW DO THESE WORK?
WITH MAGIC.
WHAT ?
YA KNOW, MAGICAL ENERGY... IF YOU WANNA SEE SOME MORE, WE HAVE MANY OF THOSE IN OUR TOWN SQUARE.
!
SNIFF SNIFF
TIK
HA ?
VHA

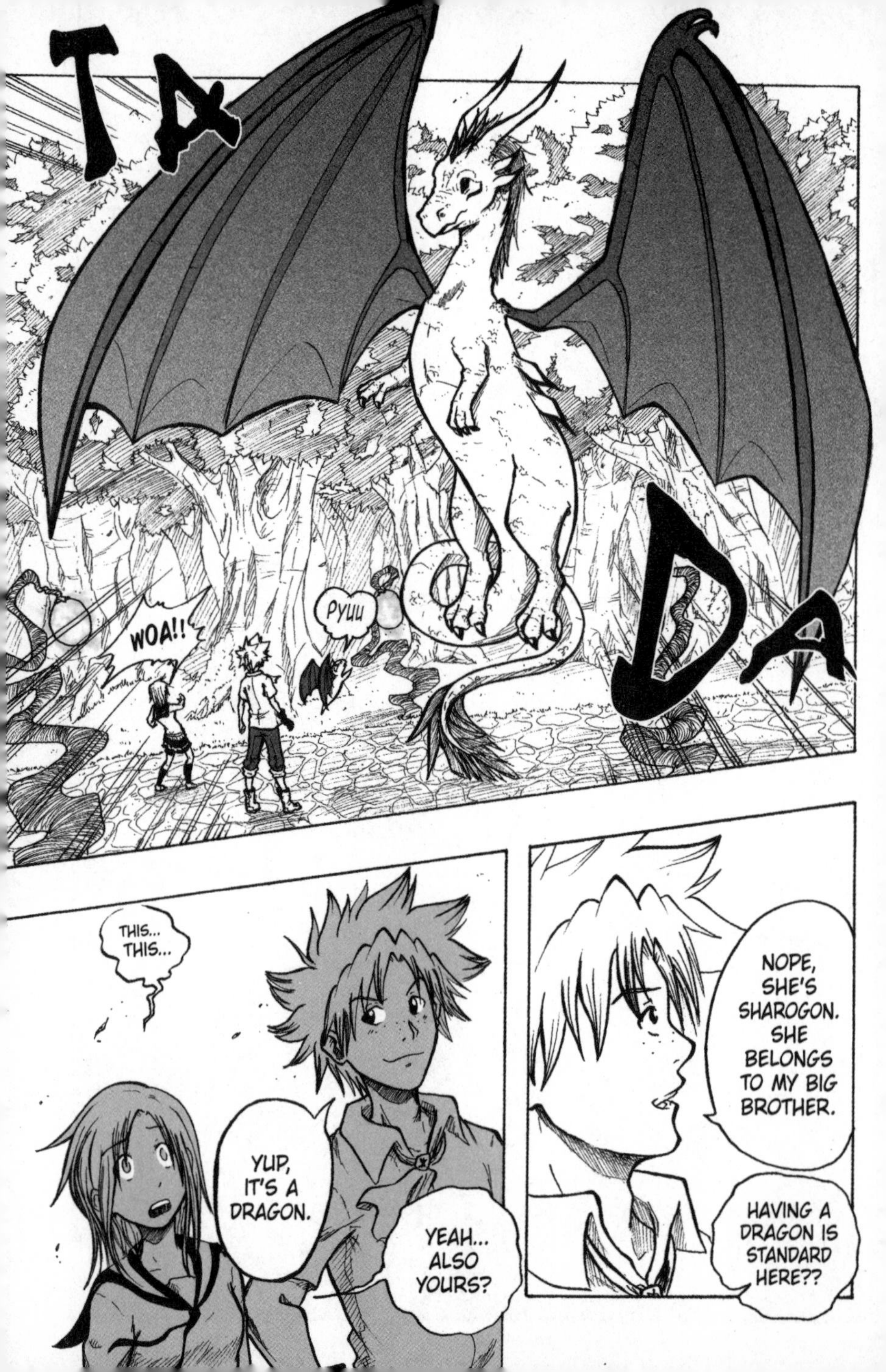
TA
WOA!!
Pyuu
DA
THIS... THIS...
YUP, IT'S A DRAGON.
YEAH... ALSO YOURS?
NOPE, SHE'S SHAROGON. SHE BELONGS TO MY BIG BROTHER.
HAVING A DRAGON IS STANDARD HERE??

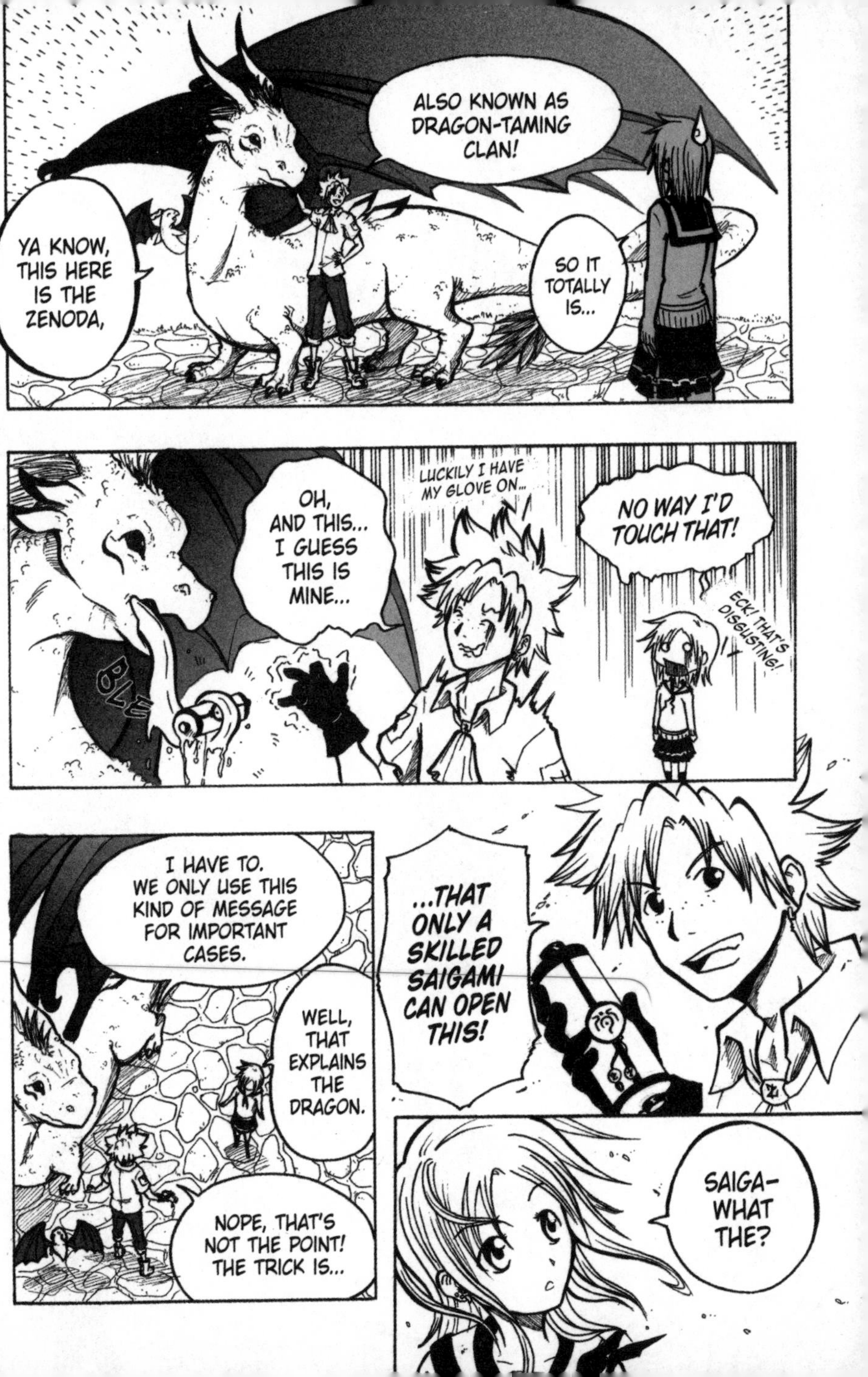
YA KNOW, THIS HERE IS THE ZENODA,
ALSO KNOWN AS DRAGON-TAMING CLAN!
SO IT TOTALLY IS...
OH, AND THIS... I GUESS THIS IS MINE...
LUCKILY I HAVE MY GLOVE ON...
NO WAY I'D TOUCH THAT!
ECK! THAT'S DISGUSTING!
I HAVE TO. WE ONLY USE THIS KIND OF MESSAGE FOR IMPORTANT CASES.
WELL, THAT EXPLAINS THE DRAGON.
NOPE, THAT'S NOT THE POINT! THE TRICK IS...
...THAT ONLY A SKILLED SAIGAMI CAN OPEN THIS!
SAIGA-WHAT THE?

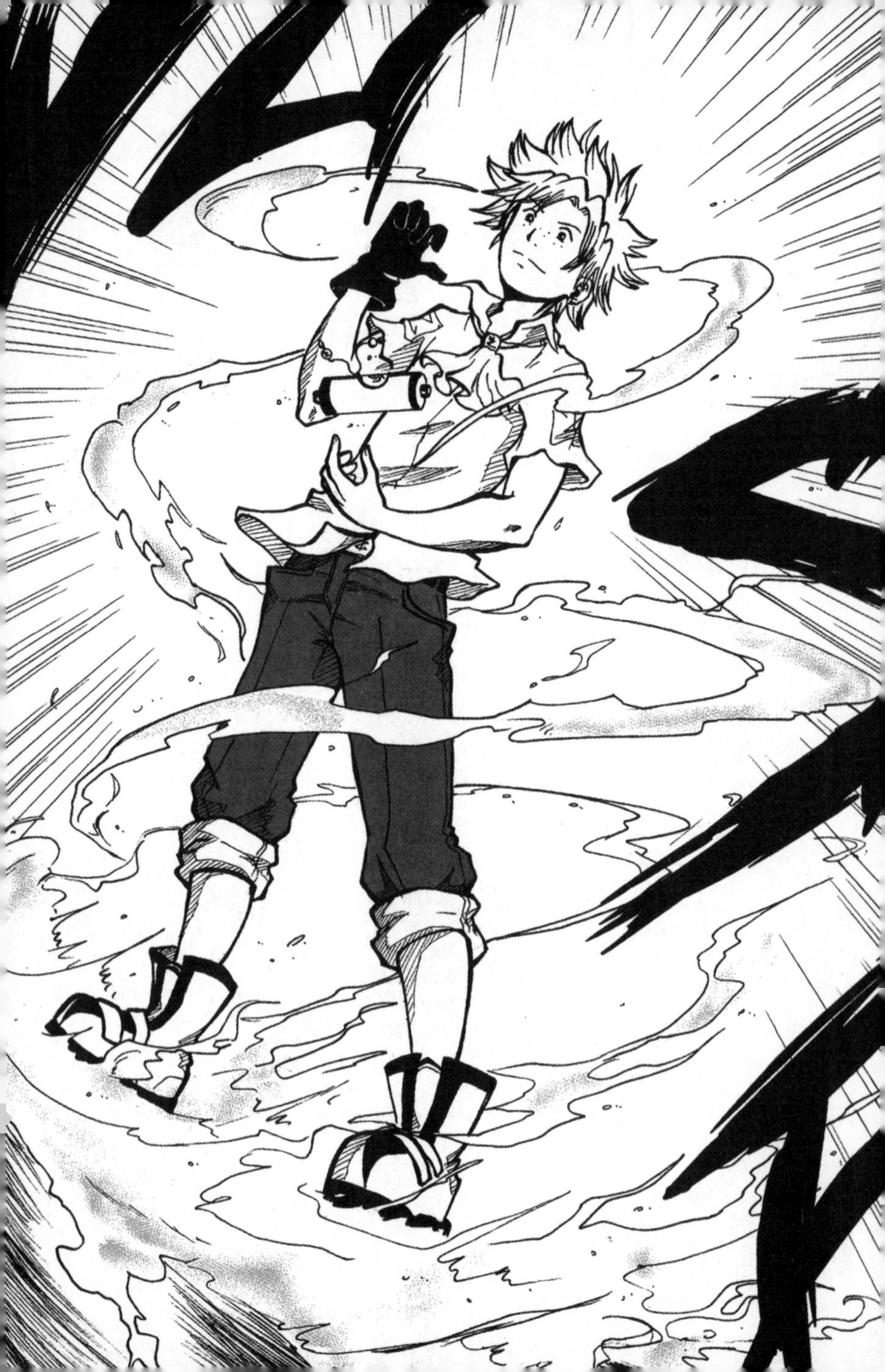

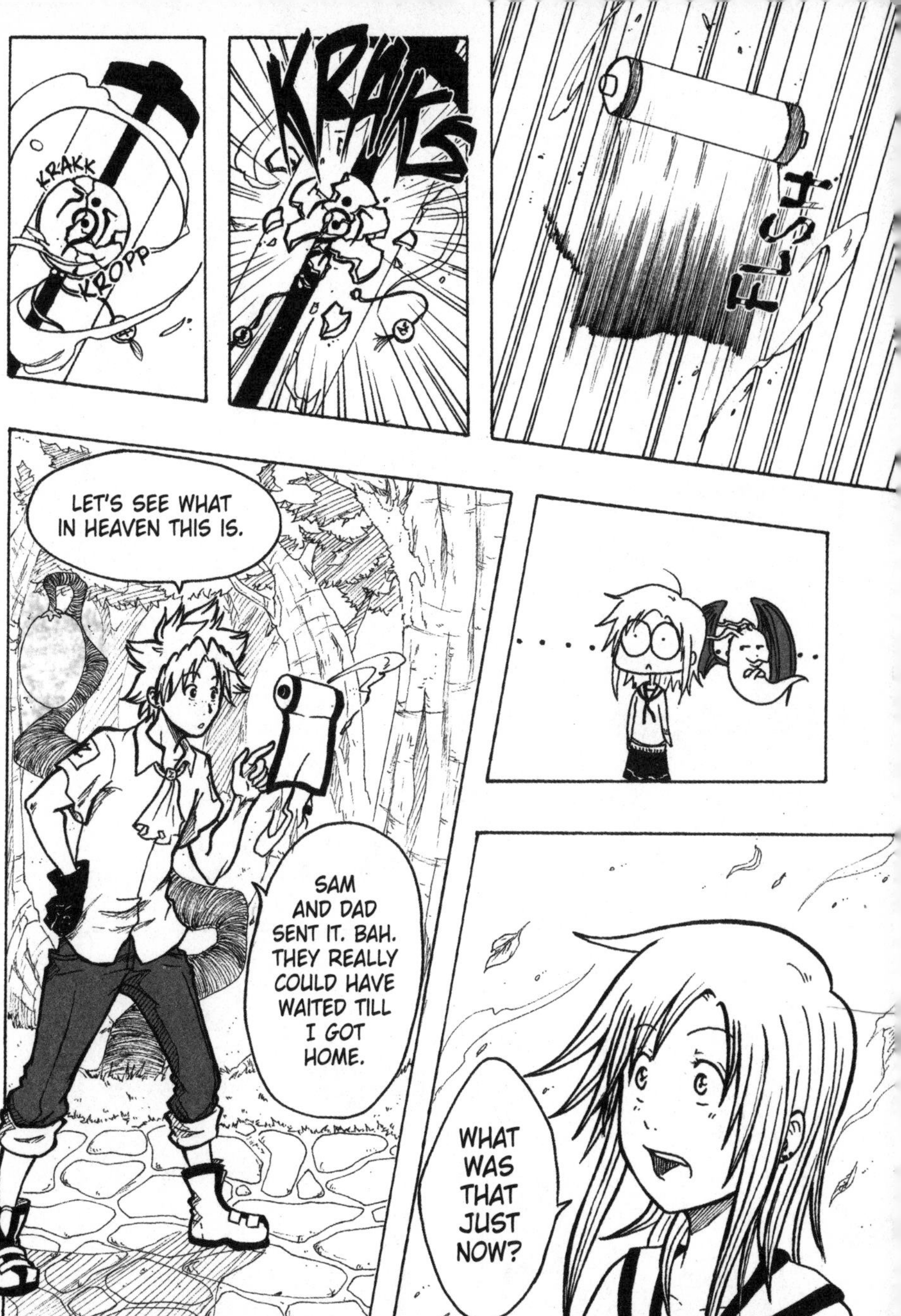
KRAKK
KROPP
KRAKS
LET'S SEE WHAT IN HEAVEN THIS IS.
SAM AND DAD SENT IT. BAH. THEY REALLY COULD HAVE WAITED TILL I GOT HOME.
WHAT WAS THAT JUST NOW?

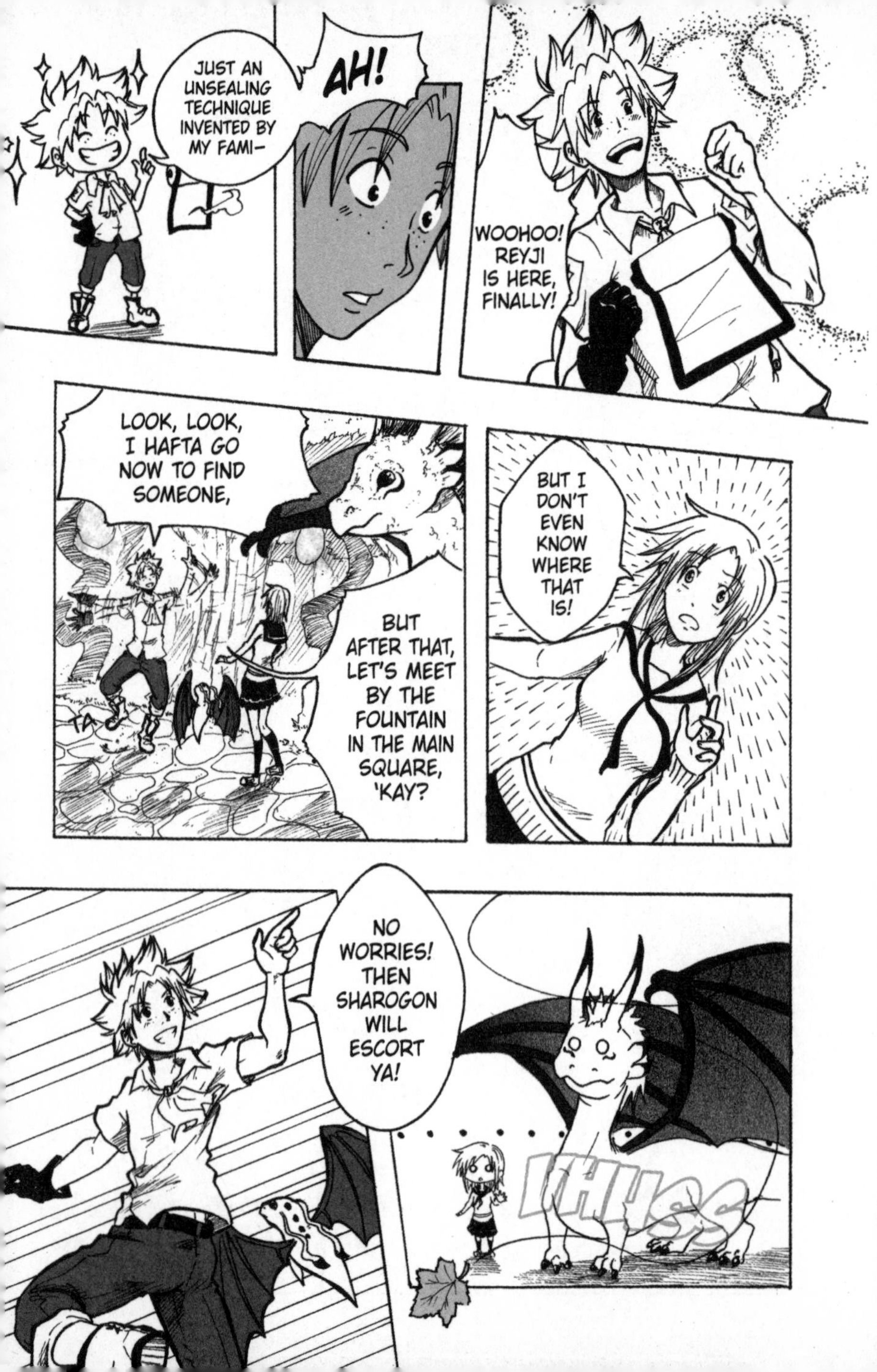
JUST AN UNSEALING TECHNIQUE INVENTED BY MY FAMI–
AH!
WOOHOO! REYJI IS HERE, FINALLY!
LOOK, LOOK, I HAFTA GO NOW TO FIND SOMEONE,
TA
BUT AFTER THAT, LET'S MEET BY THE FOUNTAIN IN THE MAIN SQUARE, 'KAY?
BUT I DON'T EVEN KNOW WHERE THAT IS!
NO WORRIES! THEN SHAROGON WILL ESCORT YA!
. . . . .
WHUSS

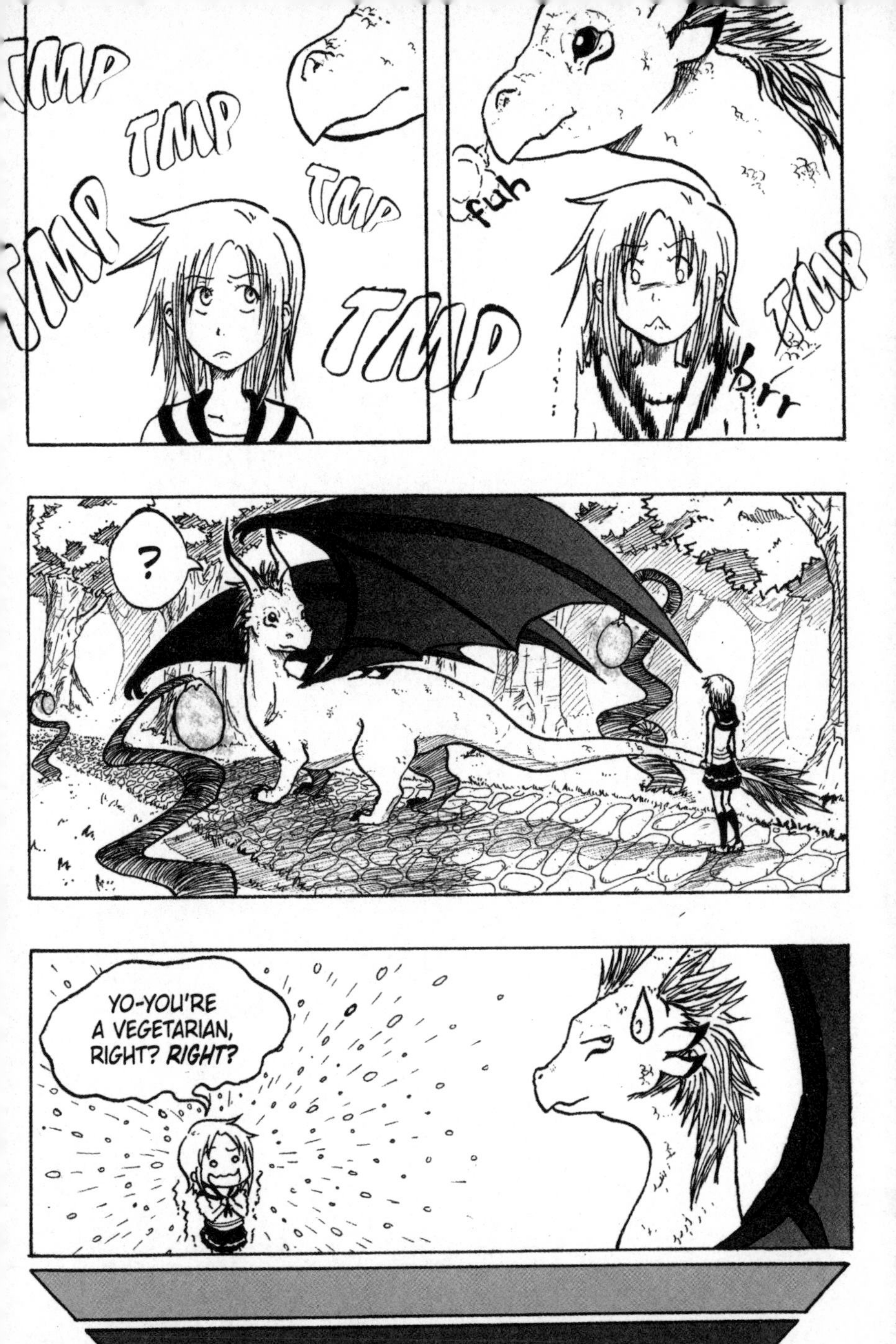
TMP
TMP
TMP
TMP
TMP
fuh
TMP
brr
?
YO-YOU'RE A VEGETARIAN, RIGHT? *RIGHT?*

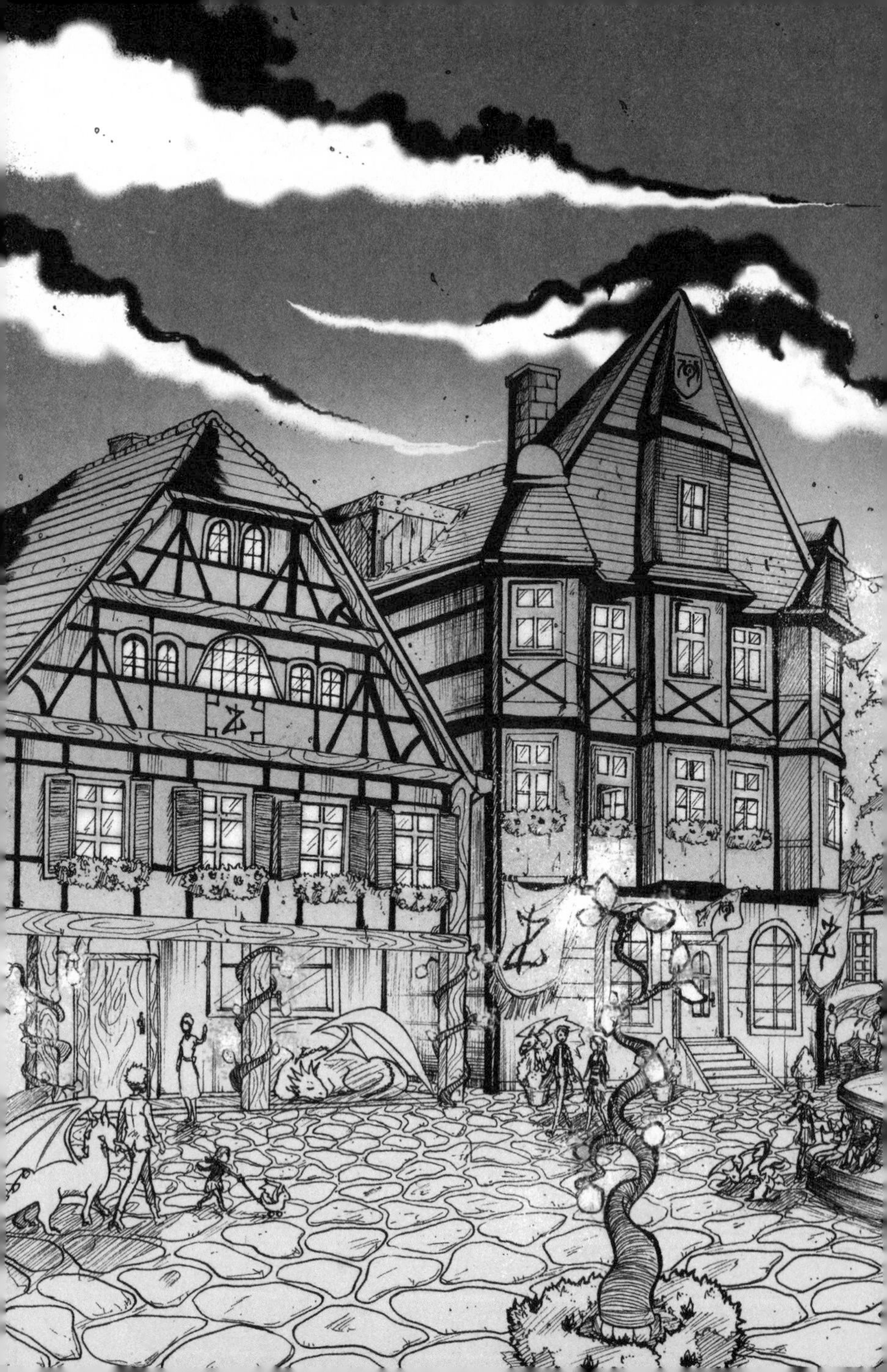

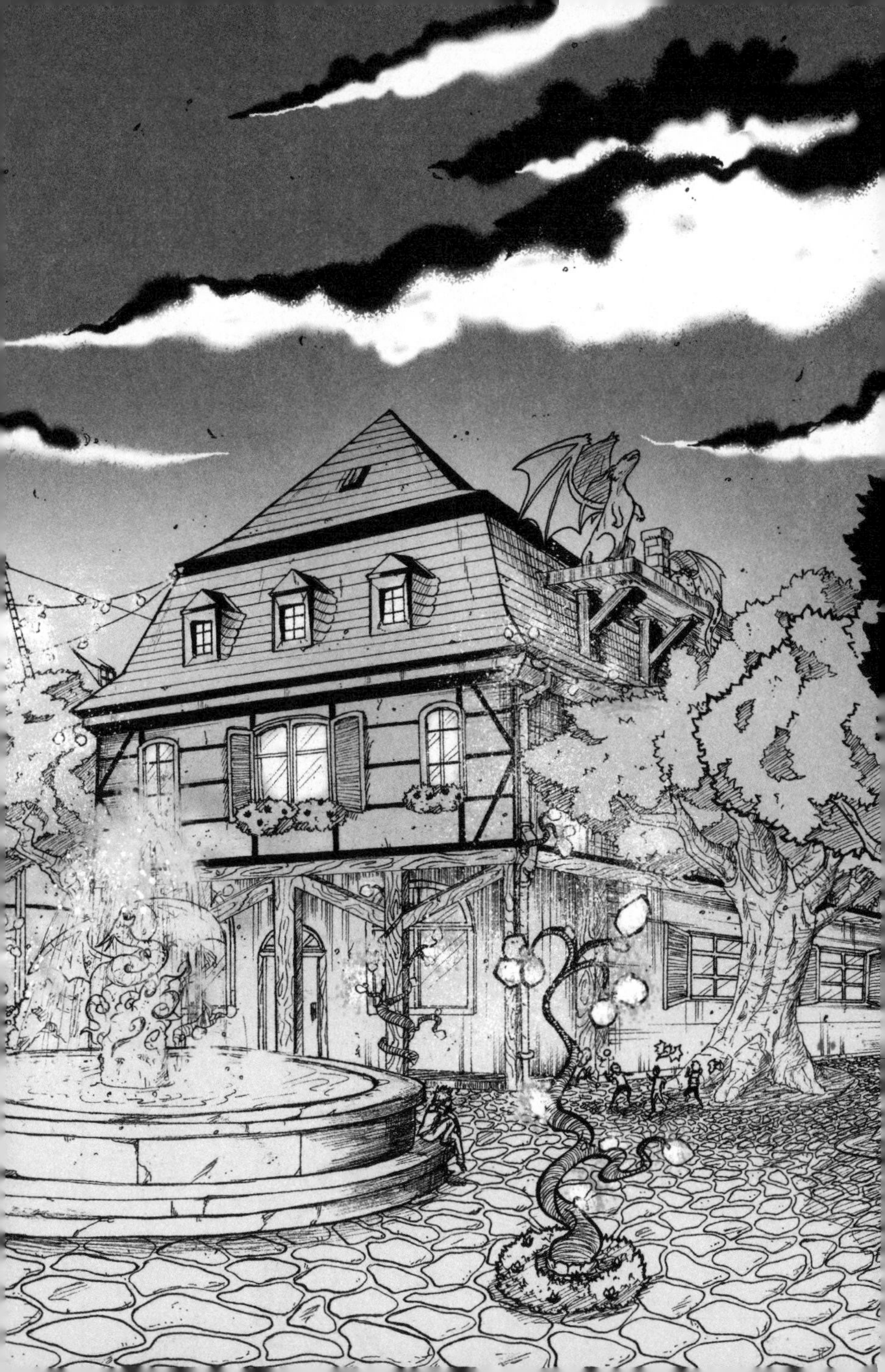

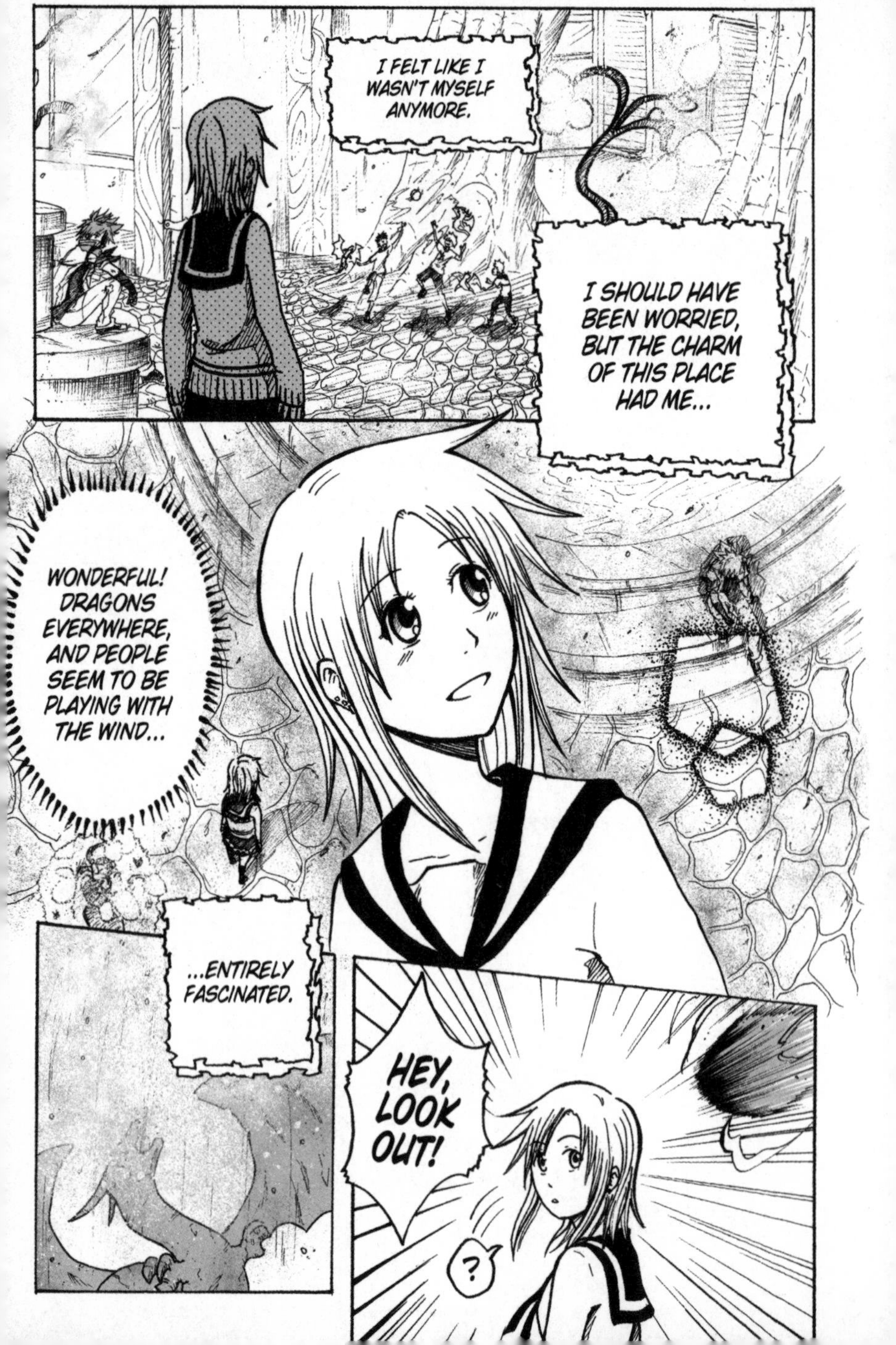
I FELT LIKE I WASN'T MYSELF ANYMORE.
I SHOULD HAVE BEEN WORRIED, BUT THE CHARM OF THIS PLACE HAD ME...
WONDERFUL! DRAGONS EVERYWHERE, AND PEOPLE SEEM TO BE PLAYING WITH THE WIND...
...ENTIRELY FASCINATED.
HEY, LOOK OUT!
?

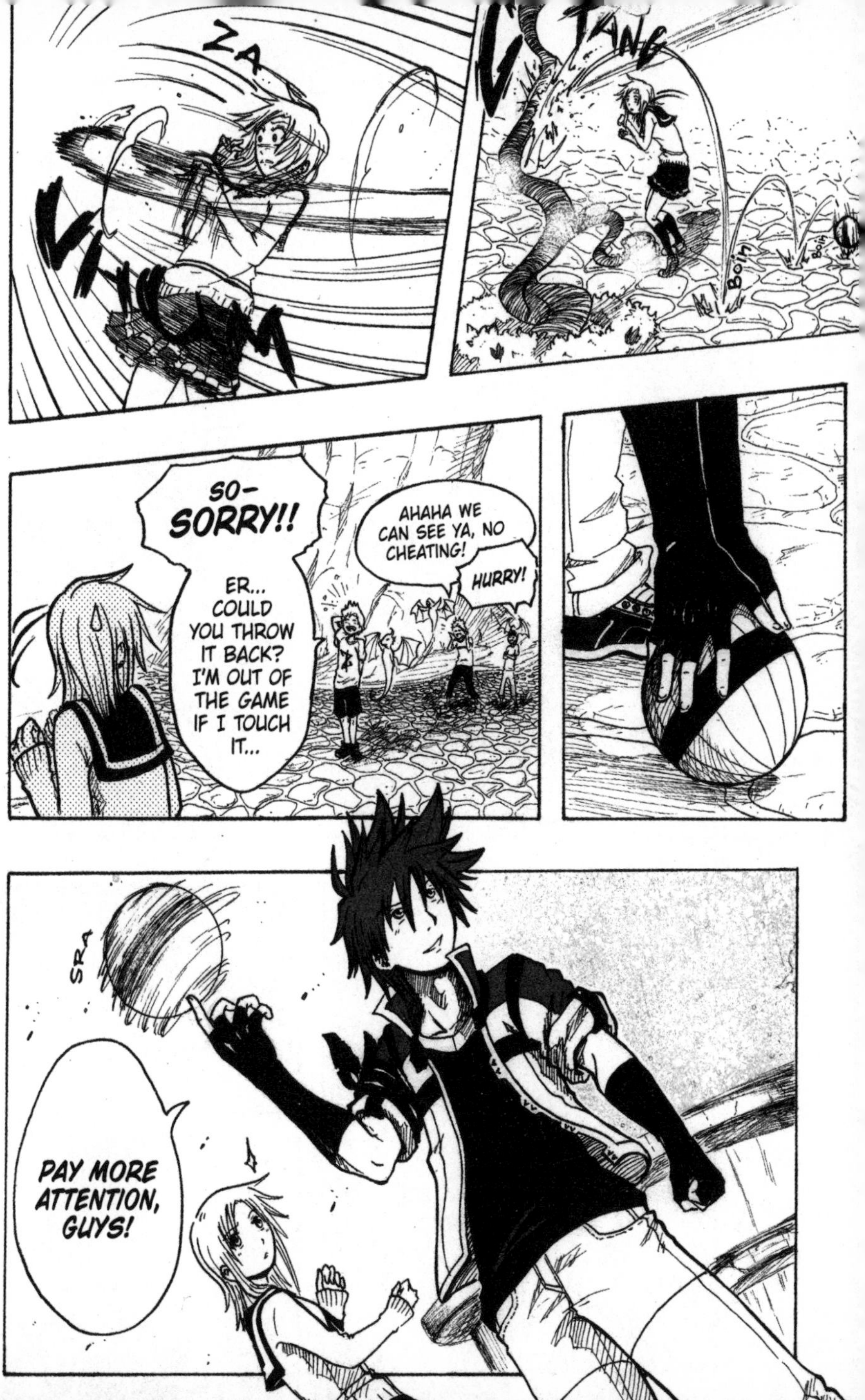
ZA
VHUUM
TANG
Boin
Boin
SO- SORRY!!
ER... COULD YOU THROW IT BACK? I'M OUT OF THE GAME IF I TOUCH IT...
AHAHA WE CAN SEE YA, NO CHEATING!
HURRY!
SRA
PAY MORE ATTENTION, GUYS!

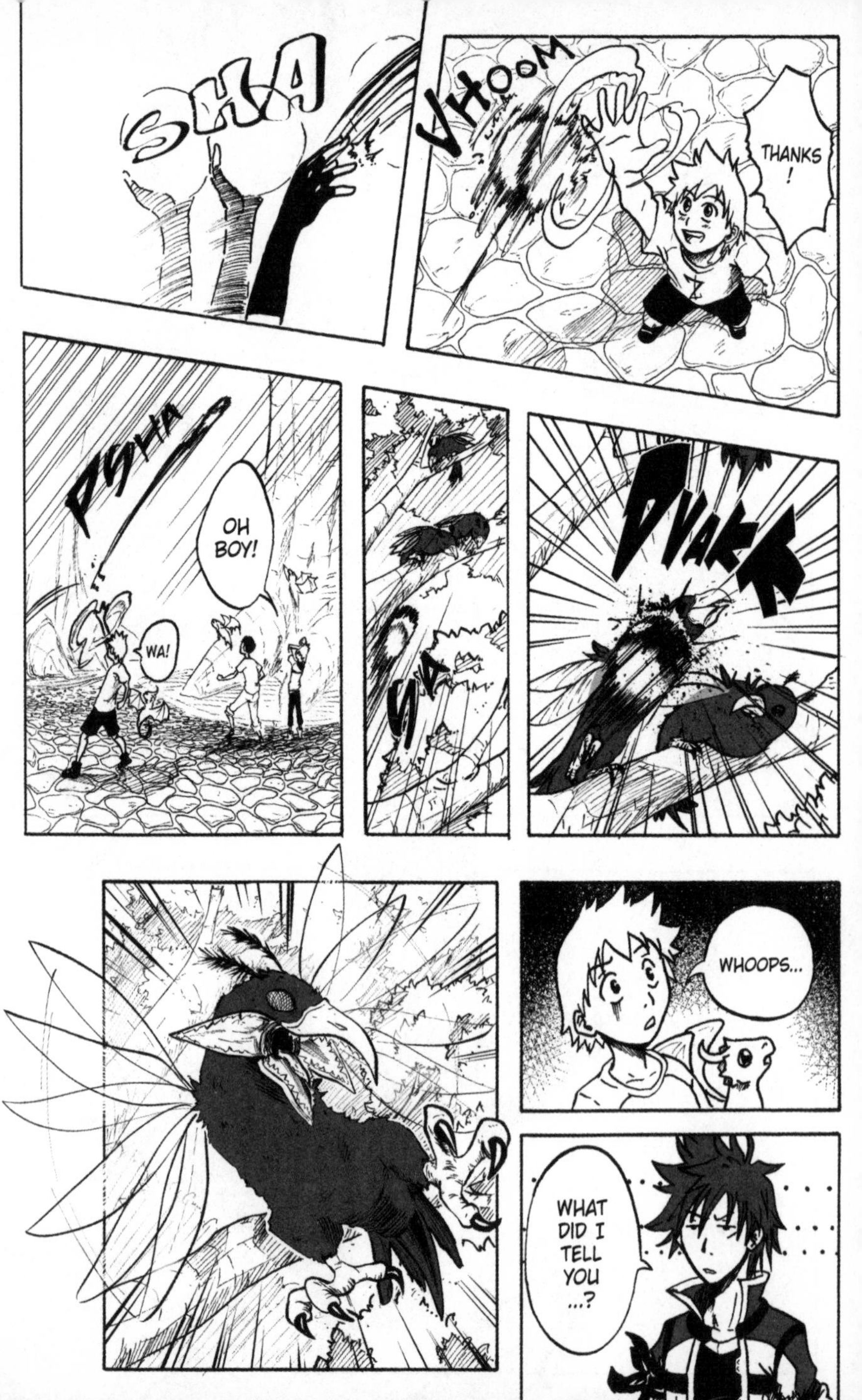
SHA
VHOOM
THANKS!
PSHA
OH BOY!
WA!
SA
DVAKK
WHOOPS...
WHAT DID I TELL YOU ...?

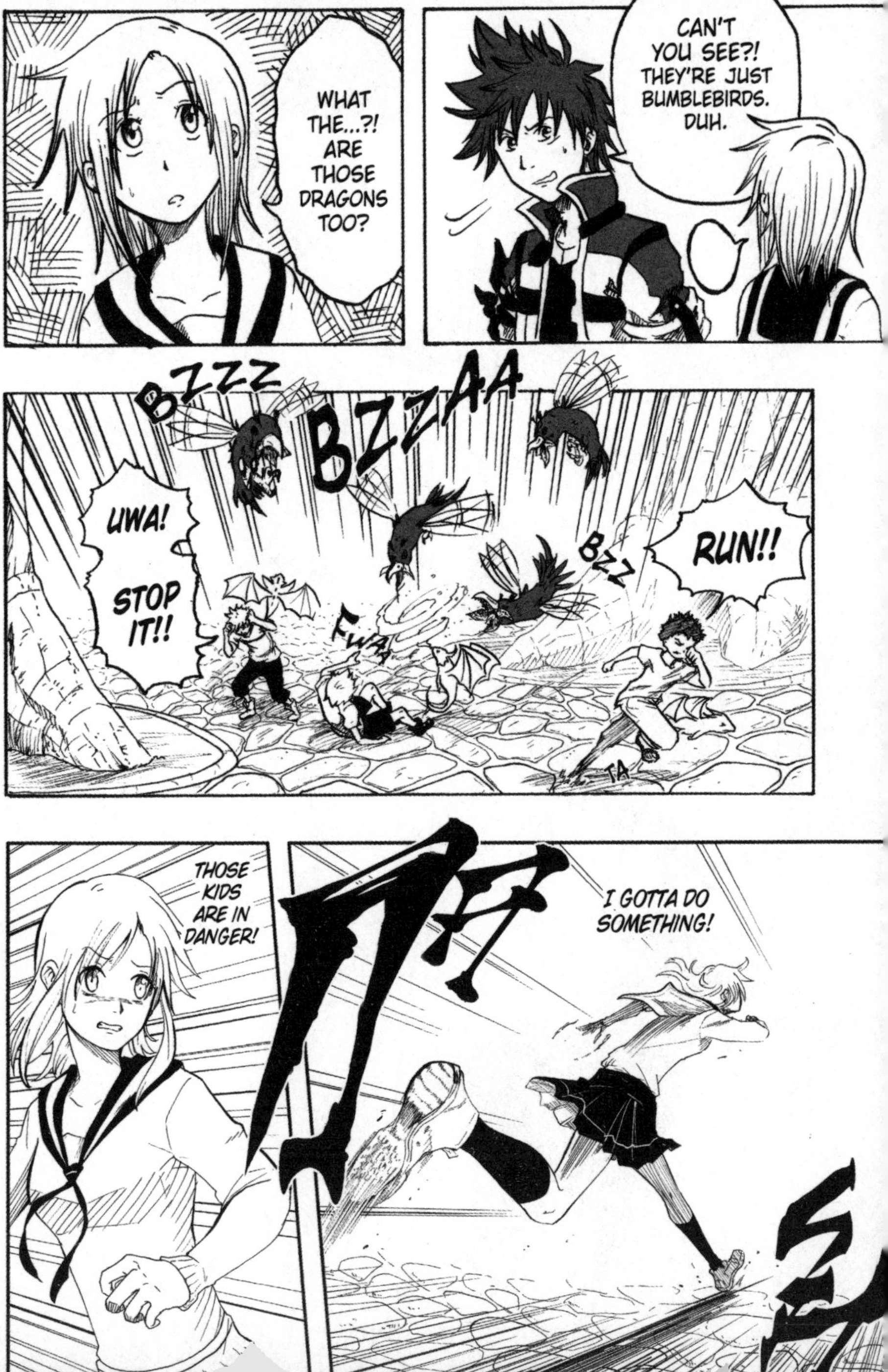
WHAT THE...?! ARE THOSE DRAGONS TOO?
CAN'T YOU SEE?! THEY'RE JUST BUMBLEBIRDS. DUH.
BZZZ
BZZAA
UWA!
STOP IT!!
BZZ
RUN!!
FWAA
TA
THOSE KIDS ARE IN DANGER!
I GOTTA DO SOMETHING!

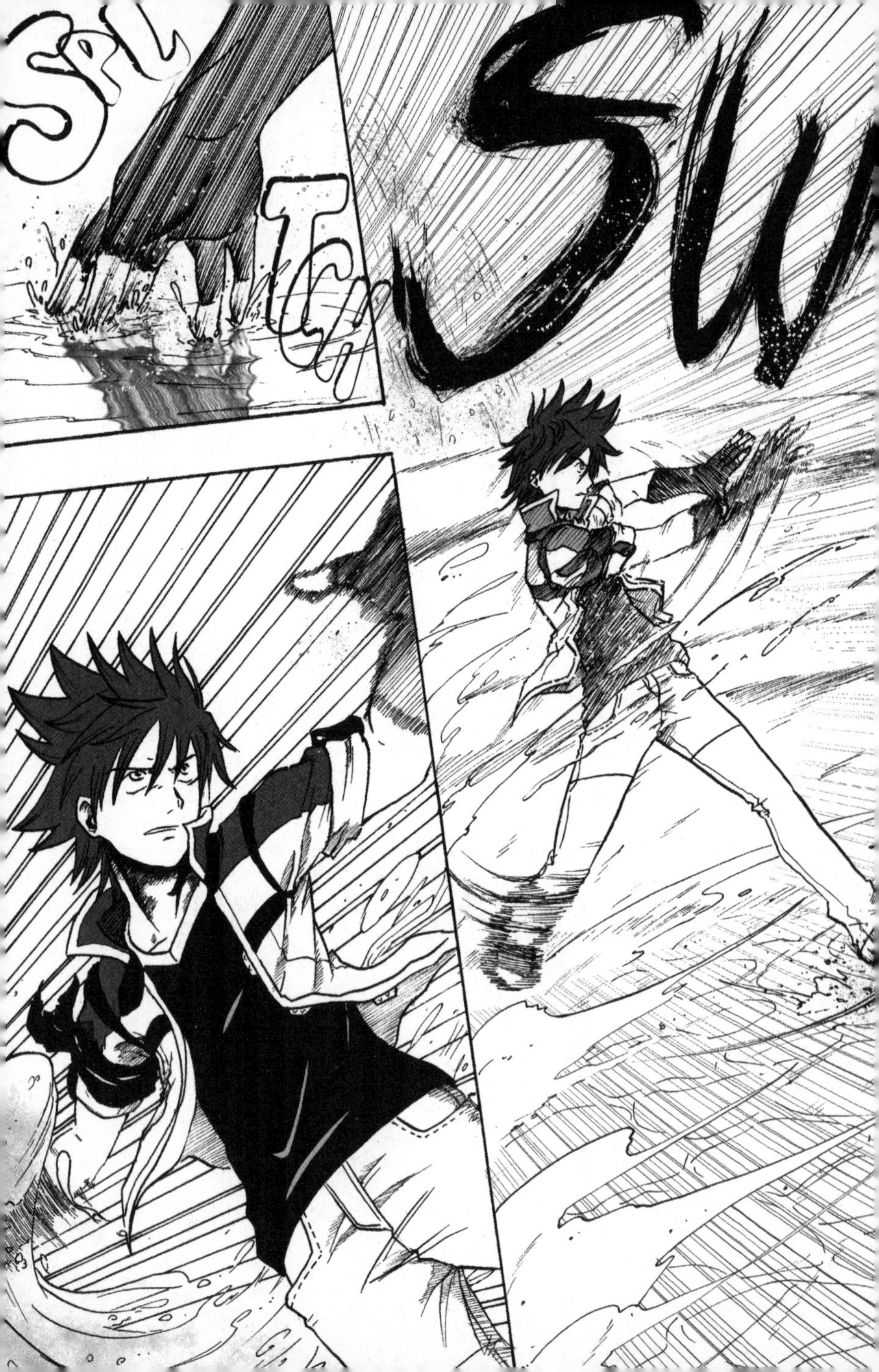
SPL
TCH
SUU

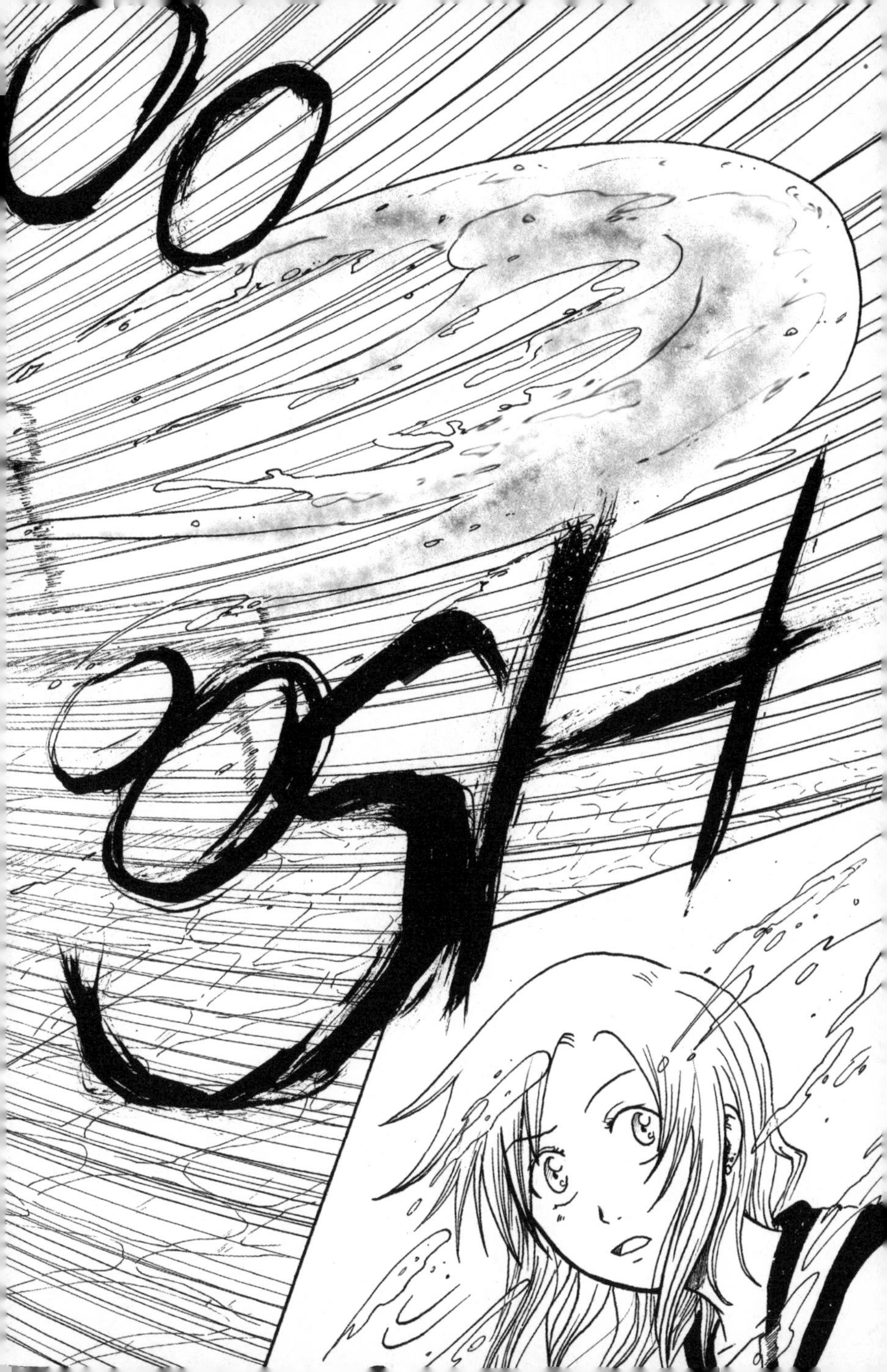

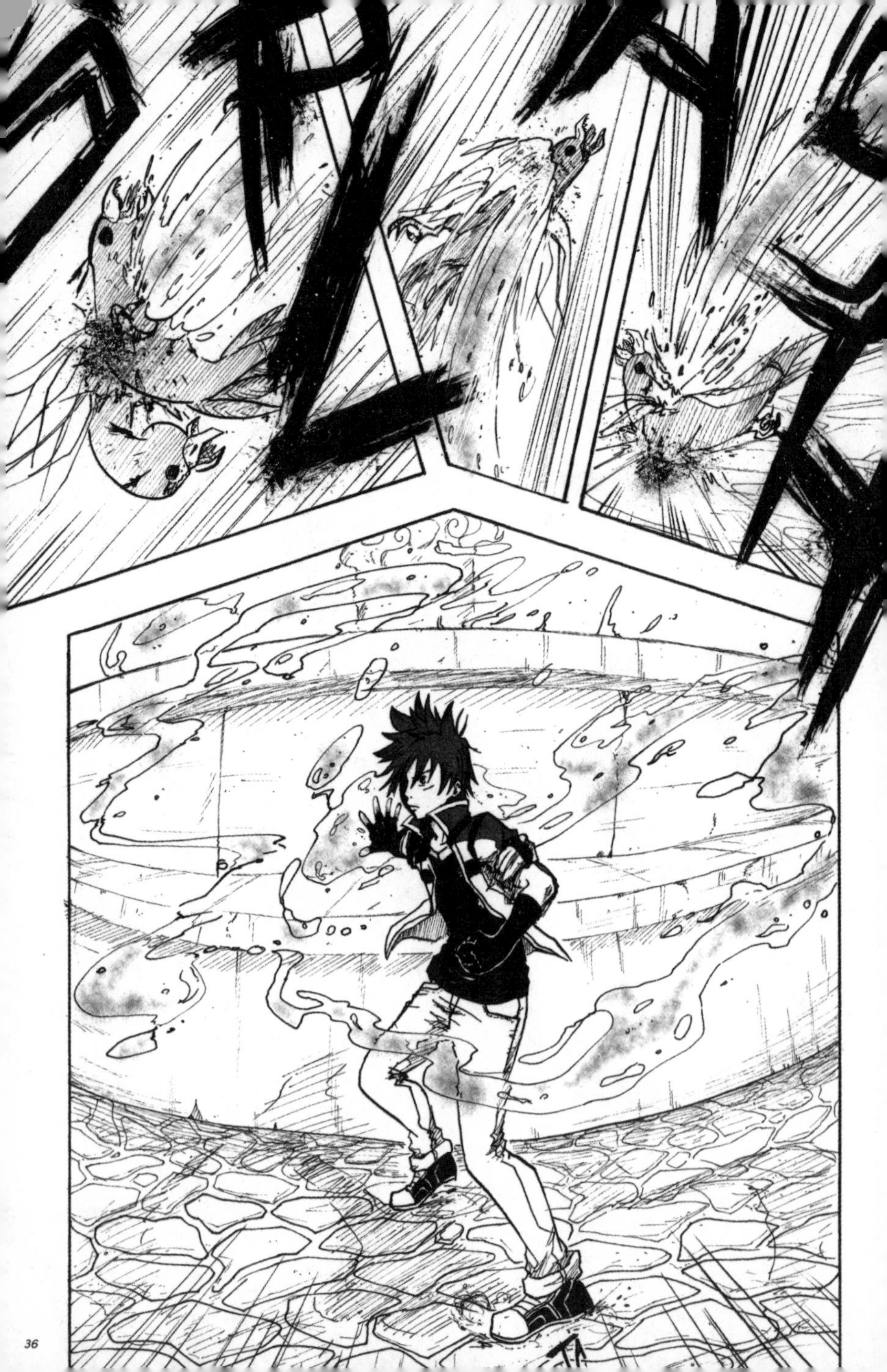

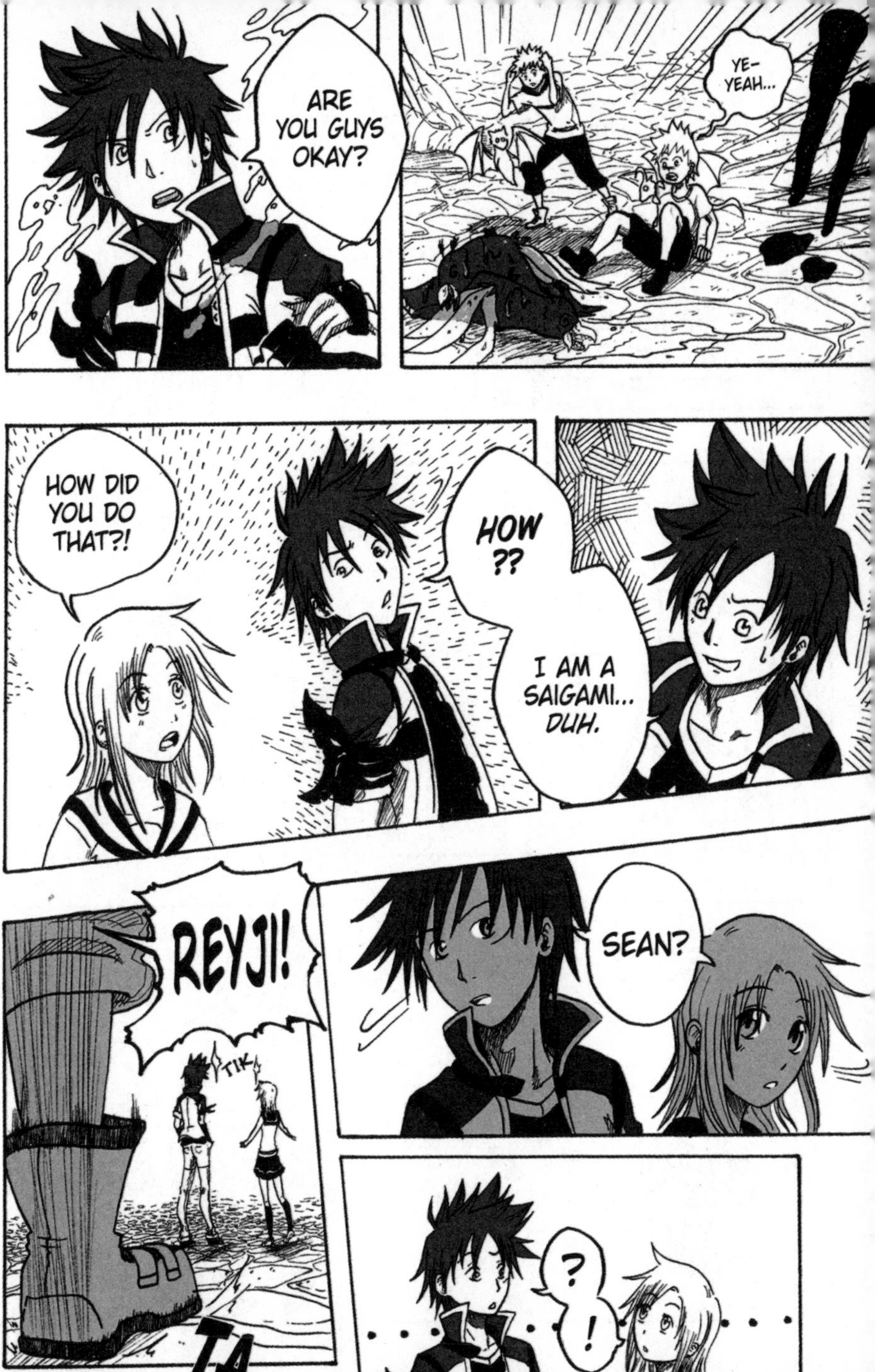
ARE YOU GUYS OKAY?
YE- YEAH...
HOW DID YOU DO THAT?!
HOW ??
I AM A SAIGAMI... DUH.
REYJI!
TIK
TA
SEAN?
?
!

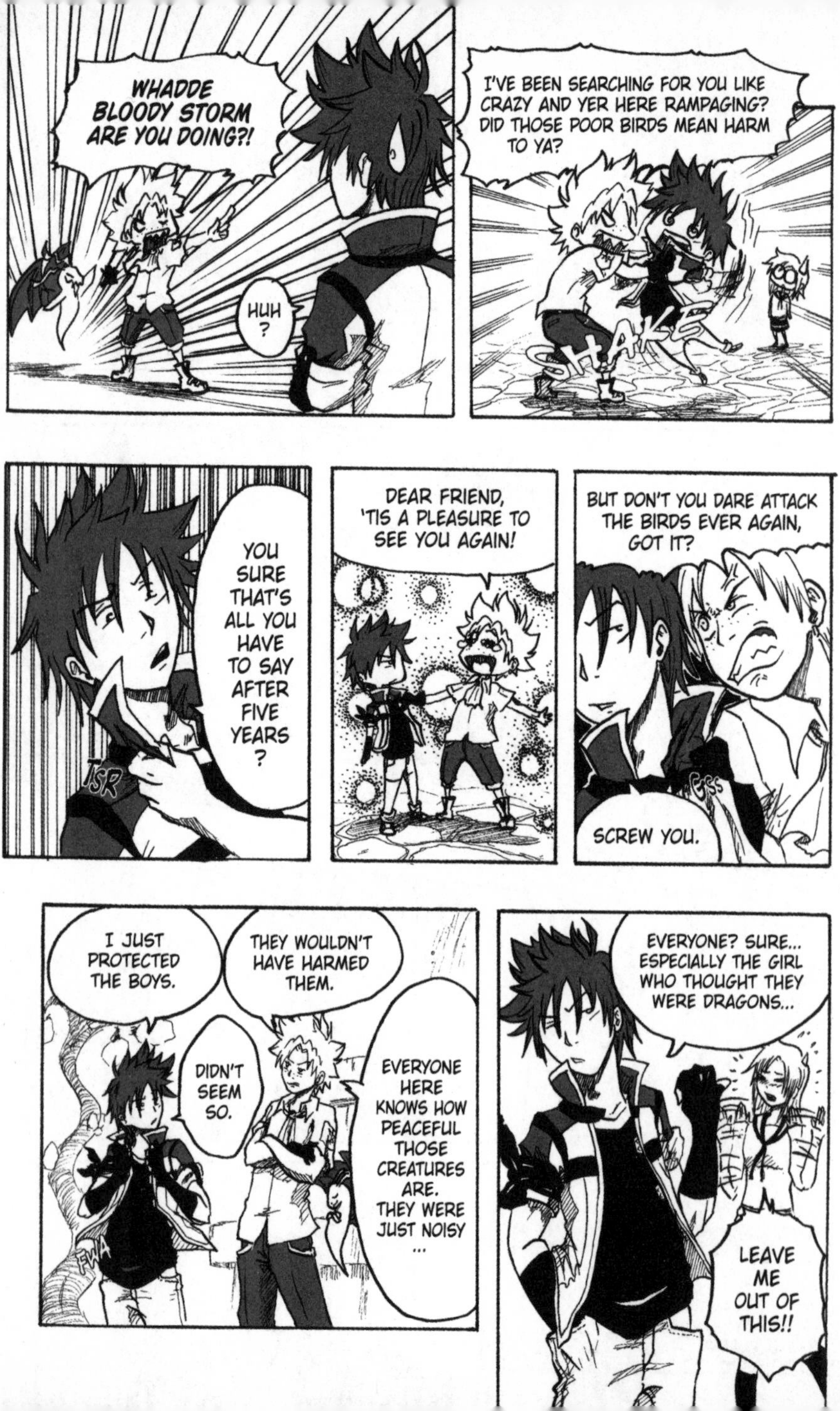
WHADDE BLOODY STORM ARE YOU DOING?!
HUH?
I'VE BEEN SEARCHING FOR YOU LIKE CRAZY AND YER HERE RAMPAGING? DID THOSE POOR BIRDS MEAN HARM TO YA?
SHAKE
YOU SURE THAT'S ALL YOU HAVE TO SAY AFTER FIVE YEARS?
TSR
DEAR FRIEND, 'TIS A PLEASURE TO SEE YOU AGAIN!
BUT DON'T YOU DARE ATTACK THE BIRDS EVER AGAIN, GOT IT?
GSS
SCREW YOU.
I JUST PROTECTED THE BOYS.
THEY WOULDN'T HAVE HARMED THEM.
DIDN'T SEEM SO.
EVERYONE HERE KNOWS HOW PEACEFUL THOSE CREATURES ARE. THEY WERE JUST NOISY ...
FWA
EVERYONE? SURE... ESPECIALLY THE GIRL WHO THOUGHT THEY WERE DRAGONS...
LEAVE ME OUT OF THIS!!

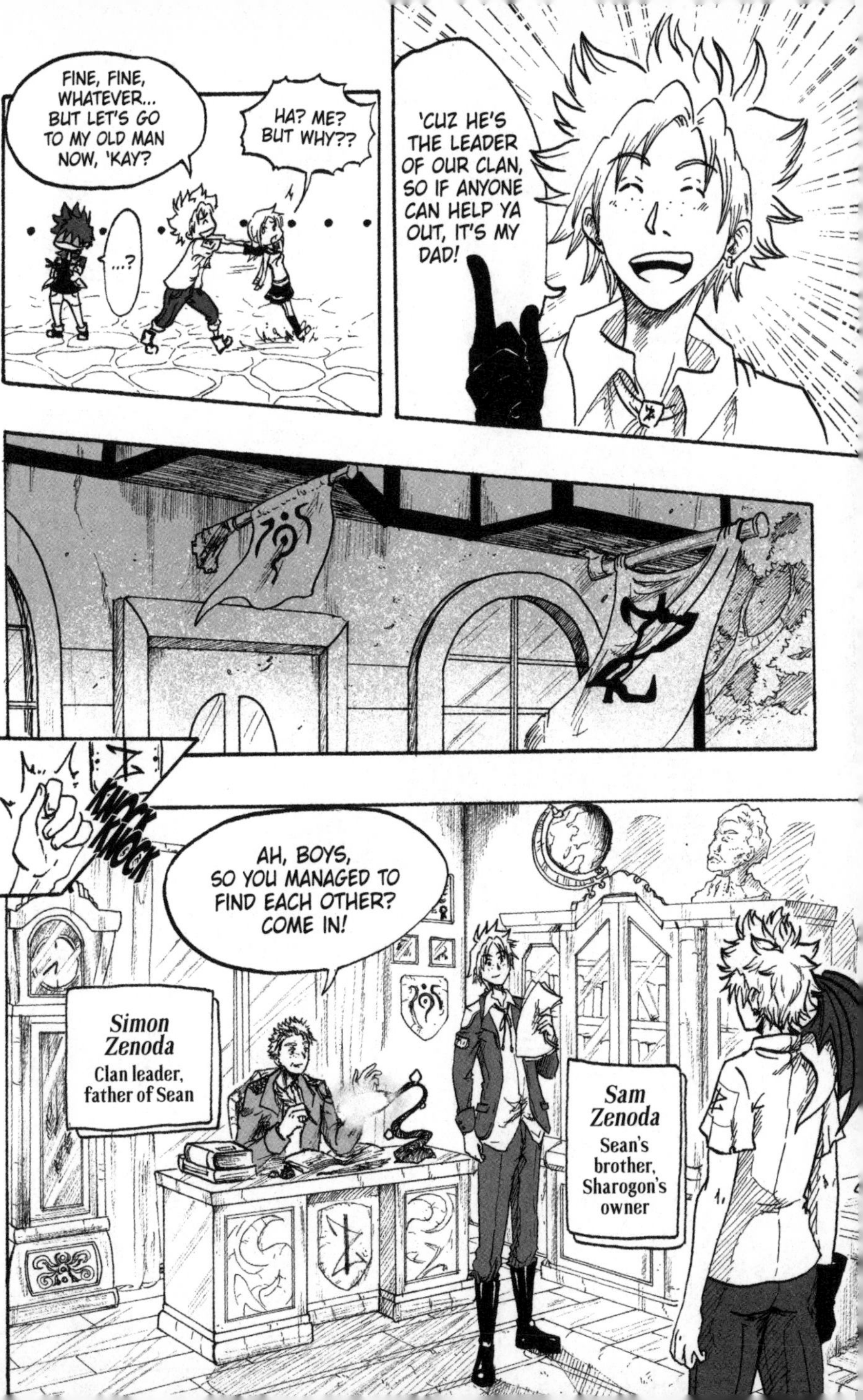
FINE, FINE, WHATEVER... BUT LET'S GO TO MY OLD MAN NOW, 'KAY?
HA? ME? BUT WHY??
...?
'CUZ HE'S THE LEADER OF OUR CLAN, SO IF ANYONE CAN HELP YA OUT, IT'S MY DAD!
KNOCK KNOCK
AH, BOYS, SO YOU MANAGED TO FIND EACH OTHER? COME IN!
Simon Zenoda
Clan leader, father of Sean
Sam Zenoda
Sean's brother, Sharogon's owner

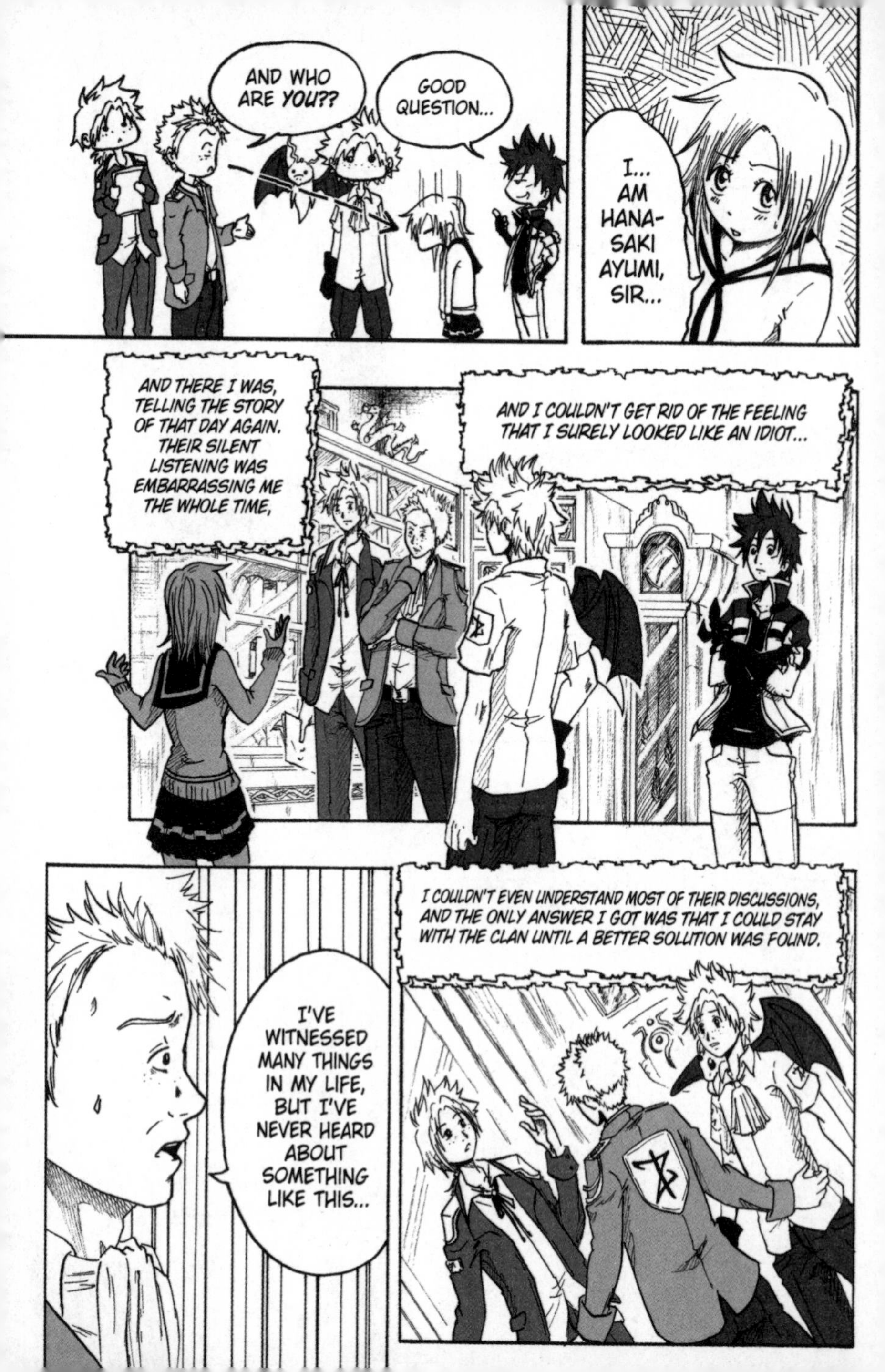
AND WHO ARE YOU??
GOOD QUESTION...
I... AM HANA-SAKI AYUMI, SIR...
AND THERE I WAS, TELLING THE STORY OF THAT DAY AGAIN. THEIR SILENT LISTENING WAS EMBARRASSING ME THE WHOLE TIME,
AND I COULDN'T GET RID OF THE FEELING THAT I SURELY LOOKED LIKE AN IDIOT...
I'VE WITNESSED MANY THINGS IN MY LIFE, BUT I'VE NEVER HEARD ABOUT SOMETHING LIKE THIS...
I COULDN'T EVEN UNDERSTAND MOST OF THEIR DISCUSSIONS, AND THE ONLY ANSWER I GOT WAS THAT I COULD STAY WITH THE CLAN UNTIL A BETTER SOLUTION WAS FOUND.

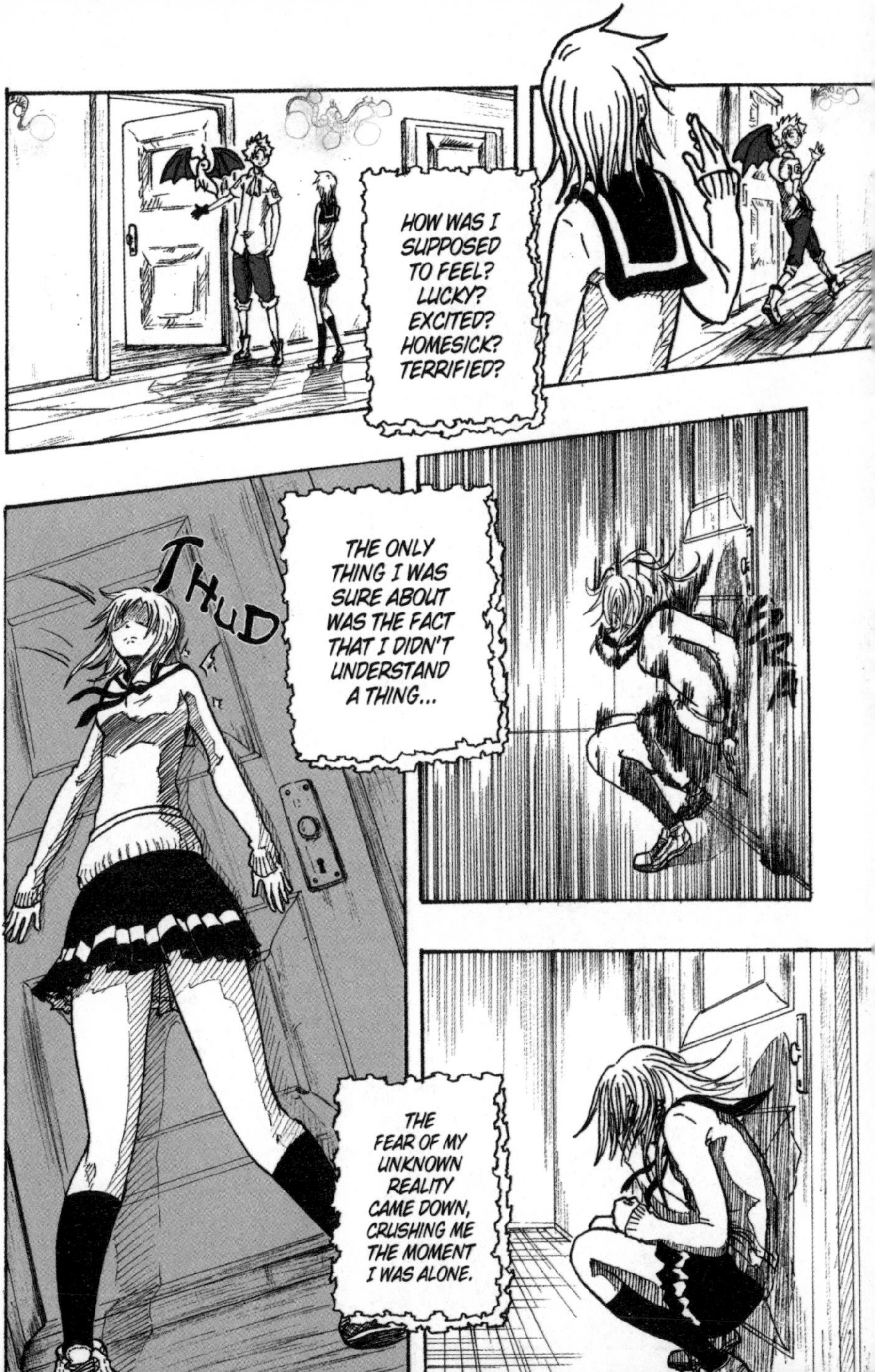
HOW WAS I SUPPOSED TO FEEL? LUCKY? EXCITED? HOMESICK? TERRIFIED?
THUD
THE ONLY THING I WAS SURE ABOUT WAS THE FACT THAT I DIDN'T UNDERSTAND A THING...
THE FEAR OF MY UNKNOWN REALITY CAME DOWN, CRUSHING ME THE MOMENT I WAS ALONE.

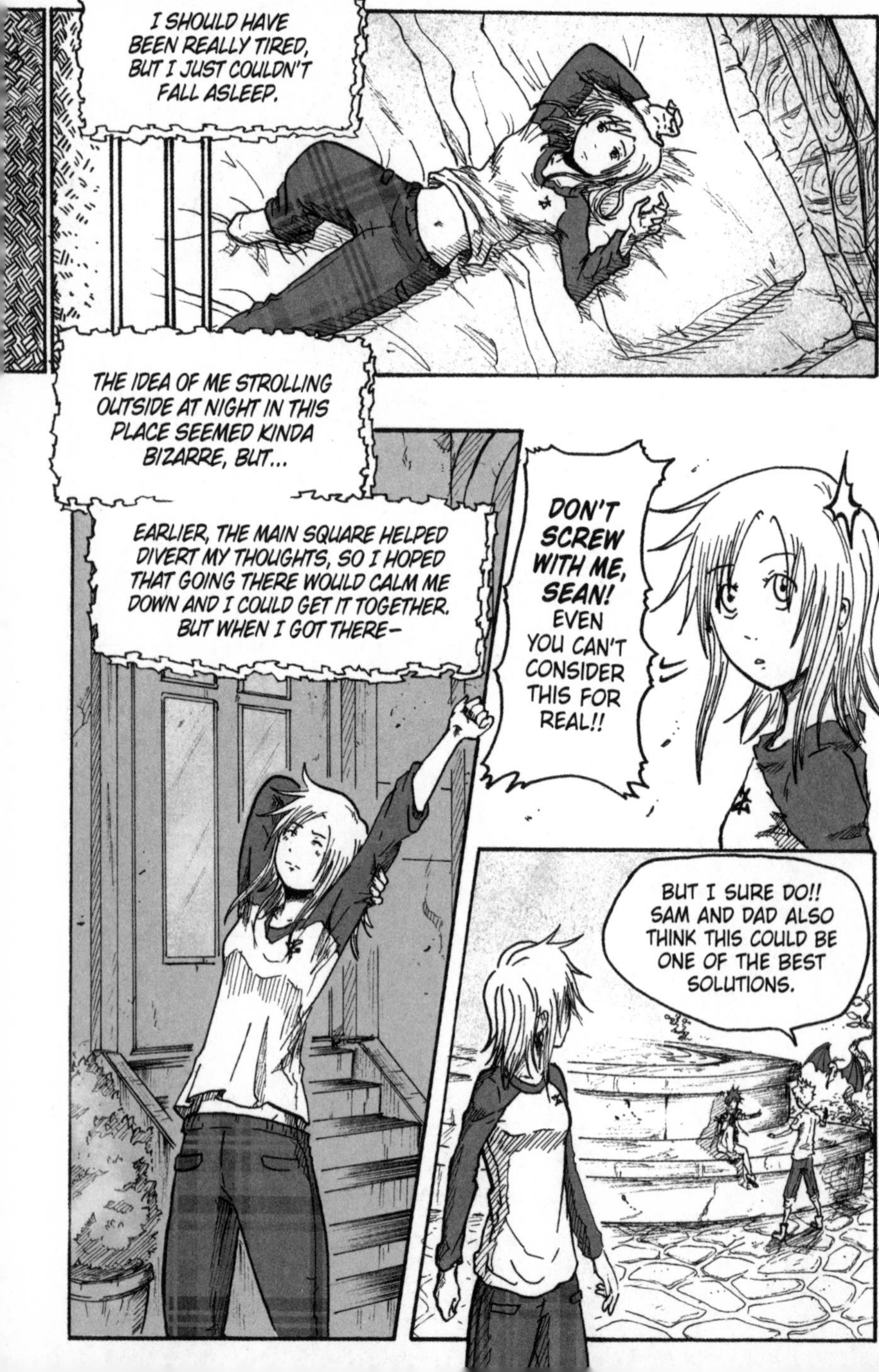
I SHOULD HAVE BEEN REALLY TIRED, BUT I JUST COULDN'T FALL ASLEEP.
THE IDEA OF ME STROLLING OUTSIDE AT NIGHT IN THIS PLACE SEEMED KINDA BIZARRE, BUT...
EARLIER, THE MAIN SQUARE HELPED DIVERT MY THOUGHTS, SO I HOPED THAT GOING THERE WOULD CALM ME DOWN AND I COULD GET IT TOGETHER. BUT WHEN I GOT THERE-
DON'T SCREW WITH ME, SEAN! EVEN YOU CAN'T CONSIDER THIS FOR REAL!!
BUT I SURE DO!! SAM AND DAD ALSO THINK THIS COULD BE ONE OF THE BEST SOLUTIONS.

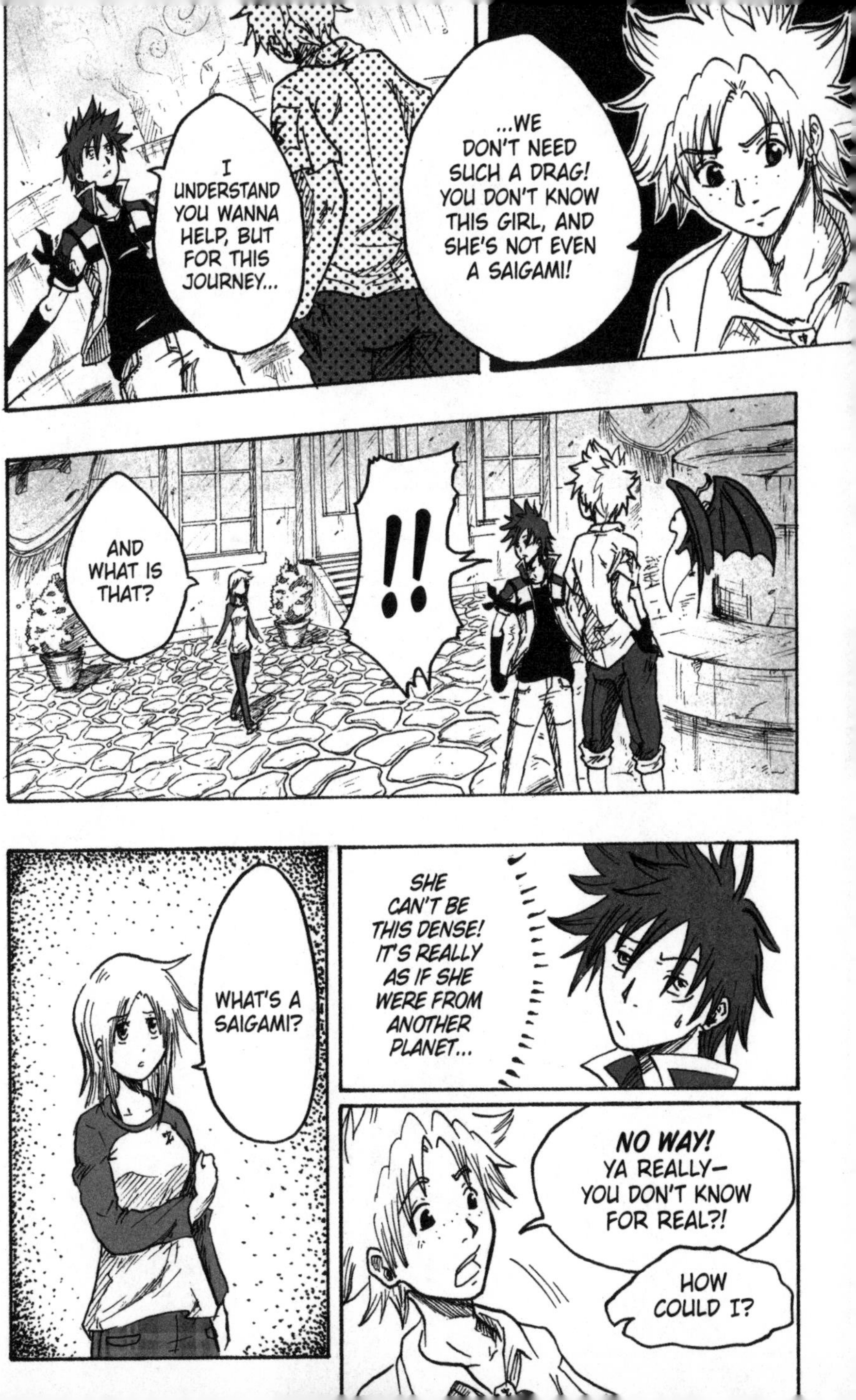
I UNDERSTAND YOU WANNA HELP, BUT FOR THIS JOURNEY...
...WE DON'T NEED SUCH A DRAG! YOU DON'T KNOW THIS GIRL, AND SHE'S NOT EVEN A SAIGAMI!
AND WHAT IS THAT?
!!
WHAT'S A SAIGAMI?
SHE CAN'T BE THIS DENSE! IT'S REALLY AS IF SHE WERE FROM ANOTHER PLANET...
NO WAY! YA REALLY— YOU DON'T KNOW FOR REAL?!
HOW COULD I?

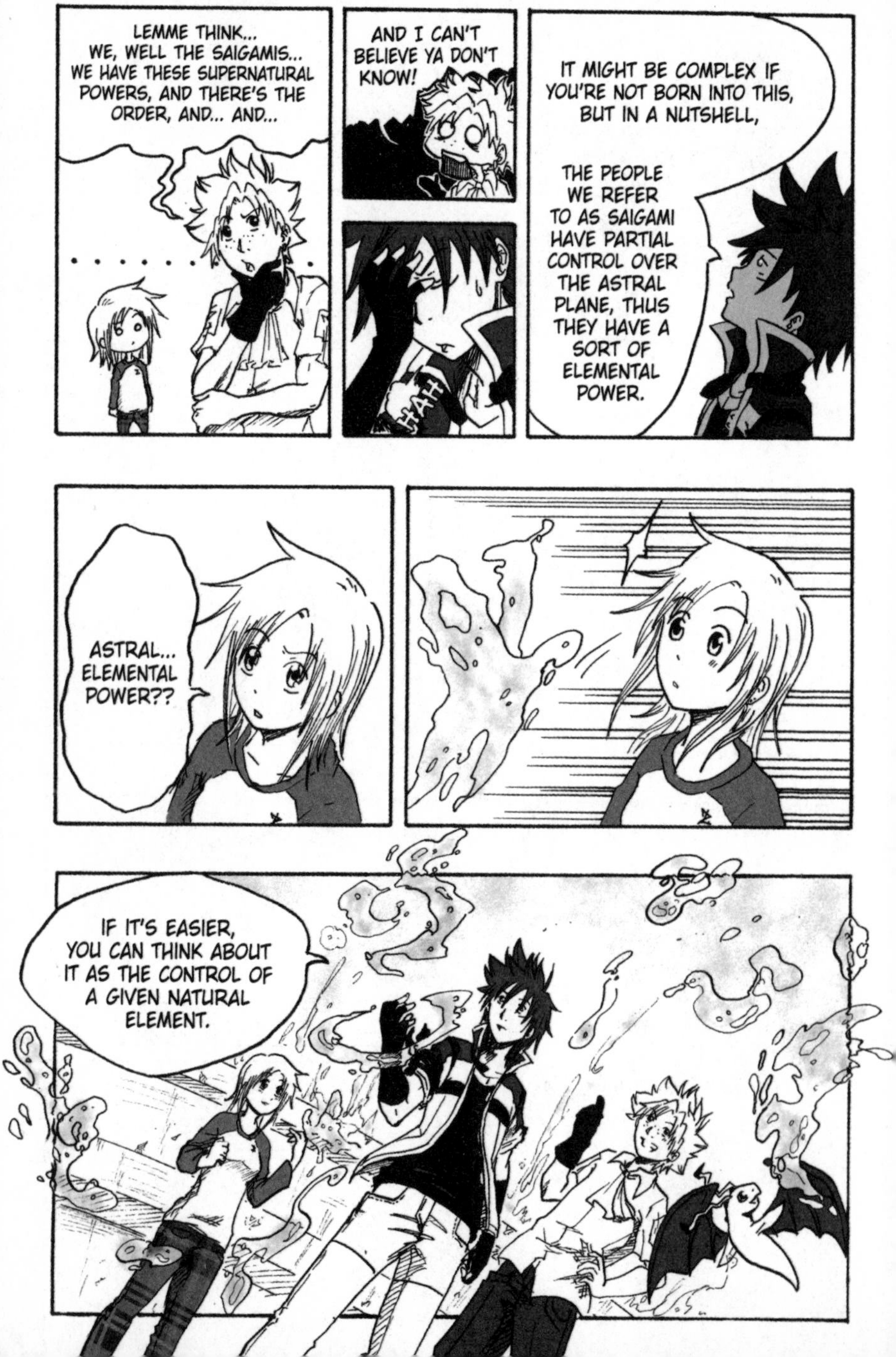
LEMME THINK... WE, WELL THE SAIGAMIS... WE HAVE THESE SUPERNATURAL POWERS, AND THERE'S THE ORDER, AND... AND...
. . . .
AND I CAN'T BELIEVE YA DON'T KNOW!
HAH
IT MIGHT BE COMPLEX IF YOU'RE NOT BORN INTO THIS, BUT IN A NUTSHELL,
THE PEOPLE WE REFER TO AS SAIGAMI HAVE PARTIAL CONTROL OVER THE ASTRAL PLANE, THUS THEY HAVE A SORT OF ELEMENTAL POWER.
ASTRAL... ELEMENTAL POWER??
IF IT'S EASIER, YOU CAN THINK ABOUT IT AS THE CONTROL OF A GIVEN NATURAL ELEMENT.

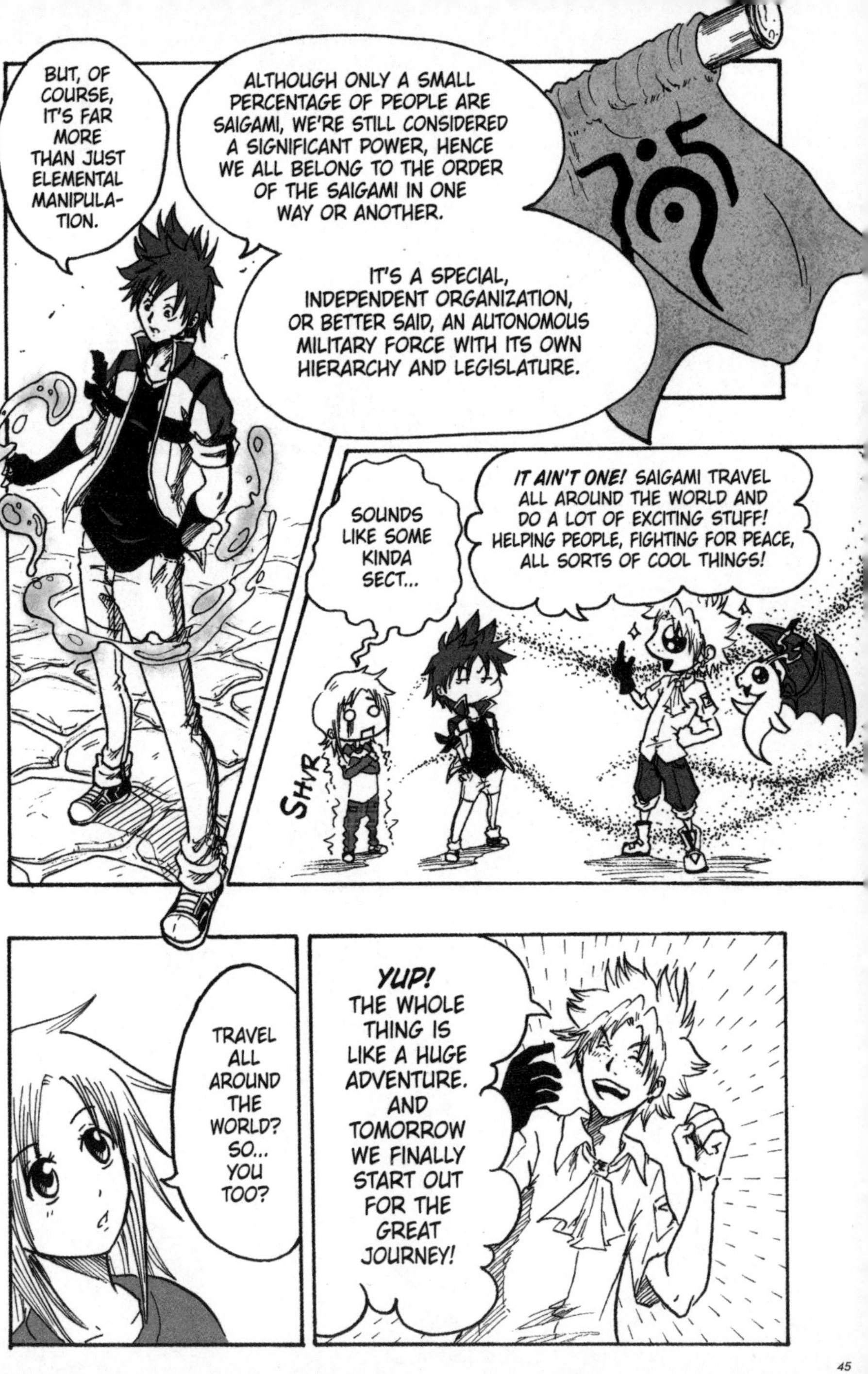
BUT, OF COURSE, IT'S FAR MORE THAN JUST ELEMENTAL MANIPULA-TION.
ALTHOUGH ONLY A SMALL PERCENTAGE OF PEOPLE ARE SAIGAMI, WE'RE STILL CONSIDERED A SIGNIFICANT POWER, HENCE WE ALL BELONG TO THE ORDER OF THE SAIGAMI IN ONE WAY OR ANOTHER.
IT'S A SPECIAL, INDEPENDENT ORGANIZATION, OR BETTER SAID, AN AUTONOMOUS MILITARY FORCE WITH ITS OWN HIERARCHY AND LEGISLATURE.
SOUNDS LIKE SOME KINDA SECT...
IT AIN'T ONE! SAIGAMI TRAVEL ALL AROUND THE WORLD AND DO A LOT OF EXCITING STUFF! HELPING PEOPLE, FIGHTING FOR PEACE, ALL SORTS OF COOL THINGS!
SHVR
TRAVEL ALL AROUND THE WORLD? SO... YOU TOO?
YUP! THE WHOLE THING IS LIKE A HUGE ADVENTURE. AND TOMORROW WE FINALLY START OUT FOR THE GREAT JOURNEY!

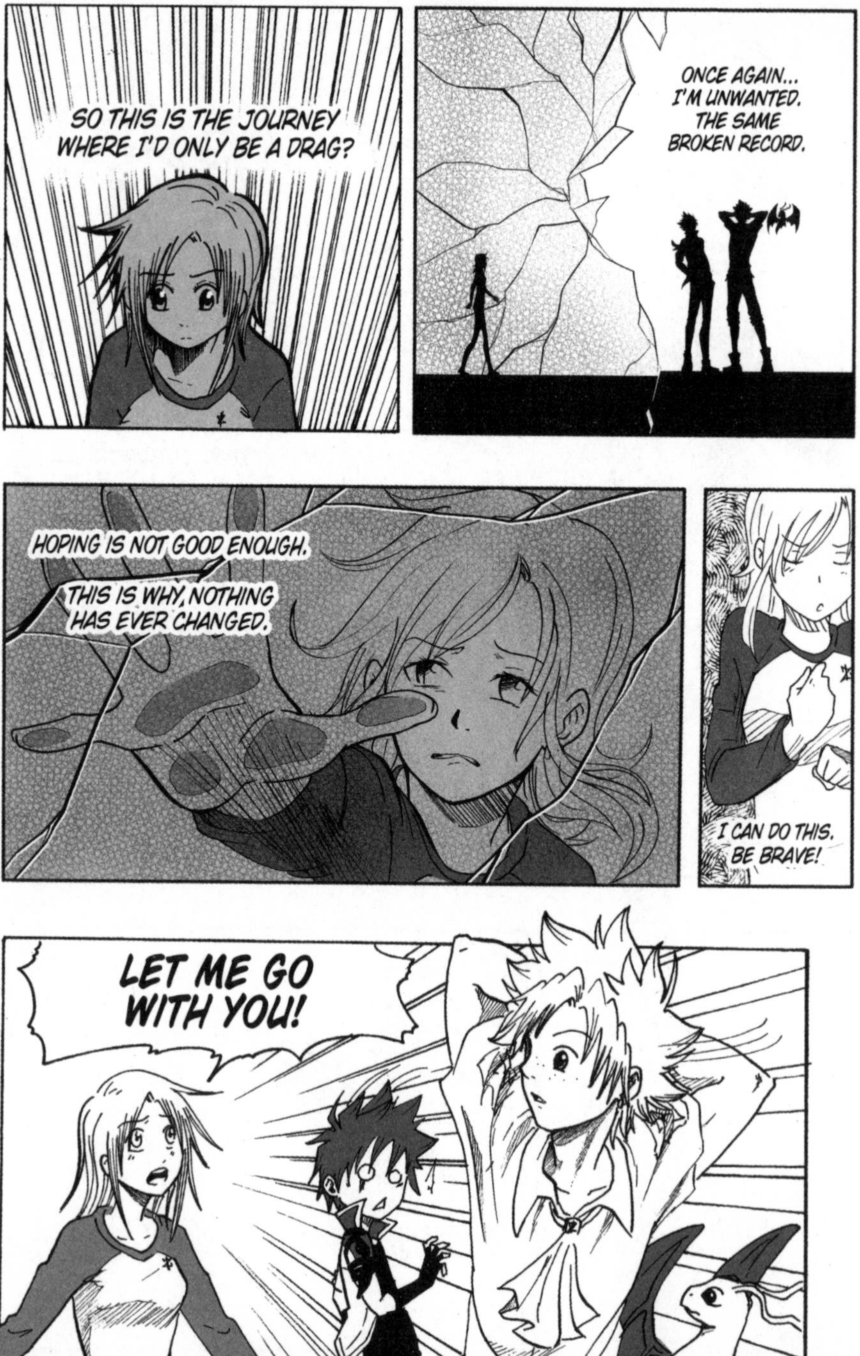
SO THIS IS THE JOURNEY WHERE I'D ONLY BE A DRAG?
ONCE AGAIN... I'M UNWANTED. THE SAME BROKEN RECORD.
HOPING IS NOT GOOD ENOUGH.
THIS IS WHY, NOTHING HAS EVER CHANGED.
I CAN DO THIS. BE BRAVE!
LET ME GO WITH YOU!

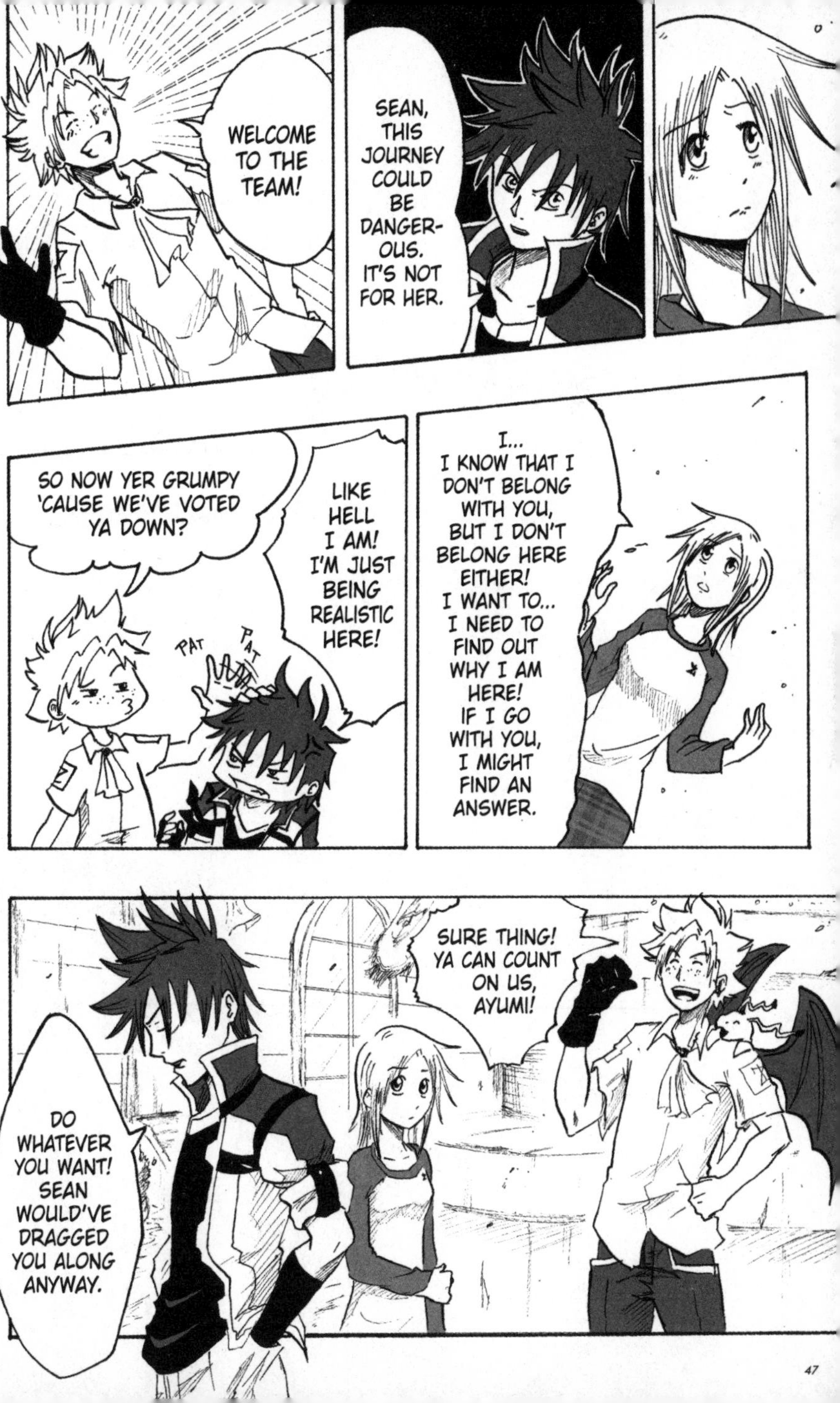
WELCOME TO THE TEAM!
SEAN, THIS JOURNEY COULD BE DANGER-OUS. IT'S NOT FOR HER.
SO NOW YER GRUMPY 'CAUSE WE'VE VOTED YA DOWN?
PAT
PAT
LIKE HELL I AM! I'M JUST BEING REALISTIC HERE!
I... I KNOW THAT I DON'T BELONG WITH YOU, BUT I DON'T BELONG HERE EITHER! I WANT TO... I NEED TO FIND OUT WHY I AM HERE! IF I GO WITH YOU, I MIGHT FIND AN ANSWER.
DO WHATEVER YOU WANT! SEAN WOULD'VE DRAGGED YOU ALONG ANYWAY.
SURE THING! YA CAN COUNT ON US, AYUMI!

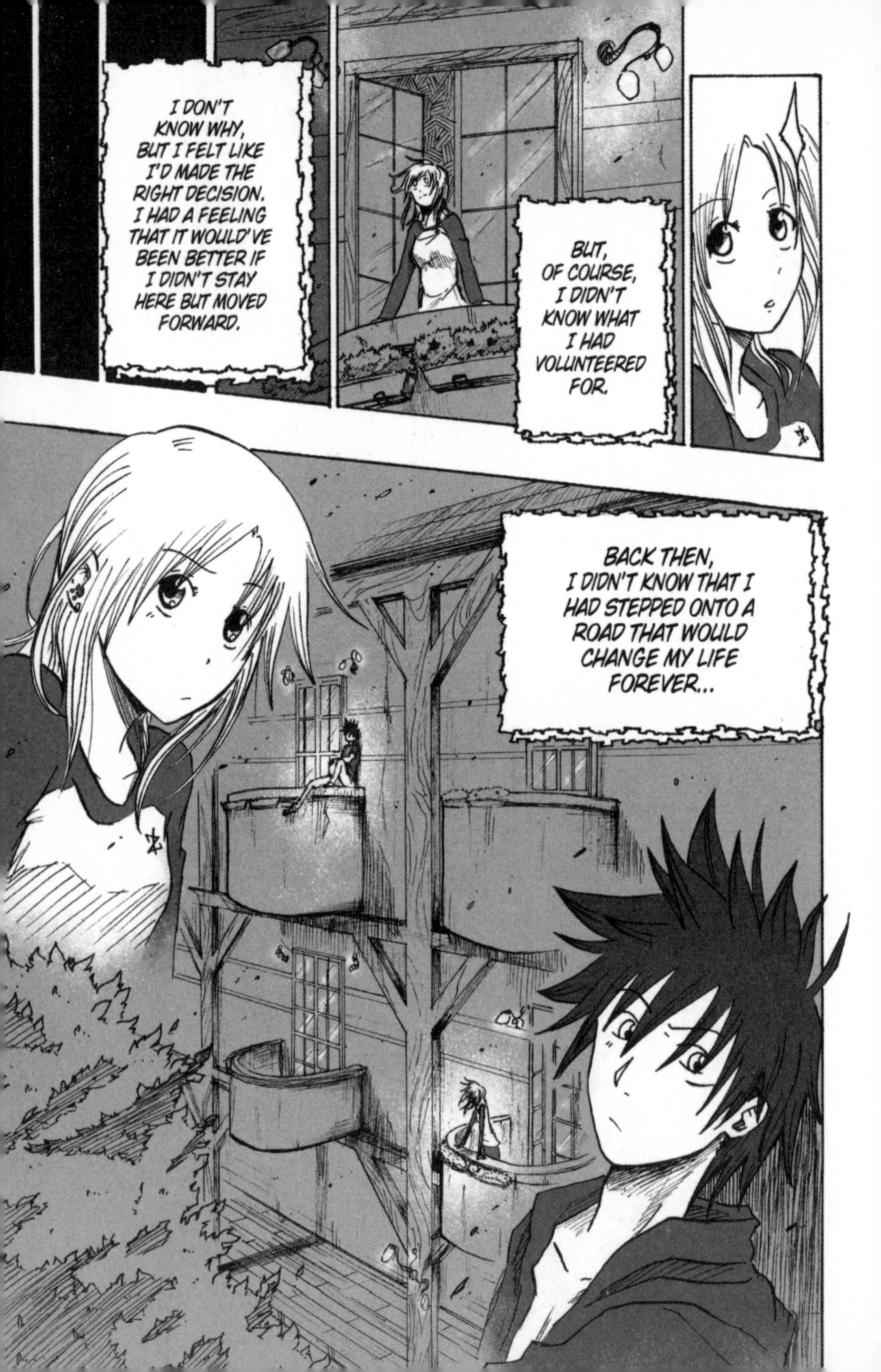
I DON'T KNOW WHY, BUT I FELT LIKE I'D MADE THE RIGHT DECISION. I HAD A FEELING THAT IT WOULD'VE BEEN BETTER IF I DIDN'T STAY HERE BUT MOVED FORWARD.
BUT, OF COURSE, I DIDN'T KNOW WHAT I HAD VOLUNTEERED FOR.
BACK THEN, I DIDN'T KNOW THAT I HAD STEPPED ONTO A ROAD THAT WOULD CHANGE MY LIFE FOREVER...

SAIGAMI

Chapter 2: **Awakening Flames**

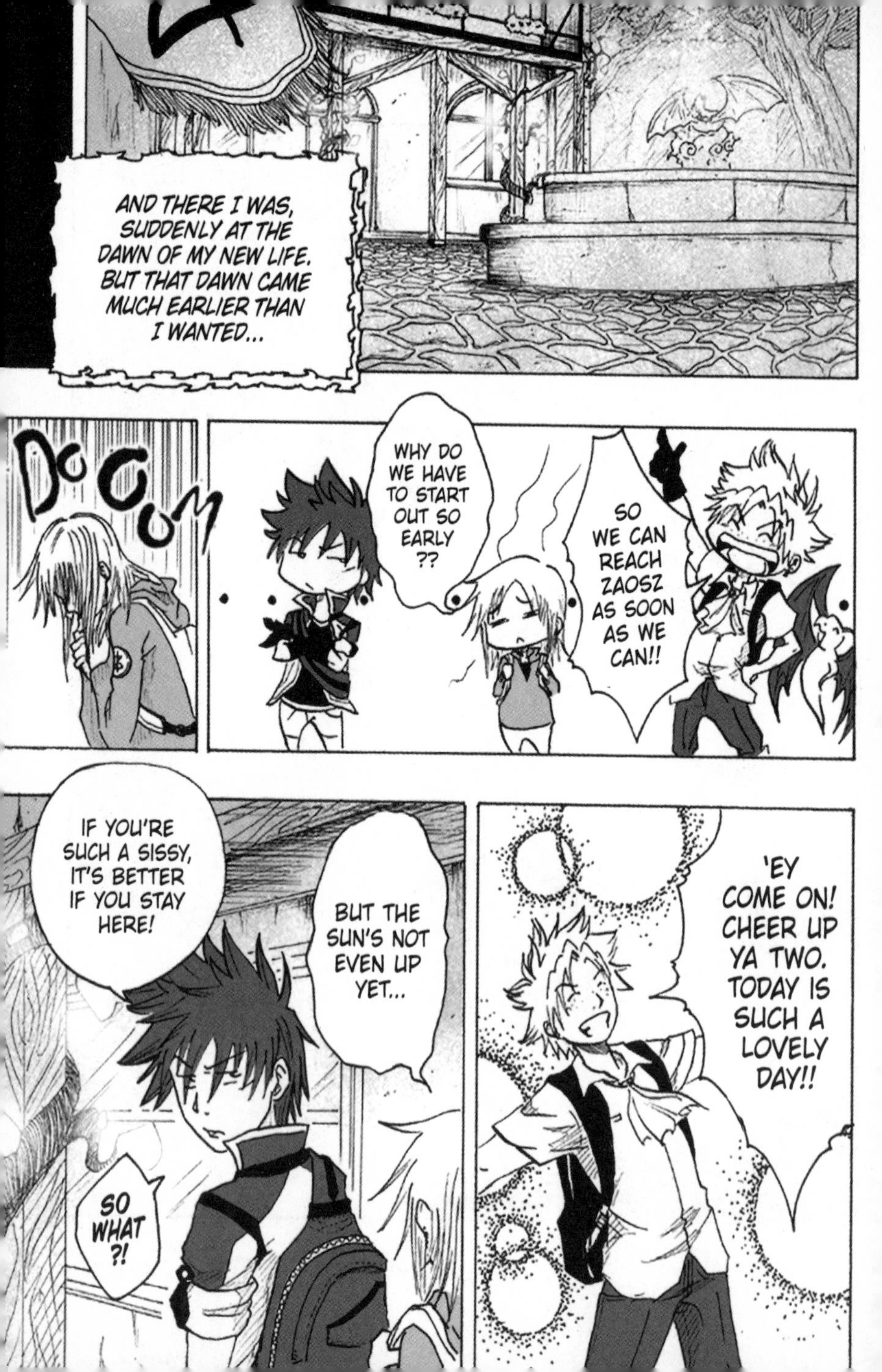
AND THERE I WAS, SUDDENLY AT THE DAWN OF MY NEW LIFE. BUT THAT DAWN CAME MUCH EARLIER THAN I WANTED...
DOOOM
WHY DO WE HAVE TO START OUT SO EARLY ??
SO WE CAN REACH ZAOSZ AS SOON AS WE CAN!!
IF YOU'RE SUCH A SISSY, IT'S BETTER IF YOU STAY HERE!
BUT THE SUN'S NOT EVEN UP YET...
SO WHAT ?!
'EY COME ON! CHEER UP YA TWO. TODAY IS SUCH A LOVELY DAY!!

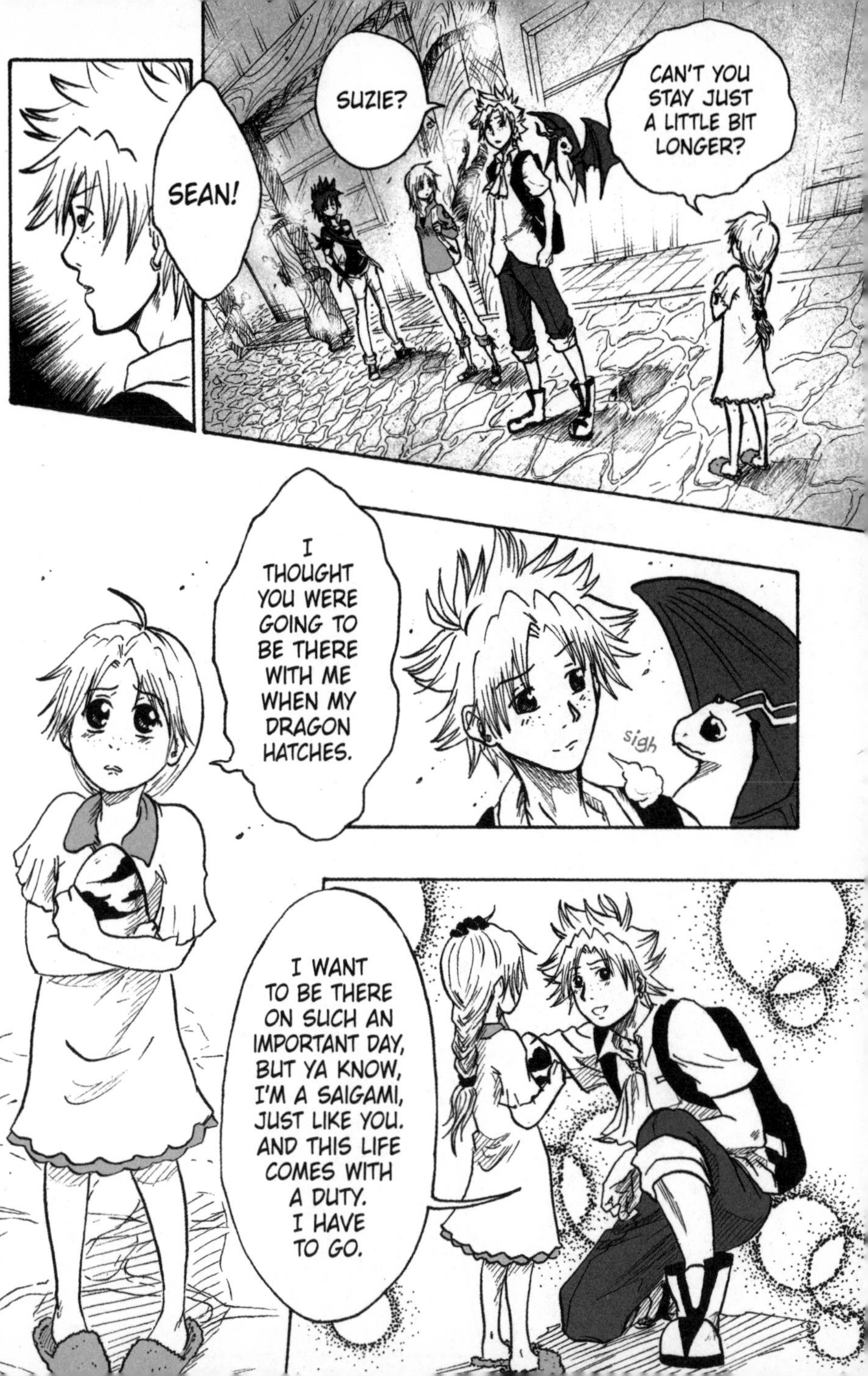
SEAN!
SUZIE?
CAN'T YOU STAY JUST A LITTLE BIT LONGER?
I THOUGHT YOU WERE GOING TO BE THERE WITH ME WHEN MY DRAGON HATCHES.
sigh
I WANT TO BE THERE ON SUCH AN IMPORTANT DAY, BUT YA KNOW, I'M A SAIGAMI, JUST LIKE YOU. AND THIS LIFE COMES WITH A DUTY. I HAVE TO GO.

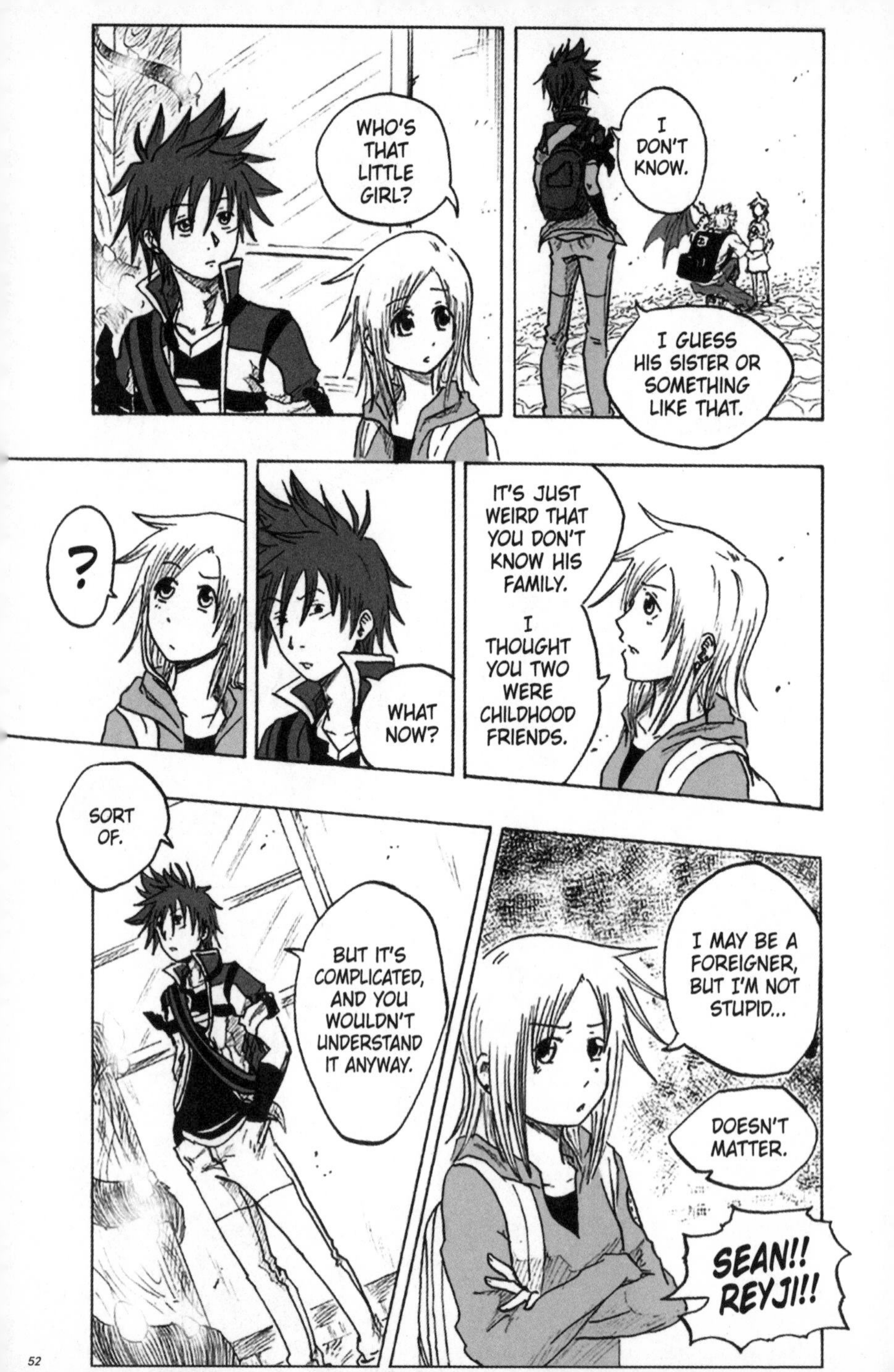
WHO'S THAT LITTLE GIRL?
I DON'T KNOW.
I GUESS HIS SISTER OR SOMETHING LIKE THAT.
?
WHAT NOW?
IT'S JUST WEIRD THAT YOU DON'T KNOW HIS FAMILY.
I THOUGHT YOU TWO WERE CHILDHOOD FRIENDS.
SORT OF.
BUT IT'S COMPLICATED, AND YOU WOULDN'T UNDERSTAND IT ANYWAY.
I MAY BE A FOREIGNER, BUT I'M NOT STUPID...
DOESN'T MATTER.
SEAN!! REYJI!!

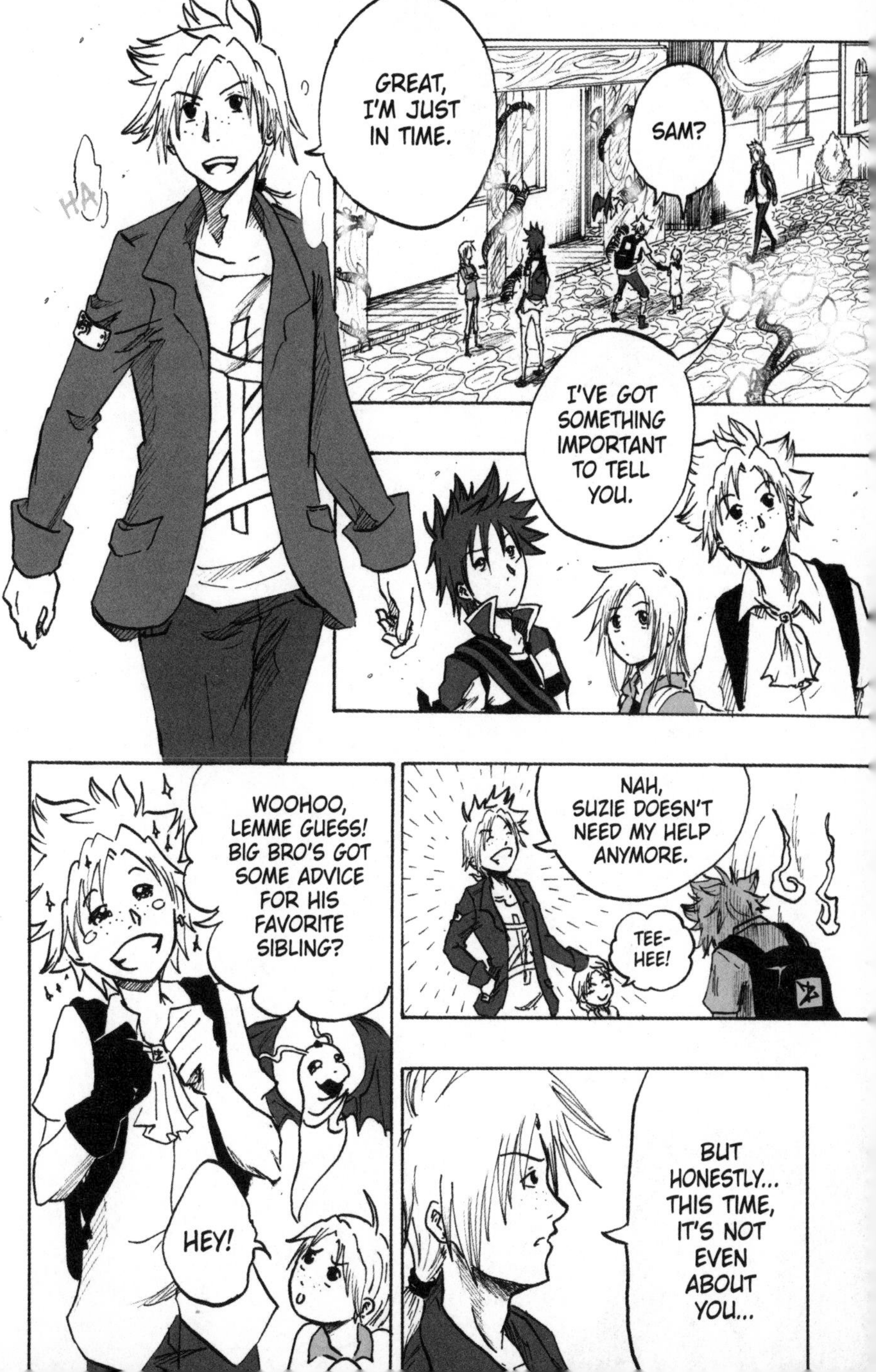
HA
GREAT, I'M JUST IN TIME.
SAM?
I'VE GOT SOMETHING IMPORTANT TO TELL YOU.
WOOHOO, LEMME GUESS! BIG BRO'S GOT SOME ADVICE FOR HIS FAVORITE SIBLING?
HEY!
NAH, SUZIE DOESN'T NEED MY HELP ANYMORE.
TEE-HEE!
BUT HONESTLY... THIS TIME, IT'S NOT EVEN ABOUT YOU...

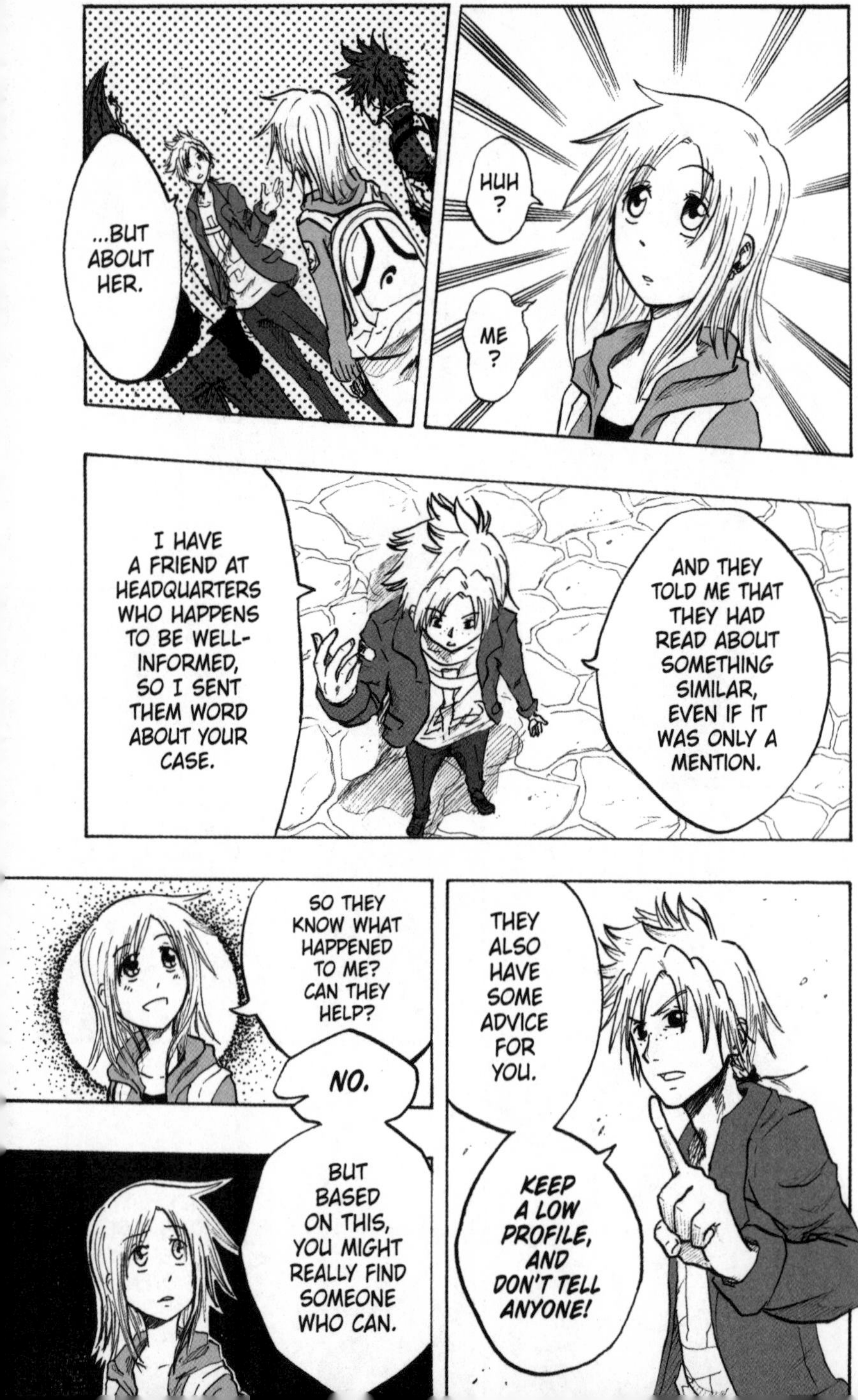
...BUT ABOUT HER.
HUH ?
ME ?
I HAVE A FRIEND AT HEADQUARTERS WHO HAPPENS TO BE WELL-INFORMED, SO I SENT THEM WORD ABOUT YOUR CASE.
AND THEY TOLD ME THAT THEY HAD READ ABOUT SOMETHING SIMILAR, EVEN IF IT WAS ONLY A MENTION.
SO THEY KNOW WHAT HAPPENED TO ME? CAN THEY HELP?
NO.
BUT BASED ON THIS, YOU MIGHT REALLY FIND SOMEONE WHO CAN.
THEY ALSO HAVE SOME ADVICE FOR YOU.
KEEP A LOW PROFILE, AND DON'T TELL ANYONE!

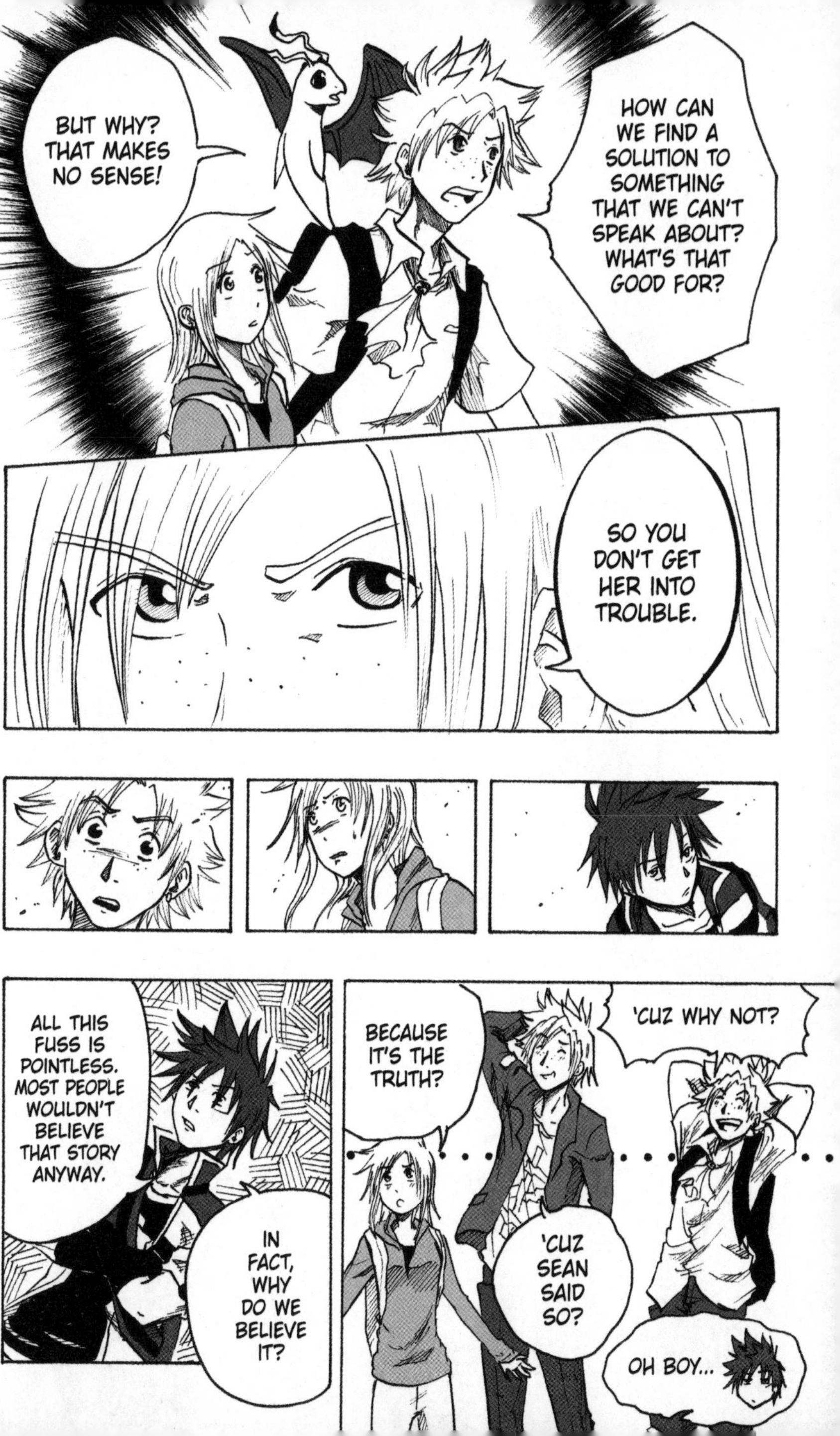
BUT WHY? THAT MAKES NO SENSE!
HOW CAN WE FIND A SOLUTION TO SOMETHING THAT WE CAN'T SPEAK ABOUT? WHAT'S THAT GOOD FOR?
SO YOU DON'T GET HER INTO TROUBLE.
ALL THIS FUSS IS POINTLESS. MOST PEOPLE WOULDN'T BELIEVE THAT STORY ANYWAY.
IN FACT, WHY DO WE BELIEVE IT?
BECAUSE IT'S THE TRUTH?
'CUZ WHY NOT?
'CUZ SEAN SAID SO?
OH BOY...

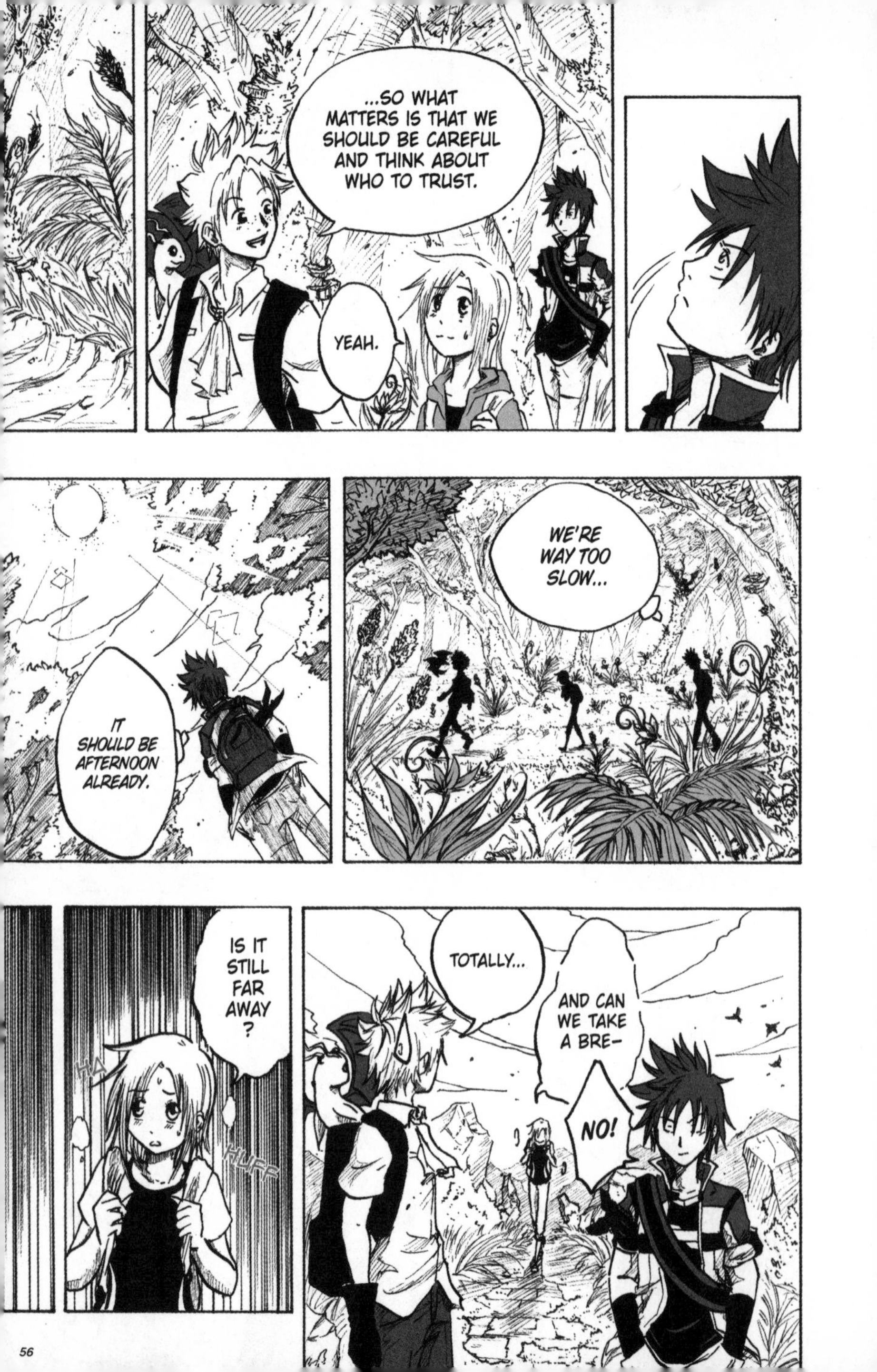
...SO WHAT MATTERS IS THAT WE SHOULD BE CAREFUL AND THINK ABOUT WHO TO TRUST.
YEAH.
IT SHOULD BE AFTERNOON ALREADY.
WE'RE WAY TOO SLOW...
IS IT STILL FAR AWAY?
HA
HUFF
TOTALLY...
AND CAN WE TAKE A BRE-
NO!

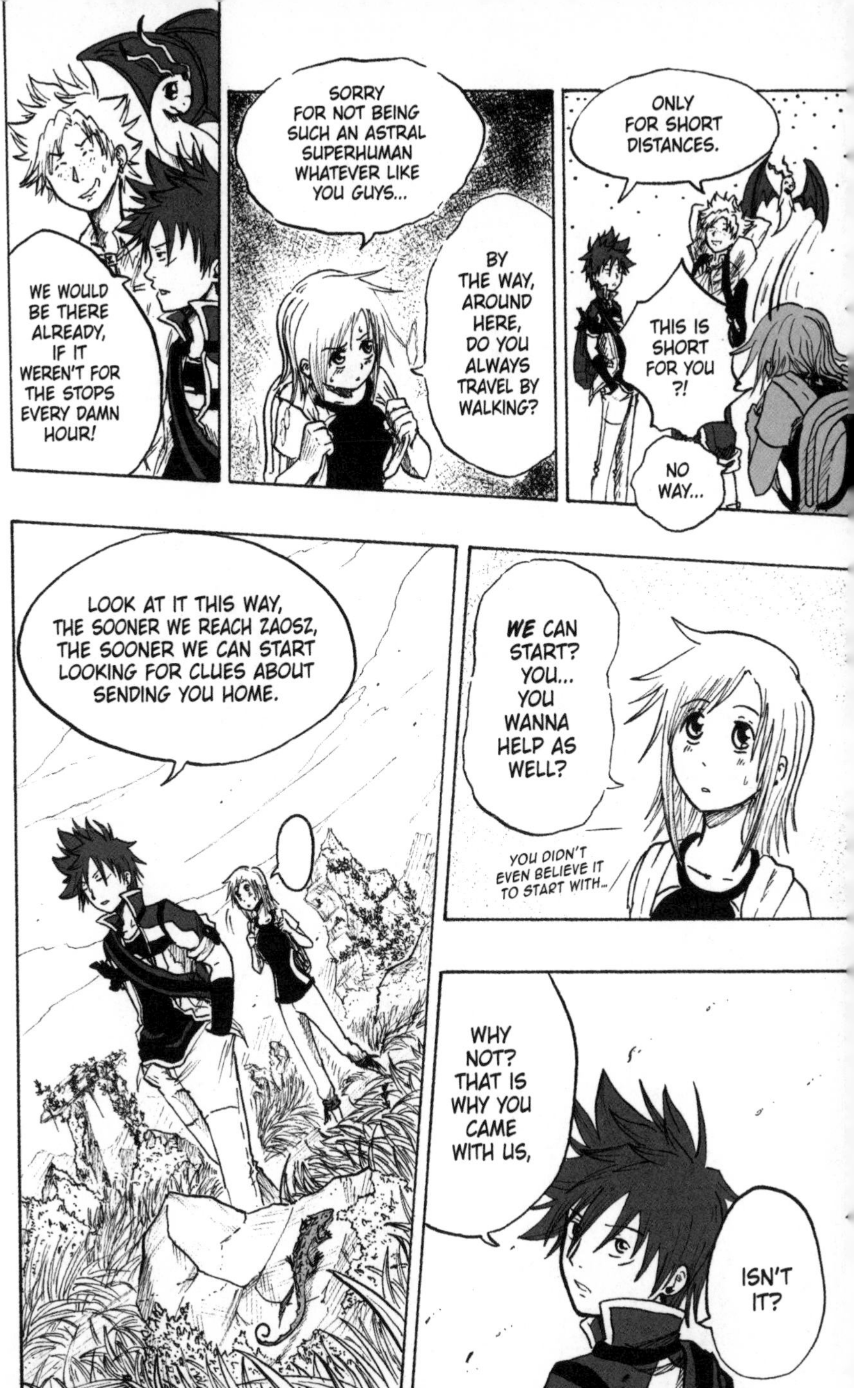
WE WOULD BE THERE ALREADY, IF IT WEREN'T FOR THE STOPS EVERY DAMN HOUR!
SORRY FOR NOT BEING SUCH AN ASTRAL SUPERHUMAN WHATEVER LIKE YOU GUYS...
BY THE WAY, AROUND HERE, DO YOU ALWAYS TRAVEL BY WALKING?
ONLY FOR SHORT DISTANCES.
THIS IS SHORT FOR YOU ?!
NO WAY...
LOOK AT IT THIS WAY, THE SOONER WE REACH ZAOSZ, THE SOONER WE CAN START LOOKING FOR CLUES ABOUT SENDING YOU HOME.
WE CAN START? YOU... YOU WANNA HELP AS WELL?
YOU DIDN'T EVEN BELIEVE IT TO START WITH...
WHY NOT? THAT IS WHY YOU CAME WITH US,
ISN'T IT?

ADMIT IT, YOU'RE ONLY HELPING TO GET RID OF HER SOONER!

THIS WAY EVERYONE GAINS SOMETHING.

DAMN RIGHT.

SHE CAN GO HOME,

WHEREVER THAT MIGHT BE.

AND WE'LL HAVE ONE LESS PROBLEM AND WON'T HAVE TO LISTEN TO HER TANTRUMS ALL DAY LONG.

BUT I HAVEN'T HAD ANY TANTRUMS TO BEGIN WITH!

YOU'RE DOING IT NOW.

BUT I'M NOT—

"ARE WE THERE YET? IS IT FAR AWAY? CAN'T WE TAKE A BREAK?"

BUT—

BUT I—

BUT THIS—

IF EVERY "BUT" WERE A STEP, WE'D ALREADY BE THERE.

YOU'RE DAMN FUNNY.

...

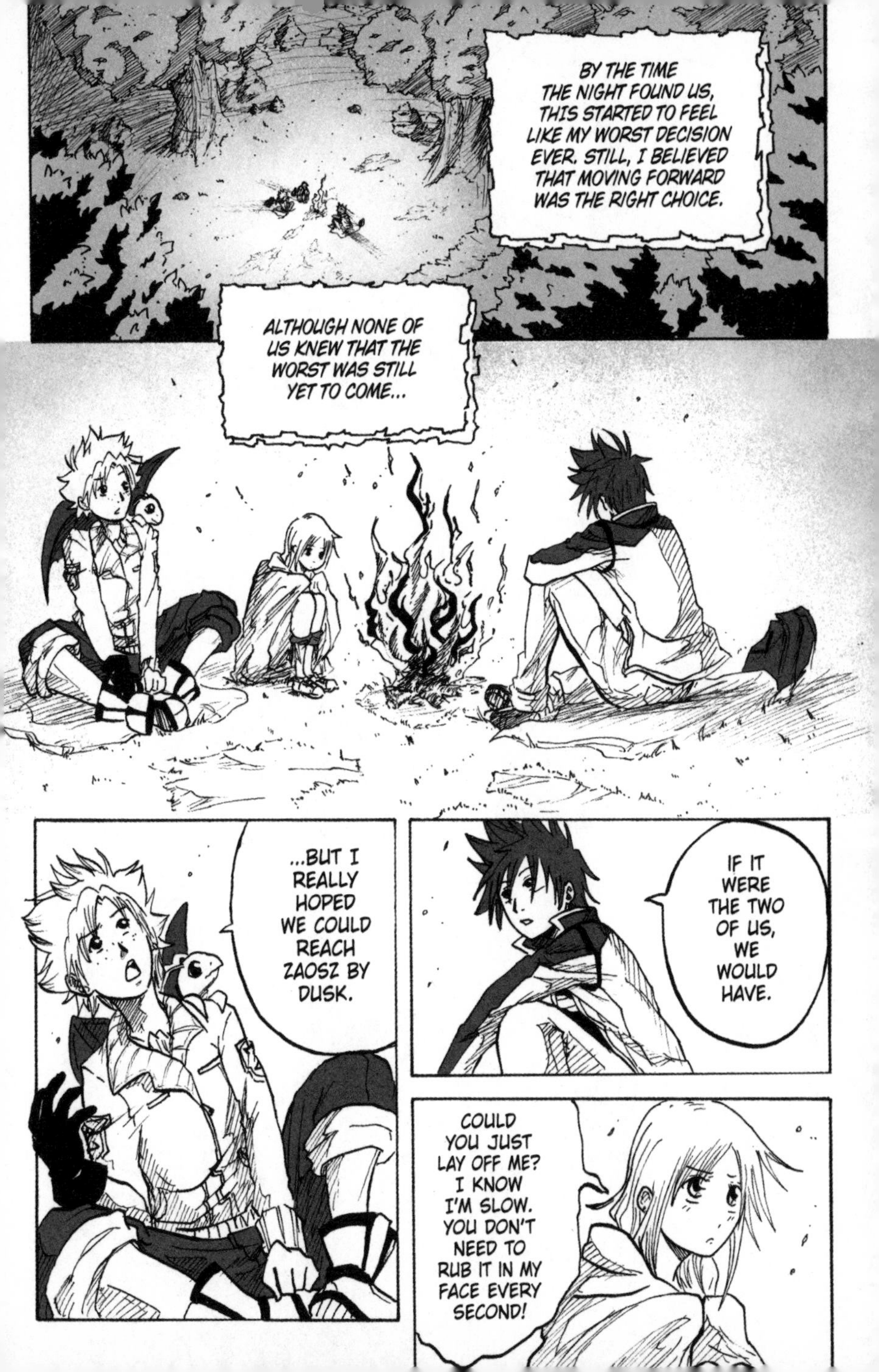
BY THE TIME THE NIGHT FOUND US, THIS STARTED TO FEEL LIKE MY WORST DECISION EVER. STILL, I BELIEVED THAT MOVING FORWARD WAS THE RIGHT CHOICE.
ALTHOUGH NONE OF US KNEW THAT THE WORST WAS STILL YET TO COME...
...BUT I REALLY HOPED WE COULD REACH ZAOSZ BY DUSK.
IF IT WERE THE TWO OF US, WE WOULD HAVE.
COULD YOU JUST LAY OFF ME? I KNOW I'M SLOW. YOU DON'T NEED TO RUB IT IN MY FACE EVERY SECOND!

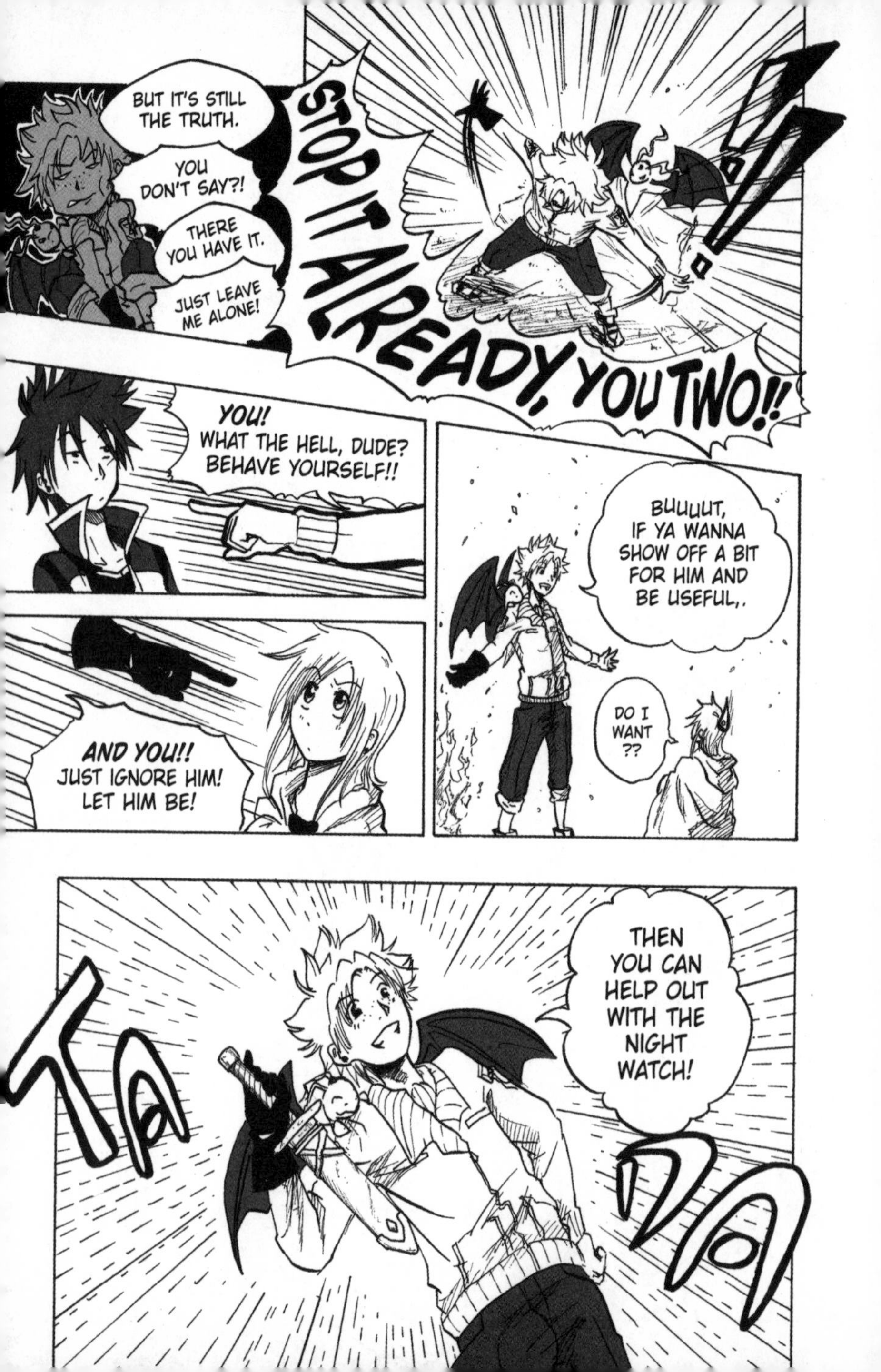
BUT IT'S STILL THE TRUTH.
YOU DON'T SAY?!
THERE YOU HAVE IT.
JUST LEAVE ME ALONE!
STOP IT ALREADY, YOU TWO!!
!!
YOU! WHAT THE HELL, DUDE? BEHAVE YOURSELF!!
AND YOU!! JUST IGNORE HIM! LET HIM BE!
BUUUUT, IF YA WANNA SHOW OFF A BIT FOR HIM AND BE USEFUL,.
DO I WANT ??
TA
THEN YOU CAN HELP OUT WITH THE NIGHT WATCH!
DA

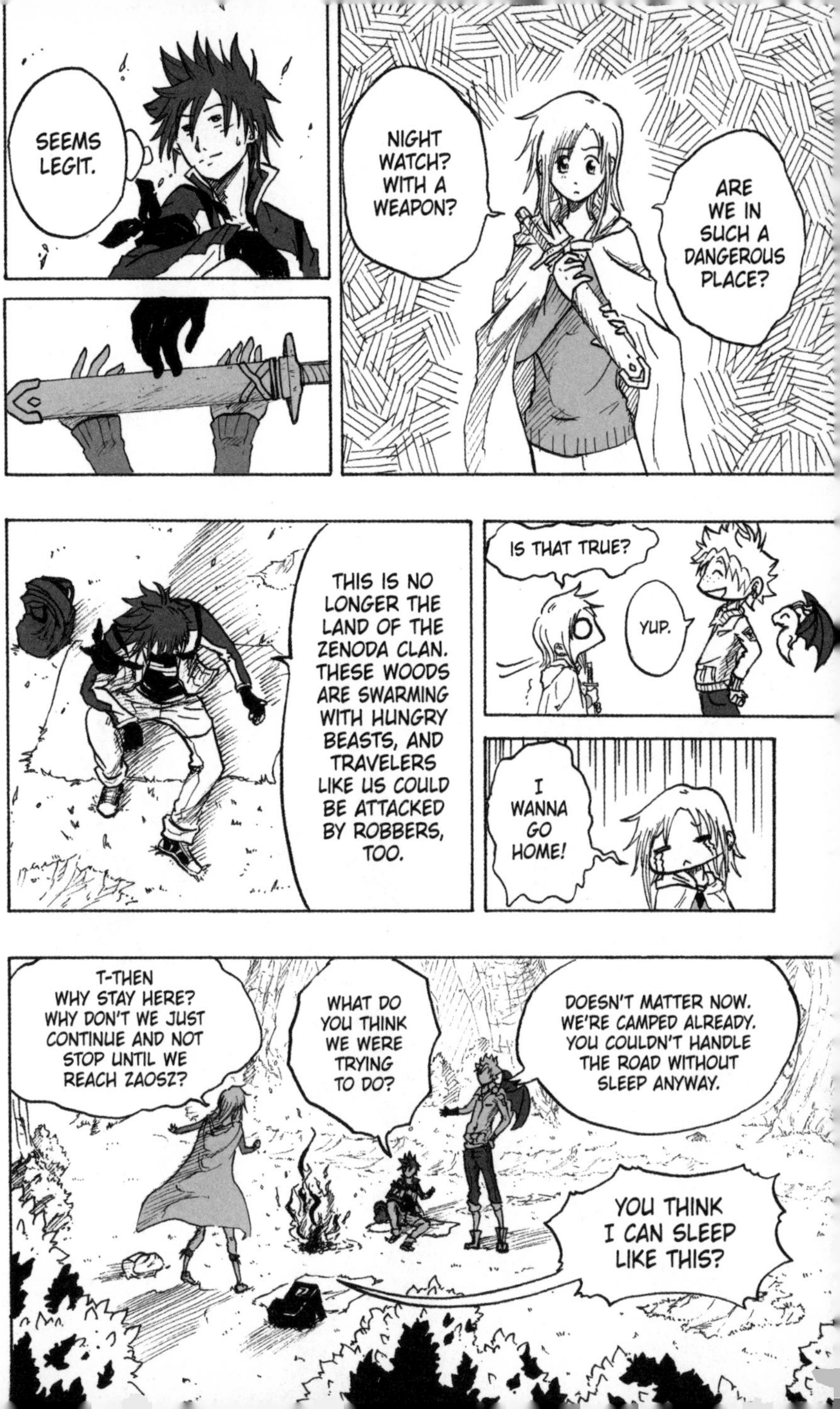
SEEMS LEGIT.
NIGHT WATCH? WITH A WEAPON?
ARE WE IN SUCH A DANGEROUS PLACE?
THIS IS NO LONGER THE LAND OF THE ZENODA CLAN. THESE WOODS ARE SWARMING WITH HUNGRY BEASTS, AND TRAVELERS LIKE US COULD BE ATTACKED BY ROBBERS, TOO.
IS THAT TRUE?
YUP.
I WANNA GO HOME!
T-THEN WHY STAY HERE? WHY DON'T WE JUST CONTINUE AND NOT STOP UNTIL WE REACH ZAOSZ?
WHAT DO YOU THINK WE WERE TRYING TO DO?
DOESN'T MATTER NOW. WE'RE CAMPED ALREADY. YOU COULDN'T HANDLE THE ROAD WITHOUT SLEEP ANYWAY.
YOU THINK I CAN SLEEP LIKE THIS?

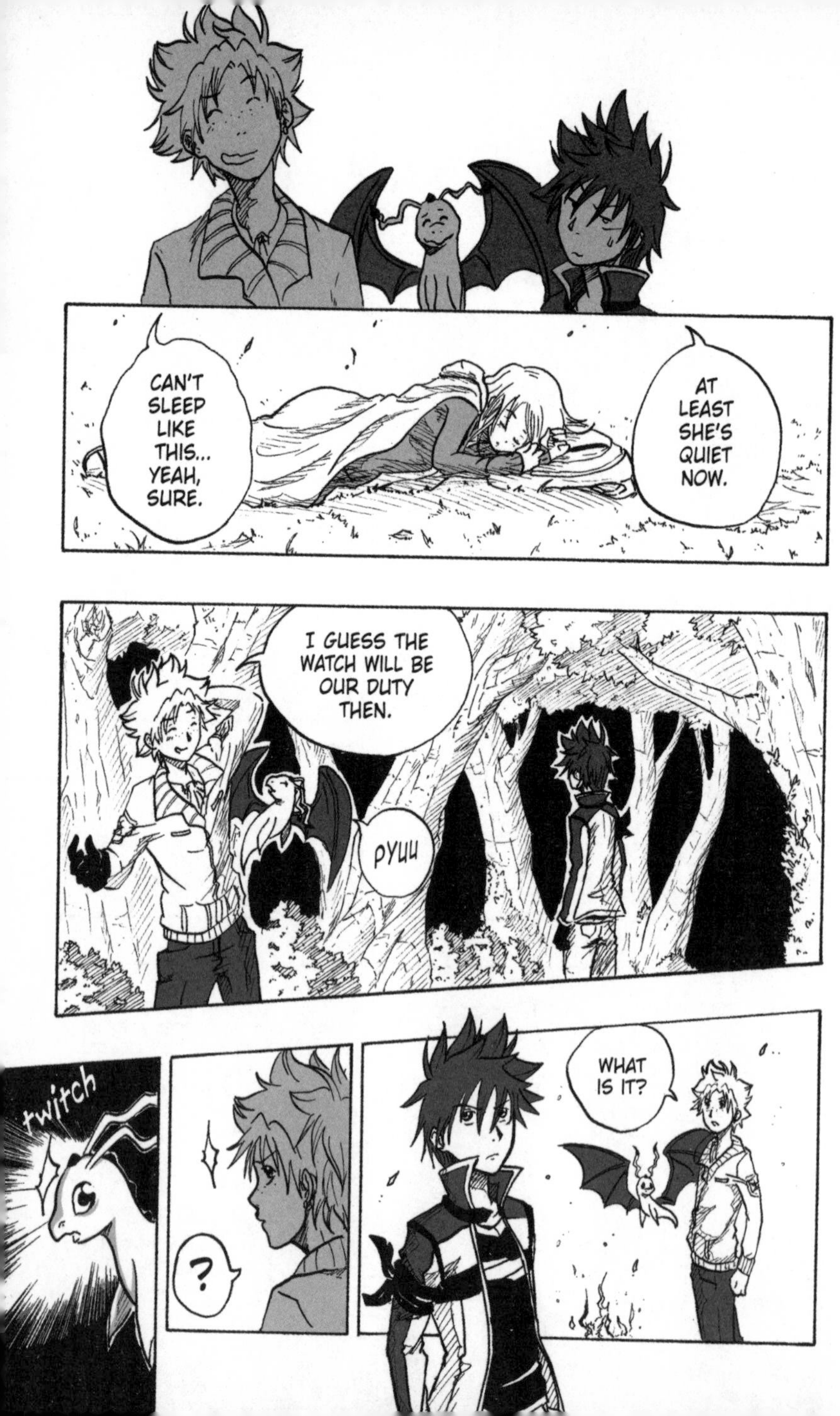
CAN'T SLEEP LIKE THIS... YEAH, SURE.
AT LEAST SHE'S QUIET NOW.
I GUESS THE WATCH WILL BE OUR DUTY THEN.
PYUU
twitch
?
WHAT IS IT?

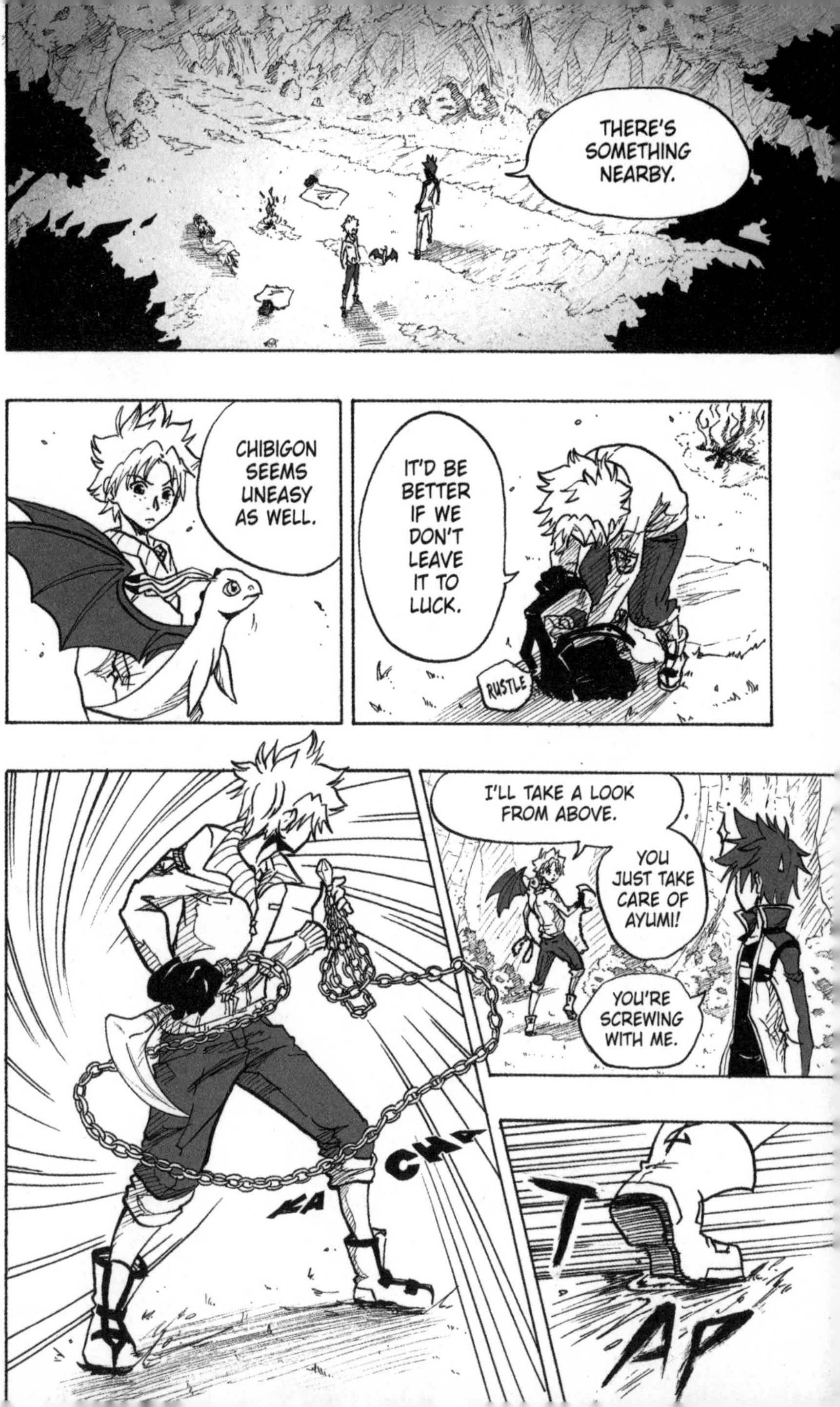
THERE'S SOMETHING NEARBY.
CHIBIGON SEEMS UNEASY AS WELL.
IT'D BE BETTER IF WE DON'T LEAVE IT TO LUCK.
RUSTLE
KA CHA
I'LL TAKE A LOOK FROM ABOVE.
YOU JUST TAKE CARE OF AYUMI!
YOU'RE SCREWING WITH ME.
TAP

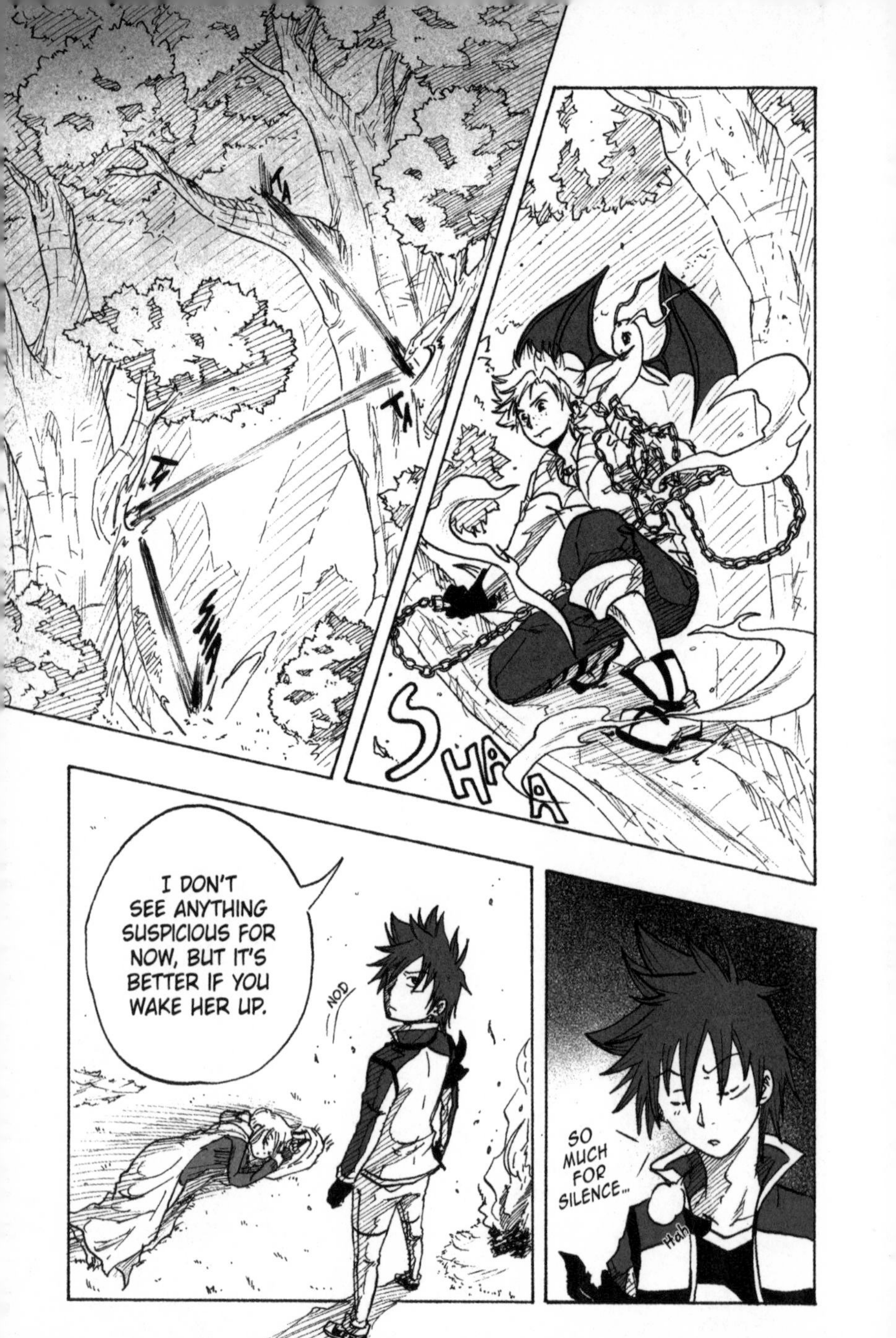
TA
TA
TA
SHA
SHAA
I DON'T SEE ANYTHING SUSPICIOUS FOR NOW, BUT IT'S BETTER IF YOU WAKE HER UP.
NOD
SO MUCH FOR SILENCE...
Hah

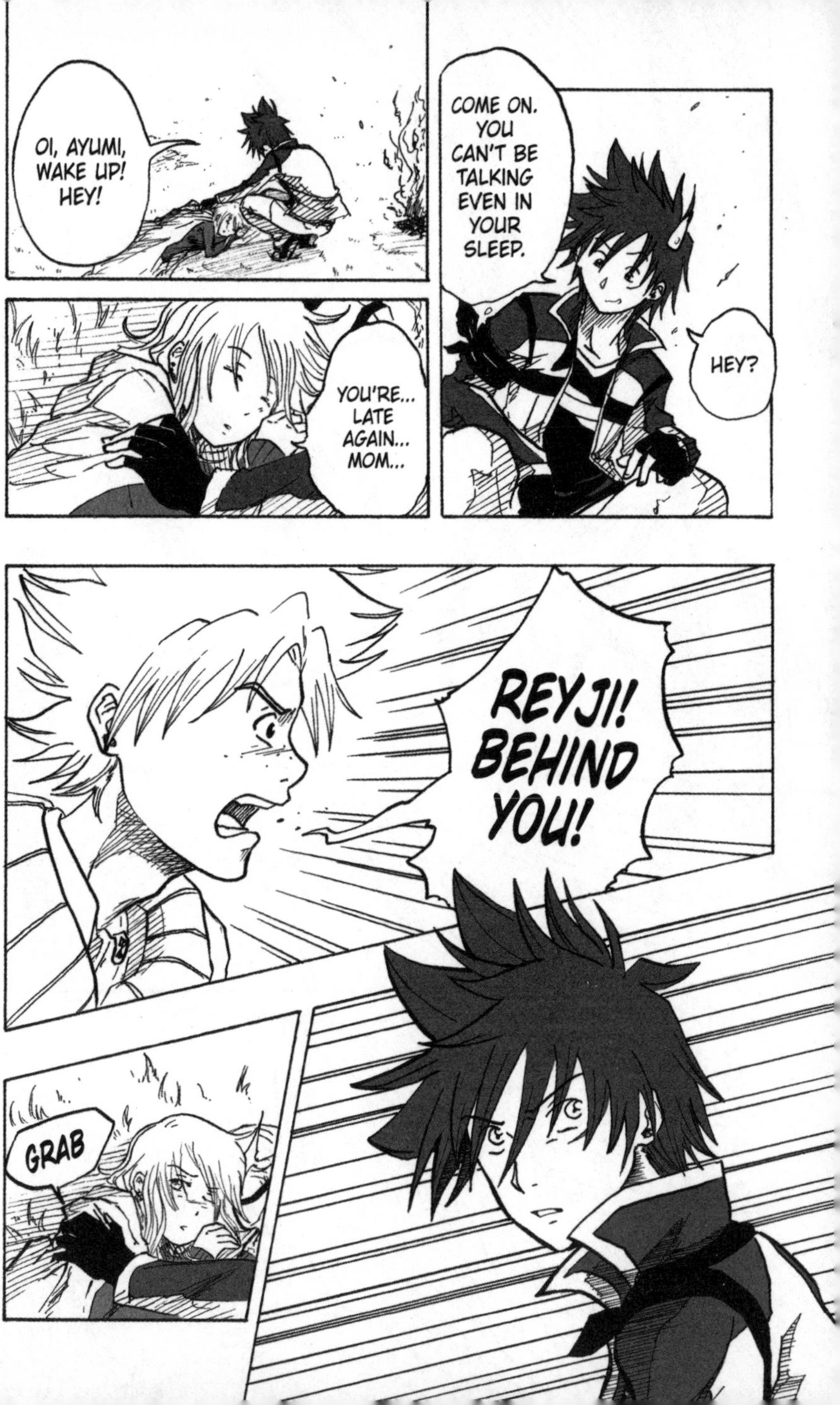
OI, AYUMI, WAKE UP! HEY!
YOU'RE... LATE AGAIN... MOM...
COME ON. YOU CAN'T BE TALKING EVEN IN YOUR SLEEP.
HEY?
REYJI! BEHIND YOU!
GRAB

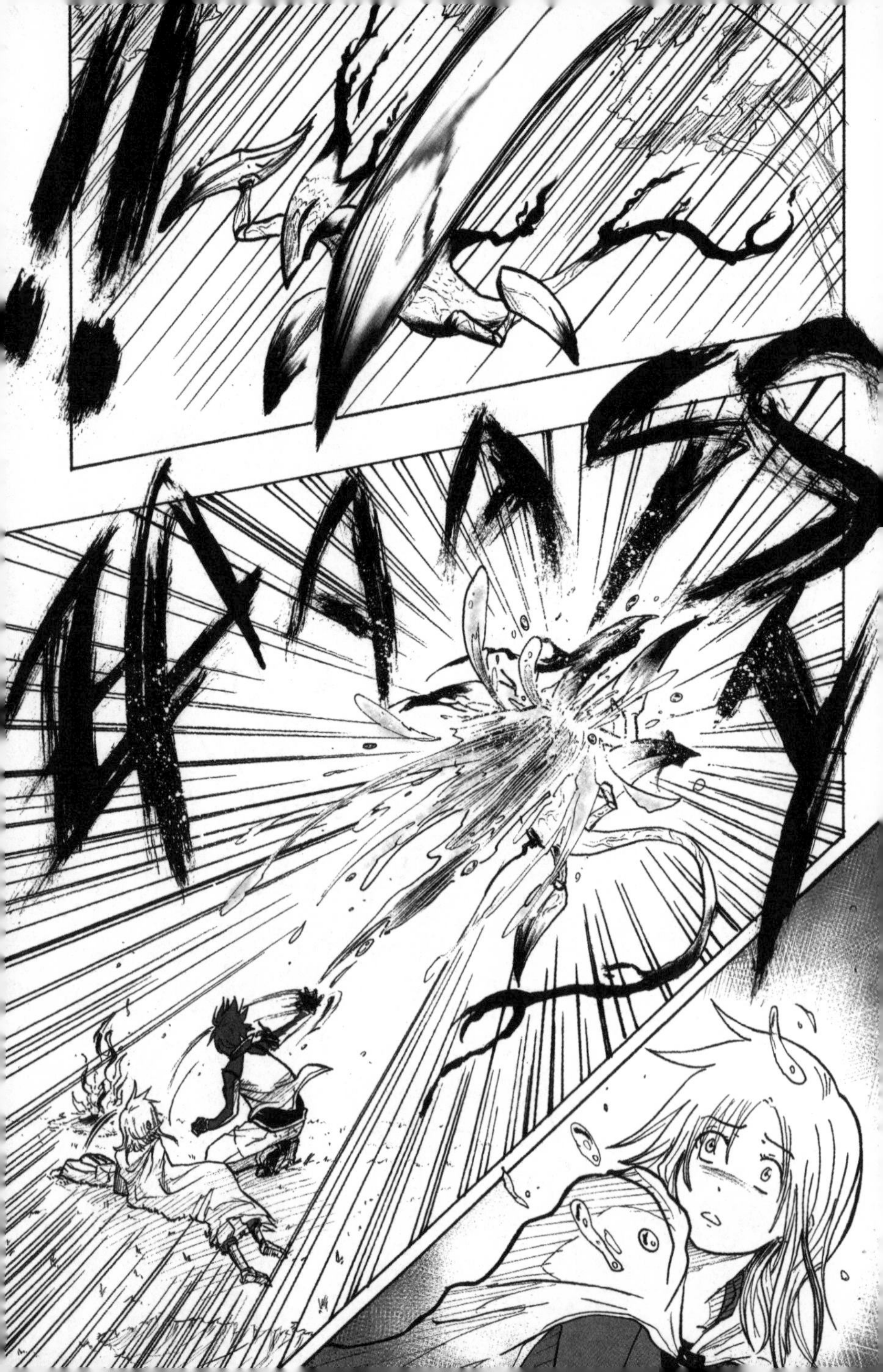

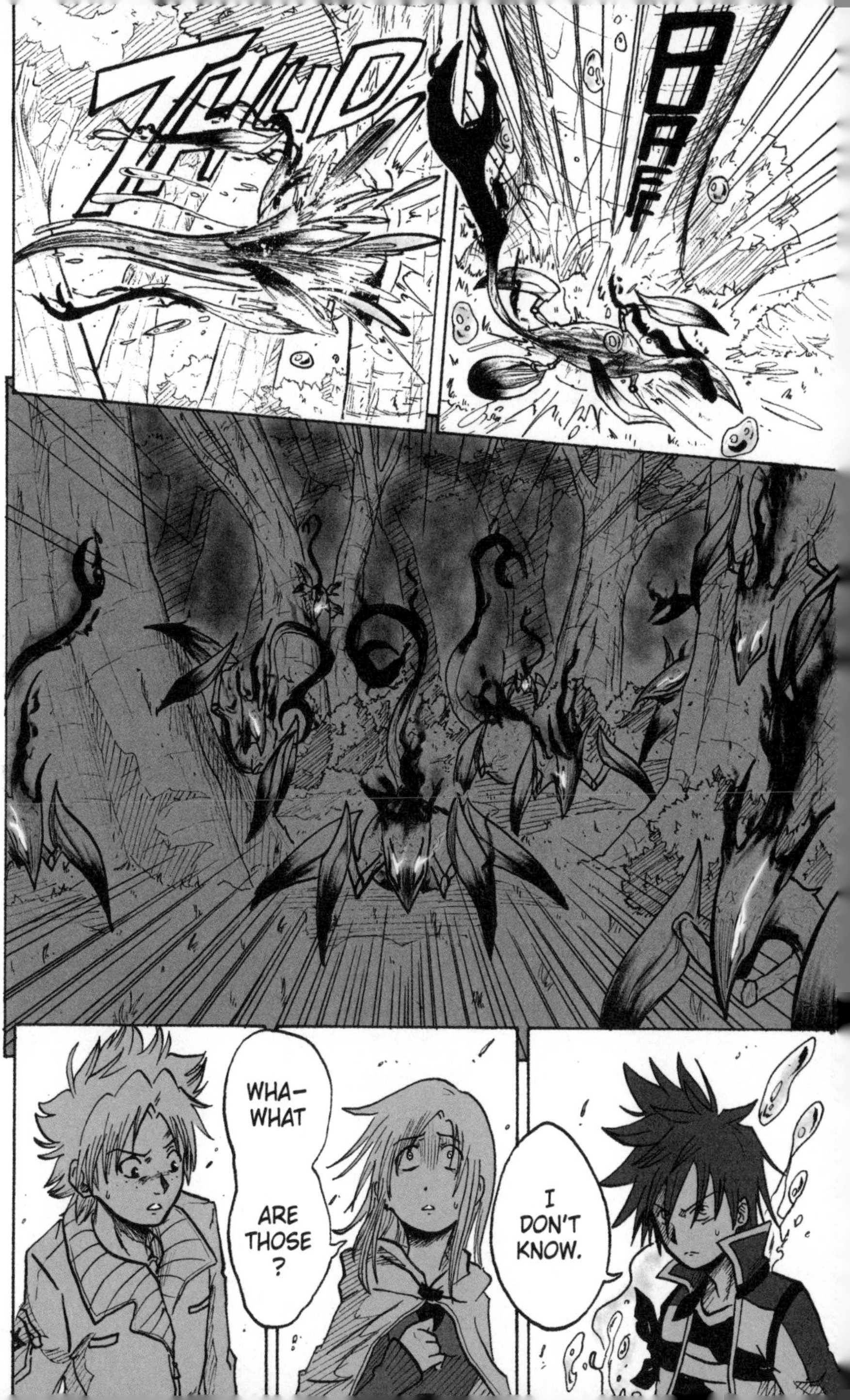

THUD
BAFF
WHA-WHAT ARE THOSE ?
I DON'T KNOW.

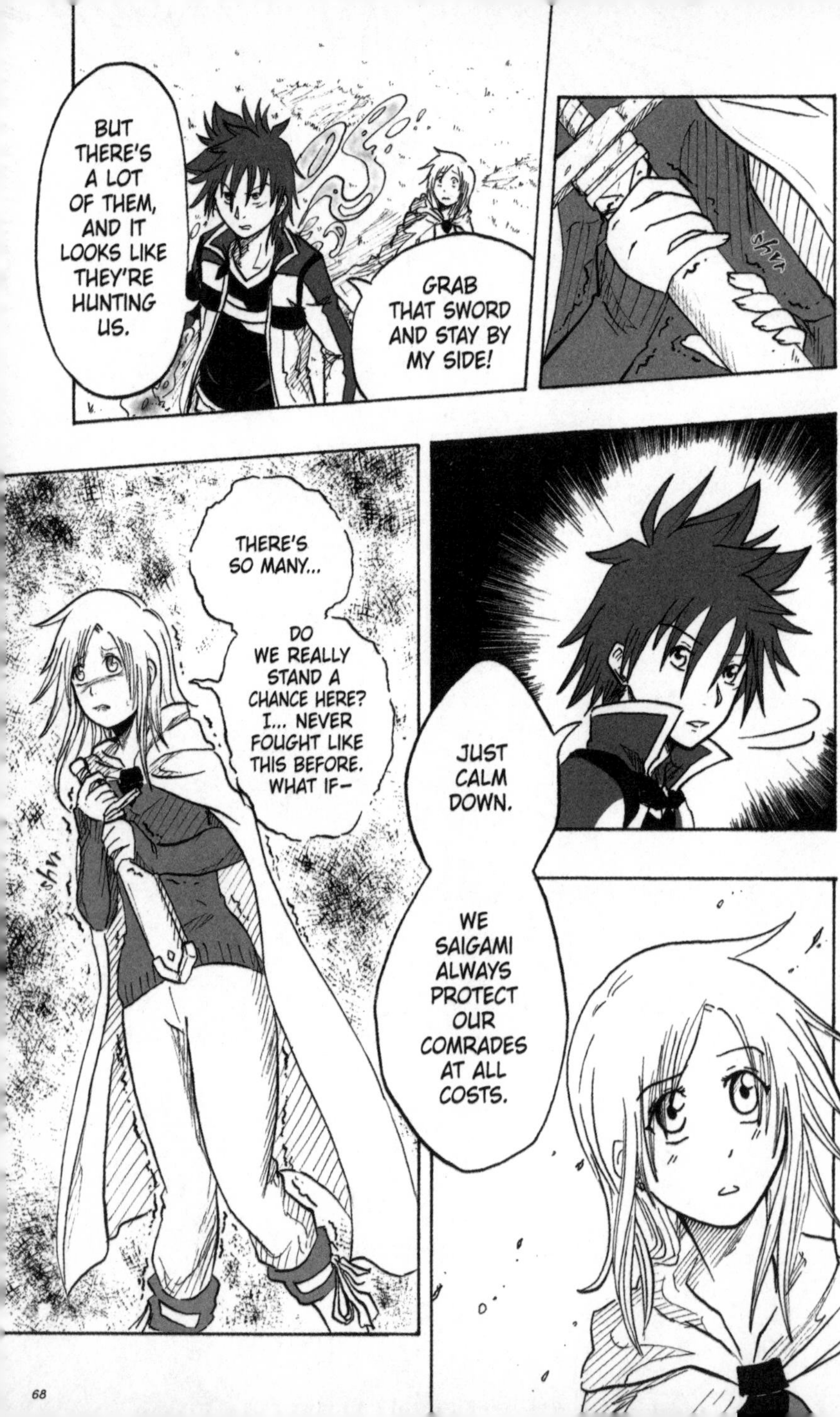
BUT THERE'S A LOT OF THEM, AND IT LOOKS LIKE THEY'RE HUNTING US.
GRAB THAT SWORD AND STAY BY MY SIDE!
shvr
THERE'S SO MANY...
DO WE REALLY STAND A CHANCE HERE? I... NEVER FOUGHT LIKE THIS BEFORE. WHAT IF–
shvr
JUST CALM DOWN.
WE SAIGAMI ALWAYS PROTECT OUR COMRADES AT ALL COSTS.

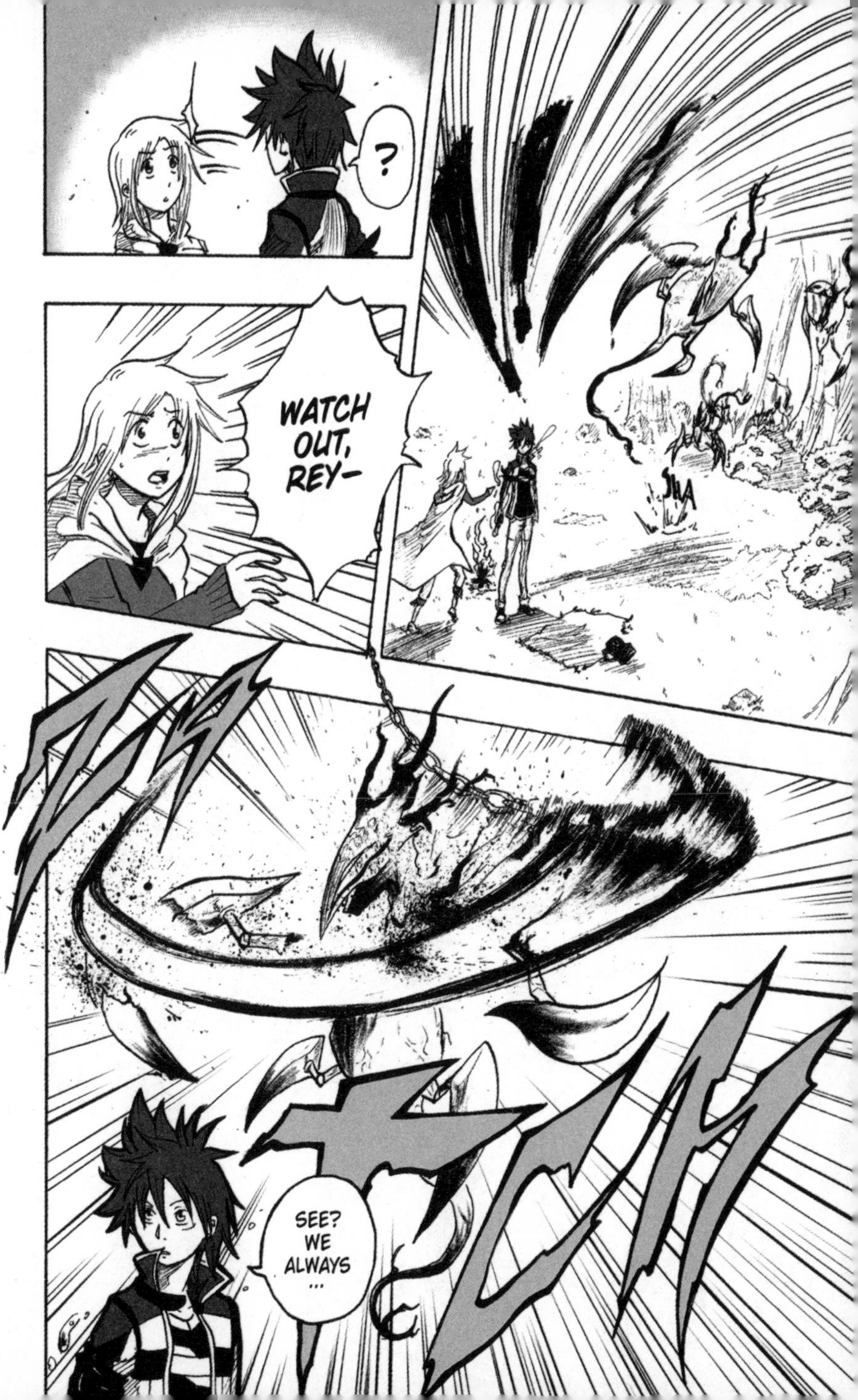
?
WATCH OUT, REY-
SEE? WE ALWAYS ...

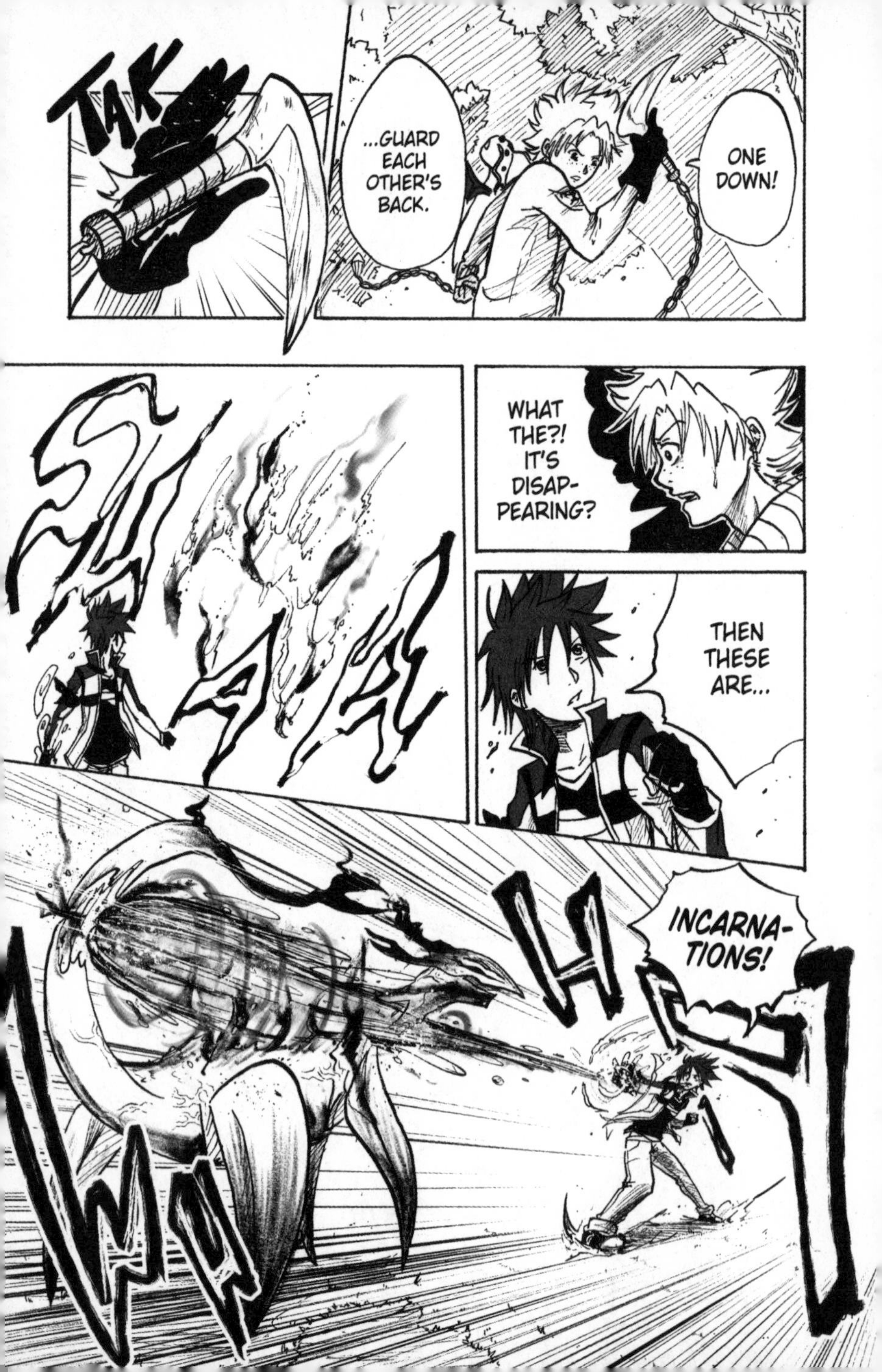
TAK
...GUARD EACH OTHER'S BACK.
ONE DOWN!
WHAT THE?! IT'S DISAP-PEARING?
THEN THESE ARE...
INCARNA-TIONS!

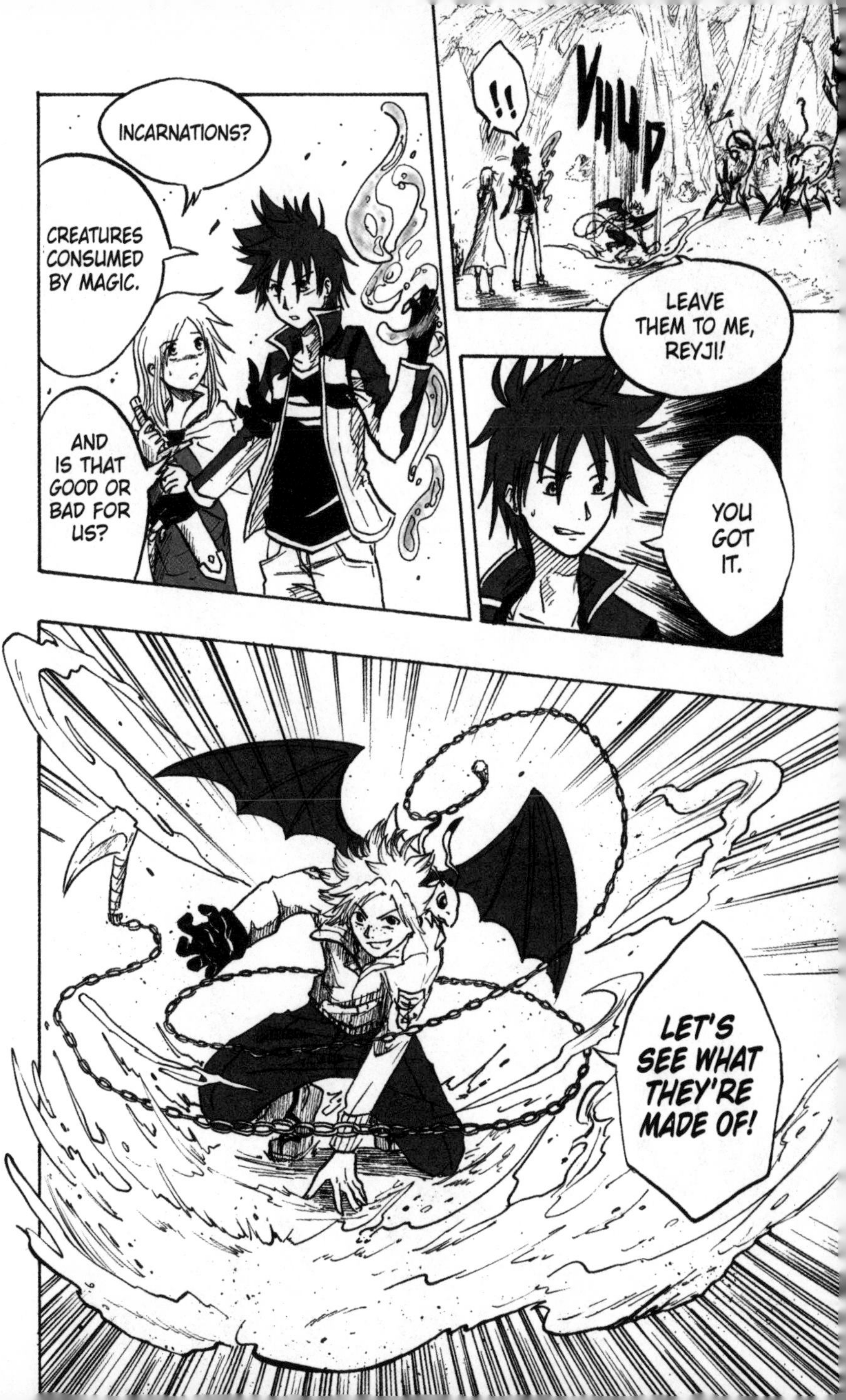
INCARNATIONS?
CREATURES CONSUMED BY MAGIC.
AND IS THAT GOOD OR BAD FOR US?
!!
VHUD
LEAVE THEM TO ME, REYJI!
YOU GOT IT.
LET'S SEE WHAT THEY'RE MADE OF!

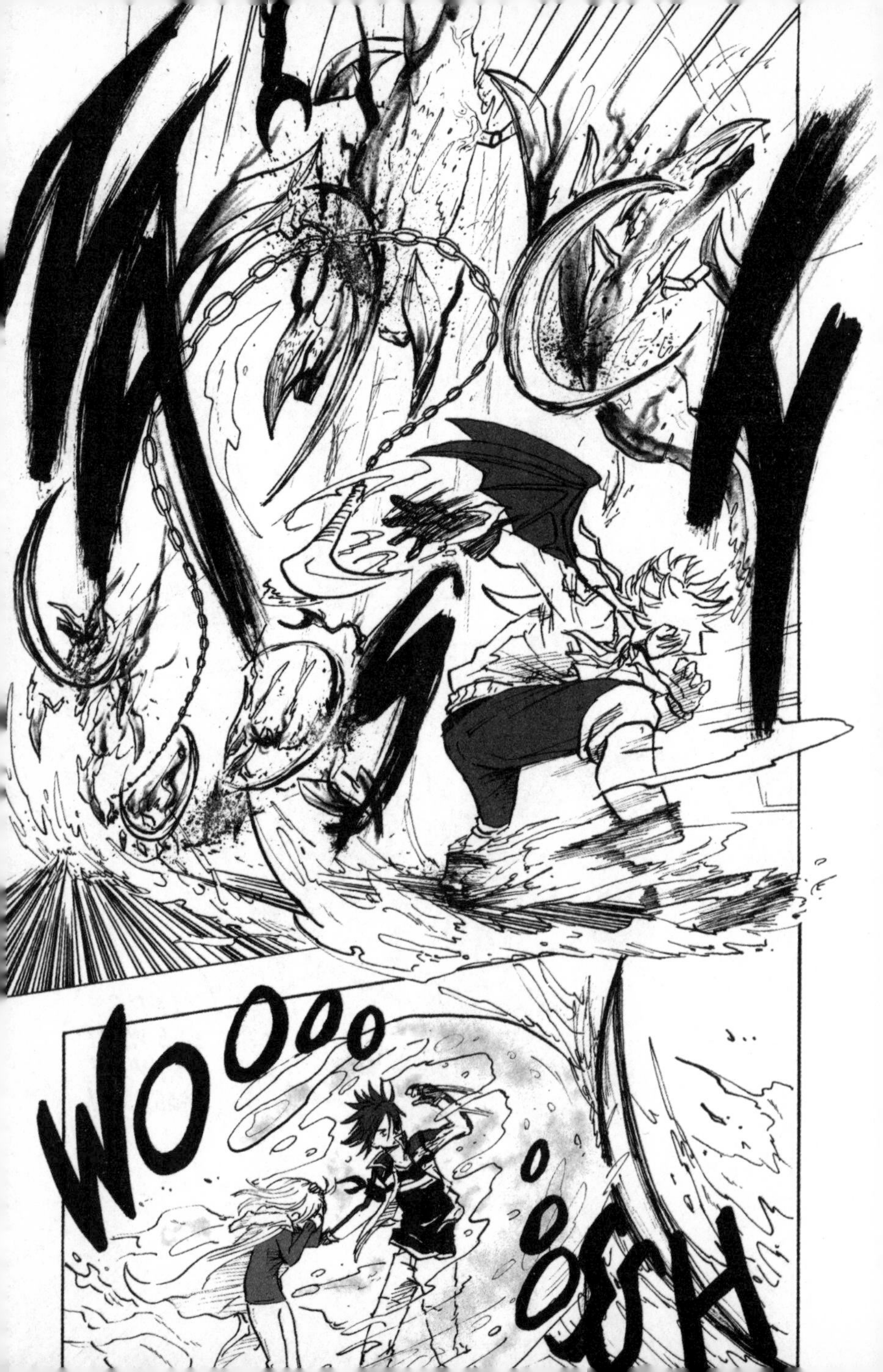
WOOOOOOOOSH

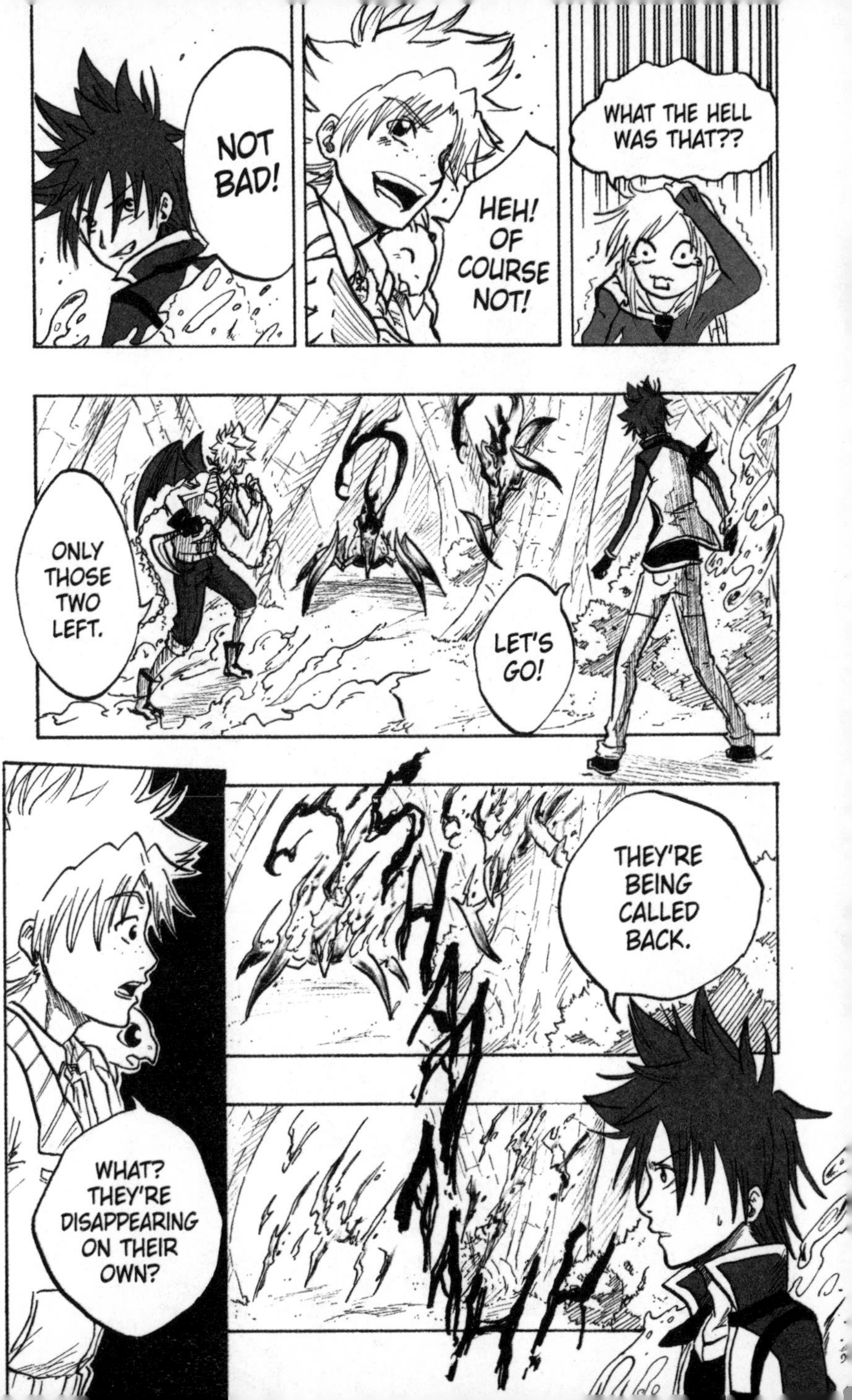
NOT BAD!
HEH! OF COURSE NOT!
WHAT THE HELL WAS THAT??
ONLY THOSE TWO LEFT.
LET'S GO!
WHAT? THEY'RE DISAPPEARING ON THEIR OWN?
THEY'RE BEING CALLED BACK.

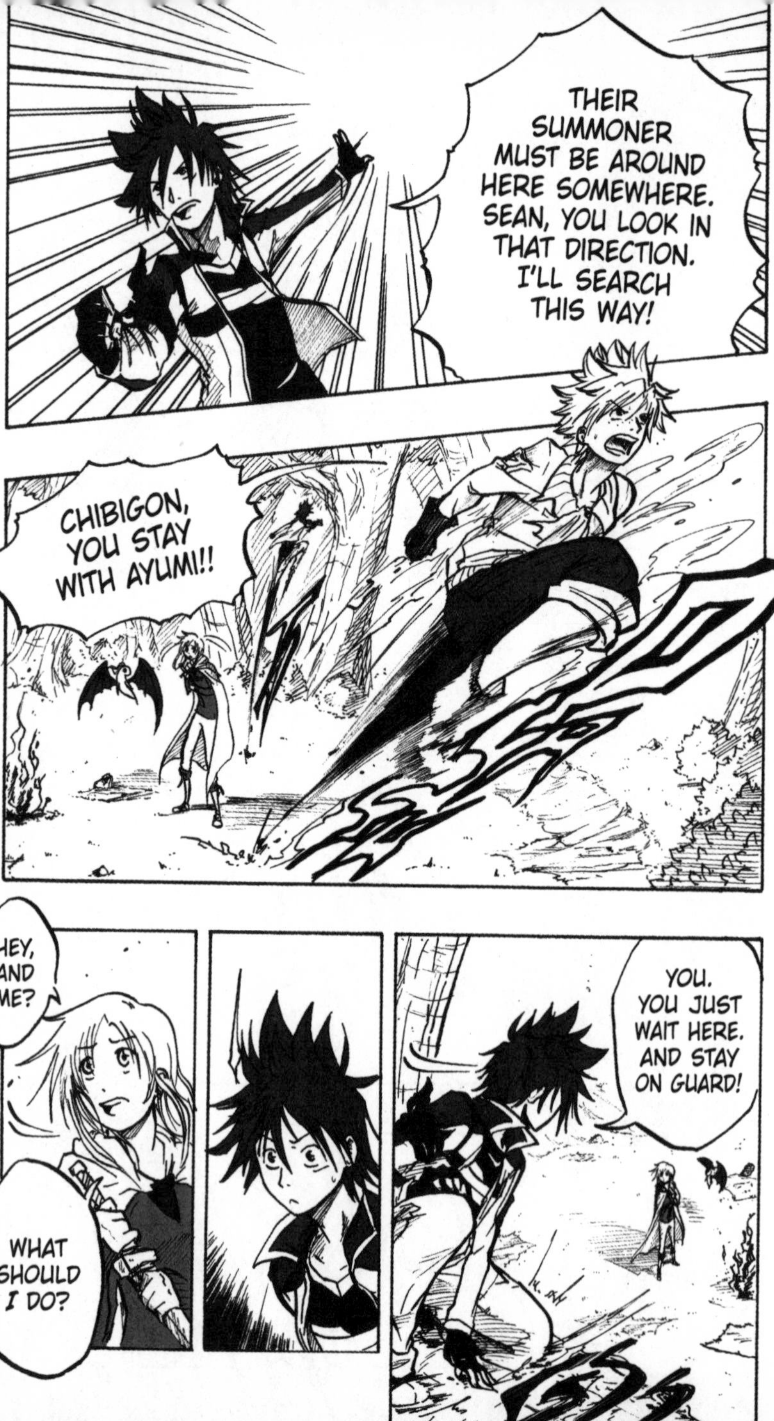
THEIR SUMMONER MUST BE AROUND HERE SOMEWHERE. SEAN, YOU LOOK IN THAT DIRECTION. I'LL SEARCH THIS WAY!
CHIBIGON, YOU STAY WITH AYUMI!!
HEY, AND ME?
WHAT SHOULD I DO?
YOU. YOU JUST WAIT HERE. AND STAY ON GUARD!

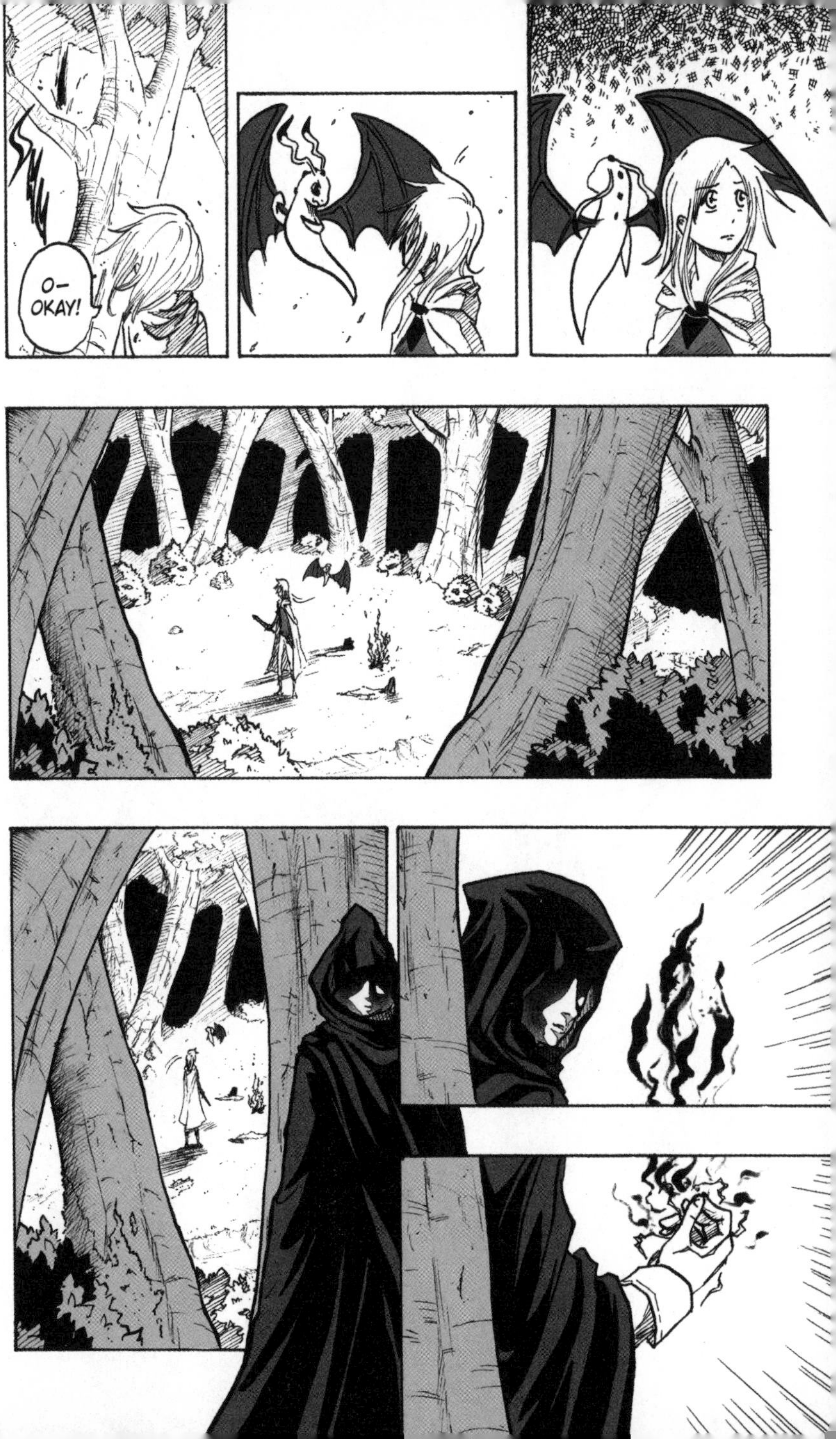
O—
OKAY!

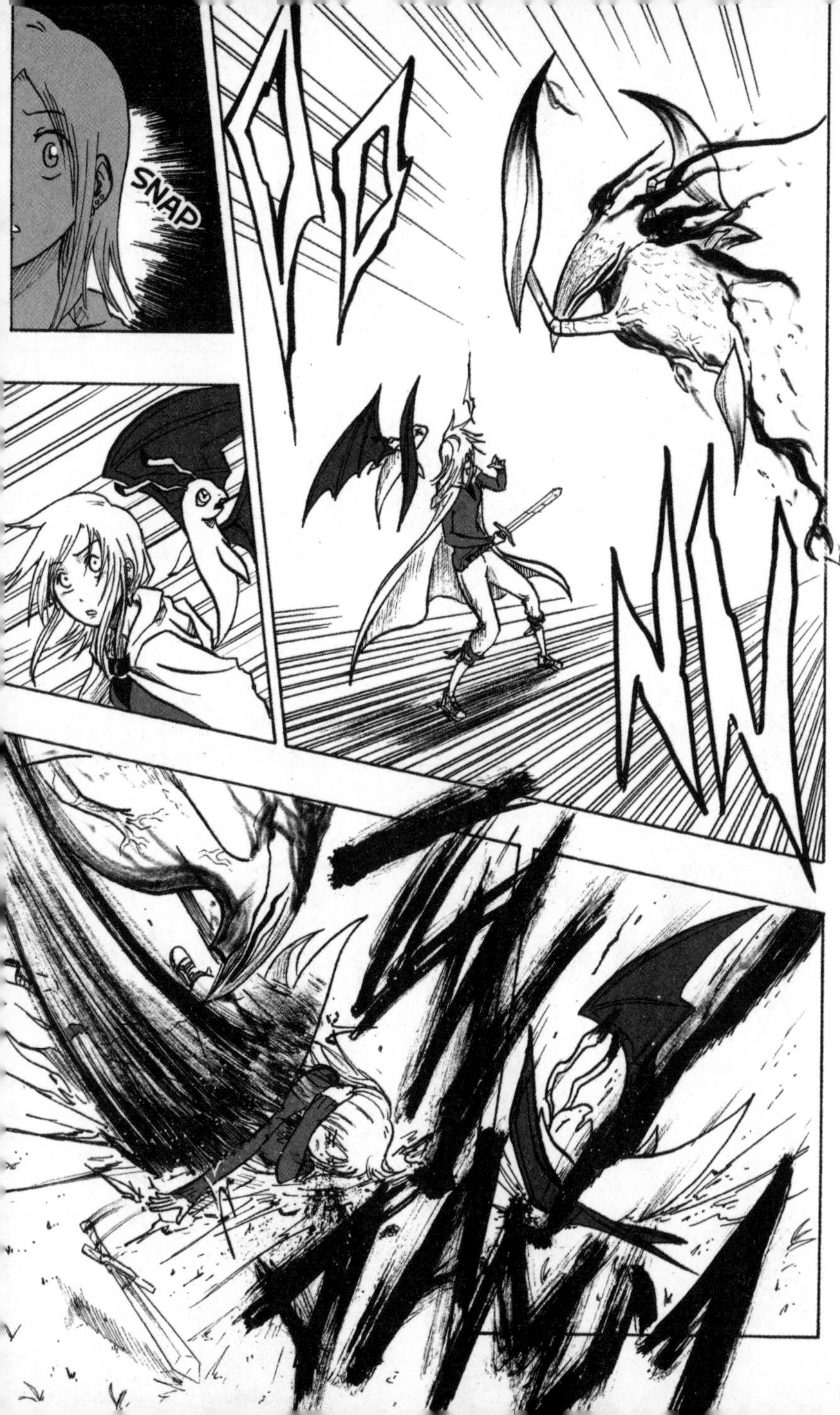
SNAP

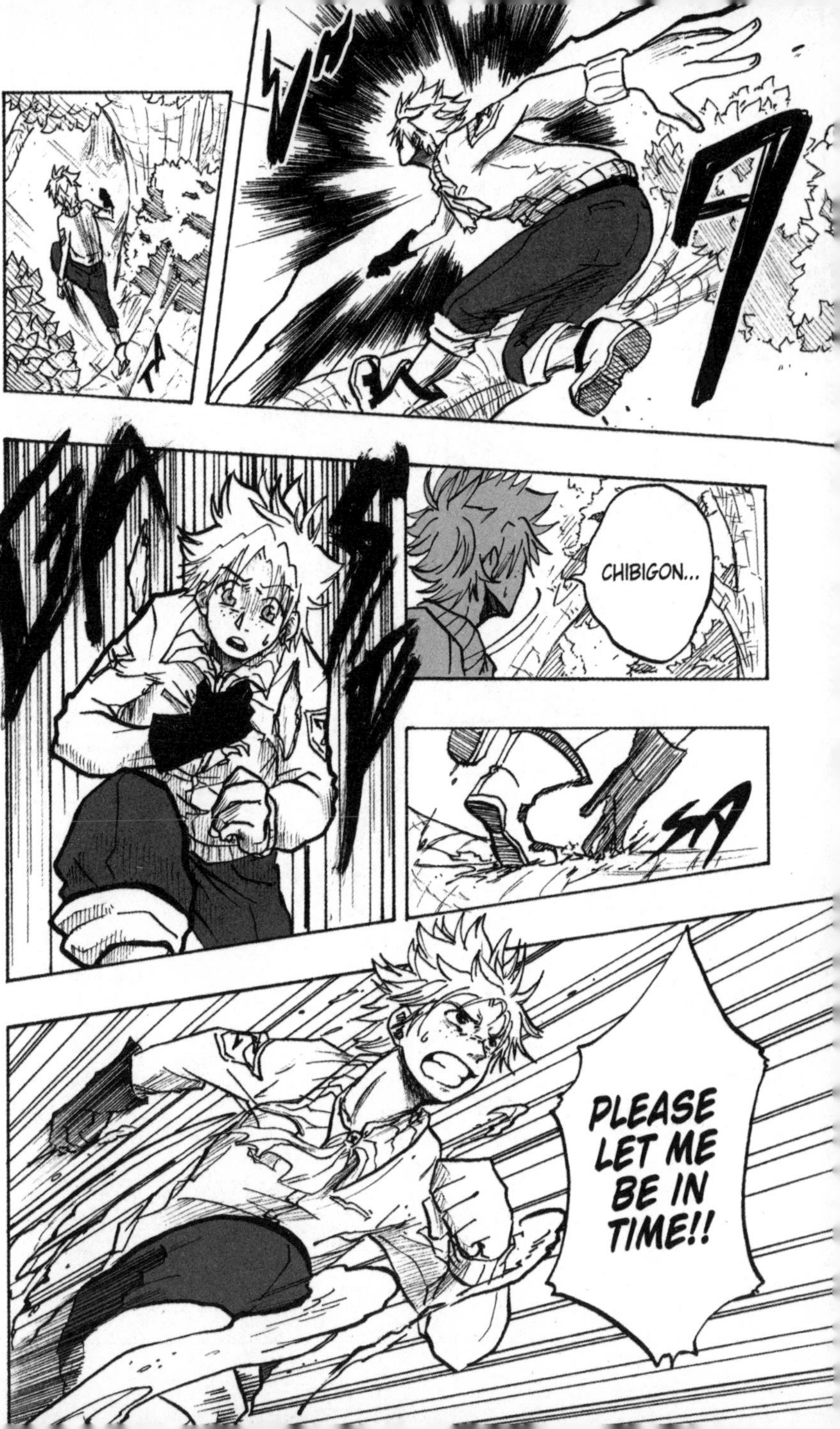
CHIBIGON...
SA
PLEASE LET ME BE IN TIME!!

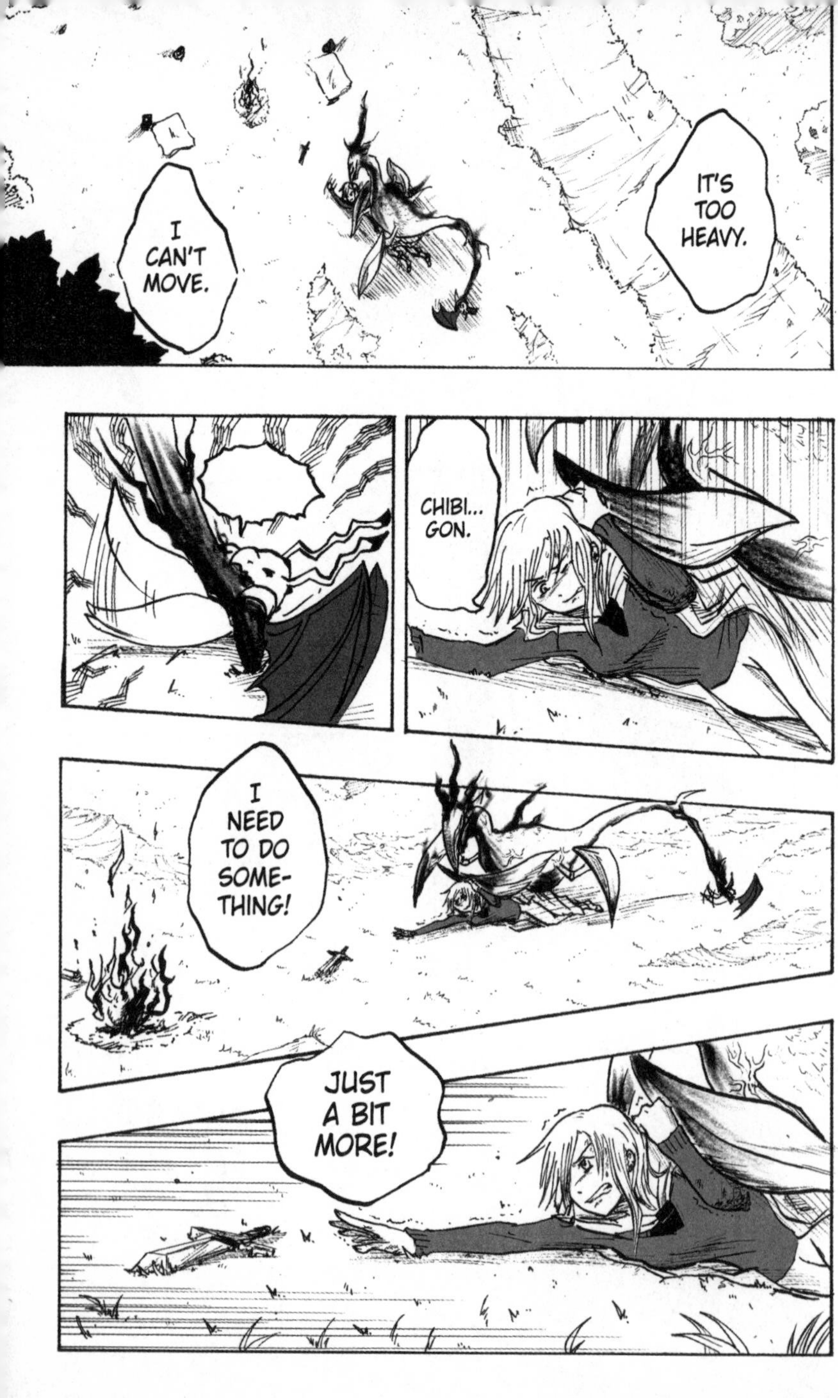
I CAN'T MOVE.
IT'S TOO HEAVY.
CHIBI... GON.
I NEED TO DO SOME-THING!
JUST A BIT MORE!

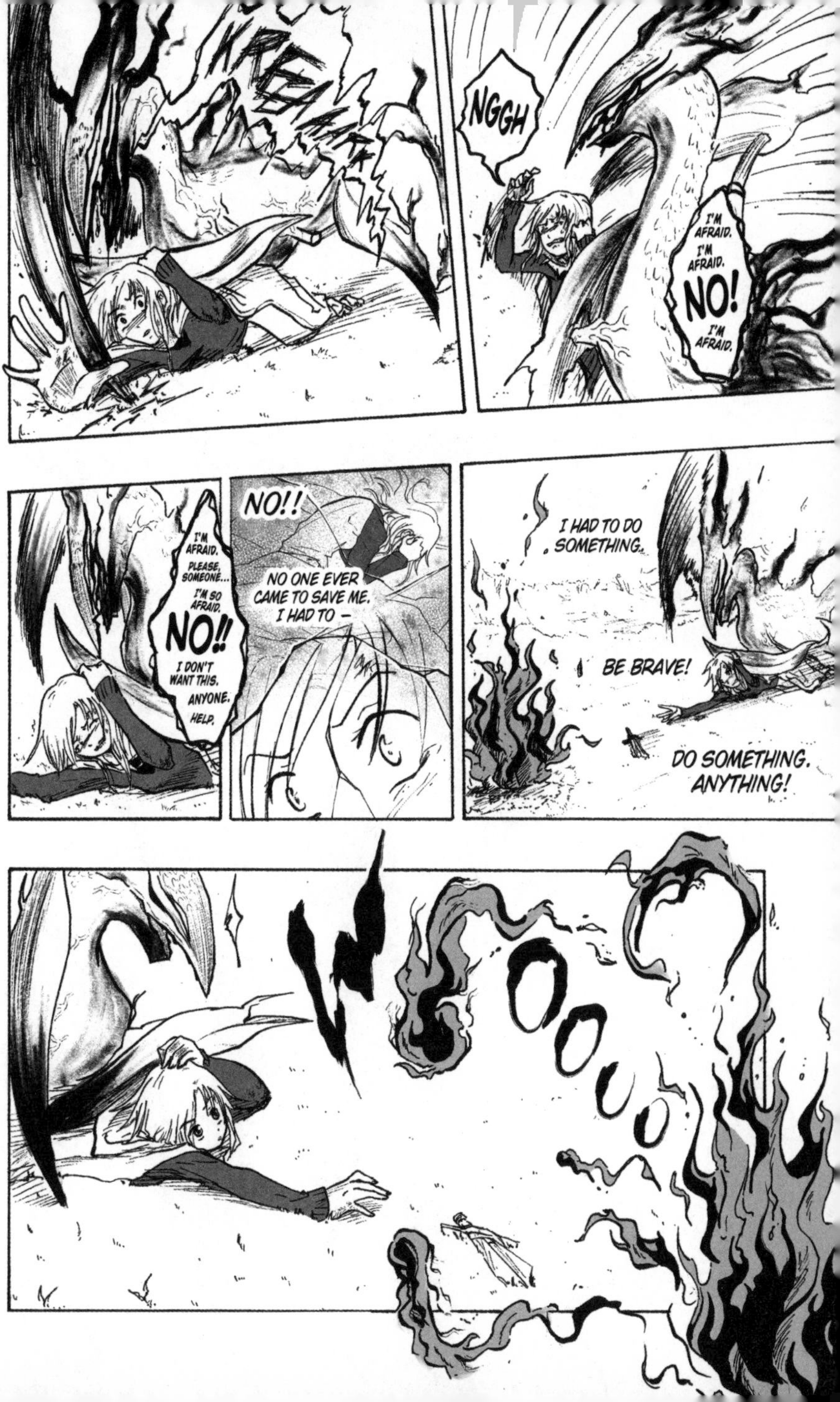
NGGH
I'M AFRAID. I'M AFRAID. NO! I'M AFRAID.
I'M AFRAID. PLEASE, SOMEONE... I'M SO AFRAID. NO!! I DON'T WANT THIS. ANYONE. HELP.
NO!!
NO ONE EVER CAME TO SAVE ME. I HAD TO –
I HAD TO DO SOMETHING.
BE BRAVE!
DO SOMETHING. ANYTHING!

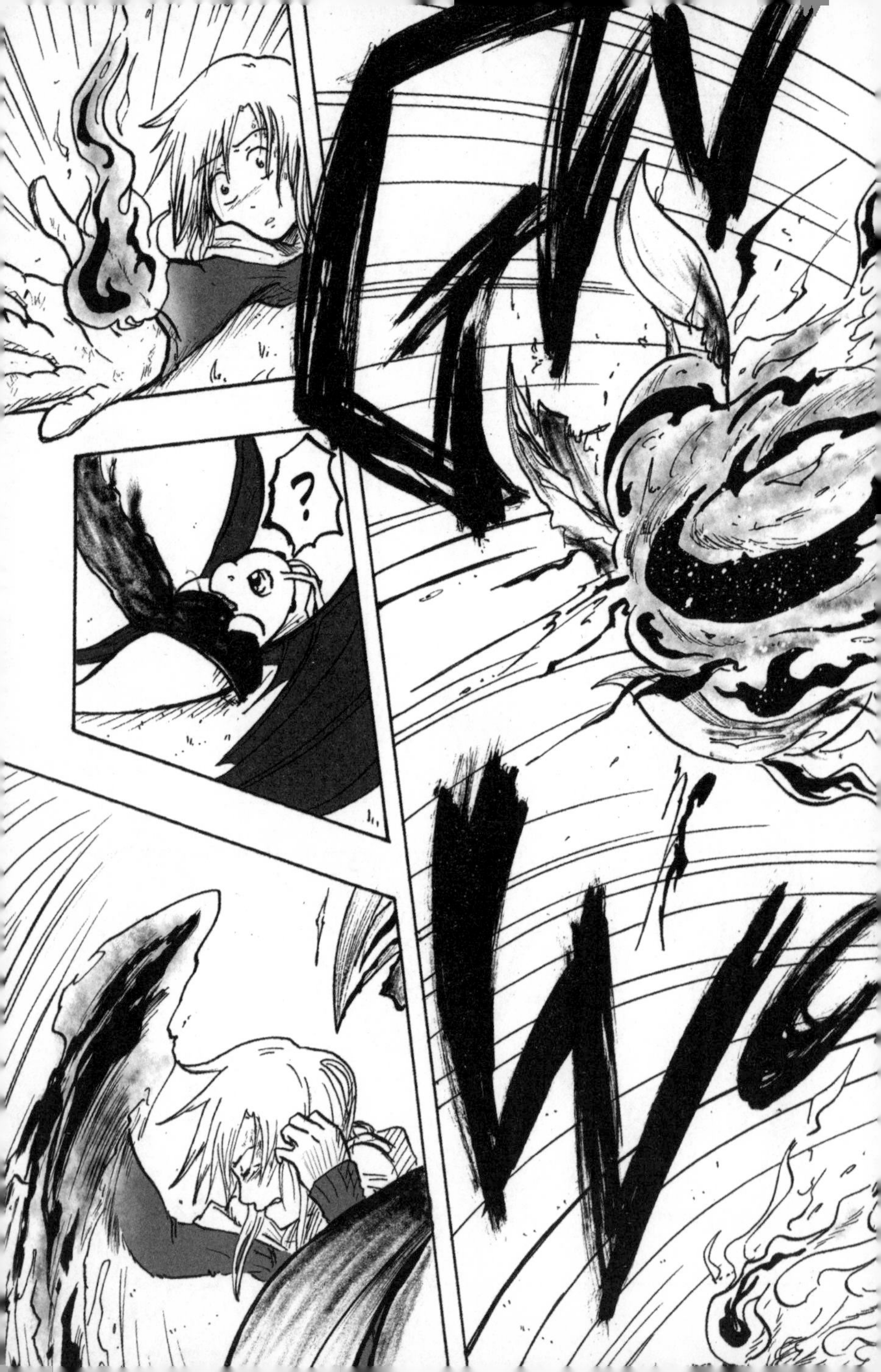
?

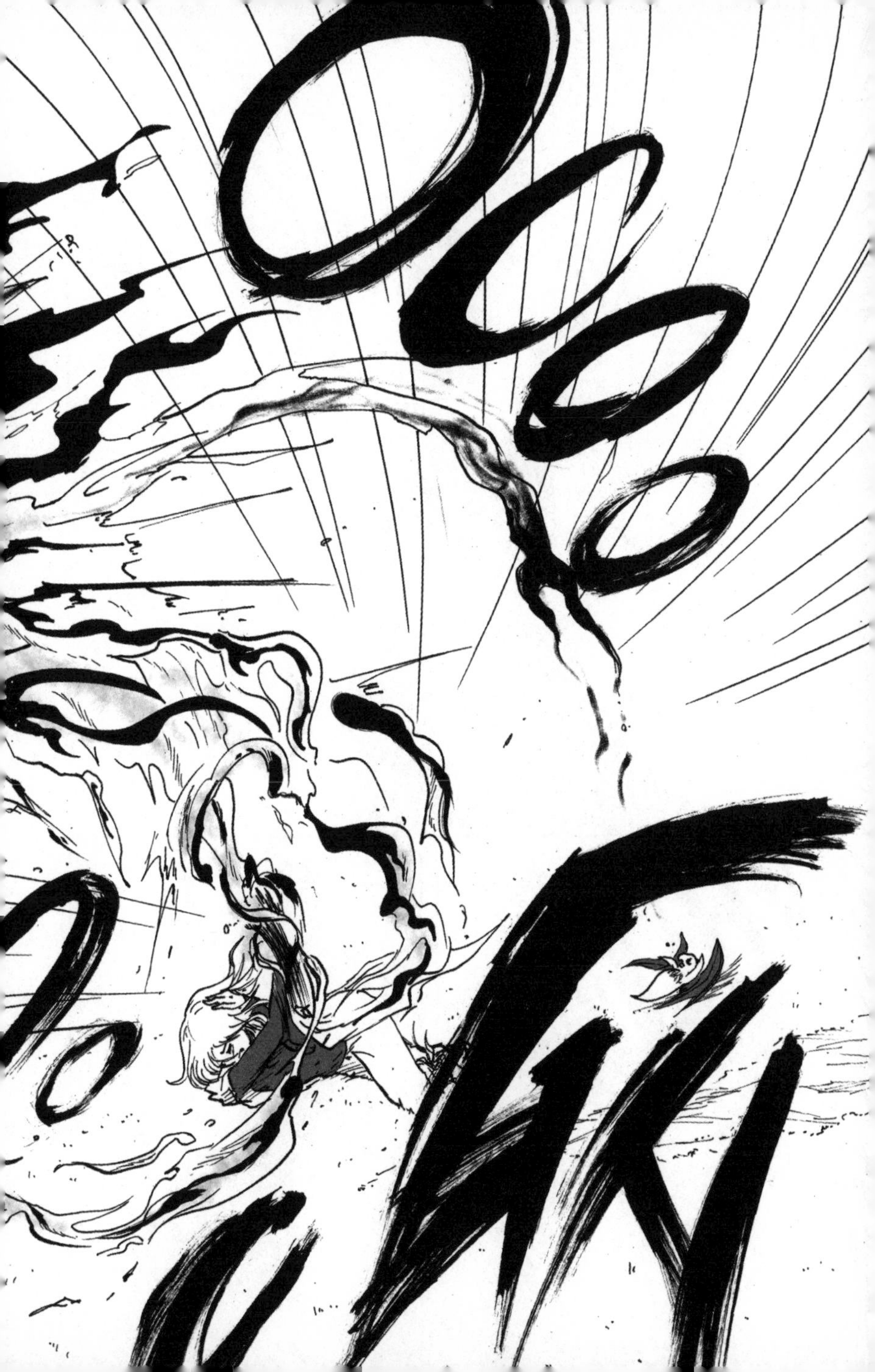

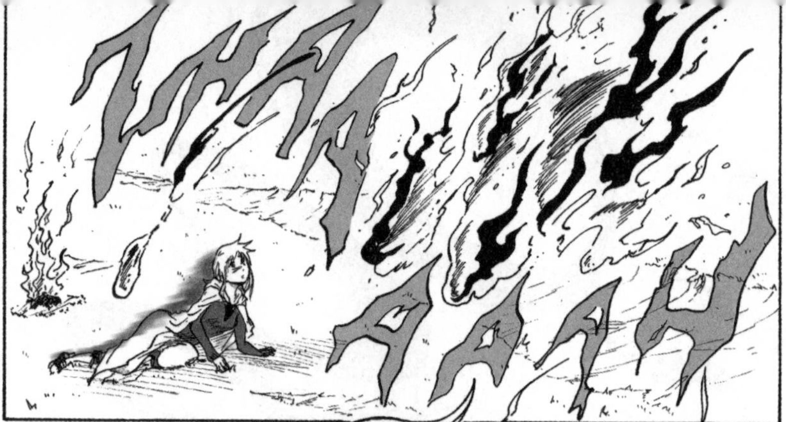
ZHAAAAAAH

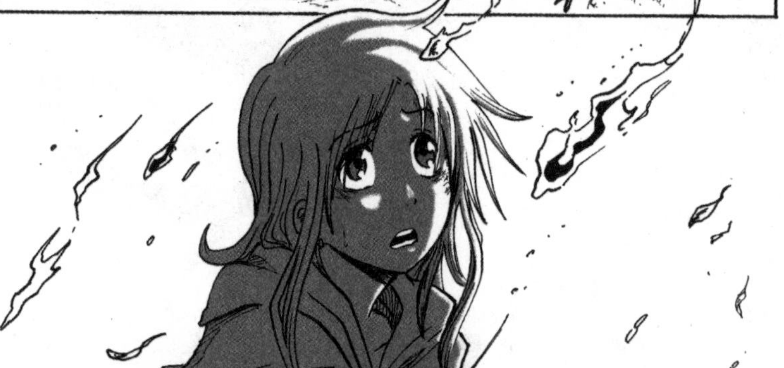

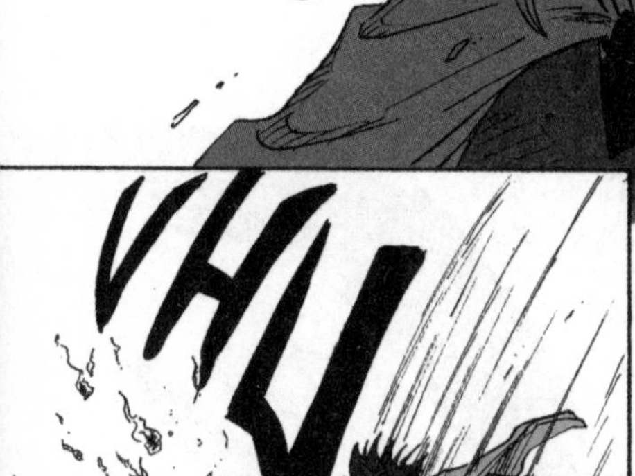
VHU

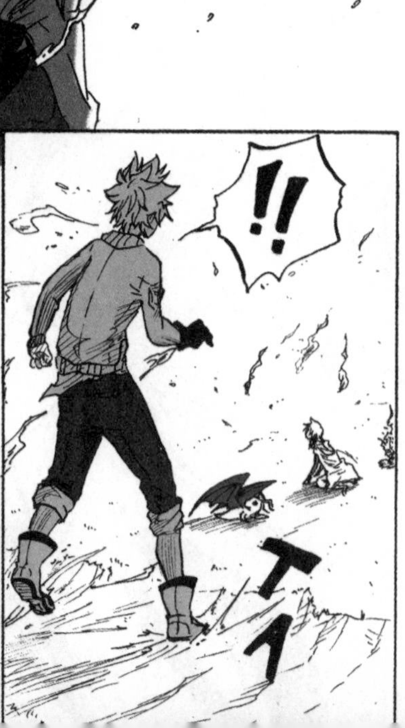
!!

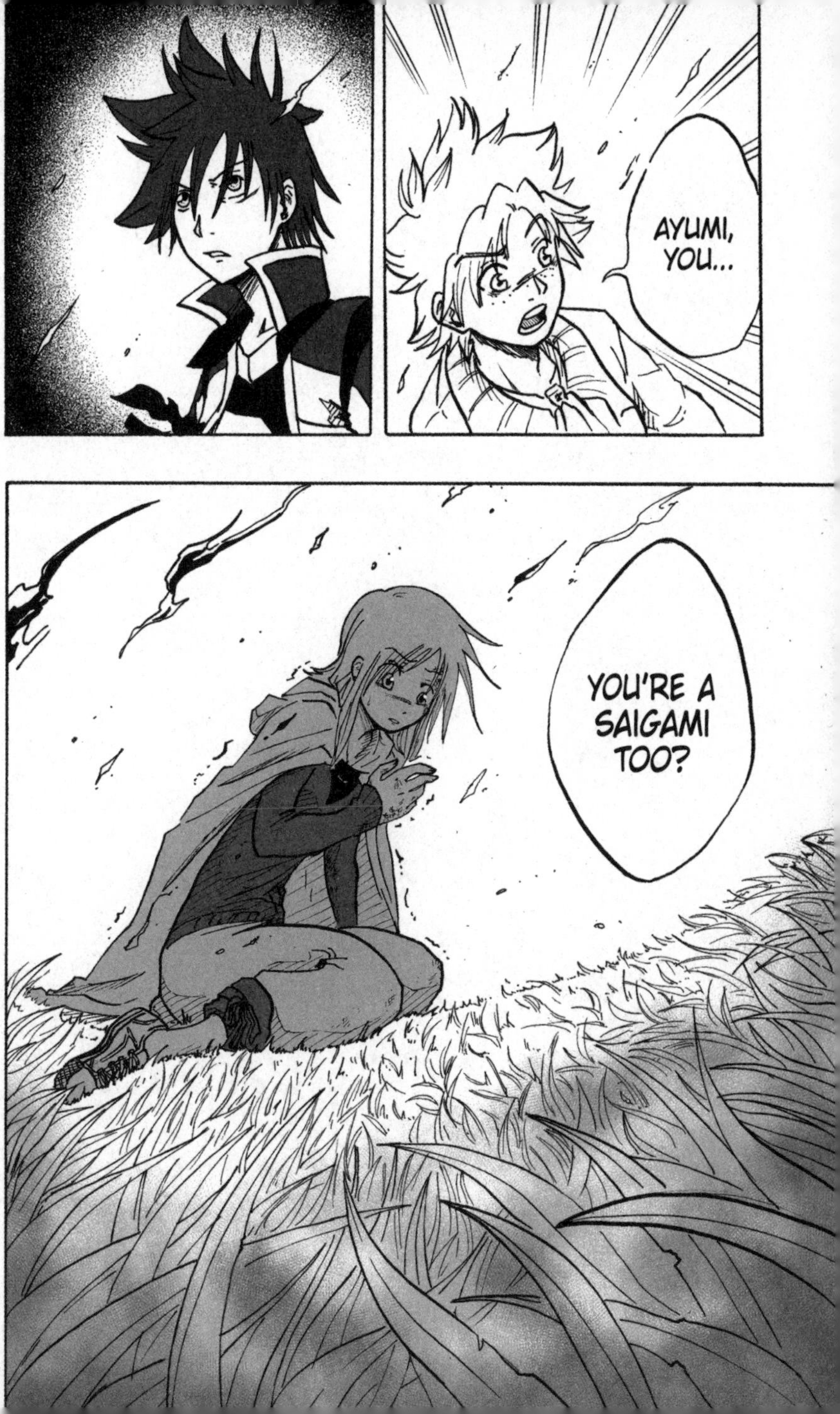
AYUMI, YOU...
YOU'RE A SAIGAMI TOO?

SAIGAMI

SAIGAMI

Chapter 3: Decisions

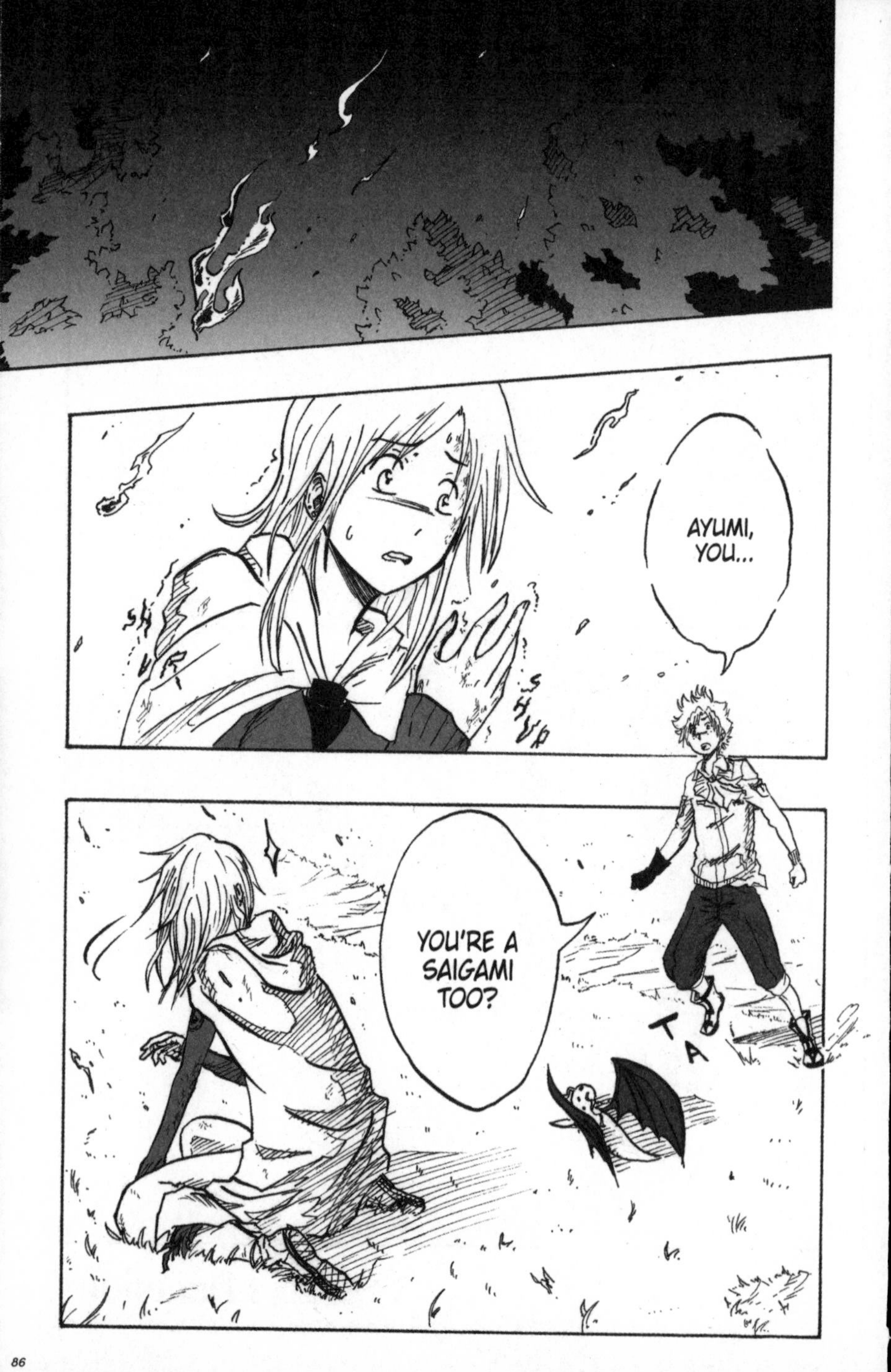
SHUR
AYUMI, YOU...
SHUR
YOU'RE A SAIGAMI TOO?
TA

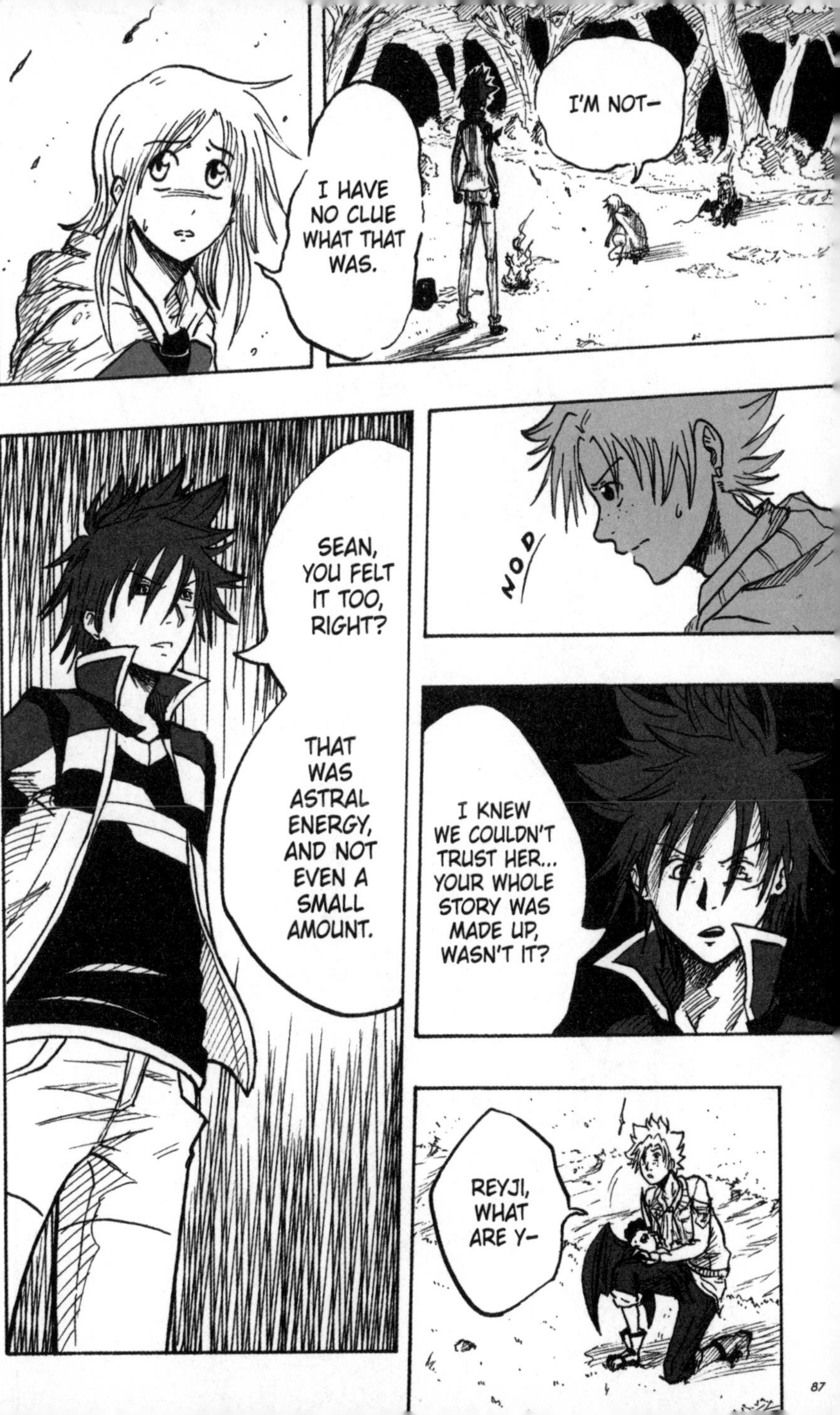
I HAVE NO CLUE WHAT THAT WAS.
I'M NOT-
SEAN, YOU FELT IT TOO, RIGHT?
THAT WAS ASTRAL ENERGY, AND NOT EVEN A SMALL AMOUNT.
NOD
I KNEW WE COULDN'T TRUST HER... YOUR WHOLE STORY WAS MADE UP, WASN'T IT?
REYJI, WHAT ARE Y-

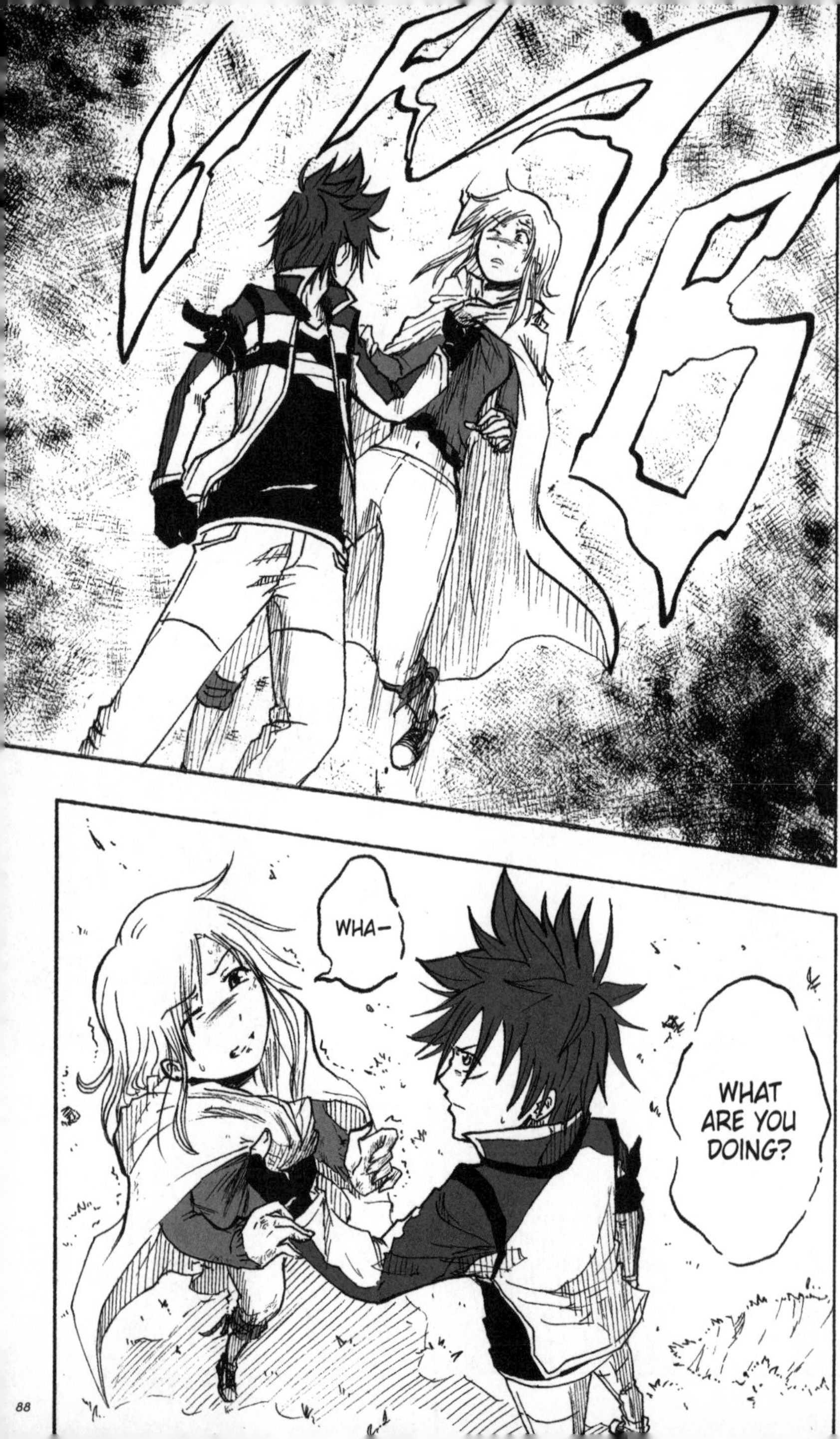
WHA-
WHAT ARE YOU DOING?

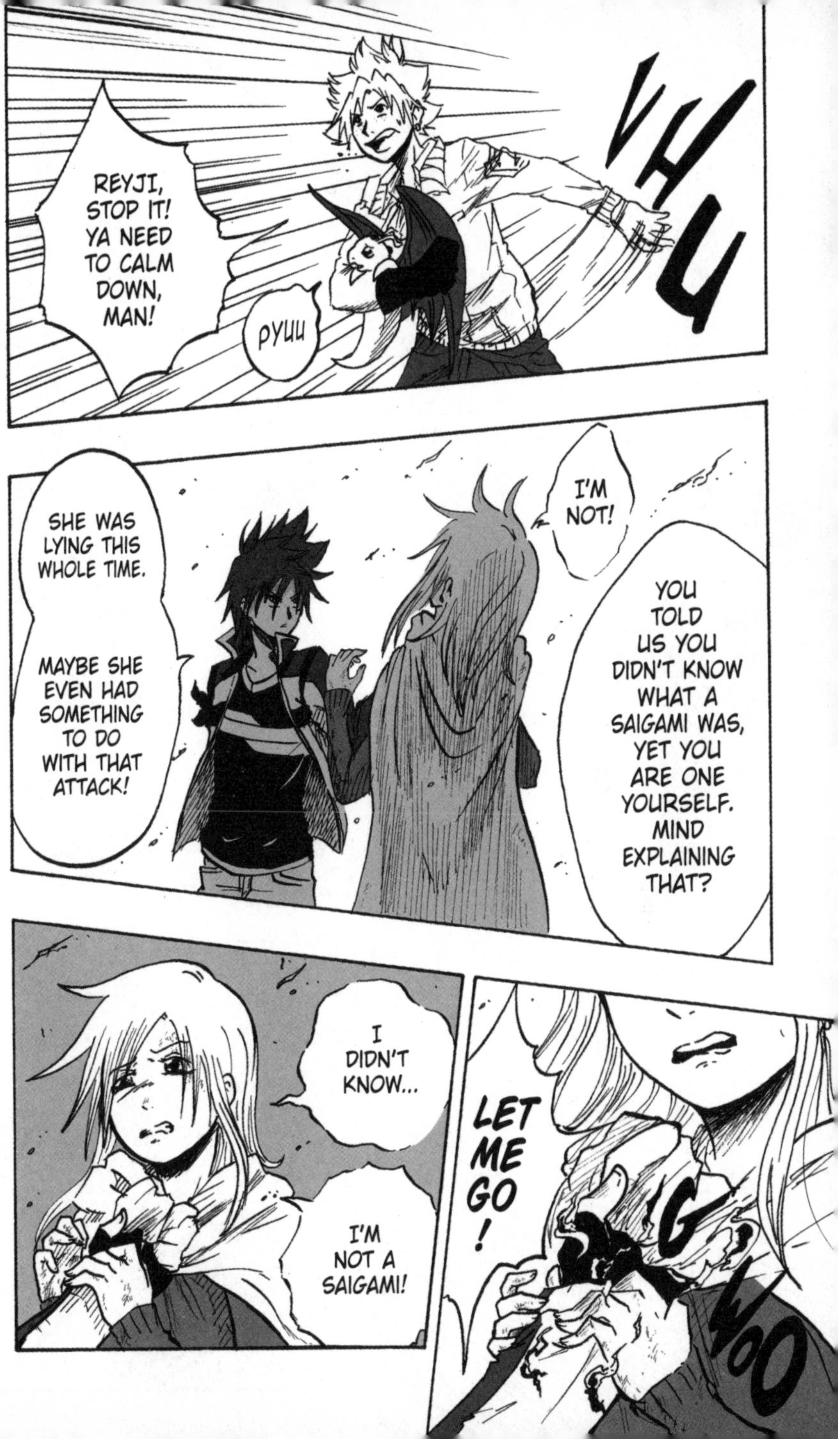
VHU
REYJI, STOP IT! YA NEED TO CALM DOWN, MAN!
PYUU
I'M NOT!
SHE WAS LYING THIS WHOLE TIME.
MAYBE SHE EVEN HAD SOMETHING TO DO WITH THAT ATTACK!
YOU TOLD US YOU DIDN'T KNOW WHAT A SAIGAMI WAS, YET YOU ARE ONE YOURSELF. MIND EXPLAINING THAT?
I DIDN'T KNOW...
I'M NOT A SAIGAMI!
LET ME GO!
GWOO

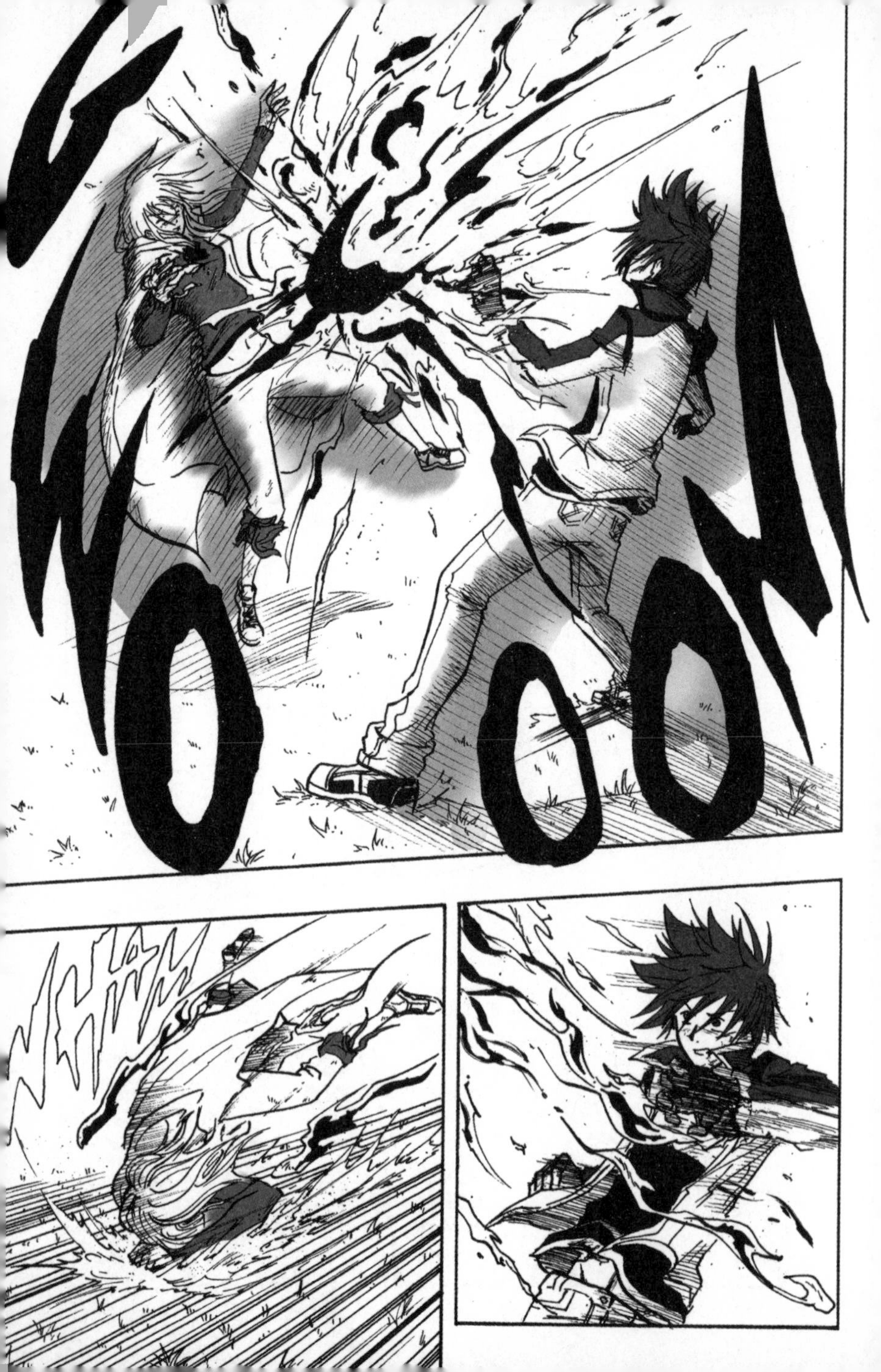
SWOOOM
WHAM

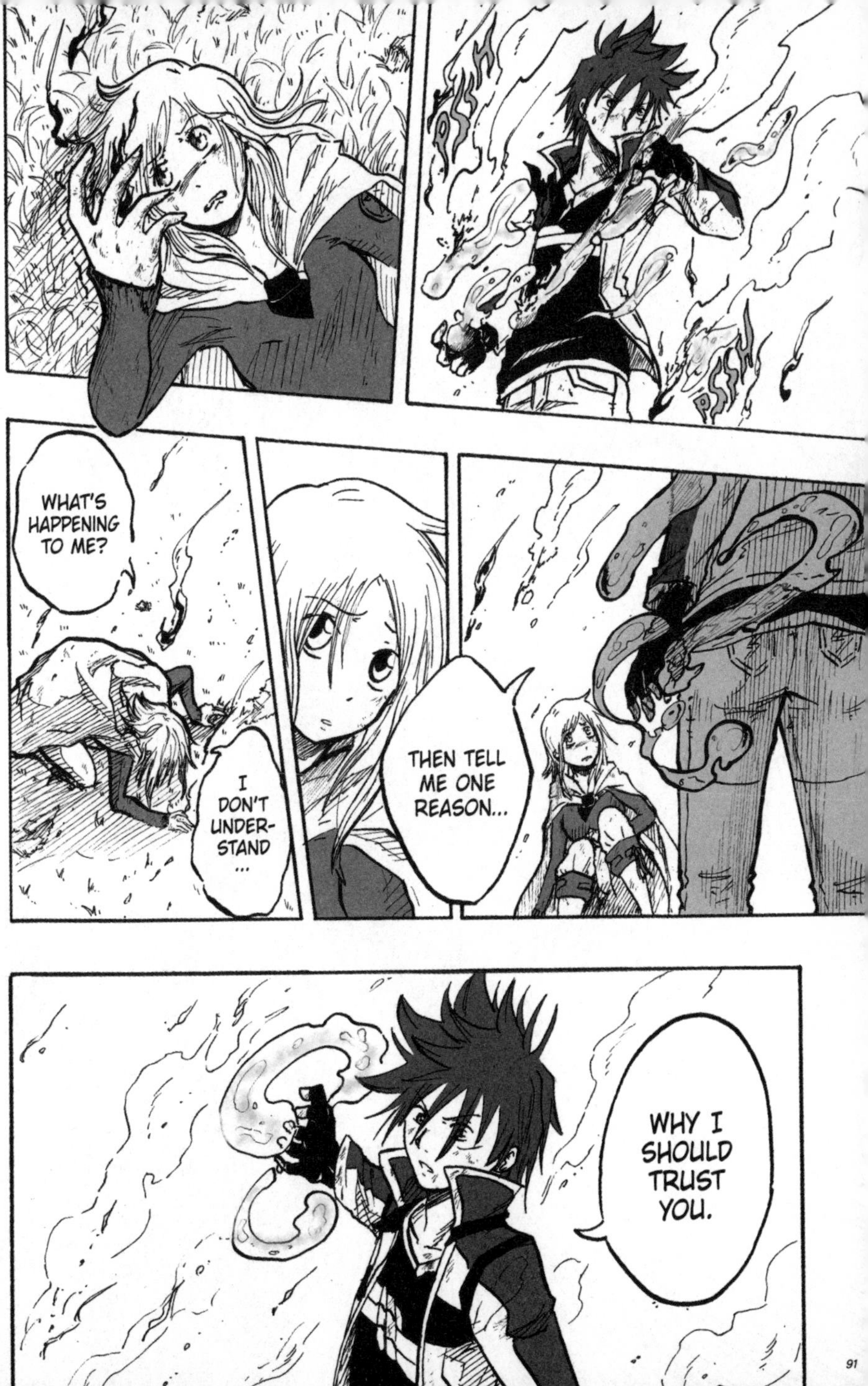
PSSH
PSSH
WHAT'S HAPPENING TO ME?
I DON'T UNDER-STAND ...
THEN TELL ME ONE REASON...
WHY I SHOULD TRUST YOU.

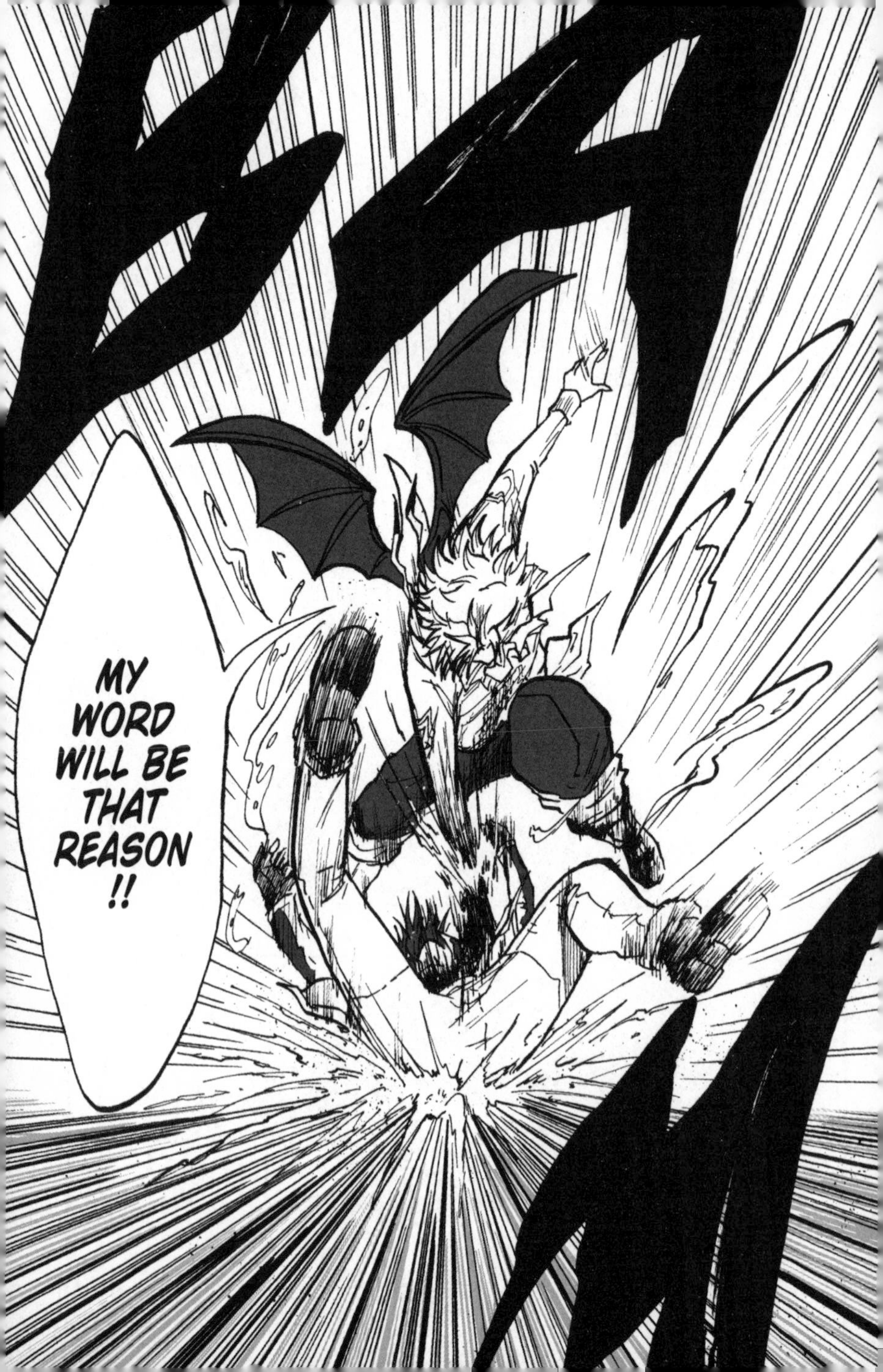
MY WORD WILL BE THAT REASON !!

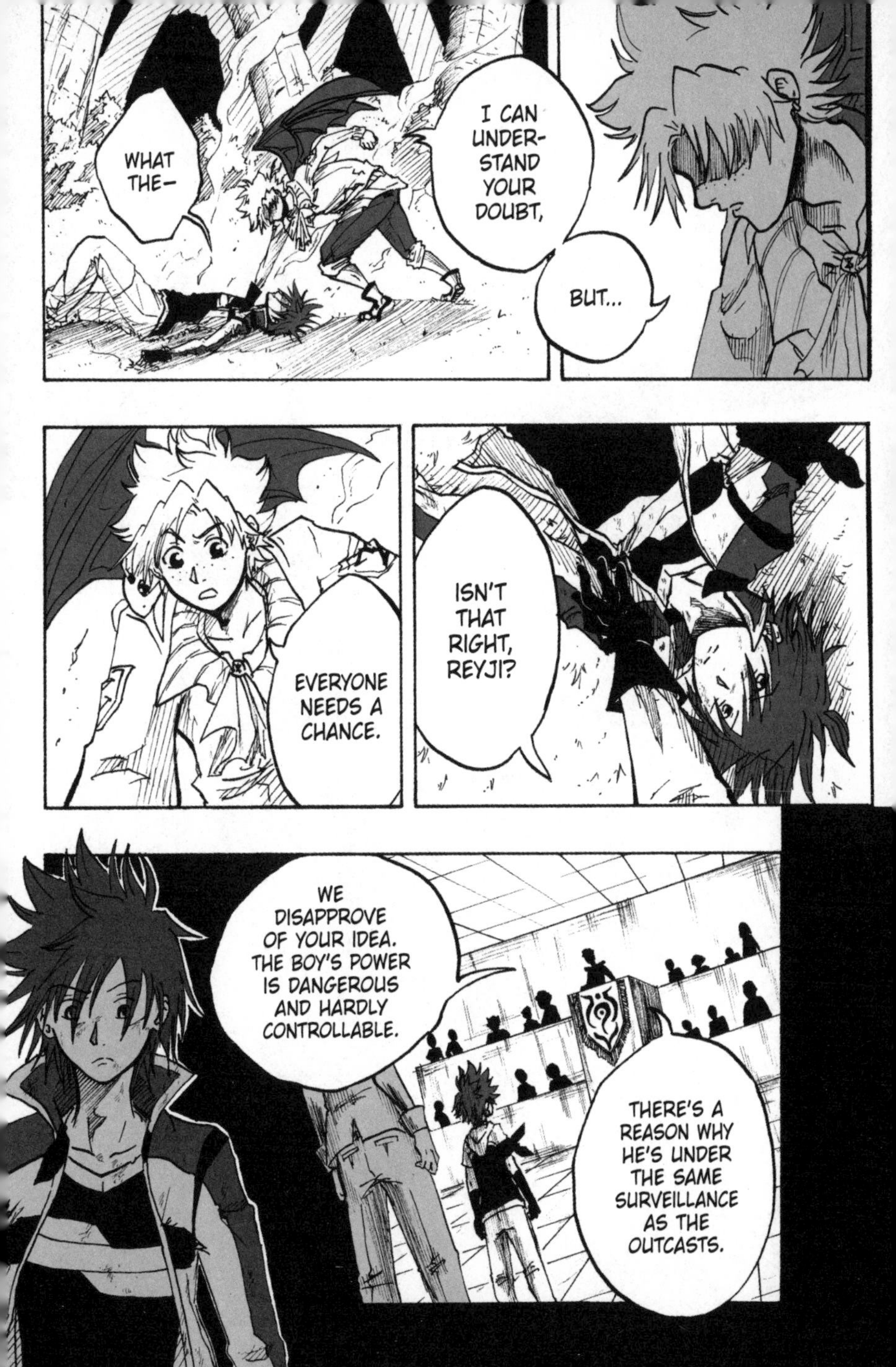
WHAT THE—
I CAN UNDERSTAND YOUR DOUBT,
BUT...
EVERYONE NEEDS A CHANCE.
ISN'T THAT RIGHT, REYJI?
WE DISAPPROVE OF YOUR IDEA. THE BOY'S POWER IS DANGEROUS AND HARDLY CONTROLLABLE.
THERE'S A REASON WHY HE'S UNDER THE SAME SURVEILLANCE AS THE OUTCASTS.

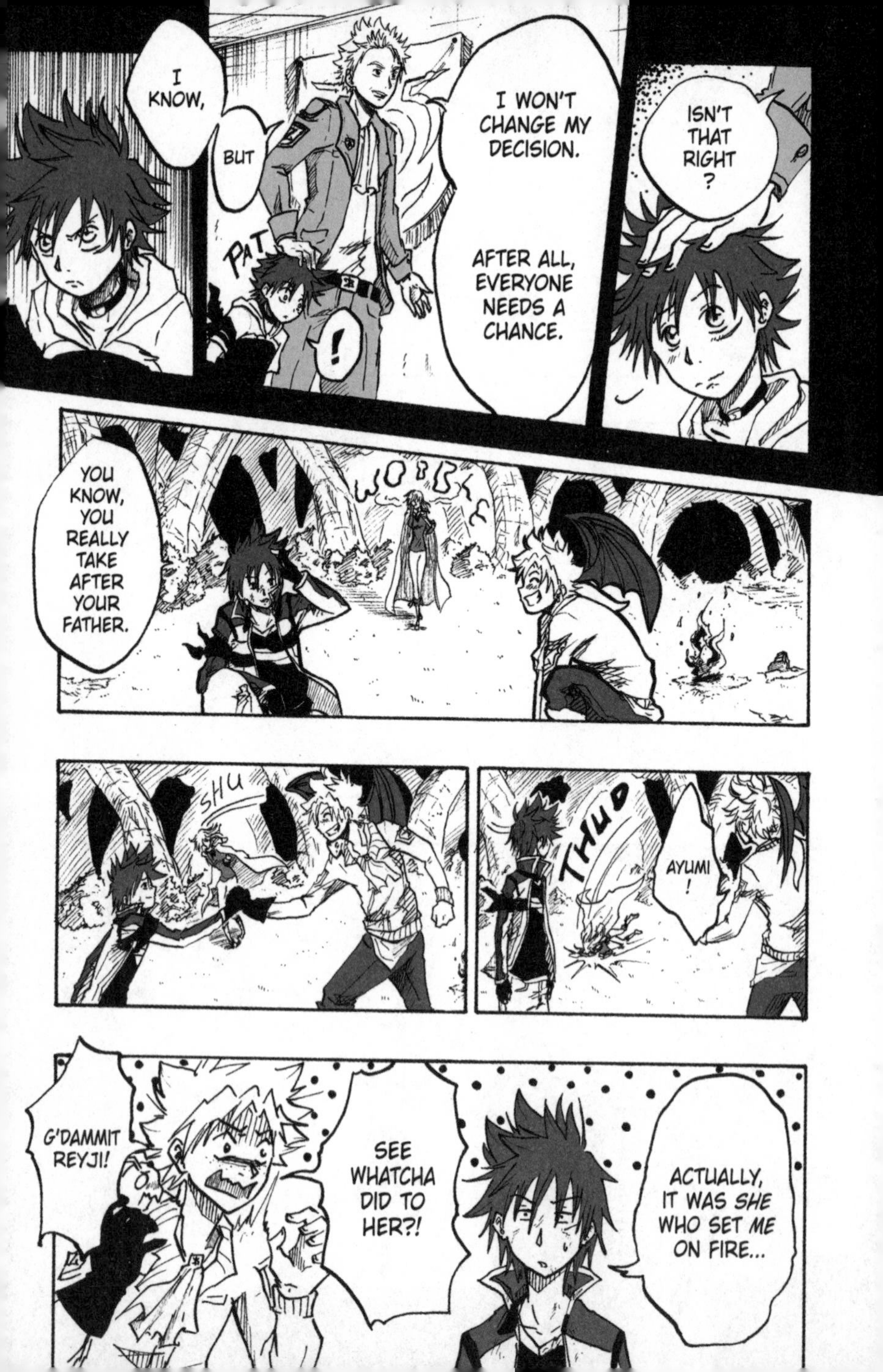
I KNOW,
BUT
PAT
!
I WON'T CHANGE MY DECISION.
AFTER ALL, EVERYONE NEEDS A CHANCE.
ISN'T THAT RIGHT?
YOU KNOW, YOU REALLY TAKE AFTER YOUR FATHER.
WOBBLE
SHU
THUD
AYUMI!
G'DAMMIT REYJI!
SEE WHATCHA DID TO HER?!
ACTUALLY, IT WAS *SHE* WHO SET ME ON FIRE...

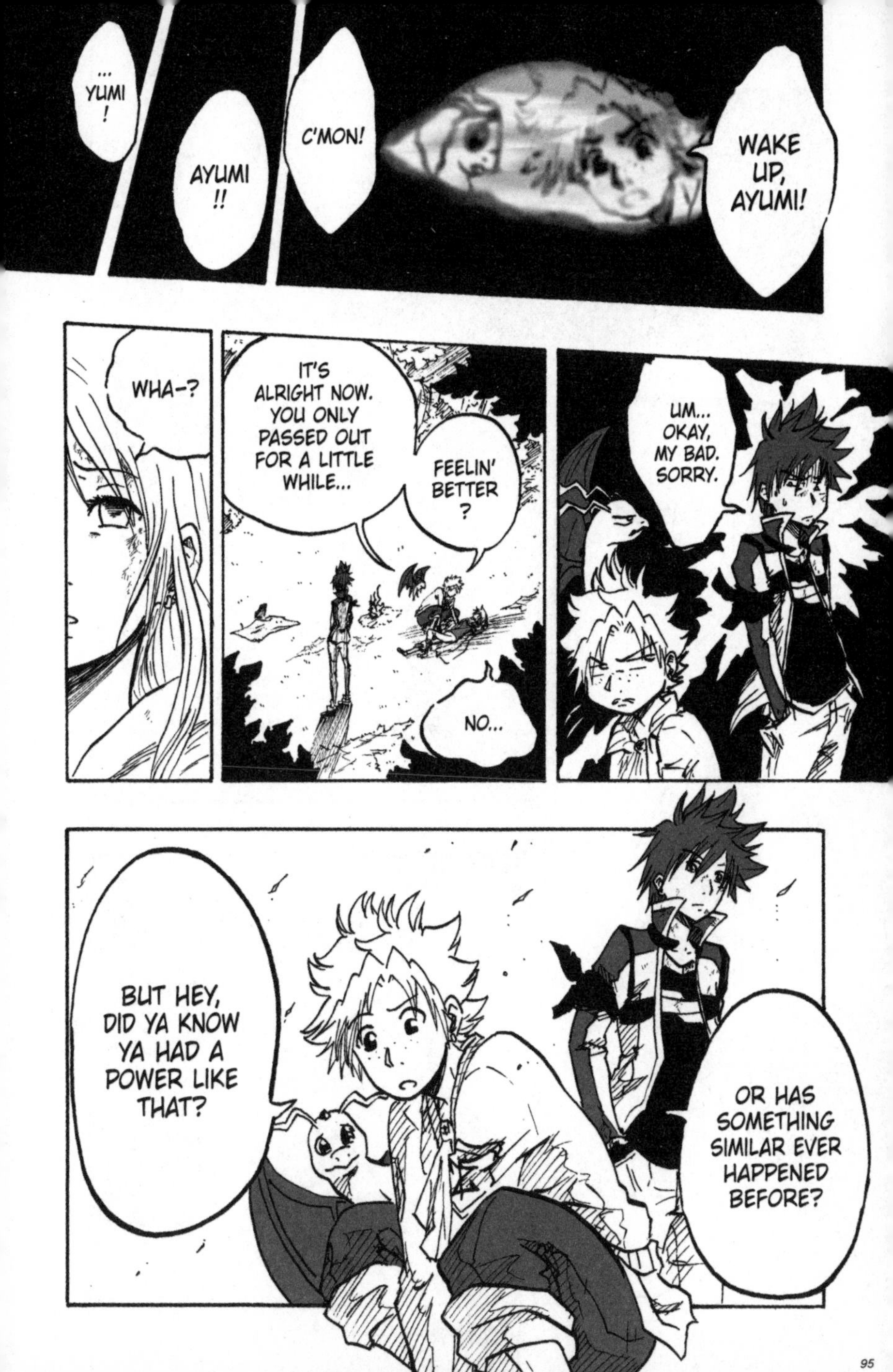
...YUMI!
AYUMI!!
C'MON!
WAKE UP, AYUMI!
WHA-?
IT'S ALRIGHT NOW. YOU ONLY PASSED OUT FOR A LITTLE WHILE...
FEELIN' BETTER?
NO...
UM... OKAY, MY BAD. SORRY.
BUT HEY, DID YA KNOW YA HAD A POWER LIKE THAT?
OR HAS SOMETHING SIMILAR EVER HAPPENED BEFORE?

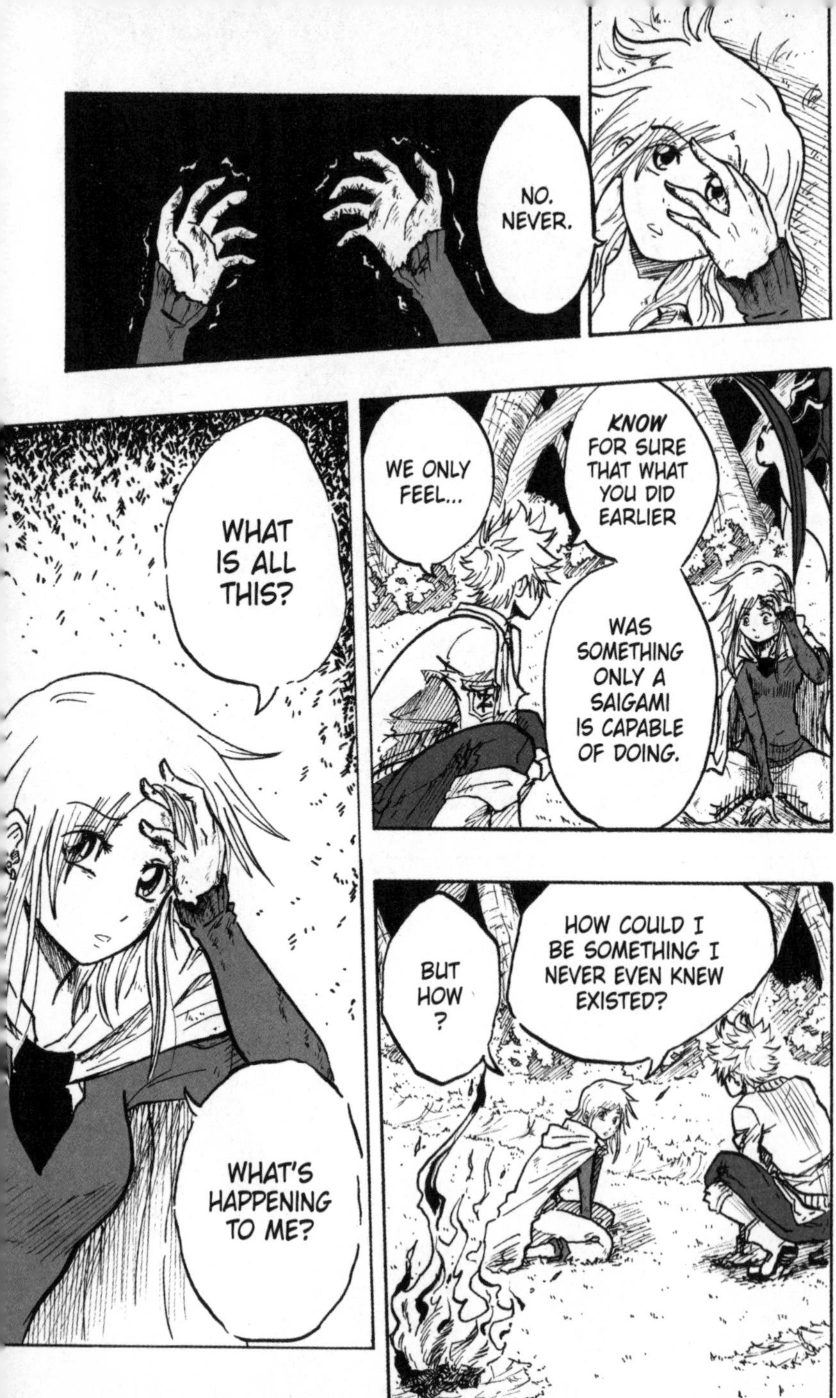
NO. NEVER.
WHAT IS ALL THIS?
WHAT'S HAPPENING TO ME?
WE ONLY FEEL...
KNOW FOR SURE THAT WHAT YOU DID EARLIER
WAS SOMETHING ONLY A SAIGAMI IS CAPABLE OF DOING.
BUT HOW?
HOW COULD I BE SOMETHING I NEVER EVEN KNEW EXISTED?

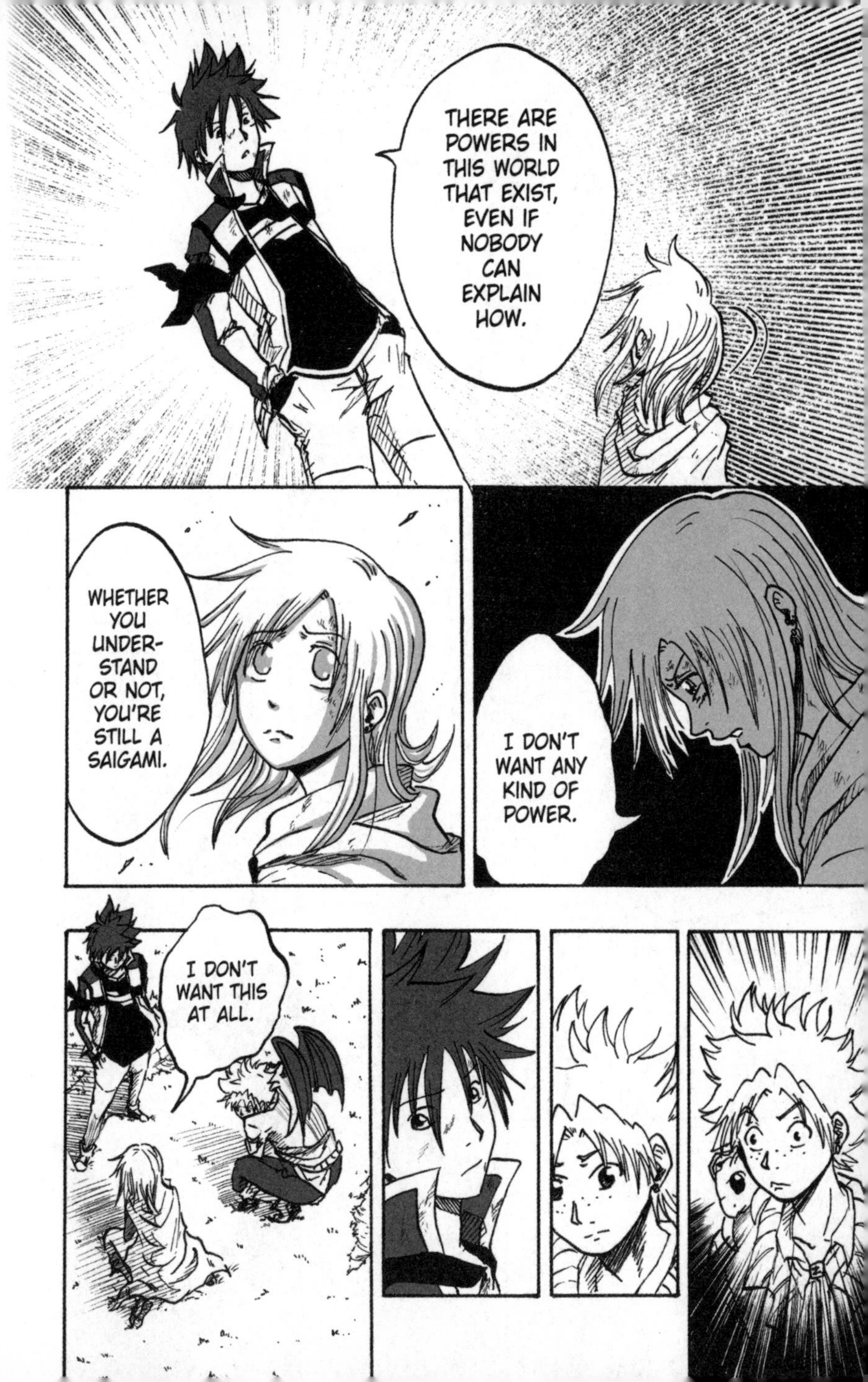
THERE ARE POWERS IN THIS WORLD THAT EXIST, EVEN IF NOBODY CAN EXPLAIN HOW.
WHETHER YOU UNDER-STAND OR NOT, YOU'RE STILL A SAIGAMI.
I DON'T WANT ANY KIND OF POWER.
I DON'T WANT THIS AT ALL.

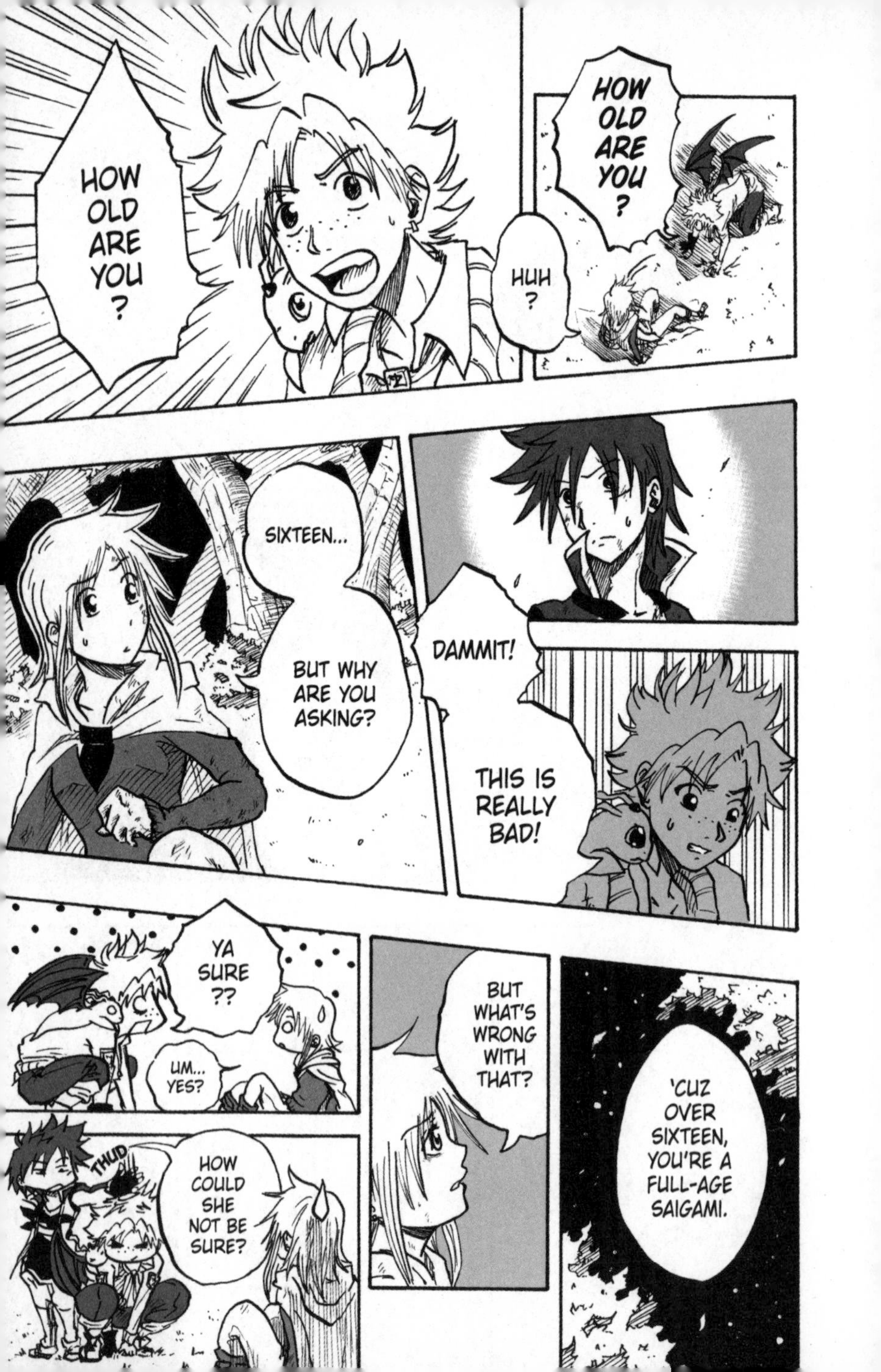
HOW OLD ARE YOU?
HOW OLD ARE YOU?
HUH?
SIXTEEN...
BUT WHY ARE YOU ASKING?
DAMMIT!
THIS IS REALLY BAD!
YA SURE??
UM... YES?
THUD
HOW COULD SHE NOT BE SURE?
BUT WHAT'S WRONG WITH THAT?
'CUZ OVER SIXTEEN, YOU'RE A FULL-AGE SAIGAMI.

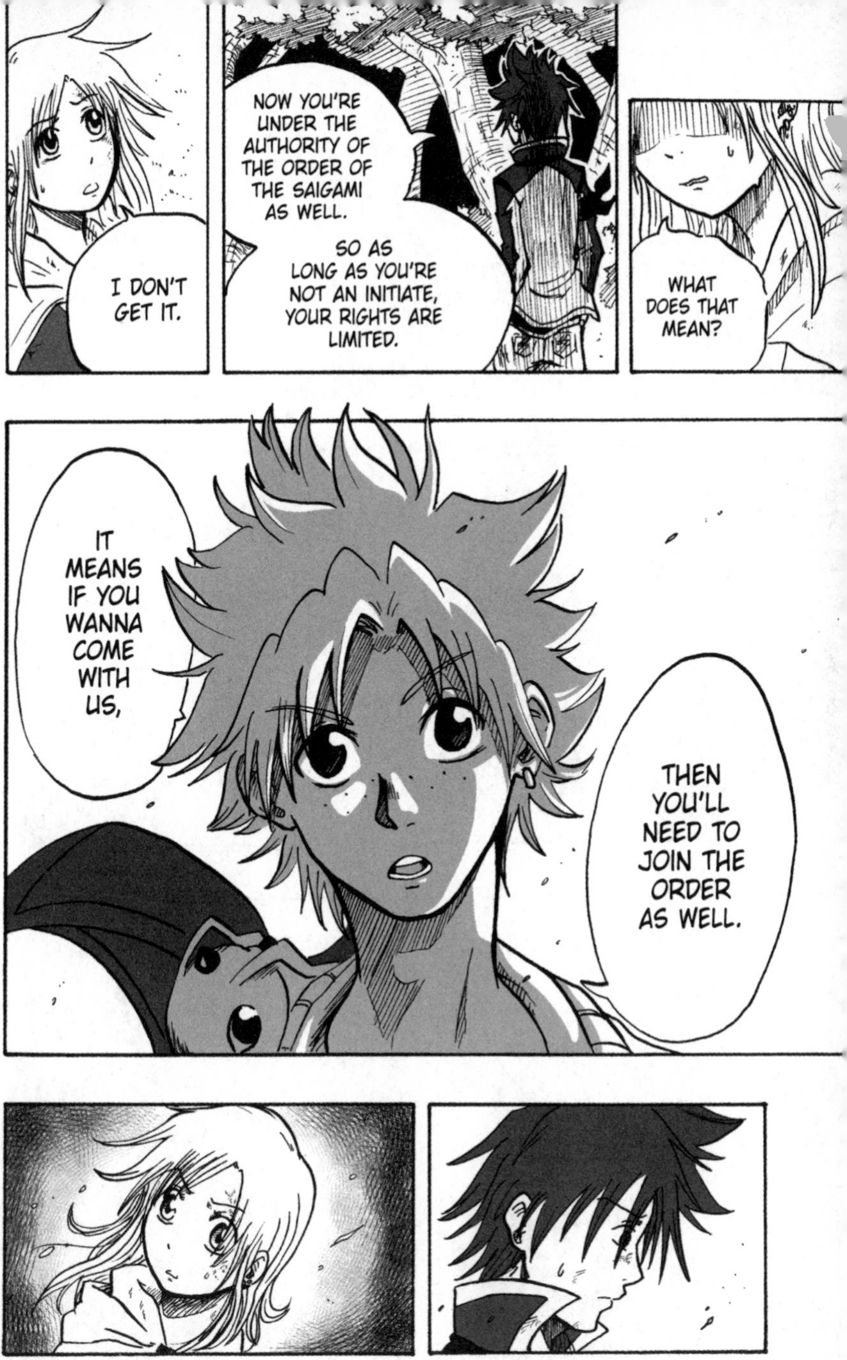
I DON'T GET IT.
NOW YOU'RE UNDER THE AUTHORITY OF THE ORDER OF THE SAIGAMI AS WELL.
SO AS LONG AS YOU'RE NOT AN INITIATE, YOUR RIGHTS ARE LIMITED.
WHAT DOES THAT MEAN?
IT MEANS IF YOU WANNA COME WITH US,
THEN YOU'LL NEED TO JOIN THE ORDER AS WELL.

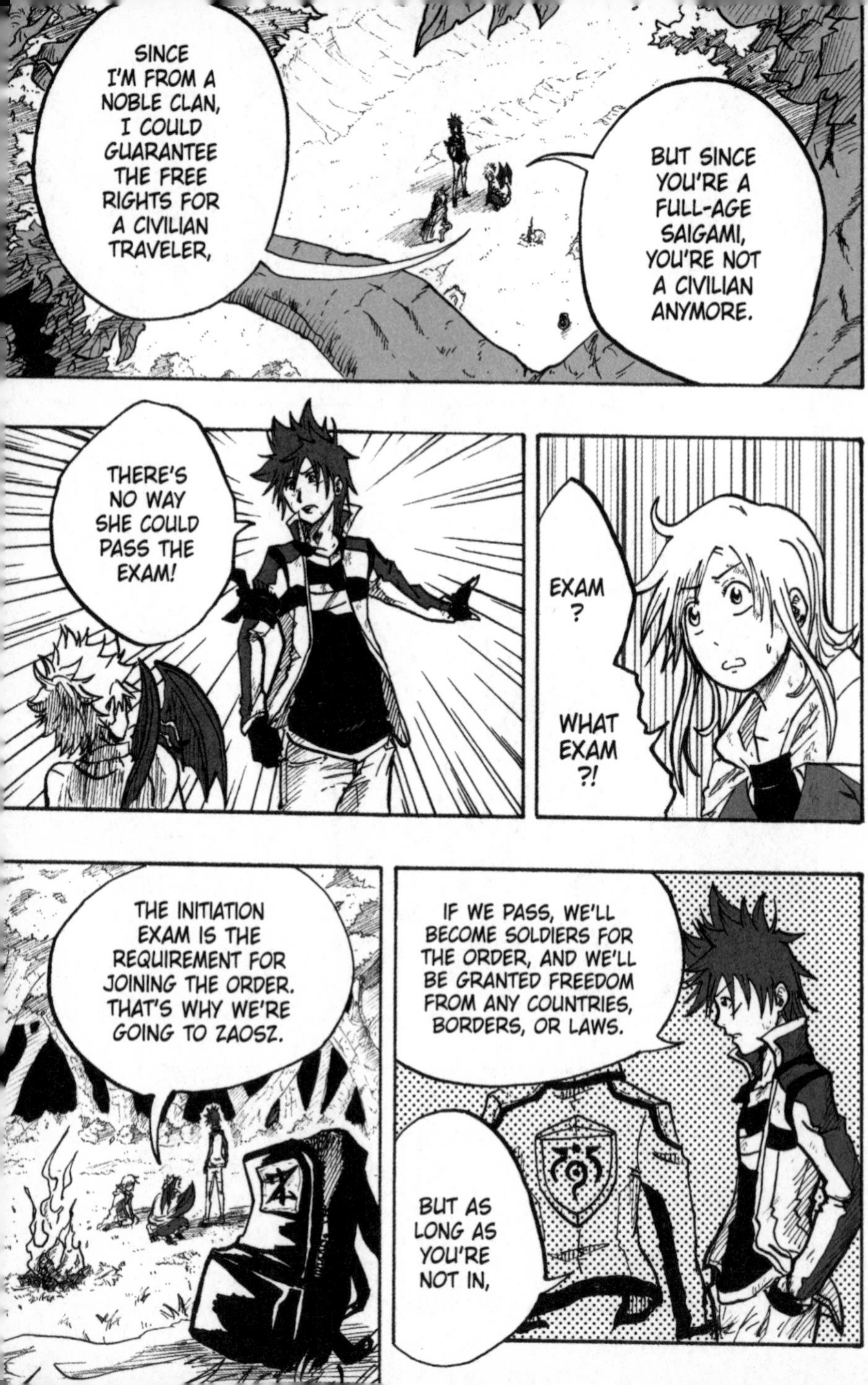
SINCE I'M FROM A NOBLE CLAN, I COULD GUARANTEE THE FREE RIGHTS FOR A CIVILIAN TRAVELER,
BUT SINCE YOU'RE A FULL-AGE SAIGAMI, YOU'RE NOT A CIVILIAN ANYMORE.
THERE'S NO WAY SHE COULD PASS THE EXAM!
EXAM?
WHAT EXAM?!
THE INITIATION EXAM IS THE REQUIREMENT FOR JOINING THE ORDER. THAT'S WHY WE'RE GOING TO ZAOSZ.
IF WE PASS, WE'LL BECOME SOLDIERS FOR THE ORDER, AND WE'LL BE GRANTED FREEDOM FROM ANY COUNTRIES, BORDERS, OR LAWS.
BUT AS LONG AS YOU'RE NOT IN,

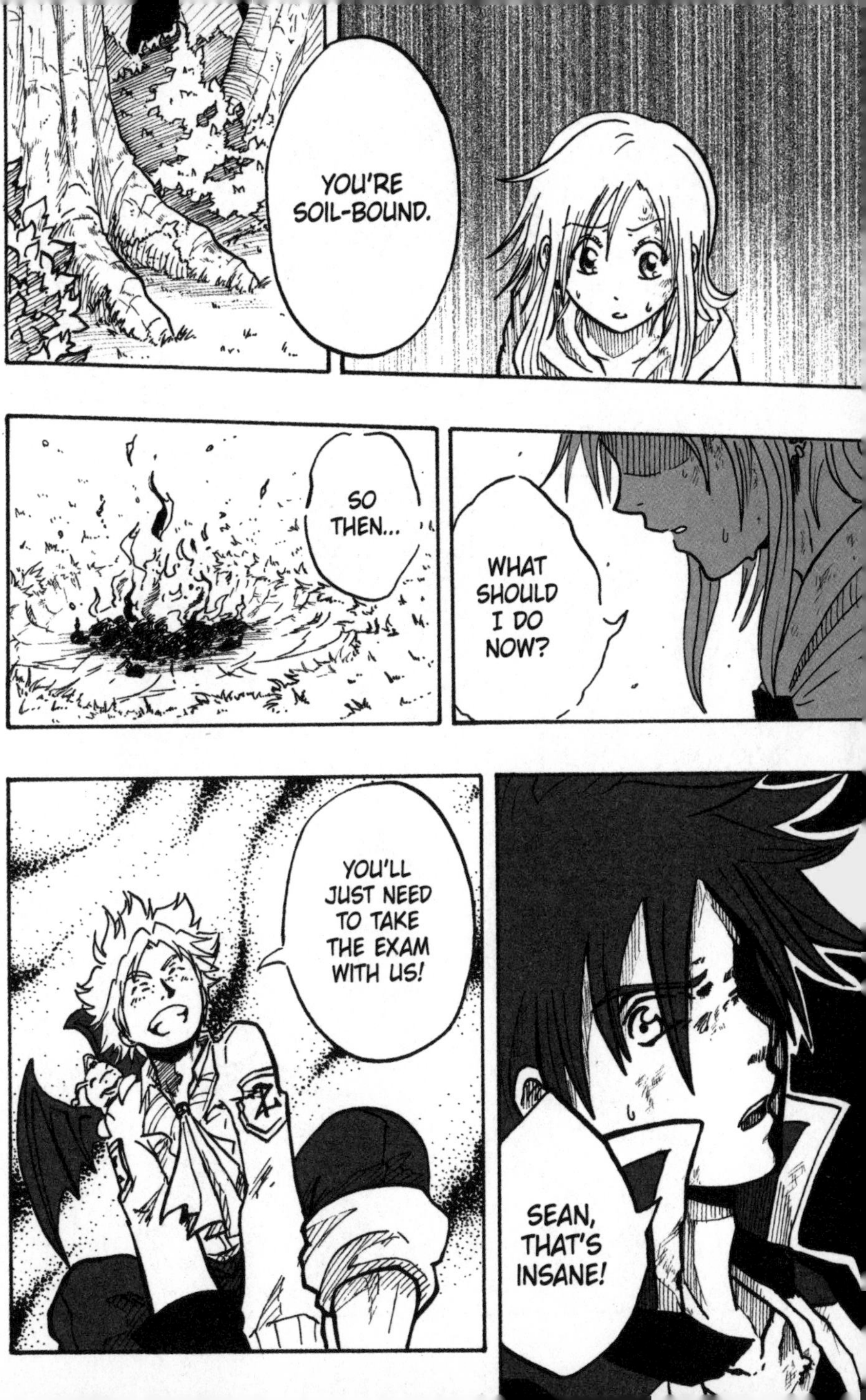
YOU'RE SOIL-BOUND.
SO THEN...
WHAT SHOULD I DO NOW?
YOU'LL JUST NEED TO TAKE THE EXAM WITH US!
SEAN, THAT'S INSANE!

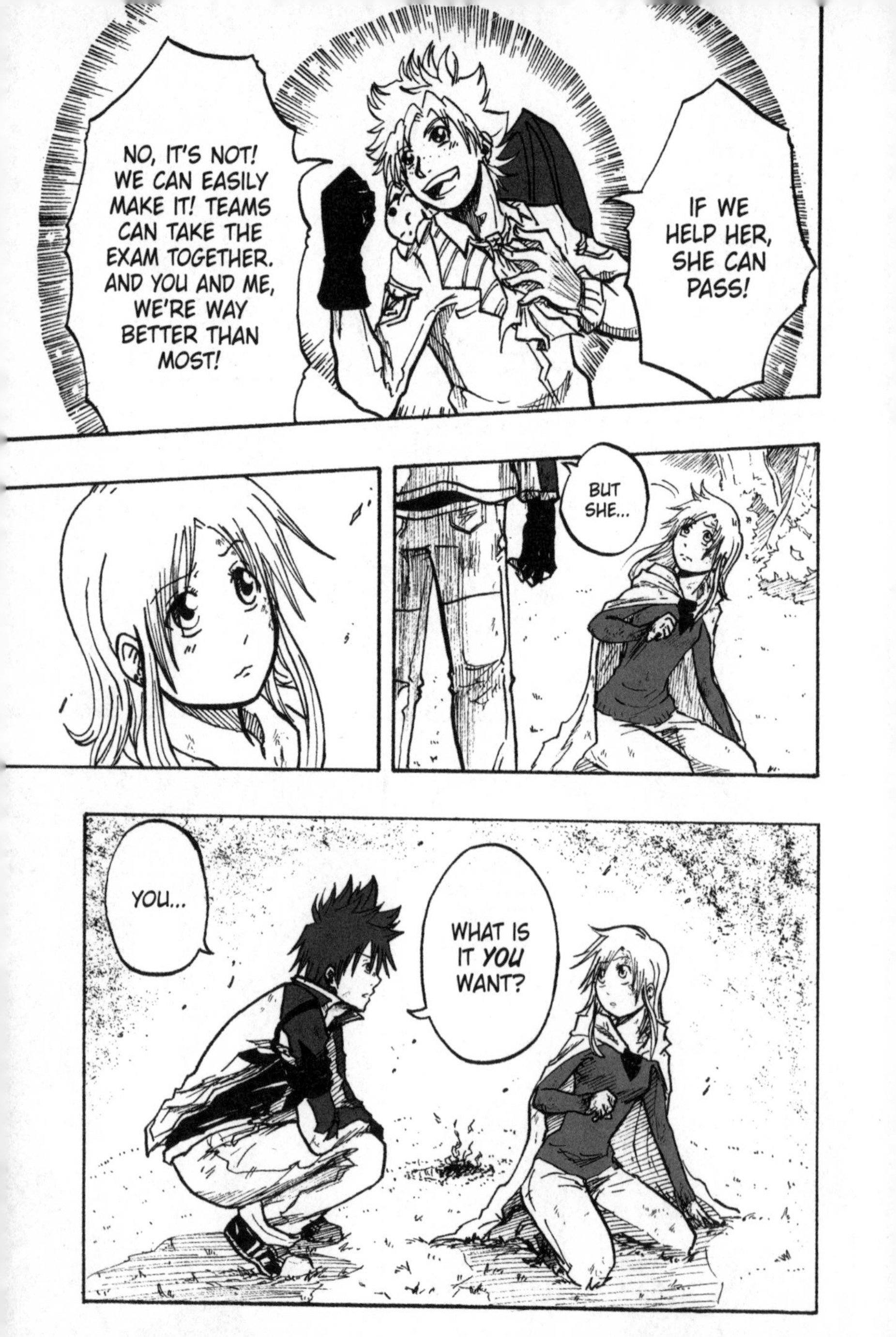
NO, IT'S NOT! WE CAN EASILY MAKE IT! TEAMS CAN TAKE THE EXAM TOGETHER. AND YOU AND ME, WE'RE WAY BETTER THAN MOST!
IF WE HELP HER, SHE CAN PASS!
BUT SHE...
YOU...
WHAT IS IT *YOU* WANT?

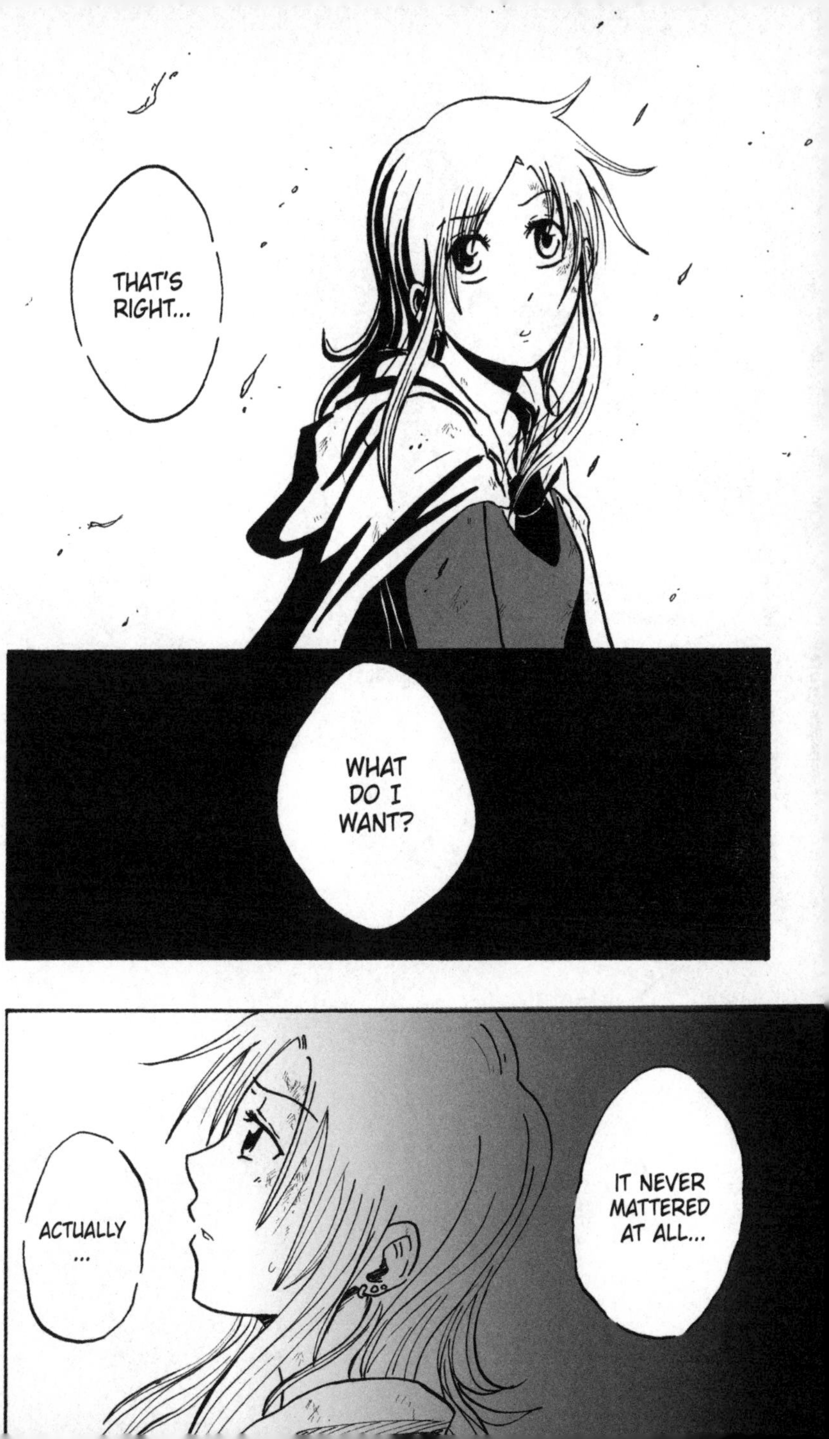
THAT'S RIGHT...
WHAT DO I WANT?
ACTUALLY ...
IT NEVER MATTERED AT ALL...

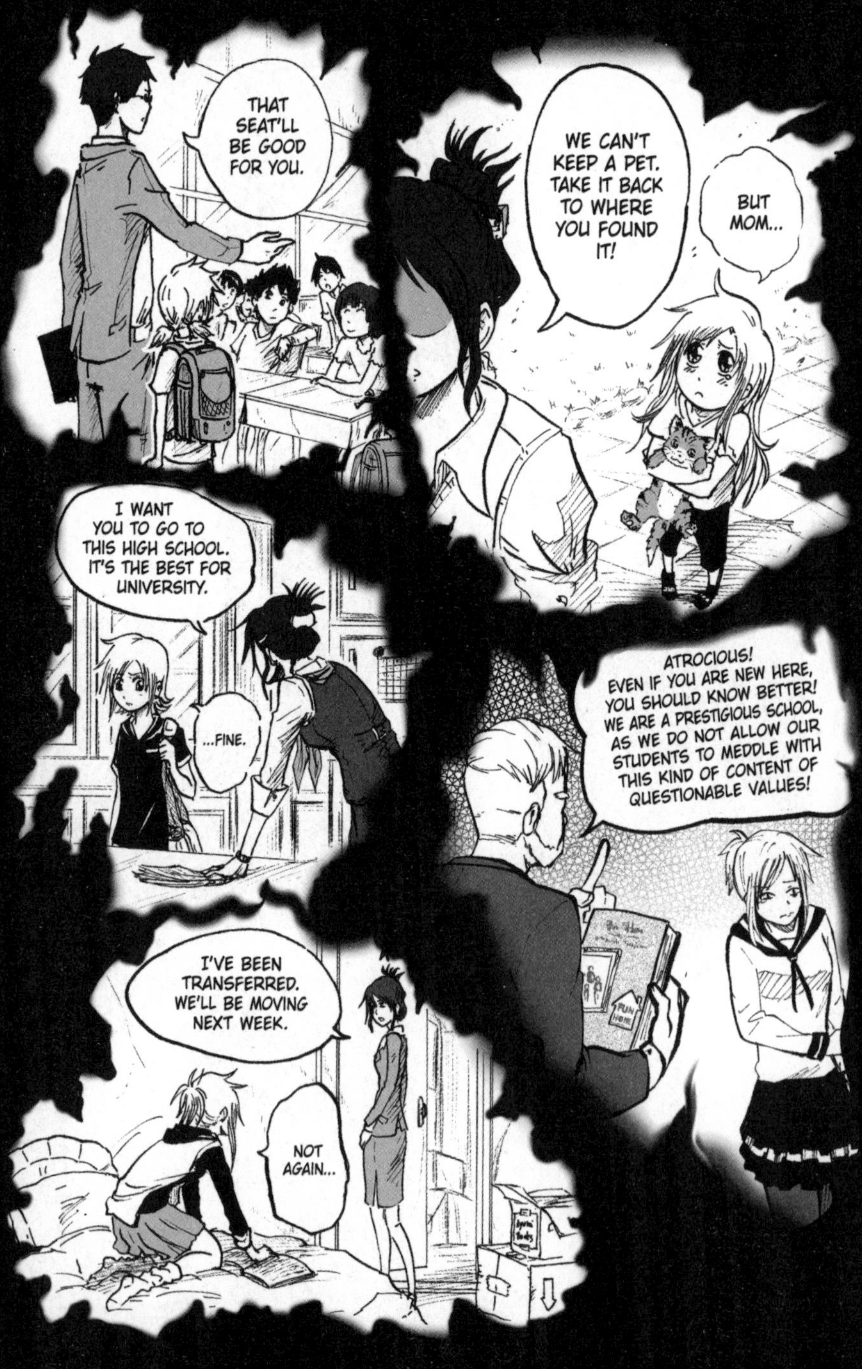
THAT SEAT'LL BE GOOD FOR YOU.
WE CAN'T KEEP A PET. TAKE IT BACK TO WHERE YOU FOUND IT!
BUT MOM...
I WANT YOU TO GO TO THIS HIGH SCHOOL. IT'S THE BEST FOR UNIVERSITY.
...FINE.
I'VE BEEN TRANSFERRED. WE'LL BE MOVING NEXT WEEK.
NOT AGAIN...
ATROCIOUS! EVEN IF YOU ARE NEW HERE, YOU SHOULD KNOW BETTER! WE ARE A PRESTIGIOUS SCHOOL, AS WE DO NOT ALLOW OUR STUDENTS TO MEDDLE WITH THIS KIND OF CONTENT OF QUESTIONABLE VALUES!

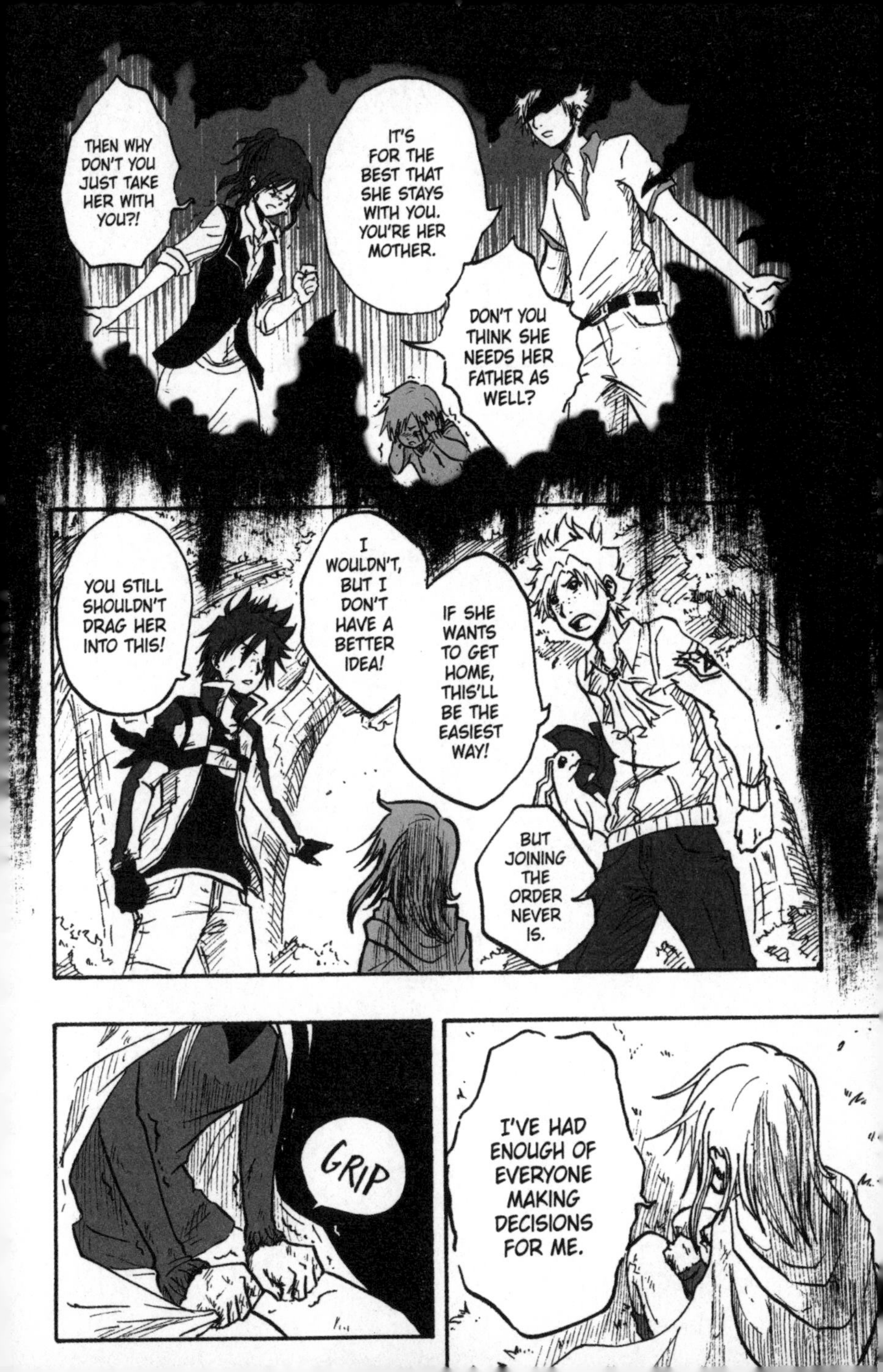
THEN WHY DON'T YOU JUST TAKE HER WITH YOU?!
IT'S FOR THE BEST THAT SHE STAYS WITH YOU. YOU'RE HER MOTHER.
DON'T YOU THINK SHE NEEDS HER FATHER AS WELL?
YOU STILL SHOULDN'T DRAG HER INTO THIS!
I WOULDN'T, BUT I DON'T HAVE A BETTER IDEA!
IF SHE WANTS TO GET HOME, THIS'LL BE THE EASIEST WAY!
BUT JOINING THE ORDER NEVER IS.
GRIP
I'VE HAD ENOUGH OF EVERYONE MAKING DECISIONS FOR ME.

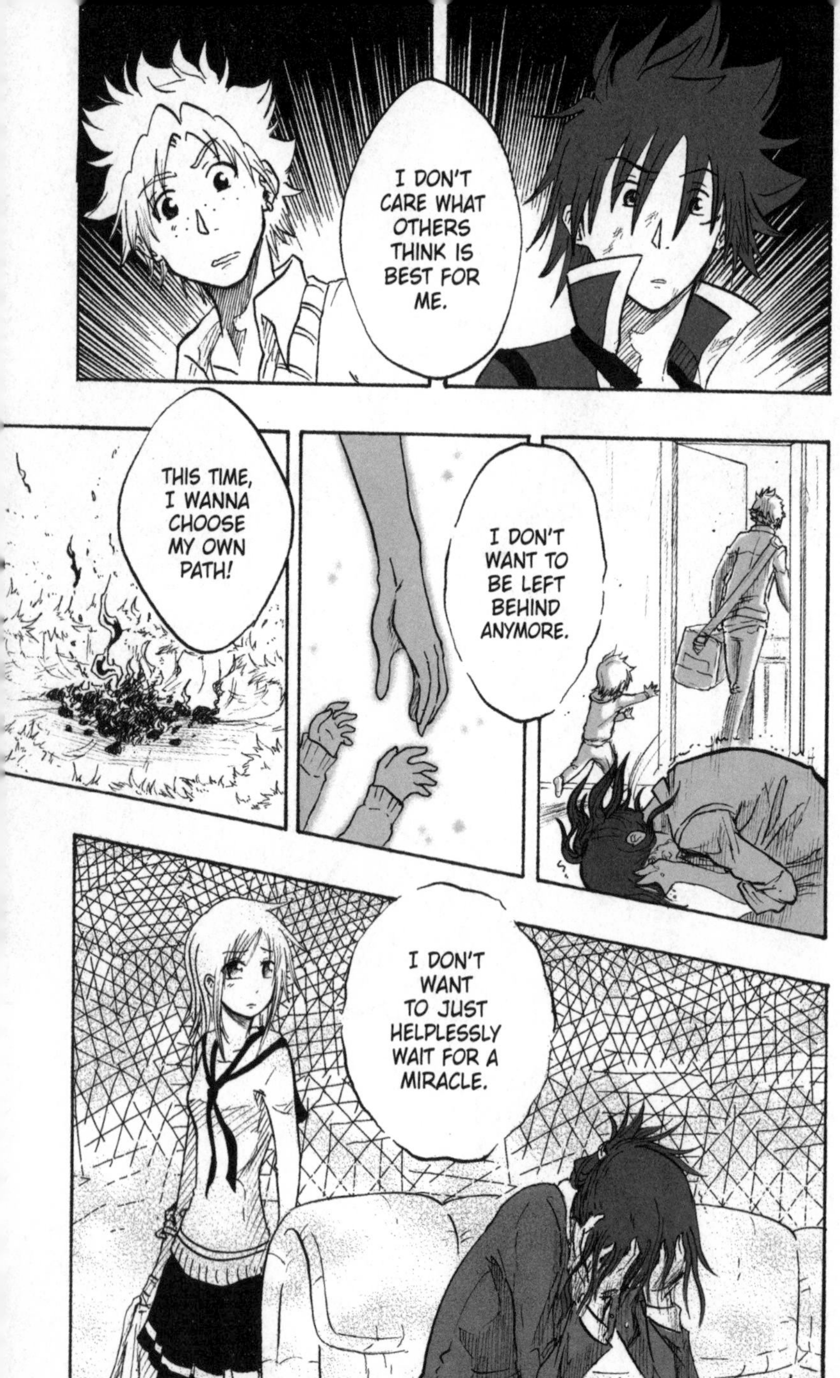
I DON'T CARE WHAT OTHERS THINK IS BEST FOR ME.
THIS TIME, I WANNA CHOOSE MY OWN PATH!
I DON'T WANT TO BE LEFT BEHIND ANYMORE.
I DON'T WANT TO JUST HELPLESSLY WAIT FOR A MIRACLE.

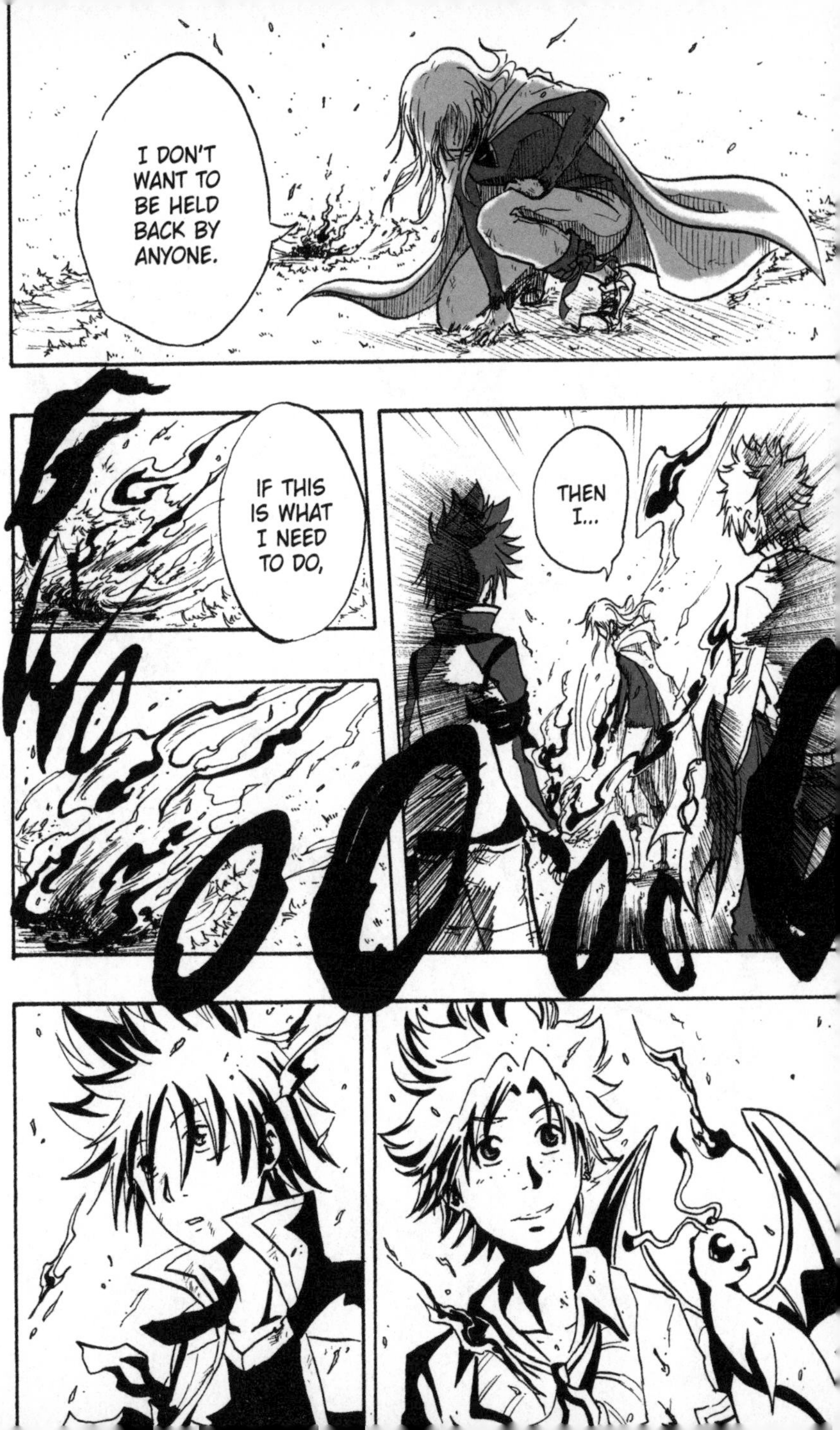
I DON'T WANT TO BE HELD BACK BY ANYONE.
IF THIS IS WHAT I NEED TO DO,
THEN I...

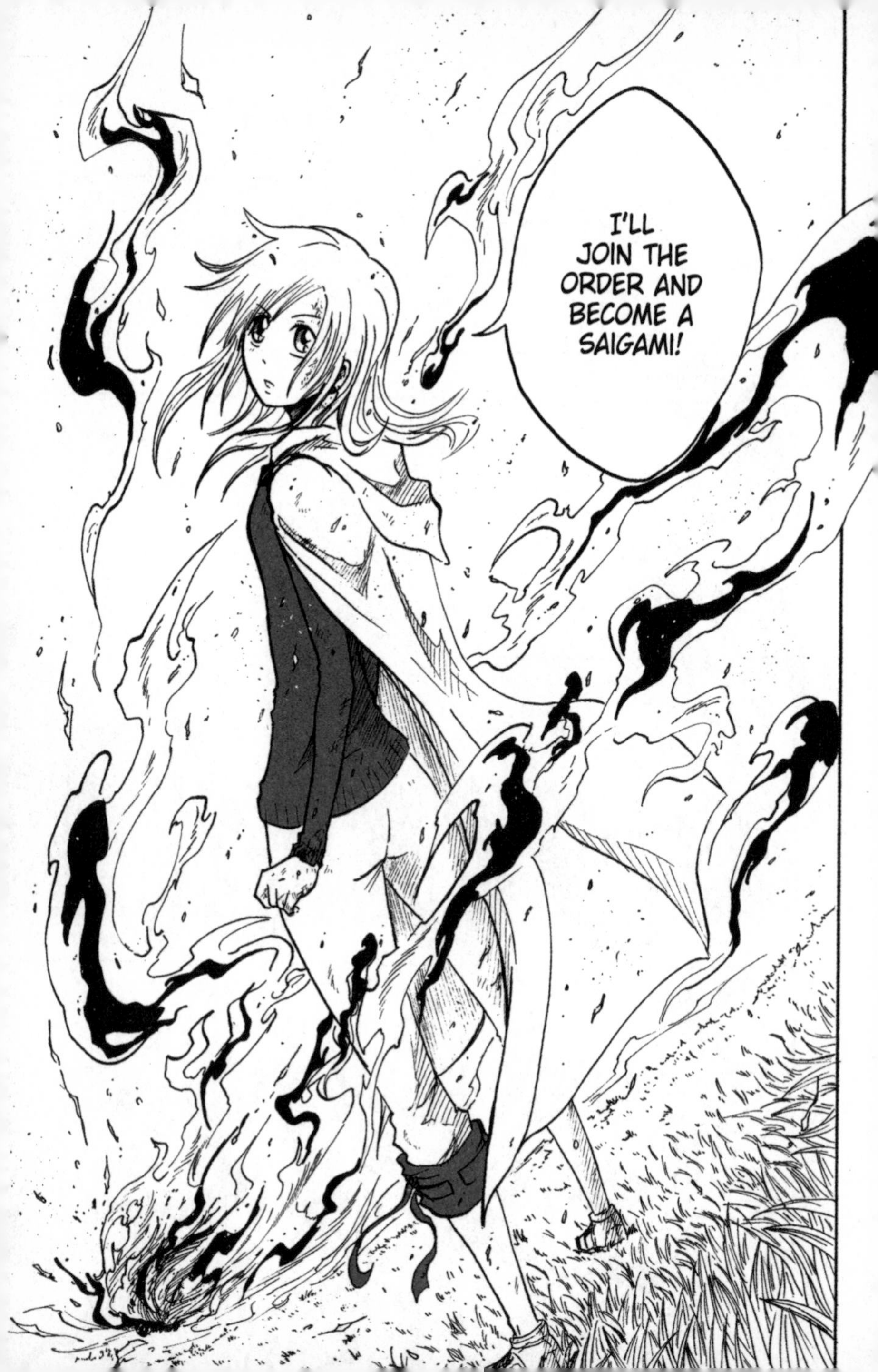
I'LL JOIN THE ORDER AND BECOME A SAIGAMI!

SAIGAMI

Chapter 4: **Welcome to Zaosz**

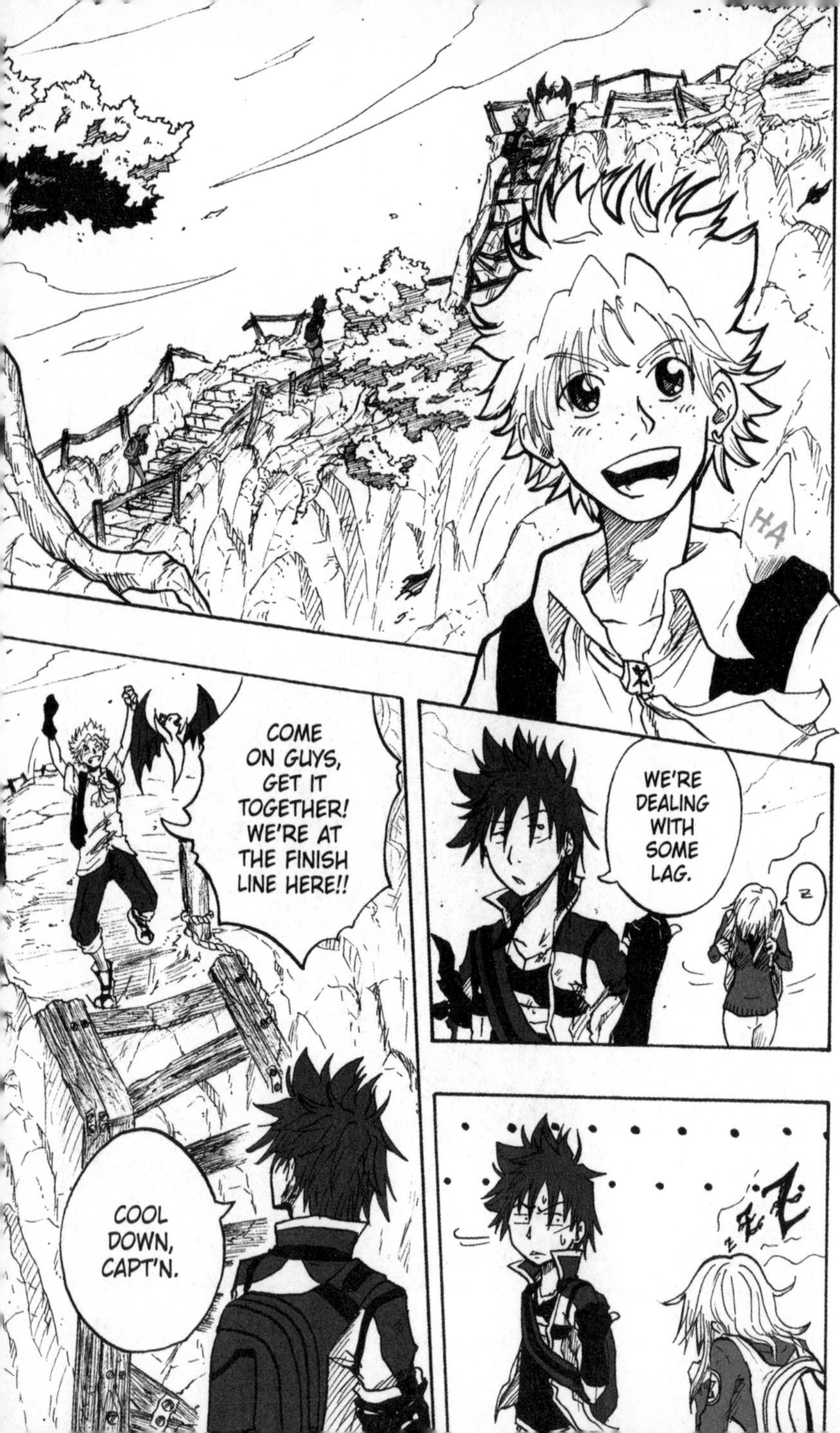
HA
COME ON GUYS, GET IT TOGETHER! WE'RE AT THE FINISH LINE HERE!!
COOL DOWN, CAPT'N.
WE'RE DEALING WITH SOME LAG.
z
• • • • • • • • • • • • • • •
z z Z

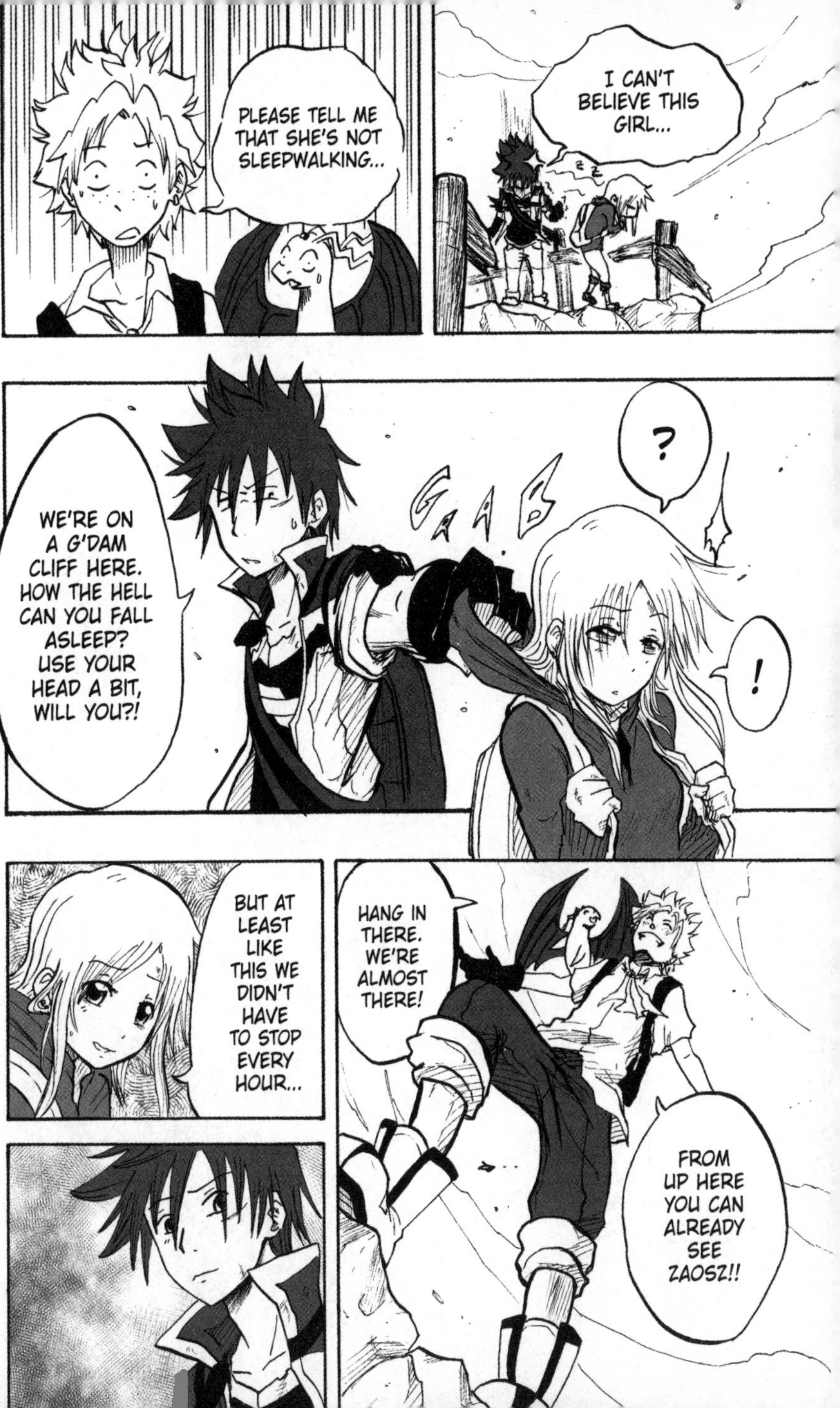
PLEASE TELL ME THAT SHE'S NOT SLEEPWALKING...
I CAN'T BELIEVE THIS GIRL...
WE'RE ON A G'DAM CLIFF HERE. HOW THE HELL CAN YOU FALL ASLEEP? USE YOUR HEAD A BIT, WILL YOU?!
GRAB
?
!
BUT AT LEAST LIKE THIS WE DIDN'T HAVE TO STOP EVERY HOUR...
HANG IN THERE. WE'RE ALMOST THERE!
FROM UP HERE YOU CAN ALREADY SEE ZAOSZ!!

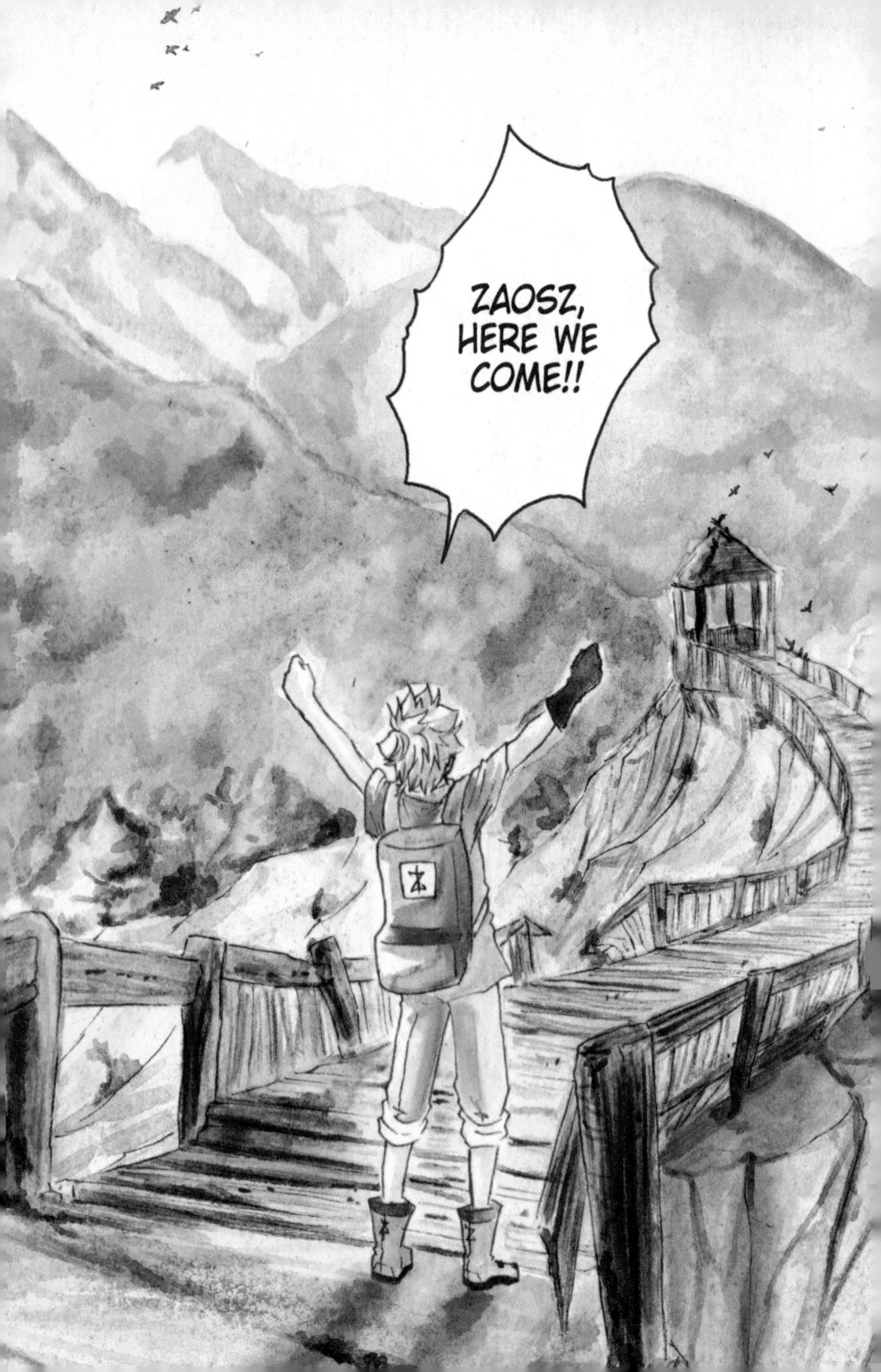
ZAOSZ, HERE WE COME!!

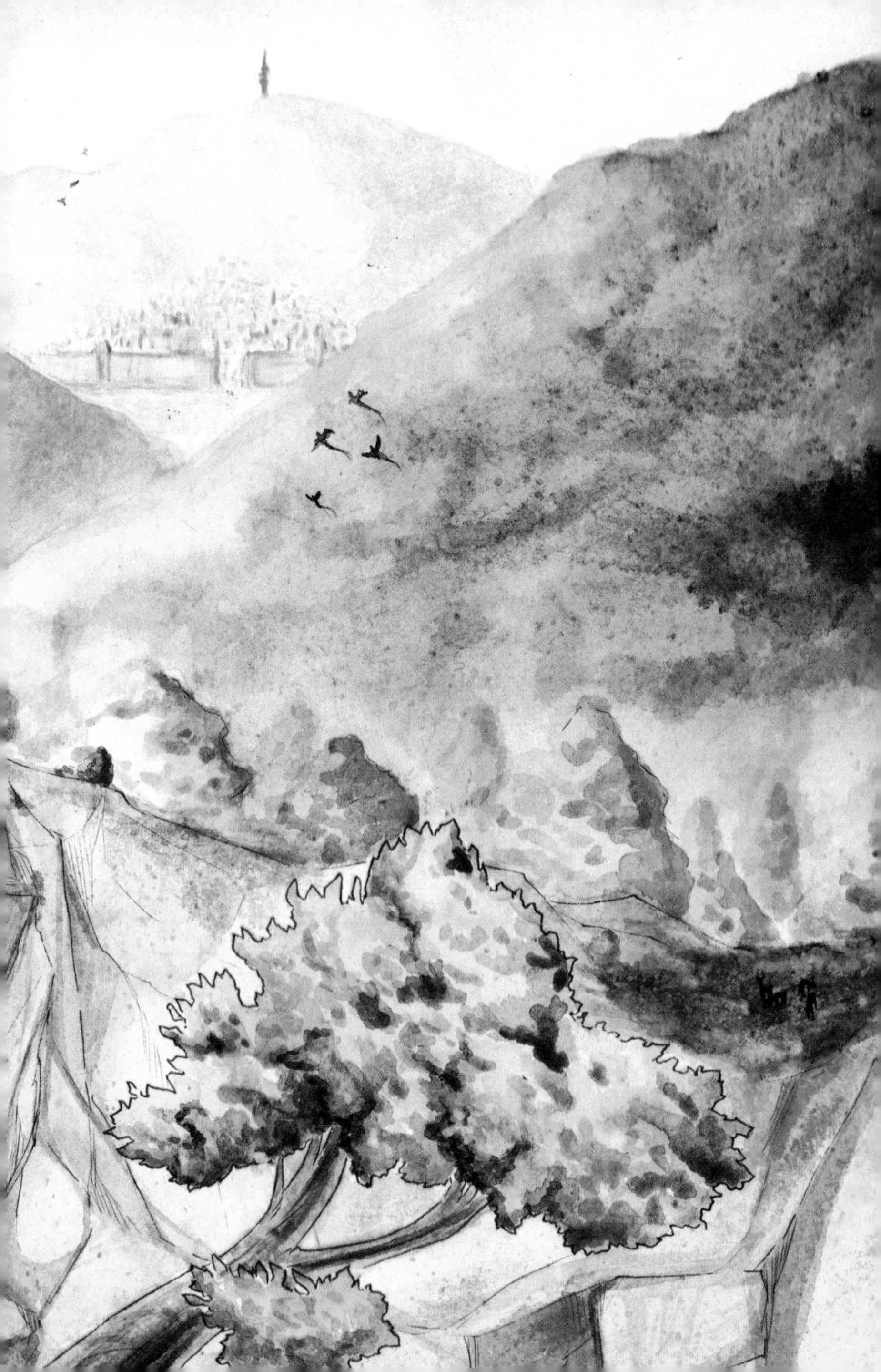

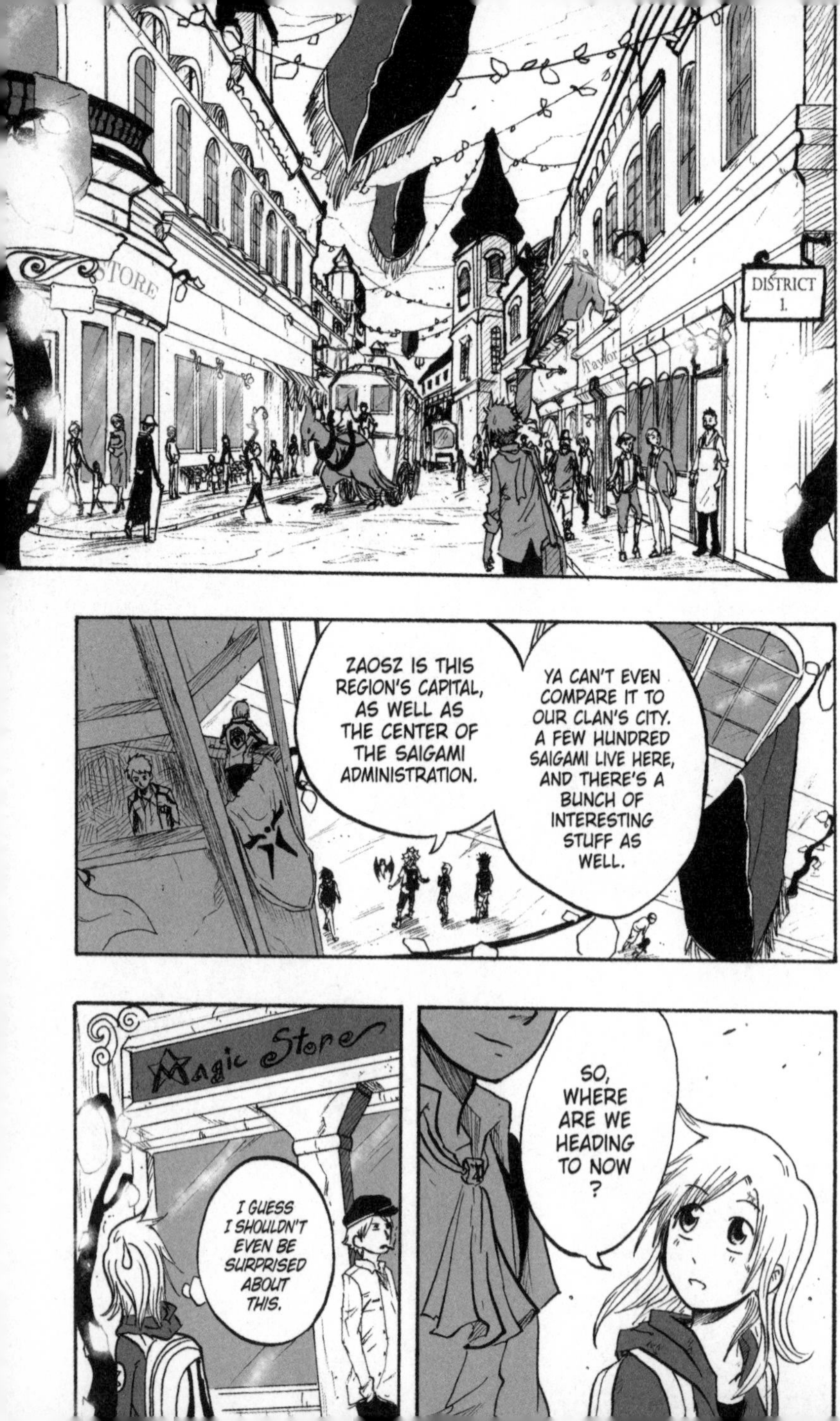
STORE
DISTRICT 1.
Taylor
ZAOSZ IS THIS REGION'S CAPITAL, AS WELL AS THE CENTER OF THE SAIGAMI ADMINISTRATION.
YA CAN'T EVEN COMPARE IT TO OUR CLAN'S CITY. A FEW HUNDRED SAIGAMI LIVE HERE, AND THERE'S A BUNCH OF INTERESTING STUFF AS WELL.
Magic Store
I GUESS I SHOULDN'T EVEN BE SURPRISED ABOUT THIS.
SO, WHERE ARE WE HEADING TO NOW?

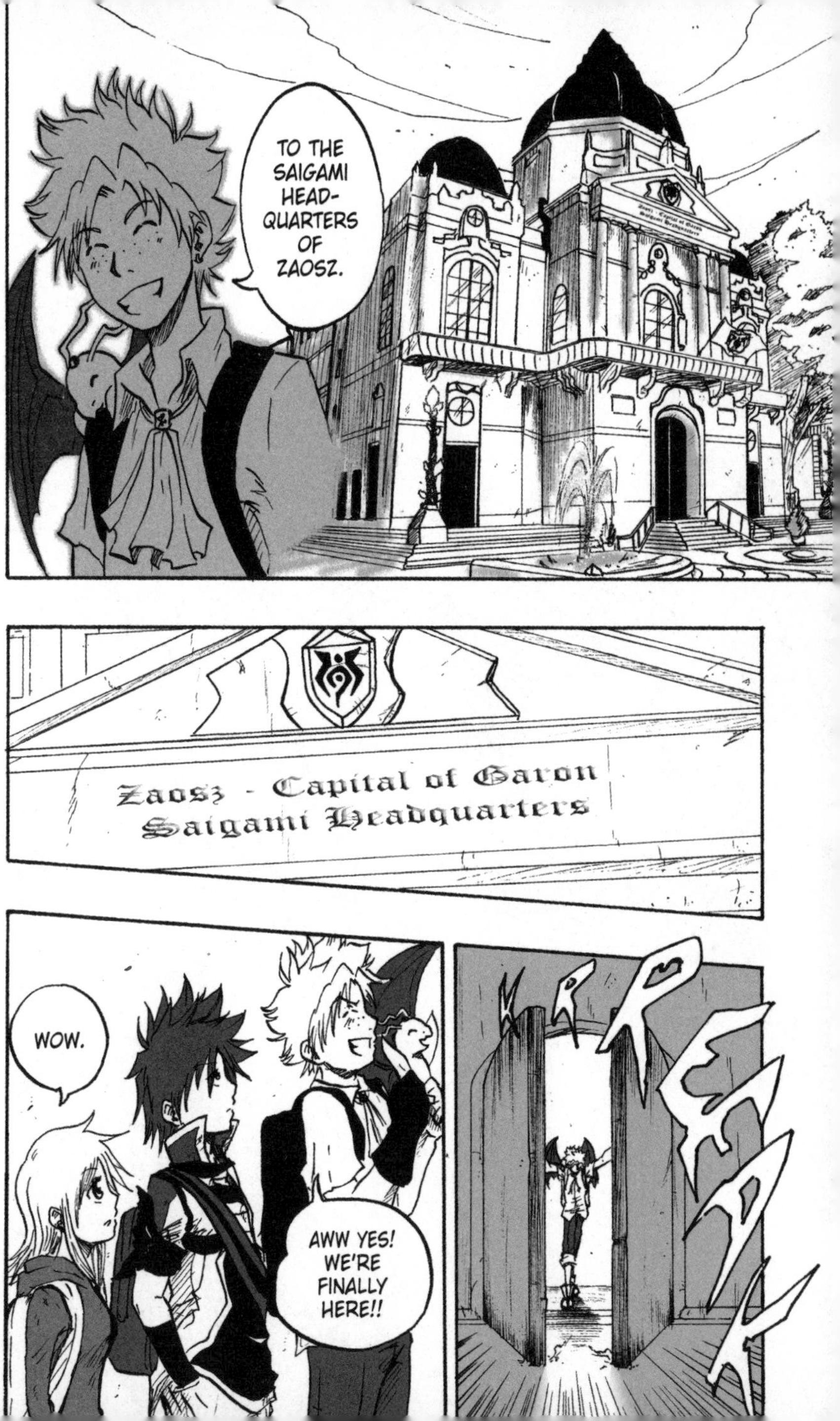
TO THE SAIGAMI HEAD-QUARTERS OF ZAOSZ.
Zaosz - Capital of Garon
Saigami Headquarters
WOW.
AWW YES! WE'RE FINALLY HERE!!

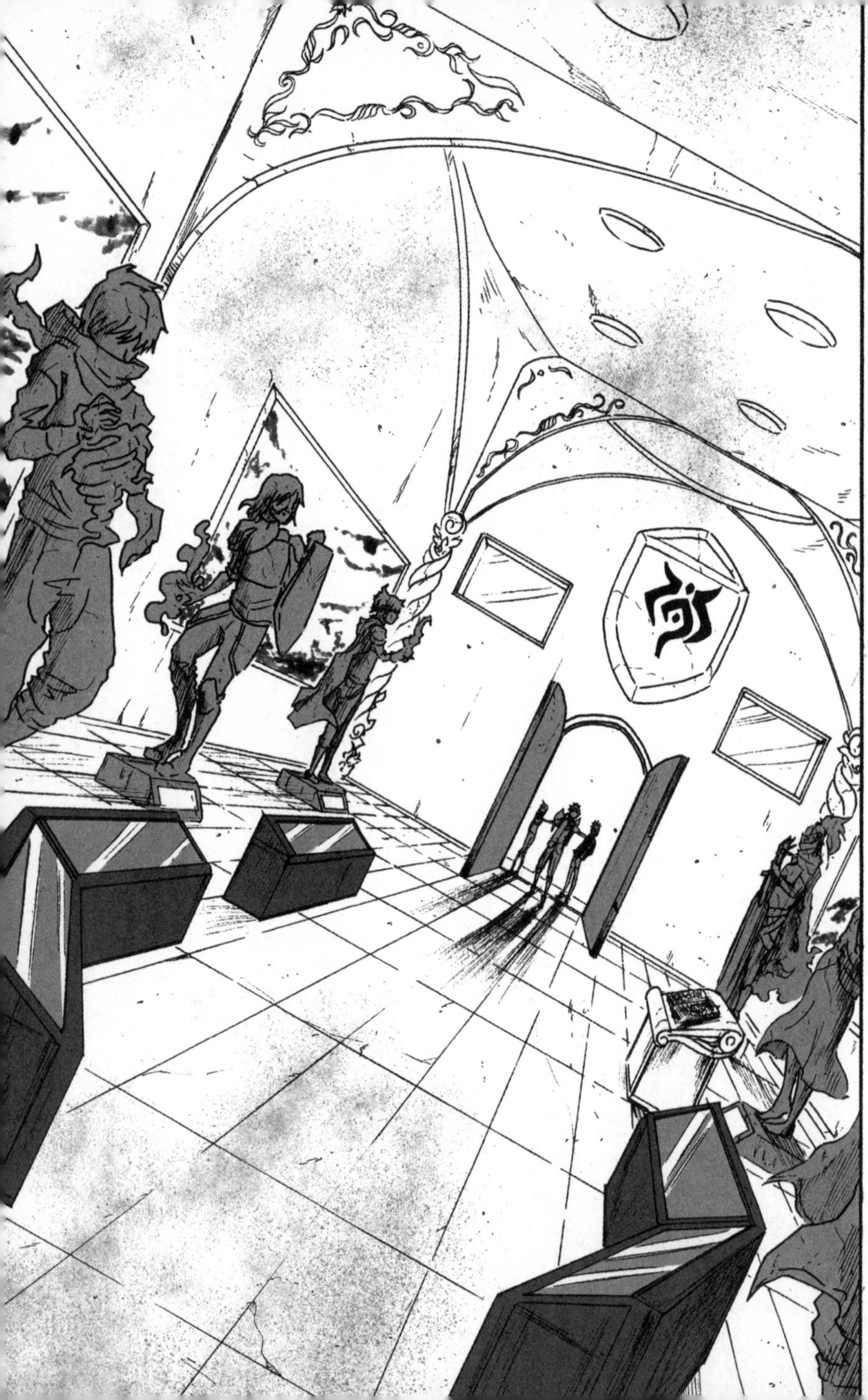

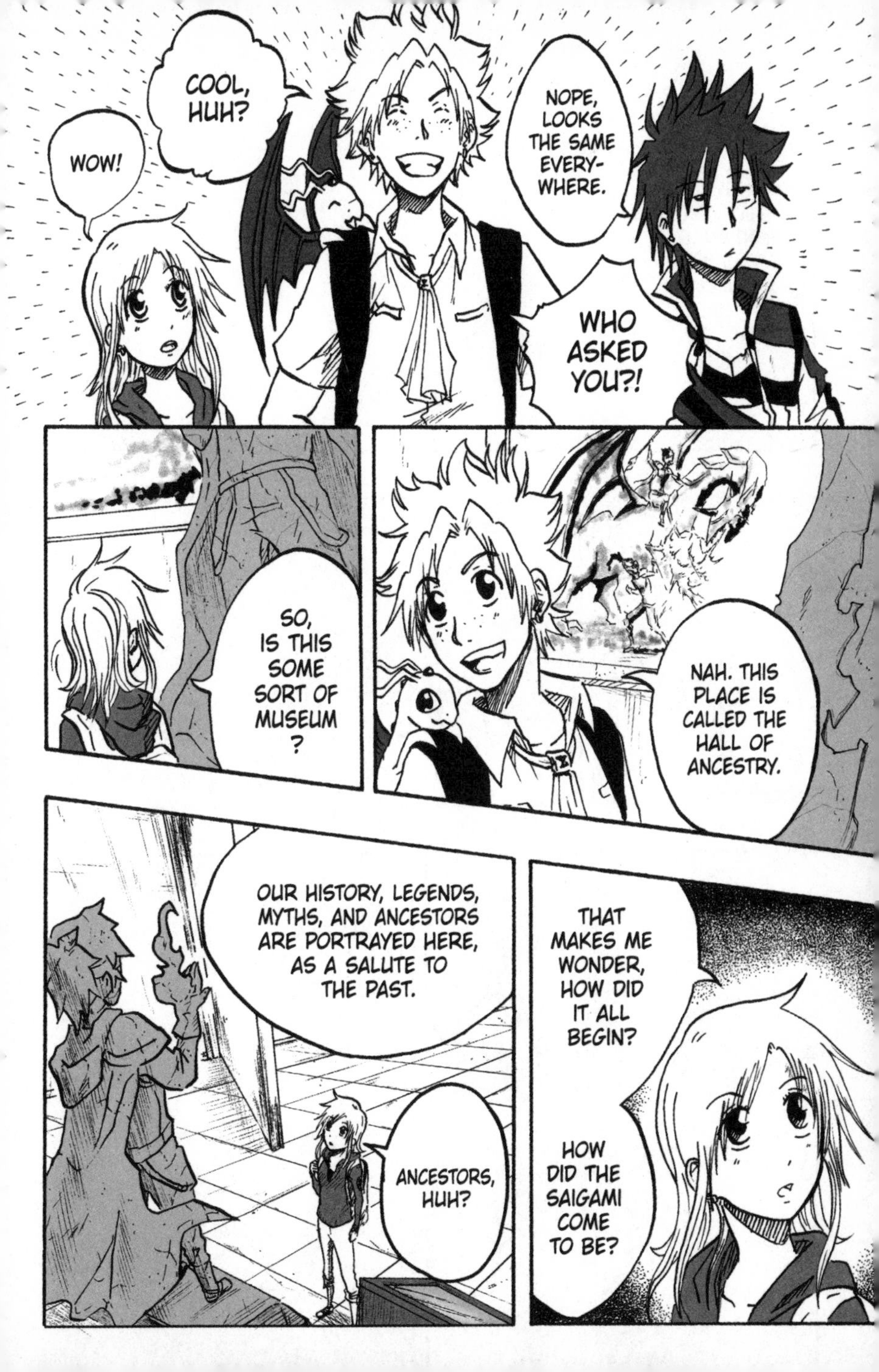
WOW!
COOL, HUH?
NOPE, LOOKS THE SAME EVERY-WHERE.
WHO ASKED YOU?!
SO, IS THIS SOME SORT OF MUSEUM ?
NAH. THIS PLACE IS CALLED THE HALL OF ANCESTRY.
OUR HISTORY, LEGENDS, MYTHS, AND ANCESTORS ARE PORTRAYED HERE, AS A SALUTE TO THE PAST.
ANCESTORS, HUH?
THAT MAKES ME WONDER, HOW DID IT ALL BEGIN?
HOW DID THE SAIGAMI COME TO BE?

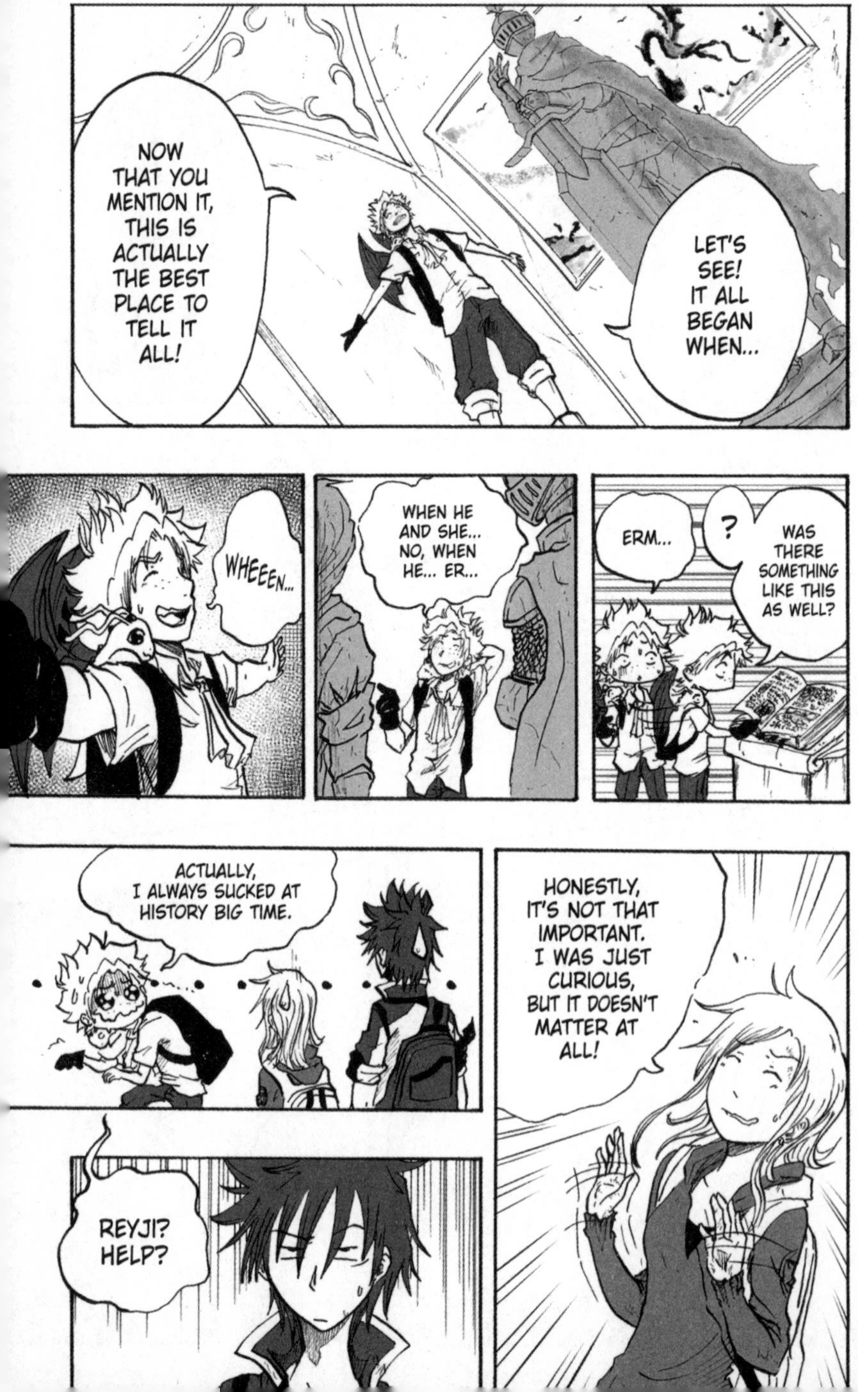
NOW THAT YOU MENTION IT, THIS IS ACTUALLY THE BEST PLACE TO TELL IT ALL!
LET'S SEE! IT ALL BEGAN WHEN...
WHEEEN...
WHEN HE AND SHE... NO, WHEN HE... ER...
ERM...
?
WAS THERE SOMETHING LIKE THIS AS WELL?
ACTUALLY, I ALWAYS SUCKED AT HISTORY BIG TIME.
REYJI? HELP?
HONESTLY, IT'S NOT THAT IMPORTANT. I WAS JUST CURIOUS, BUT IT DOESN'T MATTER AT ALL!

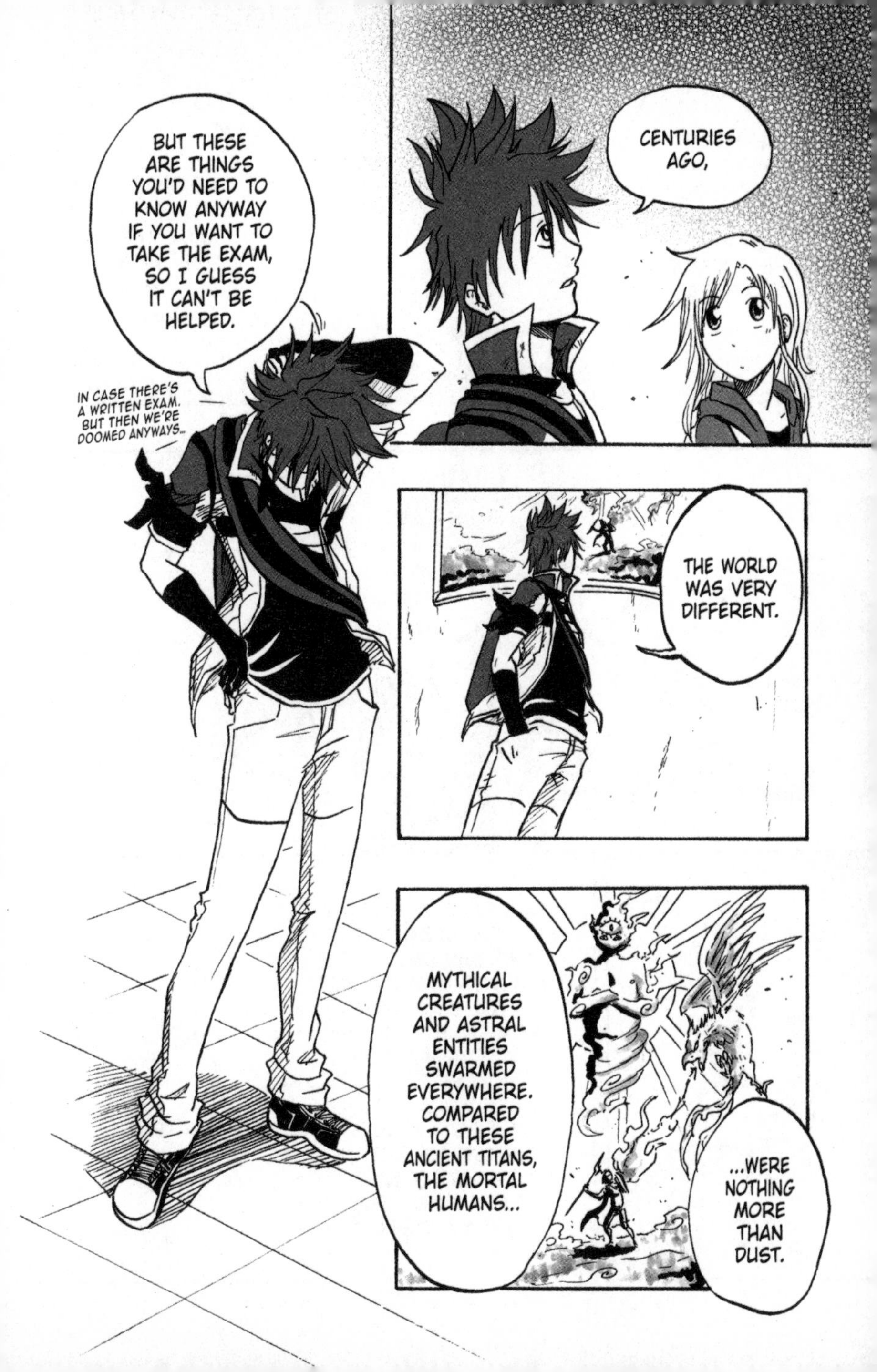
BUT THESE ARE THINGS YOU'D NEED TO KNOW ANYWAY IF YOU WANT TO TAKE THE EXAM, SO I GUESS IT CAN'T BE HELPED.
IN CASE THERE'S A WRITTEN EXAM. BUT THEN WE'RE DOOMED ANYWAYS...
CENTURIES AGO,
THE WORLD WAS VERY DIFFERENT.
MYTHICAL CREATURES AND ASTRAL ENTITIES SWARMED EVERYWHERE. COMPARED TO THESE ANCIENT TITANS, THE MORTAL HUMANS...
...WERE NOTHING MORE THAN DUST.

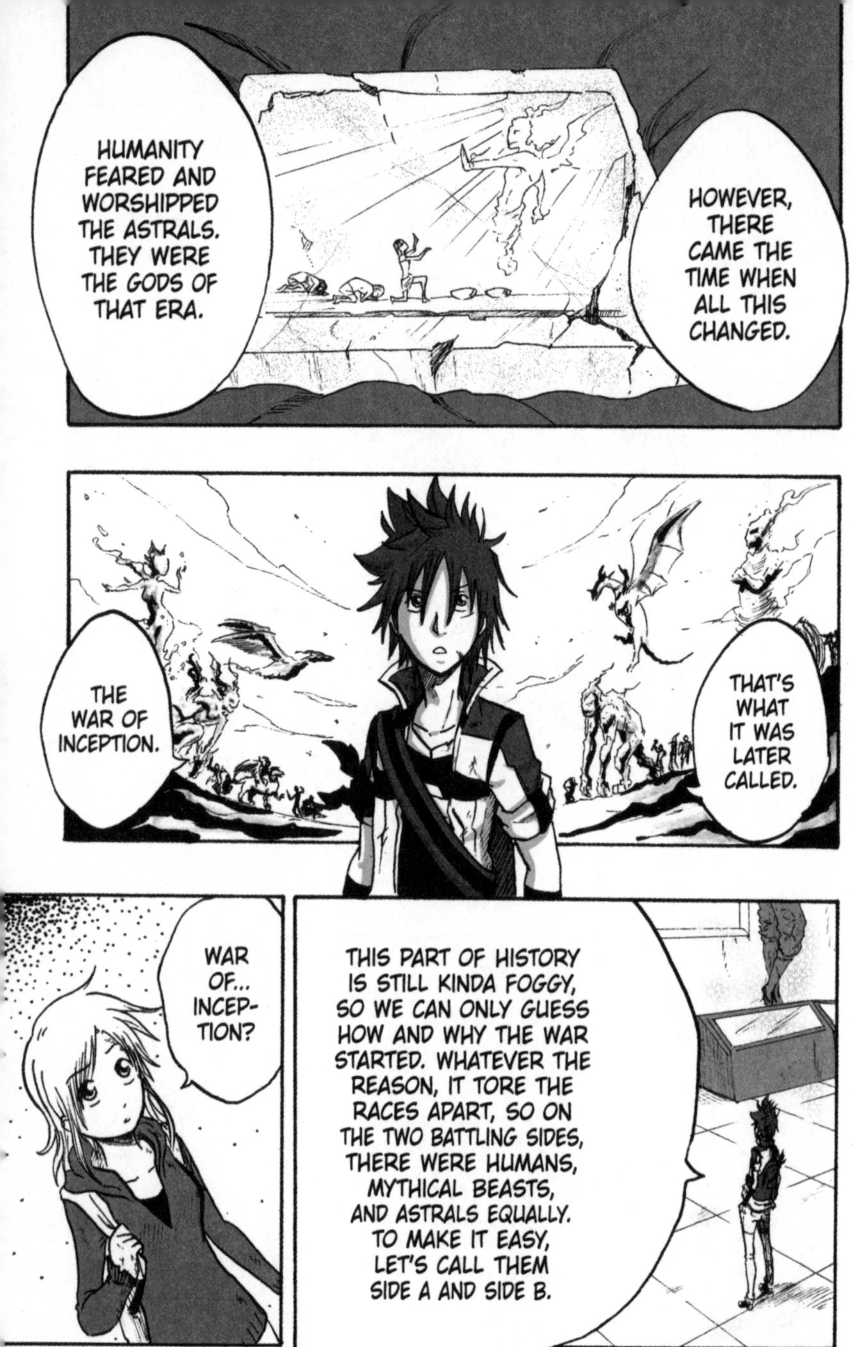
HUMANITY FEARED AND WORSHIPPED THE ASTRALS. THEY WERE THE GODS OF THAT ERA.
HOWEVER, THERE CAME THE TIME WHEN ALL THIS CHANGED.
THE WAR OF INCEPTION.
THAT'S WHAT IT WAS LATER CALLED.
WAR OF... INCEP-TION?
THIS PART OF HISTORY IS STILL KINDA FOGGY, SO WE CAN ONLY GUESS HOW AND WHY THE WAR STARTED. WHATEVER THE REASON, IT TORE THE RACES APART, SO ON THE TWO BATTLING SIDES, THERE WERE HUMANS, MYTHICAL BEASTS, AND ASTRALS EQUALLY. TO MAKE IT EASY, LET'S CALL THEM SIDE A AND SIDE B.

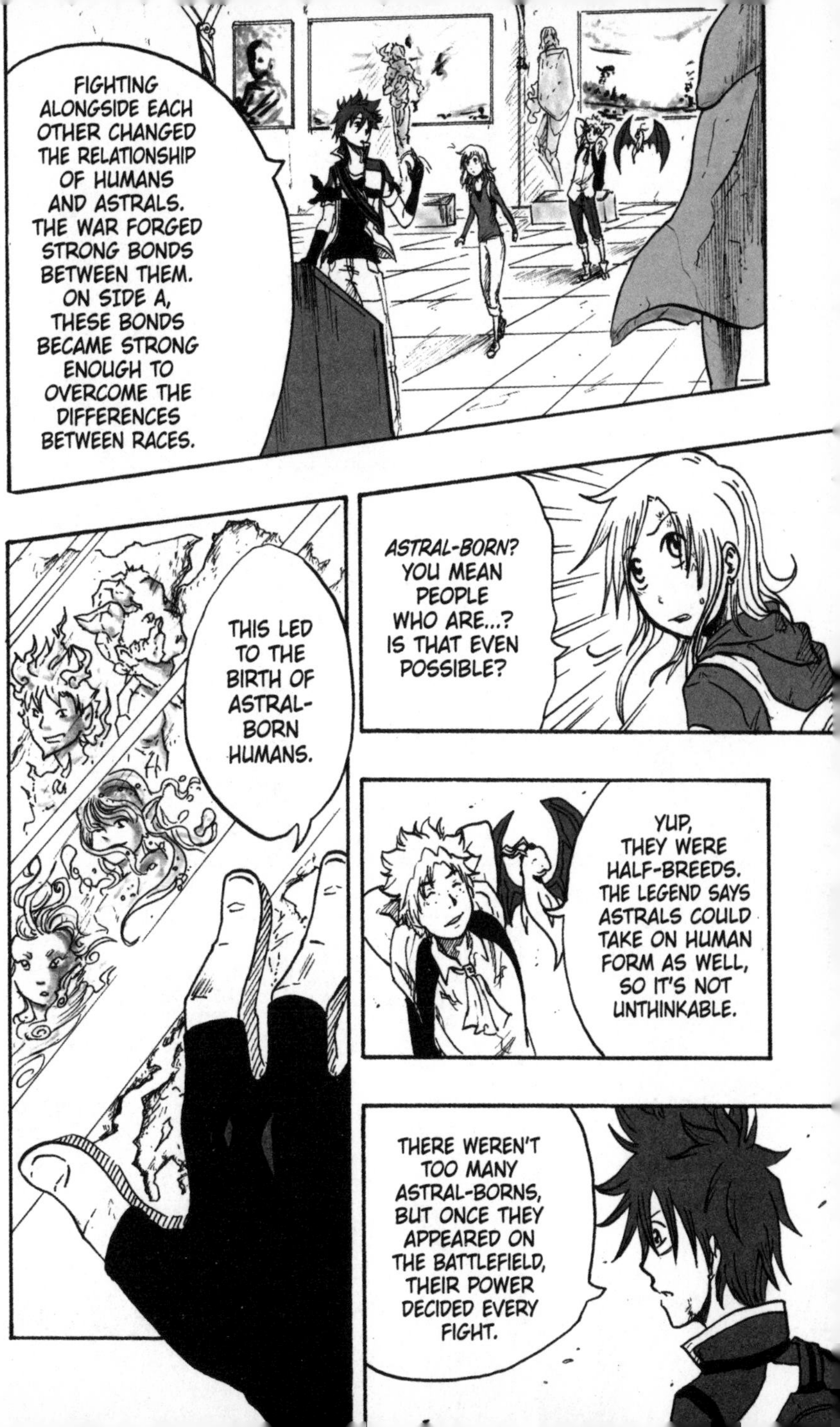
FIGHTING ALONGSIDE EACH OTHER CHANGED THE RELATIONSHIP OF HUMANS AND ASTRALS. THE WAR FORGED STRONG BONDS BETWEEN THEM. ON SIDE A, THESE BONDS BECAME STRONG ENOUGH TO OVERCOME THE DIFFERENCES BETWEEN RACES.
THIS LED TO THE BIRTH OF ASTRAL-BORN HUMANS.
ASTRAL-BORN? YOU MEAN PEOPLE WHO ARE...? IS THAT EVEN POSSIBLE?
YUP, THEY WERE HALF-BREEDS. THE LEGEND SAYS ASTRALS COULD TAKE ON HUMAN FORM AS WELL, SO IT'S NOT UNTHINKABLE.
THERE WEREN'T TOO MANY ASTRAL-BORNS, BUT ONCE THEY APPEARED ON THE BATTLEFIELD, THEIR POWER DECIDED EVERY FIGHT.

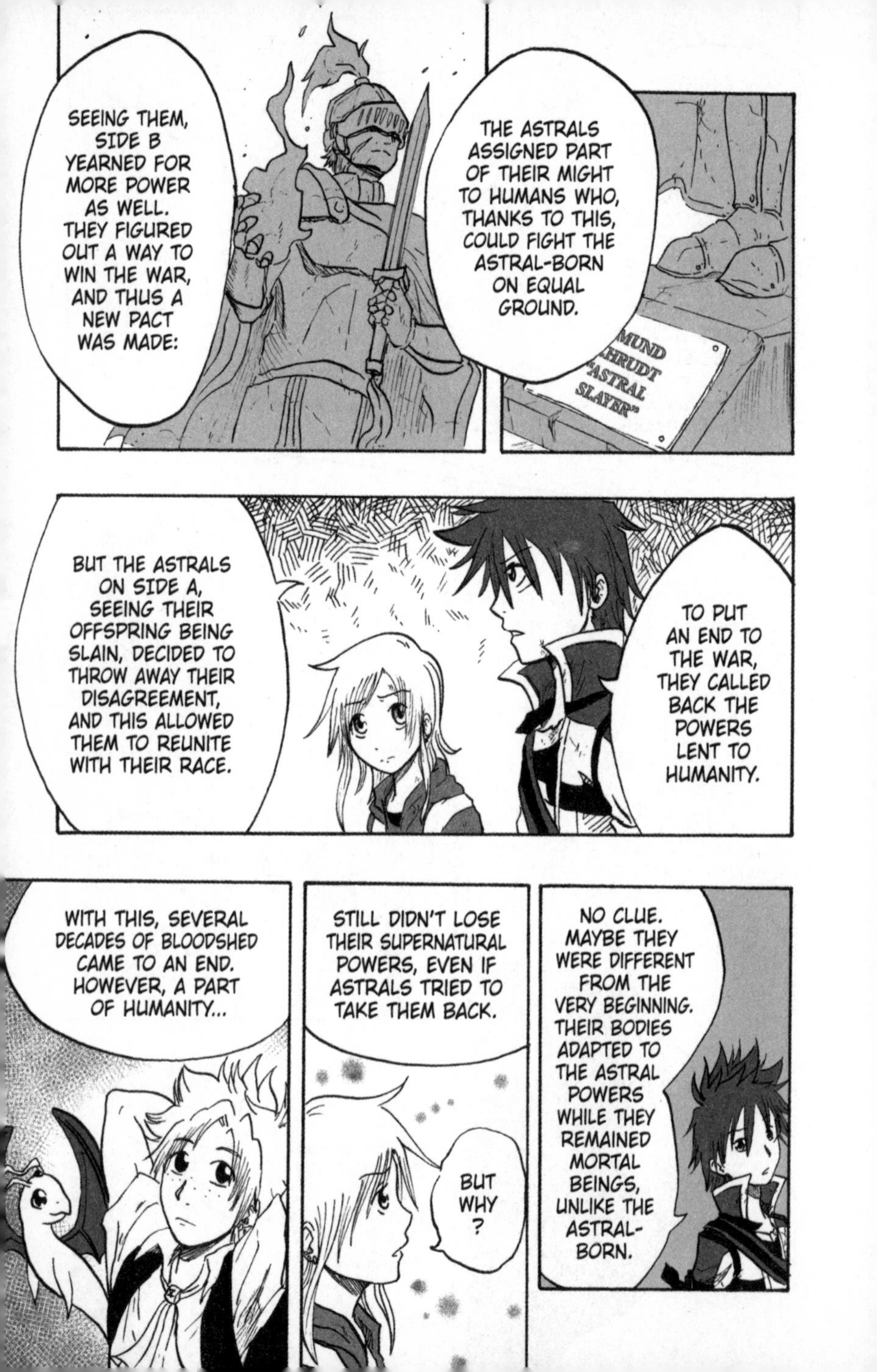
SEEING THEM, SIDE B YEARNED FOR MORE POWER AS WELL. THEY FIGURED OUT A WAY TO WIN THE WAR, AND THUS A NEW PACT WAS MADE:
THE ASTRALS ASSIGNED PART OF THEIR MIGHT TO HUMANS WHO, THANKS TO THIS, COULD FIGHT THE ASTRAL-BORN ON EQUAL GROUND.
"ASTRAL SLAYER"
BUT THE ASTRALS ON SIDE A, SEEING THEIR OFFSPRING BEING SLAIN, DECIDED TO THROW AWAY THEIR DISAGREEMENT, AND THIS ALLOWED THEM TO REUNITE WITH THEIR RACE.
TO PUT AN END TO THE WAR, THEY CALLED BACK THE POWERS LENT TO HUMANITY.
WITH THIS, SEVERAL DECADES OF BLOODSHED CAME TO AN END. HOWEVER, A PART OF HUMANITY...
STILL DIDN'T LOSE THEIR SUPERNATURAL POWERS, EVEN IF ASTRALS TRIED TO TAKE THEM BACK.
BUT WHY?
NO CLUE. MAYBE THEY WERE DIFFERENT FROM THE VERY BEGINNING. THEIR BODIES ADAPTED TO THE ASTRAL POWERS WHILE THEY REMAINED MORTAL BEINGS, UNLIKE THE ASTRAL-BORN.

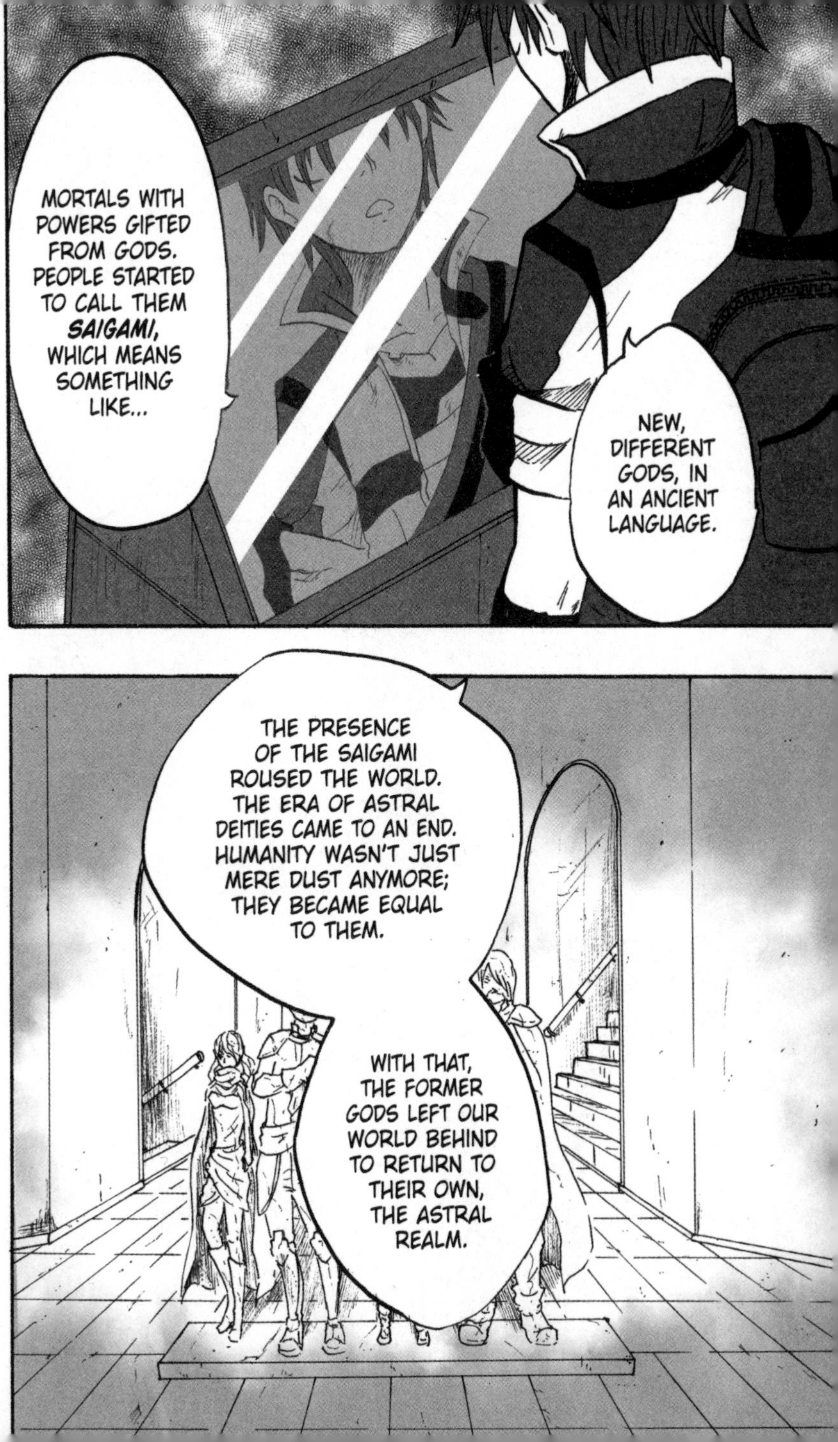
MORTALS WITH POWERS GIFTED FROM GODS. PEOPLE STARTED TO CALL THEM *SAIGAMI*, WHICH MEANS SOMETHING LIKE...
NEW, DIFFERENT GODS, IN AN ANCIENT LANGUAGE.
THE PRESENCE OF THE SAIGAMI ROUSED THE WORLD. THE ERA OF ASTRAL DEITIES CAME TO AN END. HUMANITY WASN'T JUST MERE DUST ANYMORE; THEY BECAME EQUAL TO THEM.
WITH THAT, THE FORMER GODS LEFT OUR WORLD BEHIND TO RETURN TO THEIR OWN, THE ASTRAL REALM.

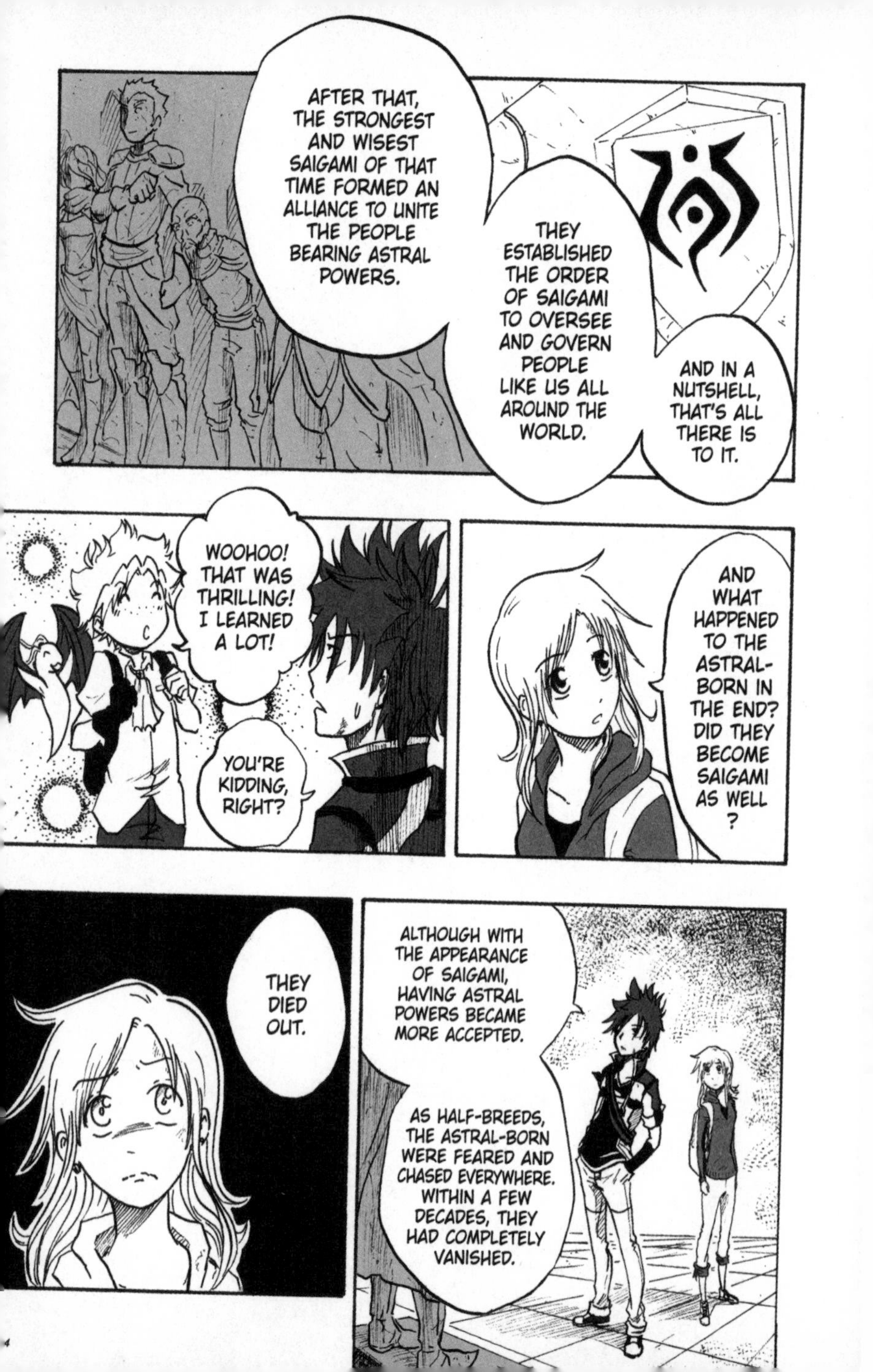
AFTER THAT, THE STRONGEST AND WISEST SAIGAMI OF THAT TIME FORMED AN ALLIANCE TO UNITE THE PEOPLE BEARING ASTRAL POWERS.
THEY ESTABLISHED THE ORDER OF SAIGAMI TO OVERSEE AND GOVERN PEOPLE LIKE US ALL AROUND THE WORLD.
AND IN A NUTSHELL, THAT'S ALL THERE IS TO IT.
WOOHOO! THAT WAS THRILLING! I LEARNED A LOT!
YOU'RE KIDDING, RIGHT?
AND WHAT HAPPENED TO THE ASTRAL-BORN IN THE END? DID THEY BECOME SAIGAMI AS WELL ?
THEY DIED OUT.
ALTHOUGH WITH THE APPEARANCE OF SAIGAMI, HAVING ASTRAL POWERS BECAME MORE ACCEPTED.
AS HALF-BREEDS, THE ASTRAL-BORN WERE FEARED AND CHASED EVERYWHERE. WITHIN A FEW DECADES, THEY HAD COMPLETELY VANISHED.

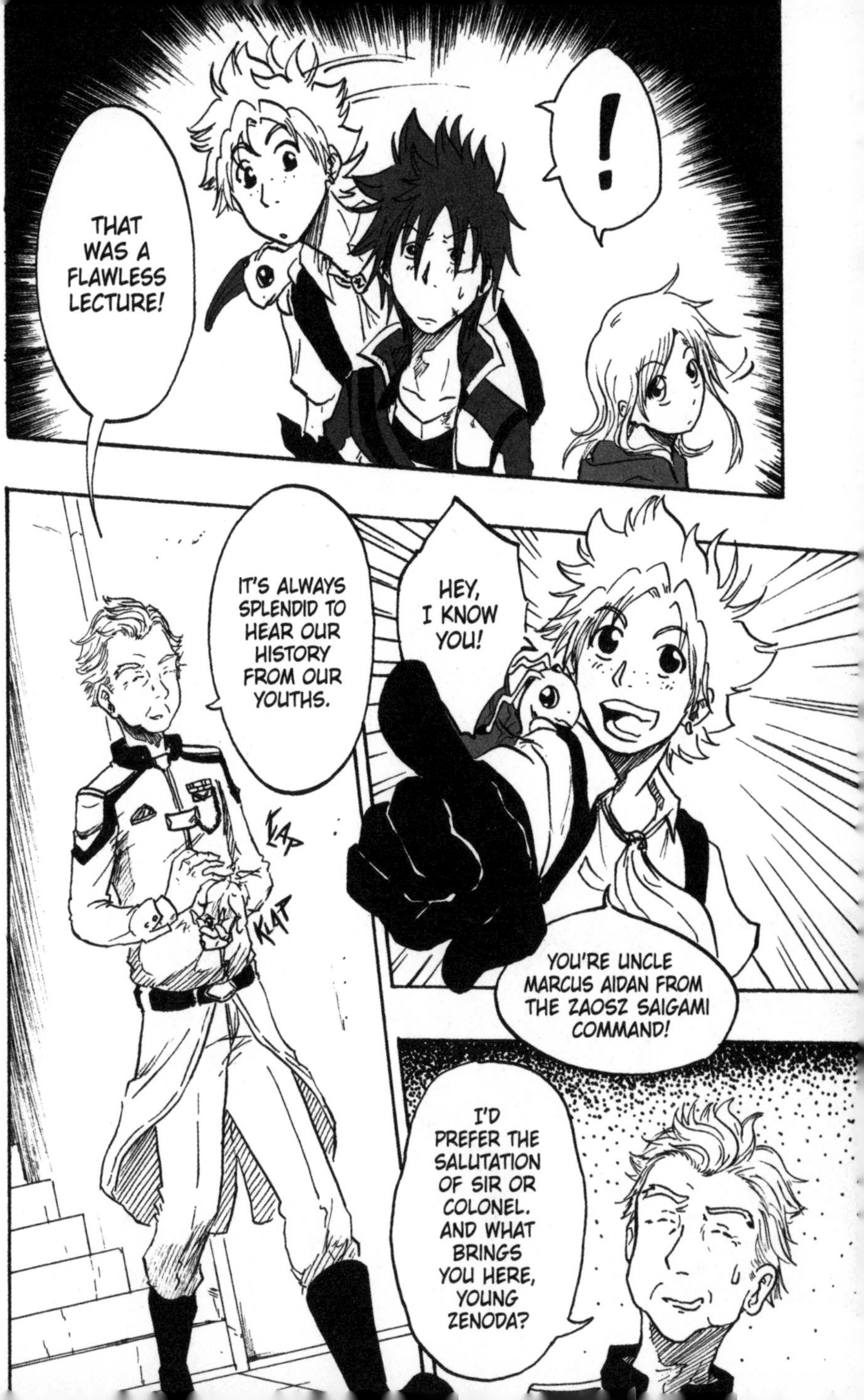
THAT WAS A FLAWLESS LECTURE!
!
IT'S ALWAYS SPLENDID TO HEAR OUR HISTORY FROM OUR YOUTHS.
KLAP
KLAP
HEY, I KNOW YOU!
YOU'RE UNCLE MARCUS AIDAN FROM THE ZAOSZ SAIGAMI COMMAND!
I'D PREFER THE SALUTATION OF SIR OR COLONEL. AND WHAT BRINGS YOU HERE, YOUNG ZENODA?

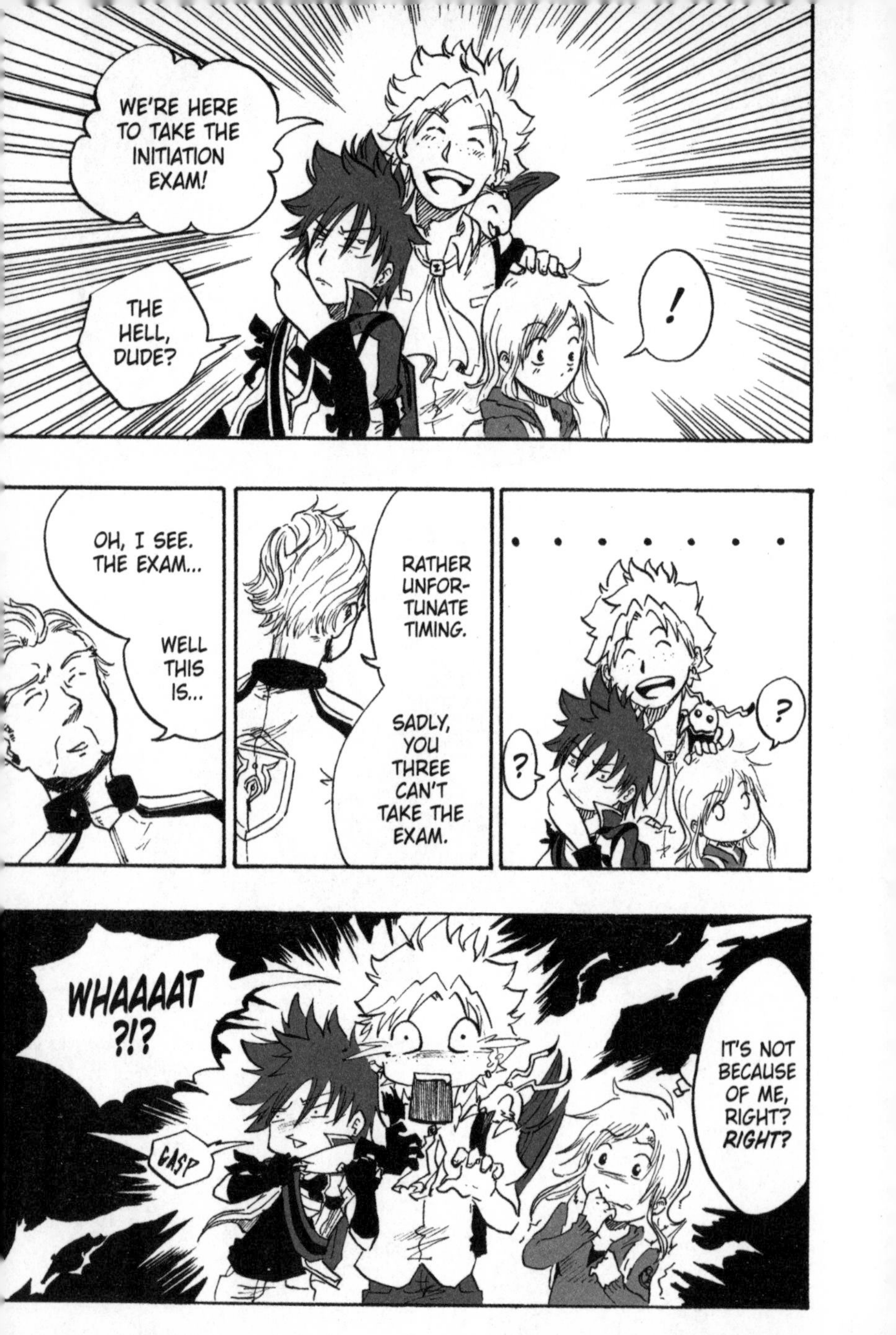
WE'RE HERE TO TAKE THE INITIATION EXAM!
THE HELL, DUDE?
!
OH, I SEE. THE EXAM...
WELL THIS IS...
RATHER UNFORTUNATE TIMING.
SADLY, YOU THREE CAN'T TAKE THE EXAM.
. . . .
?
?
WHAAAAT ?!?
GASP
IT'S NOT BECAUSE OF ME, RIGHT? *RIGHT?*

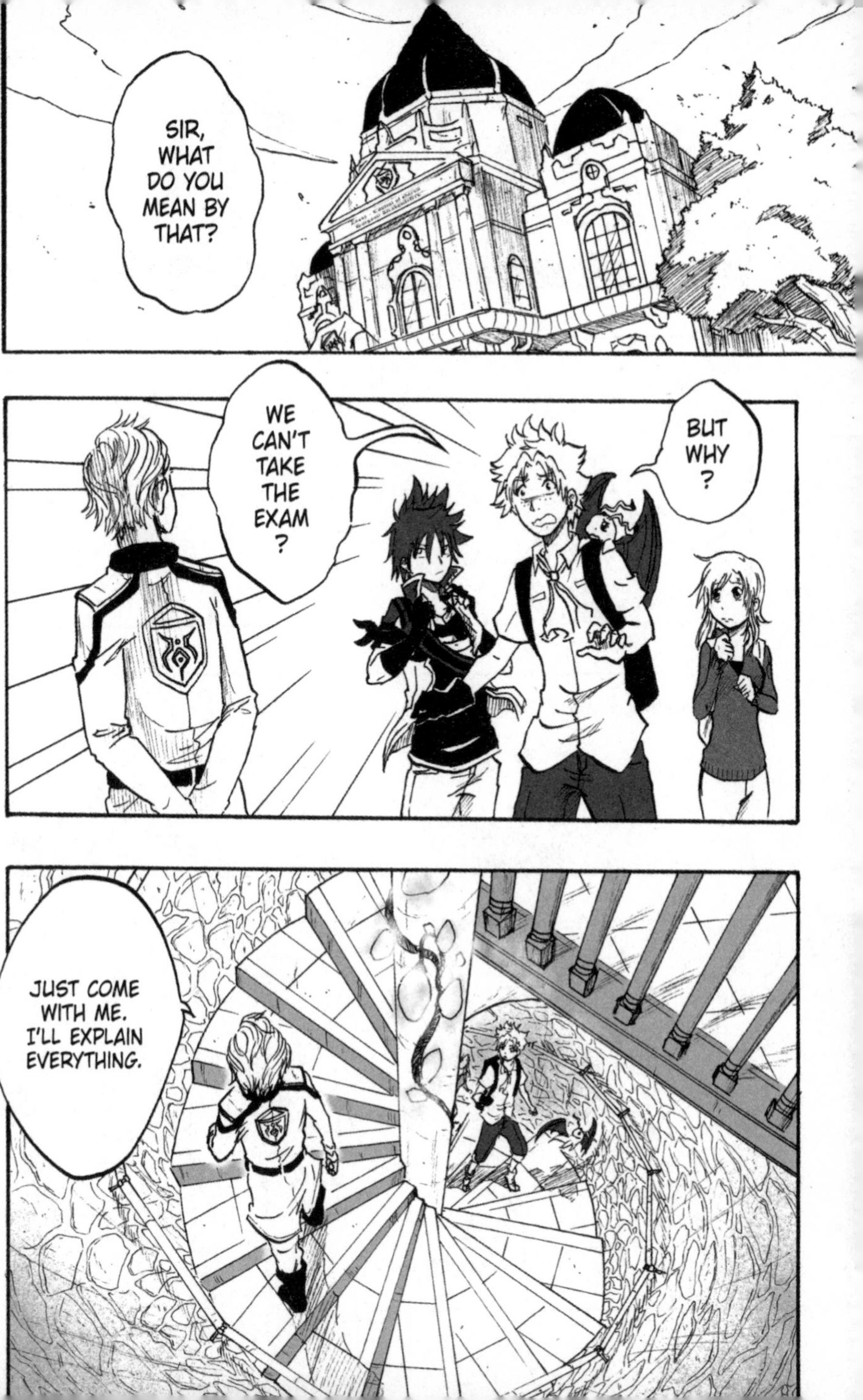
SIR, WHAT DO YOU MEAN BY THAT?
WE CAN'T TAKE THE EXAM?
BUT WHY?
JUST COME WITH ME. I'LL EXPLAIN EVERYTHING.

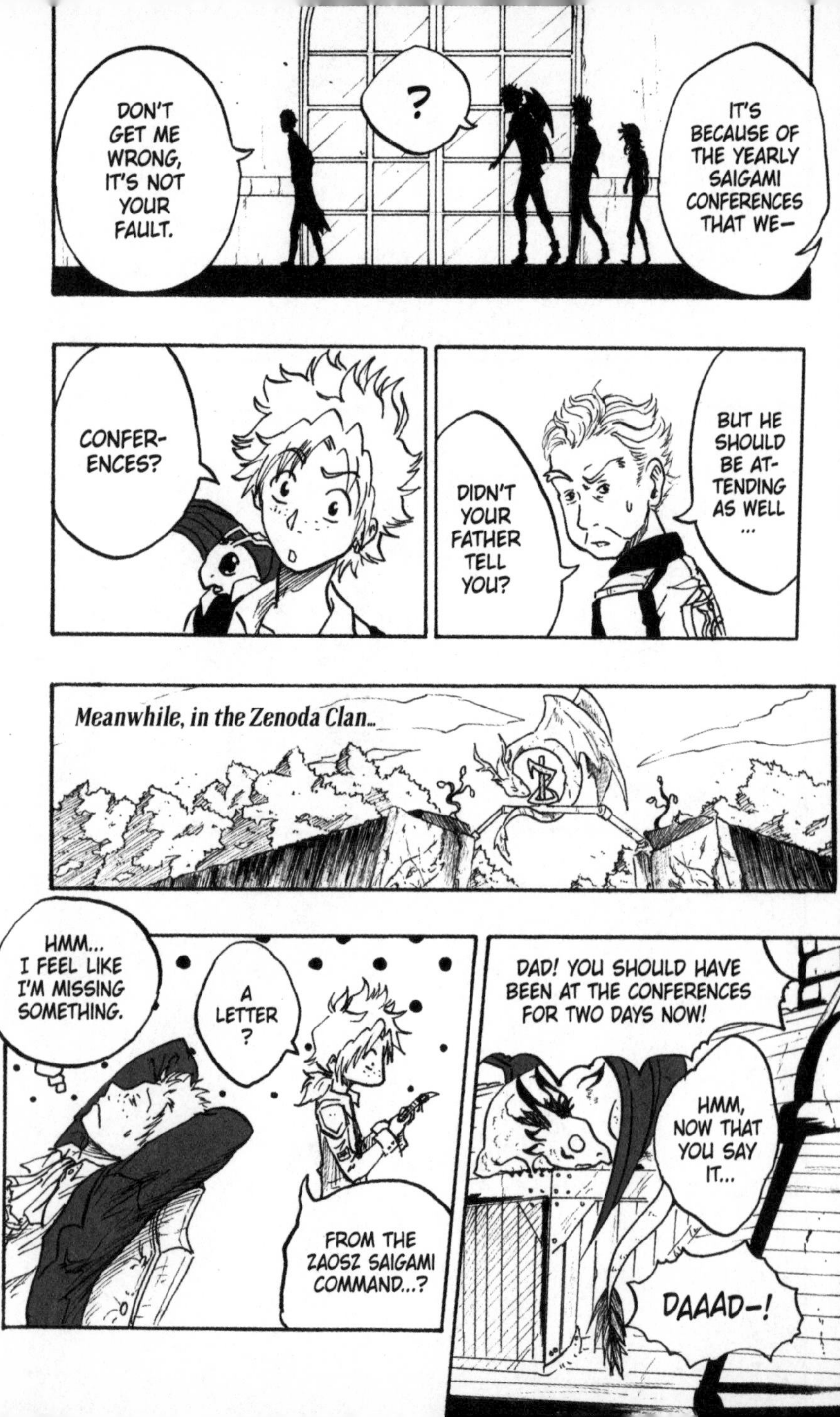
DON'T GET ME WRONG, IT'S NOT YOUR FAULT.
?
IT'S BECAUSE OF THE YEARLY SAIGAMI CONFERENCES THAT WE–
CONFER-ENCES?
DIDN'T YOUR FATHER TELL YOU?
BUT HE SHOULD BE AT-TENDING AS WELL ...
Meanwhile, in the Zenoda Clan...
HMM... I FEEL LIKE I'M MISSING SOMETHING.
A LETTER ?
FROM THE ZAOSZ SAIGAMI COMMAND...?
DAD! YOU SHOULD HAVE BEEN AT THE CONFERENCES FOR TWO DAYS NOW!
HMM, NOW THAT YOU SAY IT...
DAAAD–!

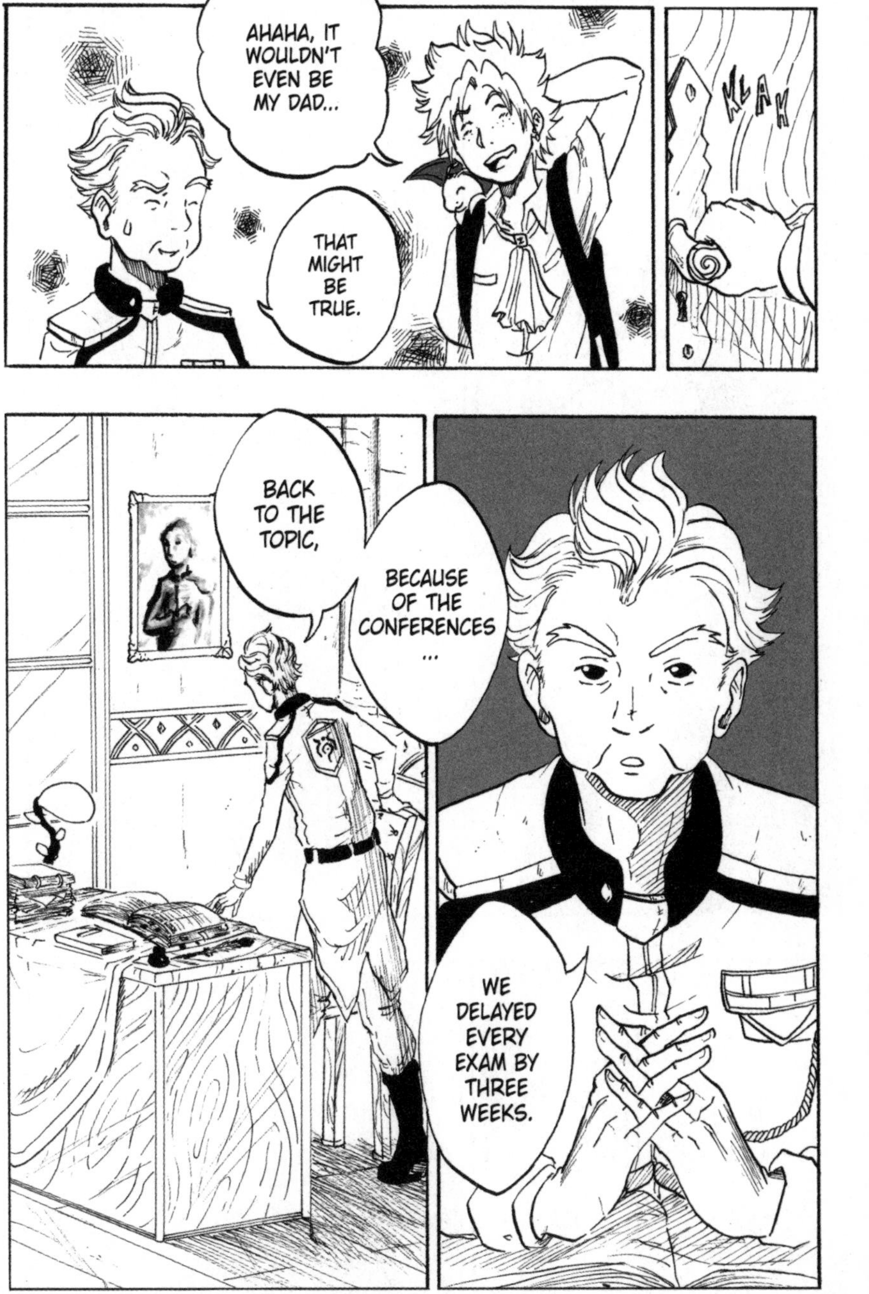
AHAHA, IT WOULDN'T EVEN BE MY DAD...
THAT MIGHT BE TRUE.
KLAK
BACK TO THE TOPIC,
BECAUSE OF THE CONFERENCES ...
WE DELAYED EVERY EXAM BY THREE WEEKS.

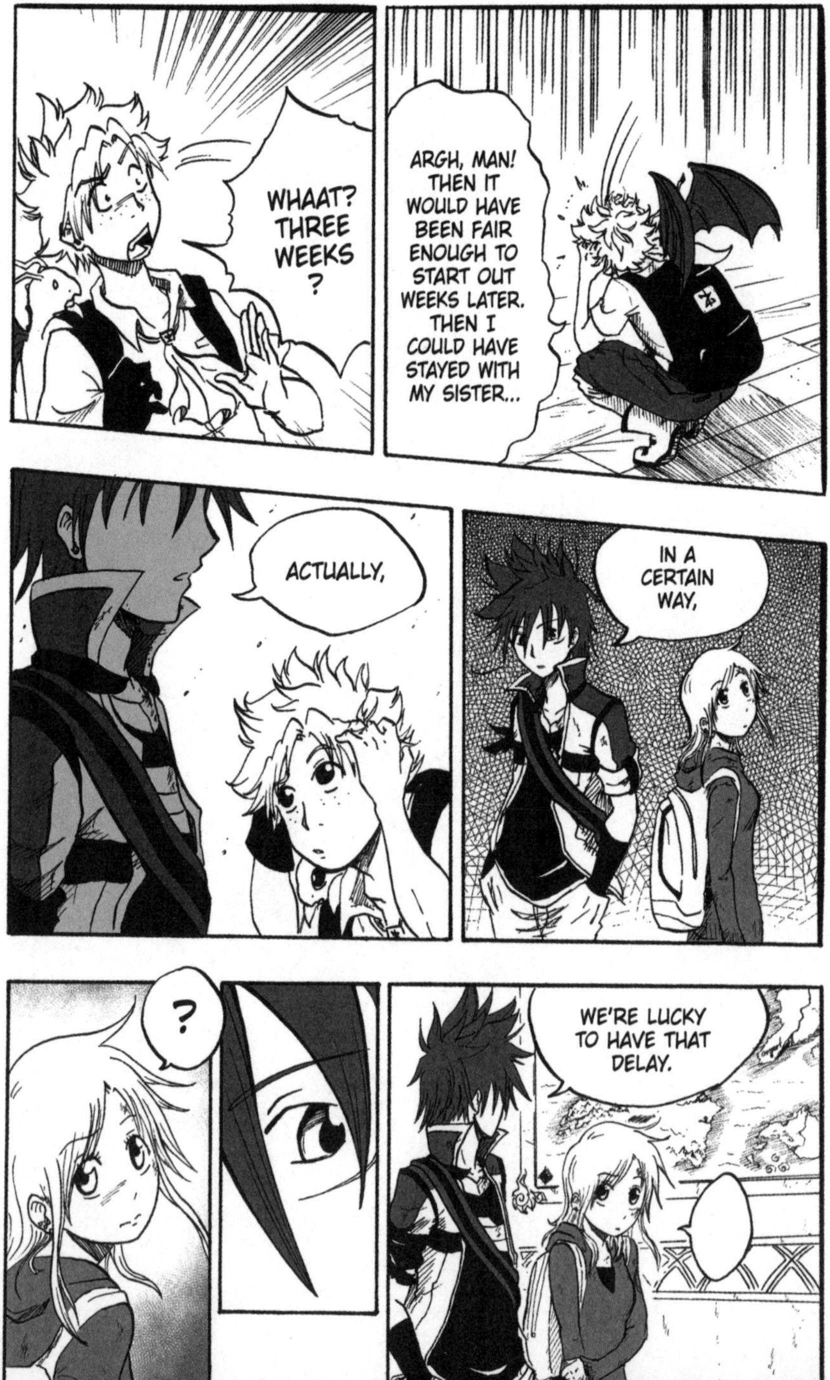
WHAAT? THREE WEEKS ?
ARGH, MAN! THEN IT WOULD HAVE BEEN FAIR ENOUGH TO START OUT WEEKS LATER. THEN I COULD HAVE STAYED WITH MY SISTER...
ACTUALLY,
IN A CERTAIN WAY,
?
WE'RE LUCKY TO HAVE THAT DELAY.

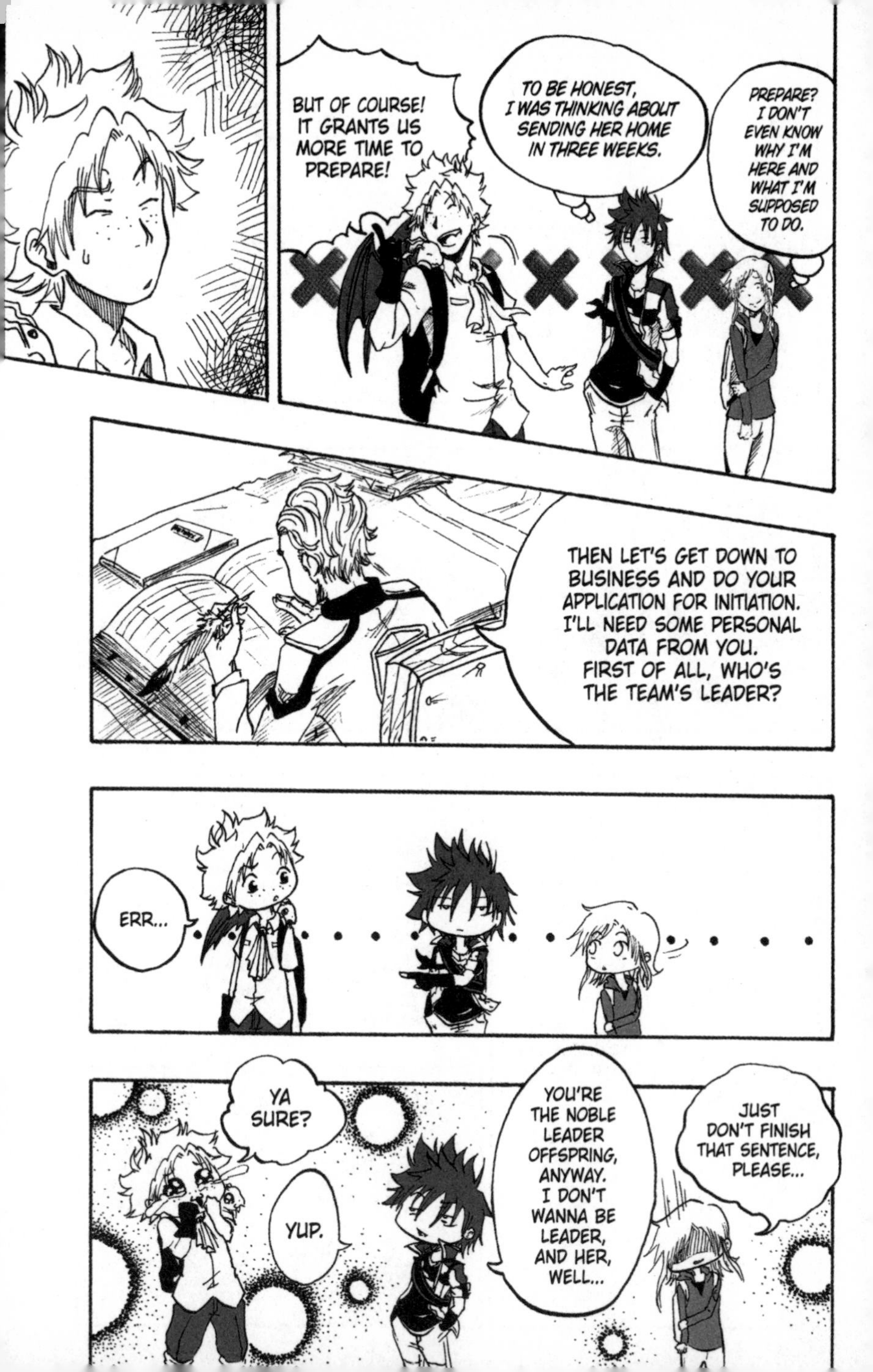
BUT OF COURSE! IT GRANTS US MORE TIME TO PREPARE!
TO BE HONEST, I WAS THINKING ABOUT SENDING HER HOME IN THREE WEEKS.
PREPARE? I DON'T EVEN KNOW WHY I'M HERE AND WHAT I'M SUPPOSED TO DO.
THEN LET'S GET DOWN TO BUSINESS AND DO YOUR APPLICATION FOR INITIATION. I'LL NEED SOME PERSONAL DATA FROM YOU. FIRST OF ALL, WHO'S THE TEAM'S LEADER?
ERR...
YA SURE?
YUP.
YOU'RE THE NOBLE LEADER OFFSPRING, ANYWAY. I DON'T WANNA BE LEADER, AND HER, WELL...
JUST DON'T FINISH THAT SENTENCE, PLEASE...

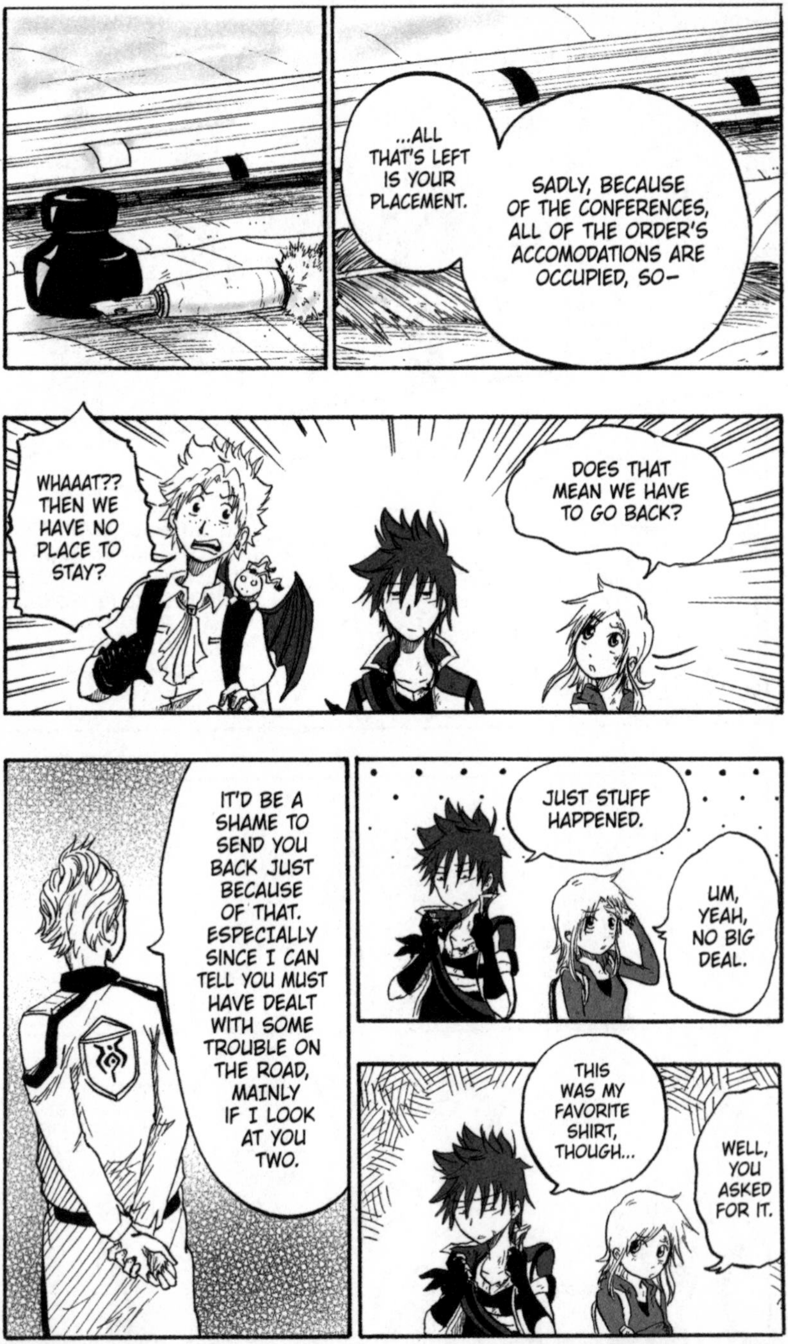
...ALL THAT'S LEFT IS YOUR PLACEMENT.
SADLY, BECAUSE OF THE CONFERENCES, ALL OF THE ORDER'S ACCOMODATIONS ARE OCCUPIED, SO—
WHAAAT?? THEN WE HAVE NO PLACE TO STAY?
DOES THAT MEAN WE HAVE TO GO BACK?
IT'D BE A SHAME TO SEND YOU BACK JUST BECAUSE OF THAT. ESPECIALLY SINCE I CAN TELL YOU MUST HAVE DEALT WITH SOME TROUBLE ON THE ROAD, MAINLY IF I LOOK AT YOU TWO.
JUST STUFF HAPPENED.
UM, YEAH, NO BIG DEAL.
THIS WAS MY FAVORITE SHIRT, THOUGH...
WELL, YOU ASKED FOR IT.

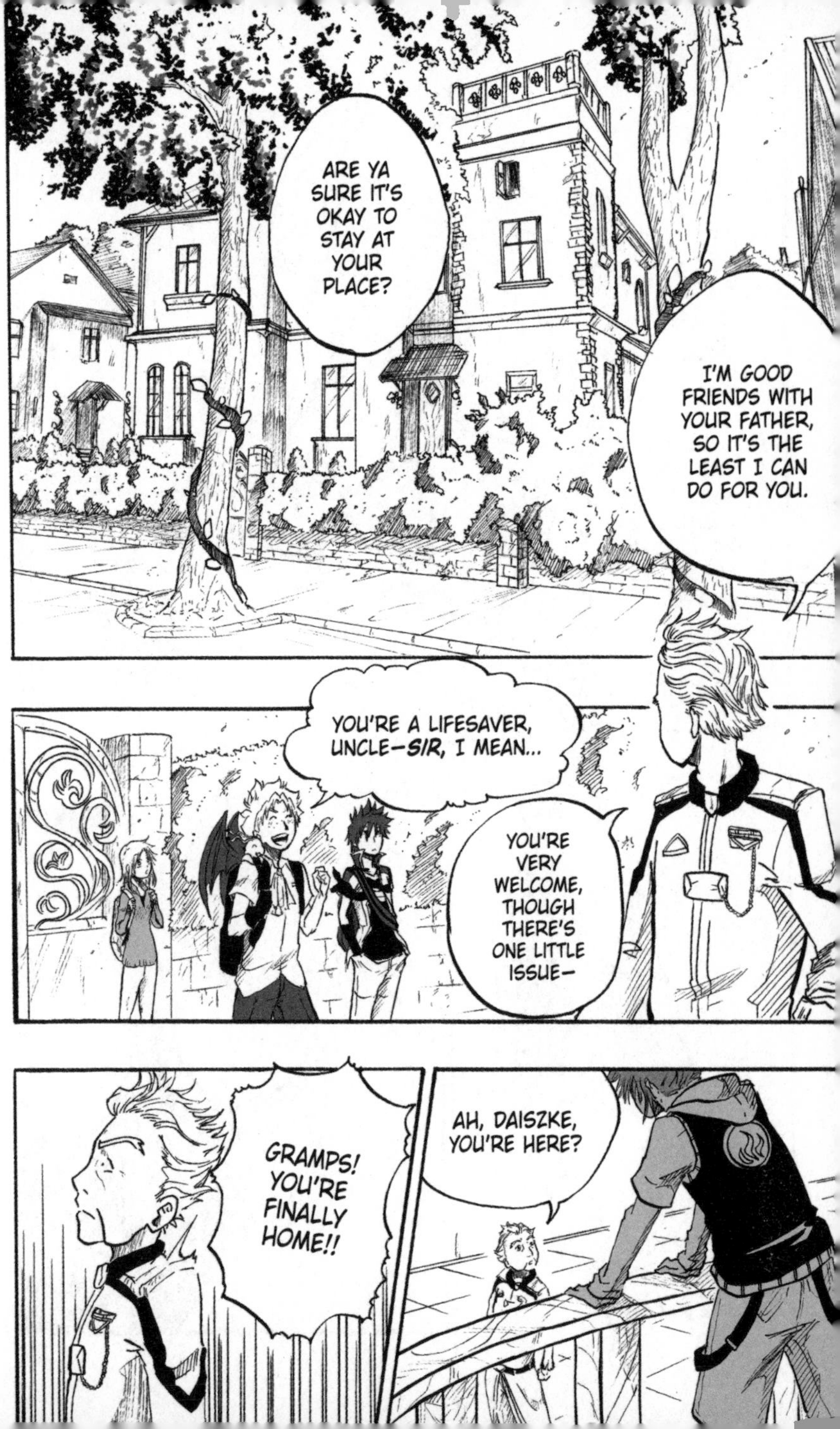
ARE YA SURE IT'S OKAY TO STAY AT YOUR PLACE?
I'M GOOD FRIENDS WITH YOUR FATHER, SO IT'S THE LEAST I CAN DO FOR YOU.
YOU'RE A LIFESAVER, UNCLE—*SIR*, I MEAN...
YOU'RE VERY WELCOME, THOUGH THERE'S ONE LITTLE ISSUE—
GRAMPS! YOU'RE FINALLY HOME!!
AH, DAISZKE, YOU'RE HERE?

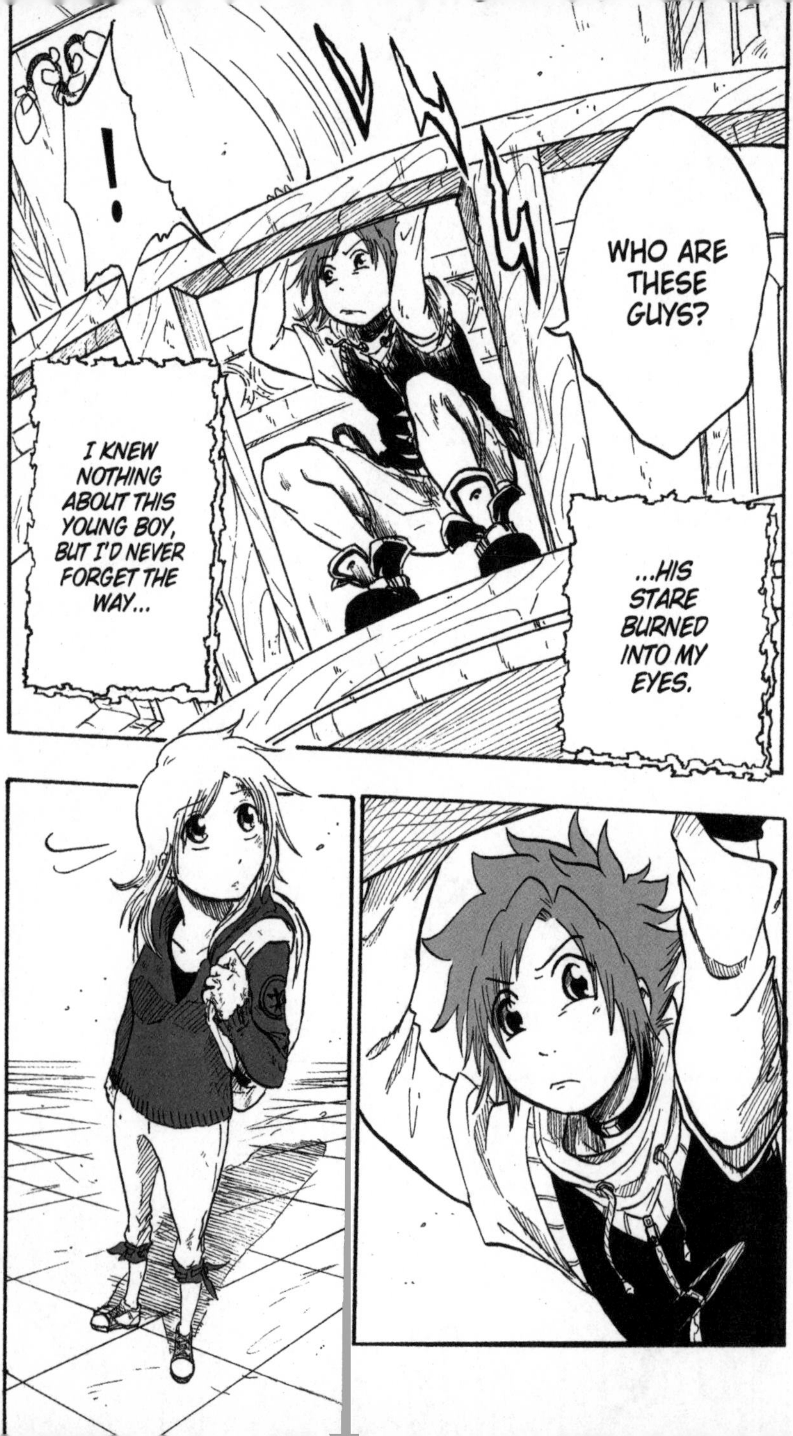
!
WHO ARE THESE GUYS?
I KNEW NOTHING ABOUT THIS YOUNG BOY, BUT I'D NEVER FORGET THE WAY...
...HIS STARE BURNED INTO MY EYES.

SAIGAMI

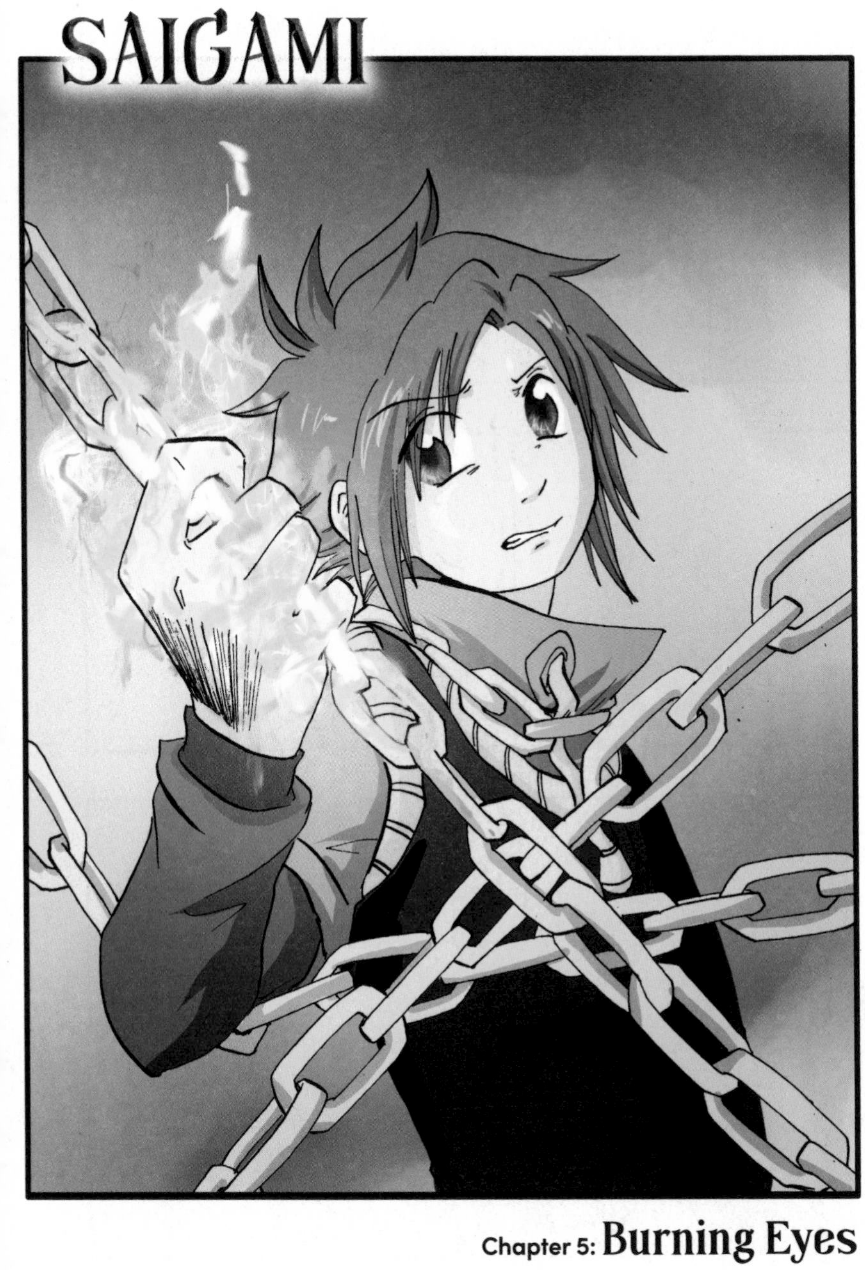

Chapter 5: Burning Eyes

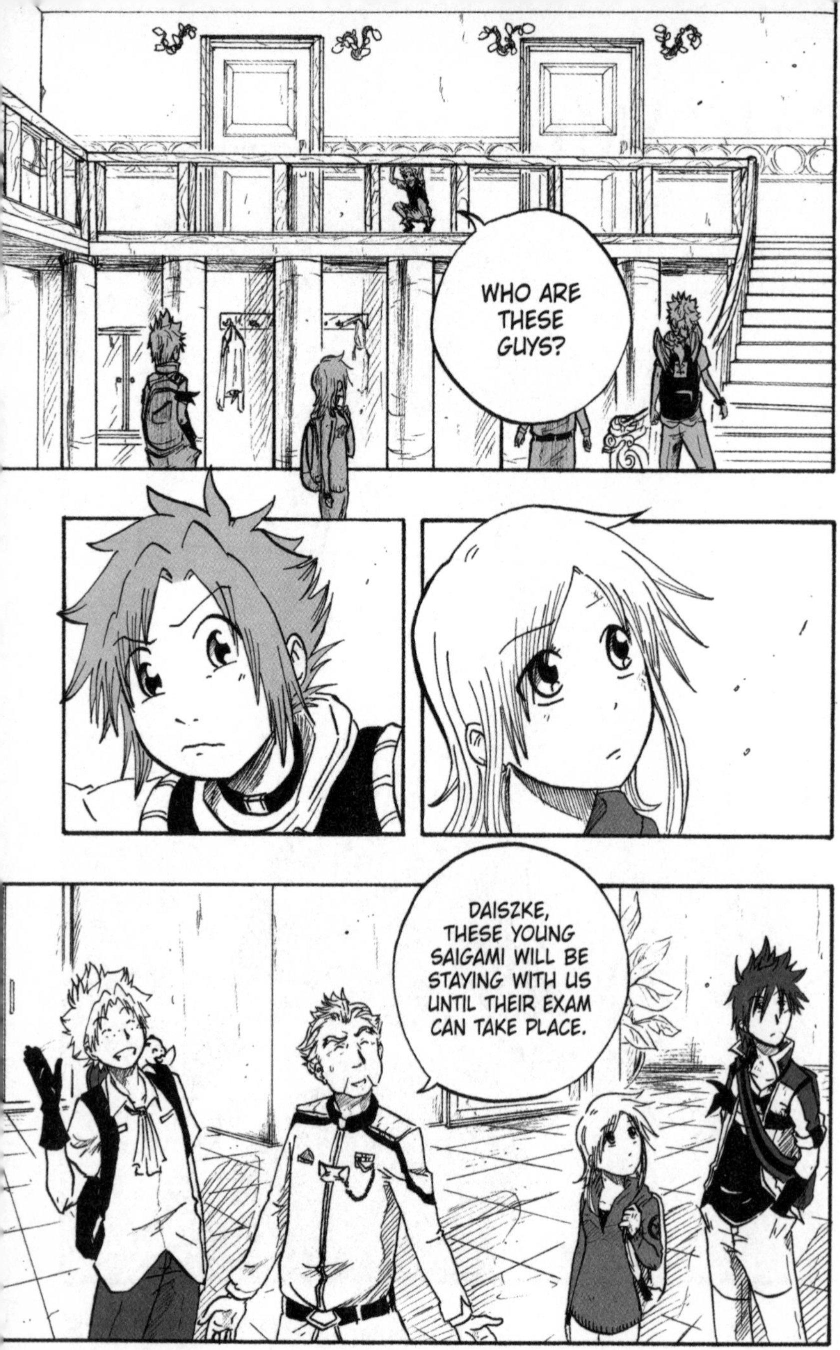
WHO ARE THESE GUYS?
DAISZKE, THESE YOUNG SAIGAMI WILL BE STAYING WITH US UNTIL THEIR EXAM CAN TAKE PLACE.

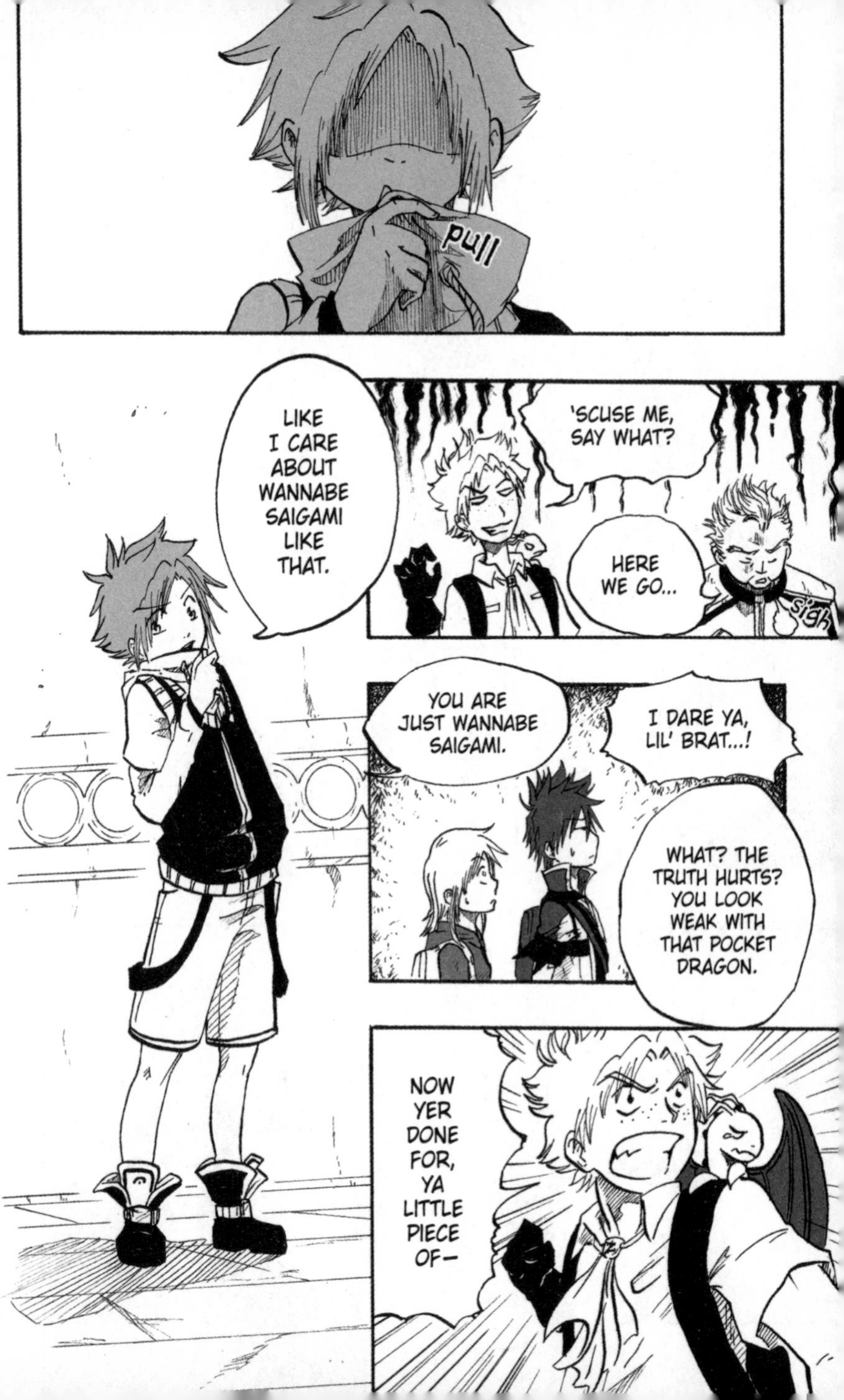
pull
LIKE I CARE ABOUT WANNABE SAIGAMI LIKE THAT.
'SCUSE ME, SAY WHAT?
HERE WE GO...
sigh
YOU ARE JUST WANNABE SAIGAMI.
I DARE YA, LIL' BRAT...!
WHAT? THE TRUTH HURTS? YOU LOOK WEAK WITH THAT POCKET DRAGON.
NOW YER DONE FOR, YA LITTLE PIECE OF—

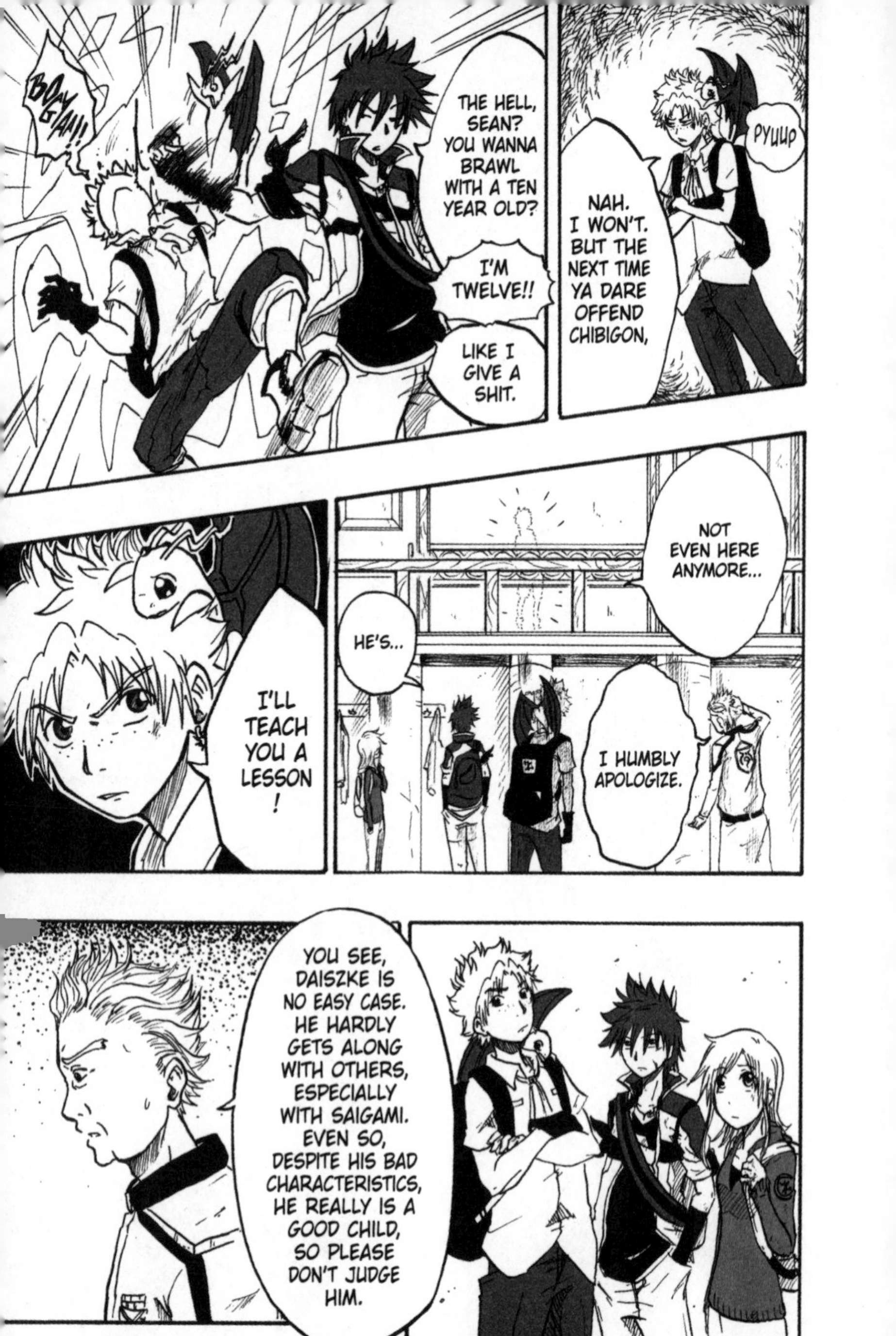
BOGYAA!!
THE HELL, SEAN? YOU WANNA BRAWL WITH A TEN YEAR OLD?
I'M TWELVE!!
LIKE I GIVE A SHIT.
PYUUP
NAH. I WON'T. BUT THE NEXT TIME YA DARE OFFEND CHIBIGON,
I'LL TEACH YOU A LESSON!
HE'S...
NOT EVEN HERE ANYMORE...
NAH.
I HUMBLY APOLOGIZE.
YOU SEE, DAISZKE IS NO EASY CASE. HE HARDLY GETS ALONG WITH OTHERS, ESPECIALLY WITH SAIGAMI. EVEN SO, DESPITE HIS BAD CHARACTERISTICS, HE REALLY IS A GOOD CHILD, SO PLEASE DON'T JUDGE HIM.

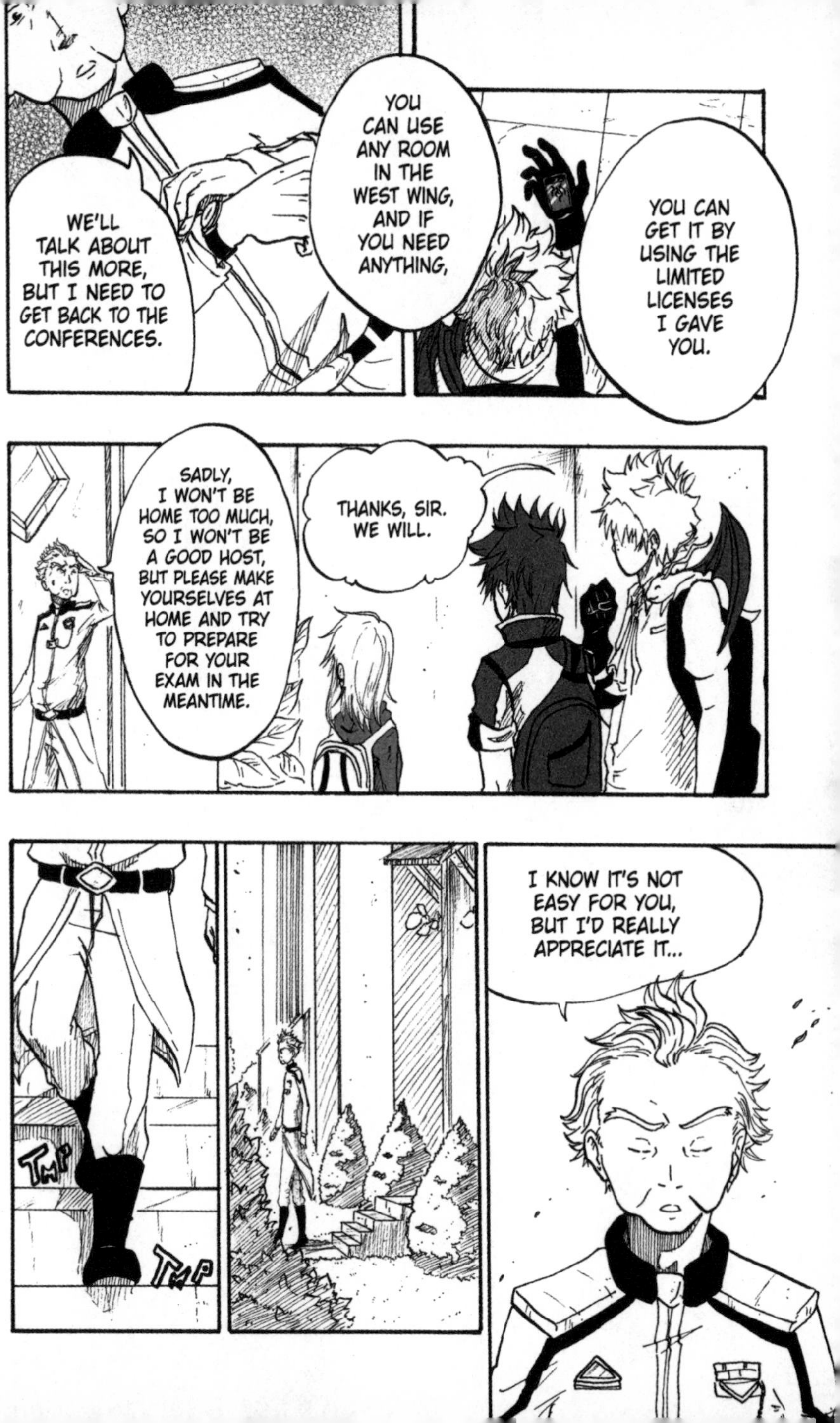
WE'LL TALK ABOUT THIS MORE, BUT I NEED TO GET BACK TO THE CONFERENCES.
YOU CAN USE ANY ROOM IN THE WEST WING, AND IF YOU NEED ANYTHING,
YOU CAN GET IT BY USING THE LIMITED LICENSES I GAVE YOU.
SADLY, I WON'T BE HOME TOO MUCH, SO I WON'T BE A GOOD HOST, BUT PLEASE MAKE YOURSELVES AT HOME AND TRY TO PREPARE FOR YOUR EXAM IN THE MEANTIME.
THANKS, SIR. WE WILL.
TMP
TMP
I KNOW IT'S NOT EASY FOR YOU, BUT I'D REALLY APPRECIATE IT...

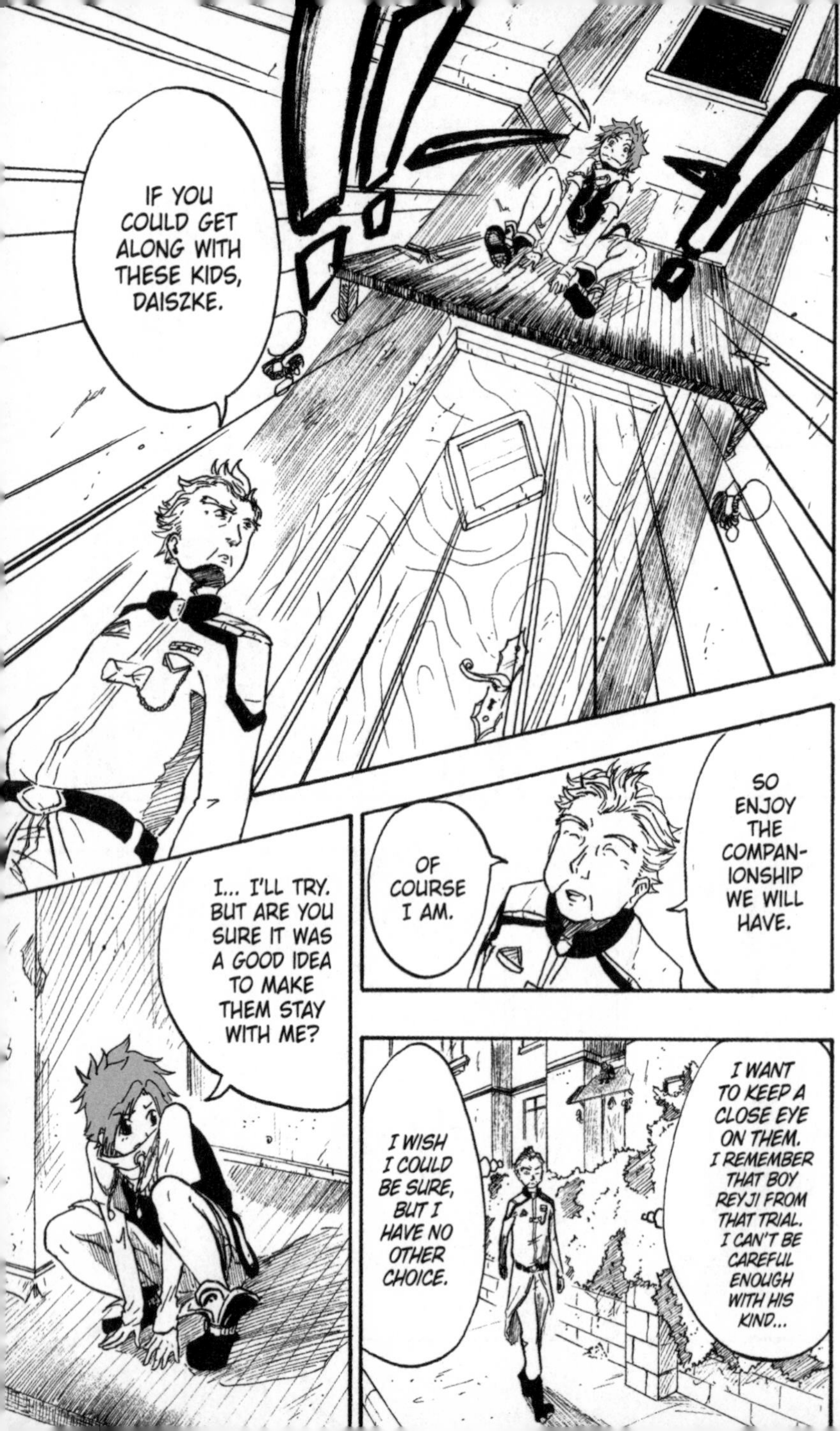
IF YOU COULD GET ALONG WITH THESE KIDS, DAISZKE.
I... I'LL TRY. BUT ARE YOU SURE IT WAS A GOOD IDEA TO MAKE THEM STAY WITH ME?
OF COURSE I AM.
SO ENJOY THE COMPANIONSHIP WE WILL HAVE.
I WISH I COULD BE SURE, BUT I HAVE NO OTHER CHOICE.
I WANT TO KEEP A CLOSE EYE ON THEM. I REMEMBER THAT BOY REYJI FROM THAT TRIAL. I CAN'T BE CAREFUL ENOUGH WITH HIS KIND...

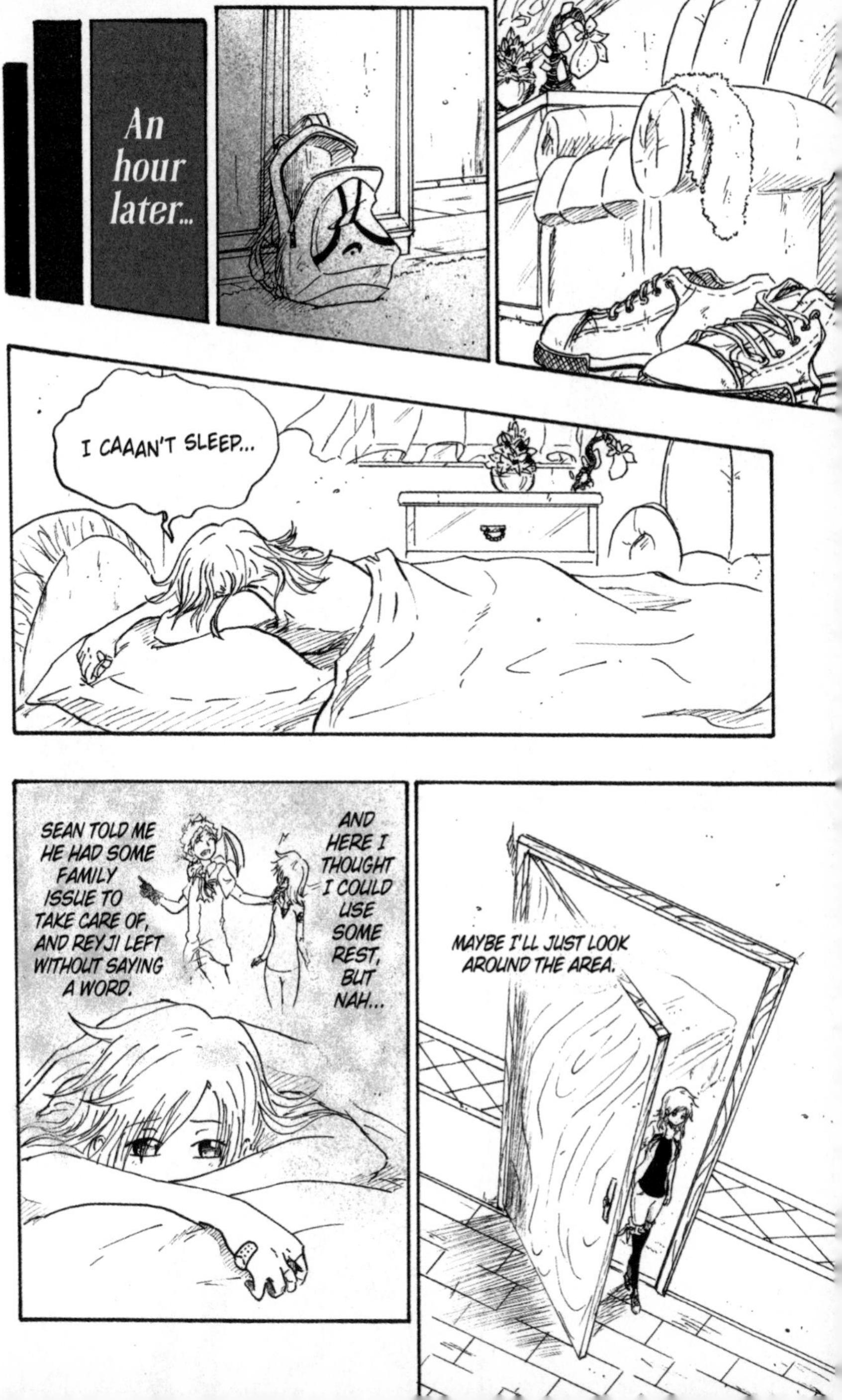
An hour later...
I CAAAN'T SLEEP...
SEAN TOLD ME HE HAD SOME FAMILY ISSUE TO TAKE CARE OF, AND REYJI LEFT WITHOUT SAYING A WORD.
AND HERE I THOUGHT I COULD USE SOME REST, BUT NAH...
MAYBE I'LL JUST LOOK AROUND THE AREA.

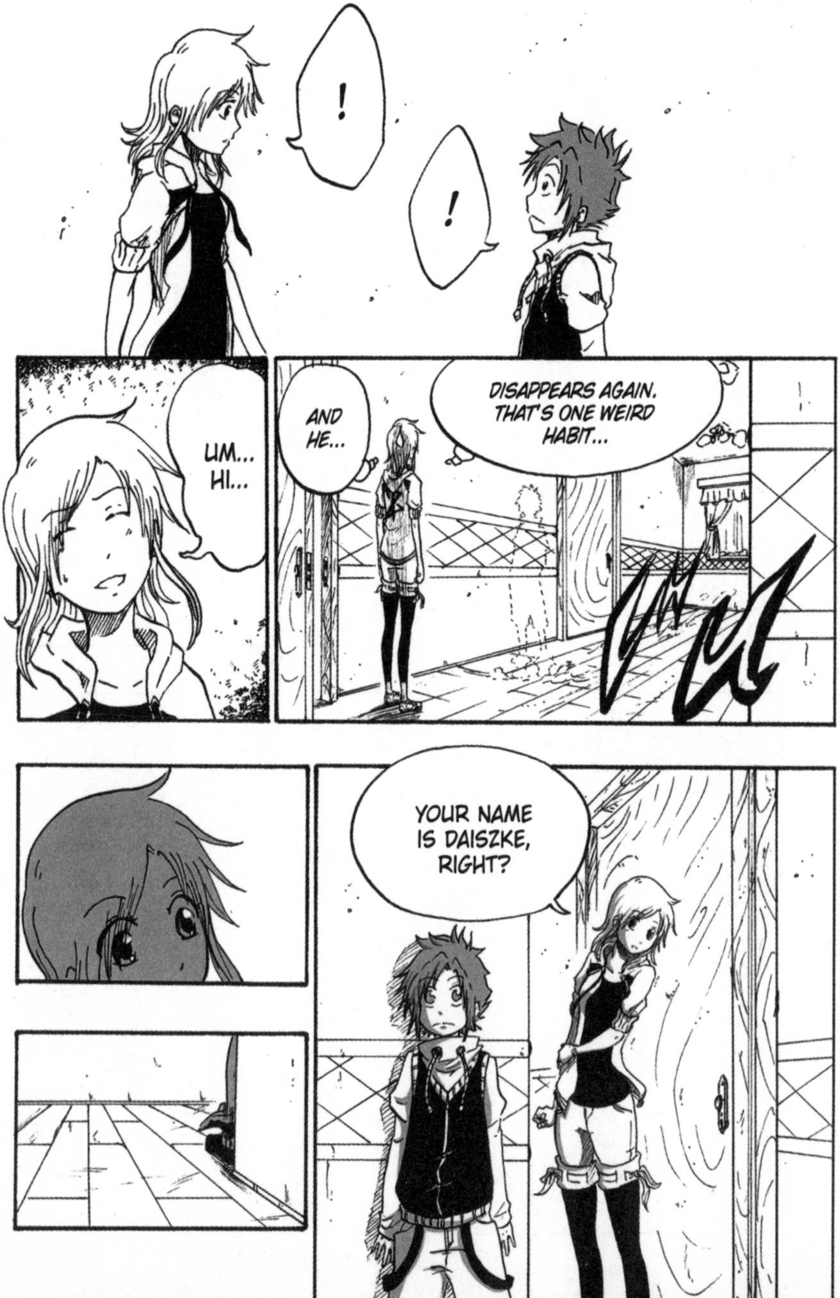
!
!
UM... HI...
AND HE...
DISAPPEARS AGAIN. THAT'S ONE WEIRD HABIT...
YOUR NAME IS DAISZKE, RIGHT?

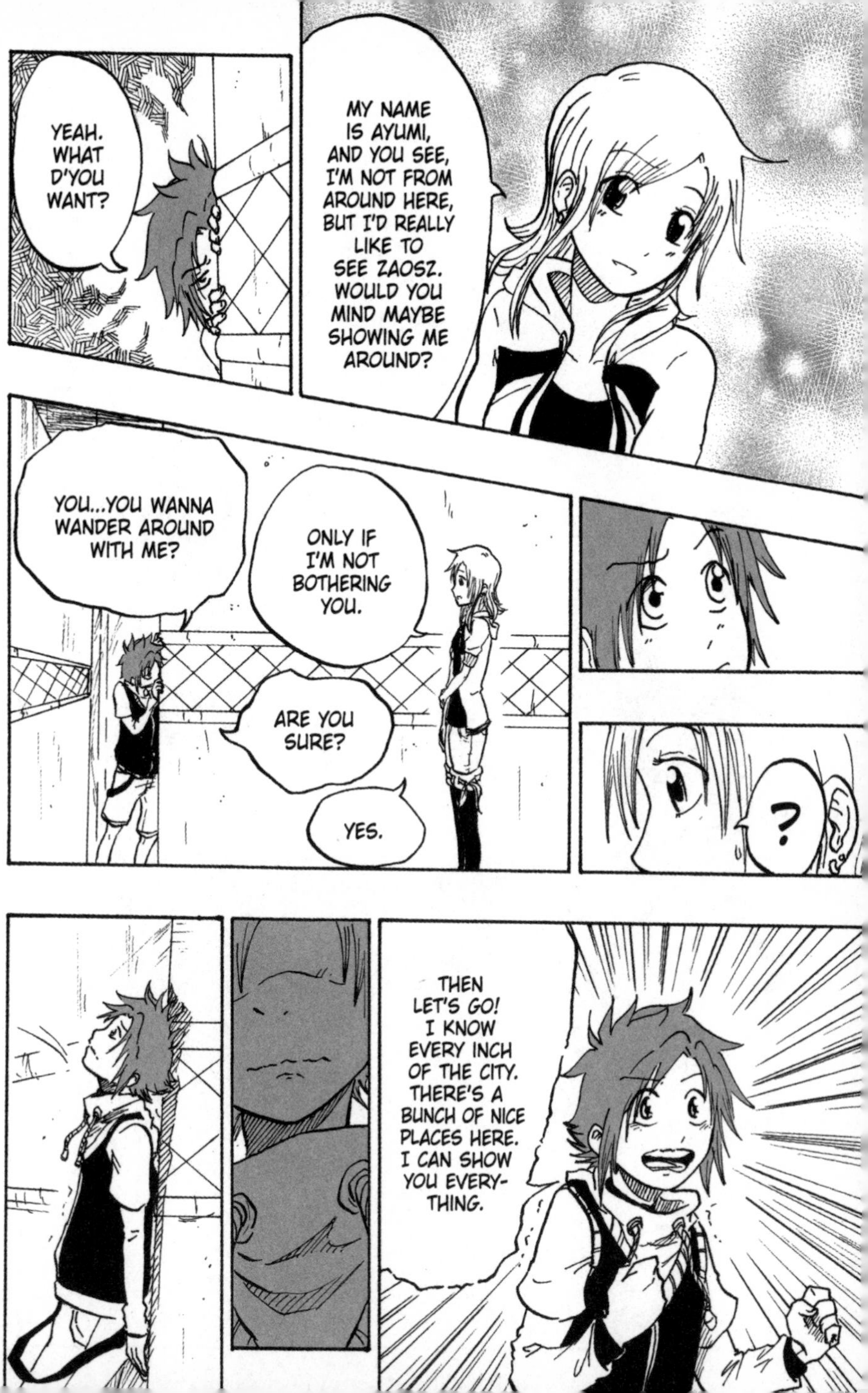
YEAH. WHAT D'YOU WANT?
MY NAME IS AYUMI, AND YOU SEE, I'M NOT FROM AROUND HERE, BUT I'D REALLY LIKE TO SEE ZAOSZ. WOULD YOU MIND MAYBE SHOWING ME AROUND?
YOU...YOU WANNA WANDER AROUND WITH ME?
ONLY IF I'M NOT BOTHERING YOU.
ARE YOU SURE?
YES.
?
THEN LET'S GO! I KNOW EVERY INCH OF THE CITY. THERE'S A BUNCH OF NICE PLACES HERE. I CAN SHOW YOU EVERY-THING.

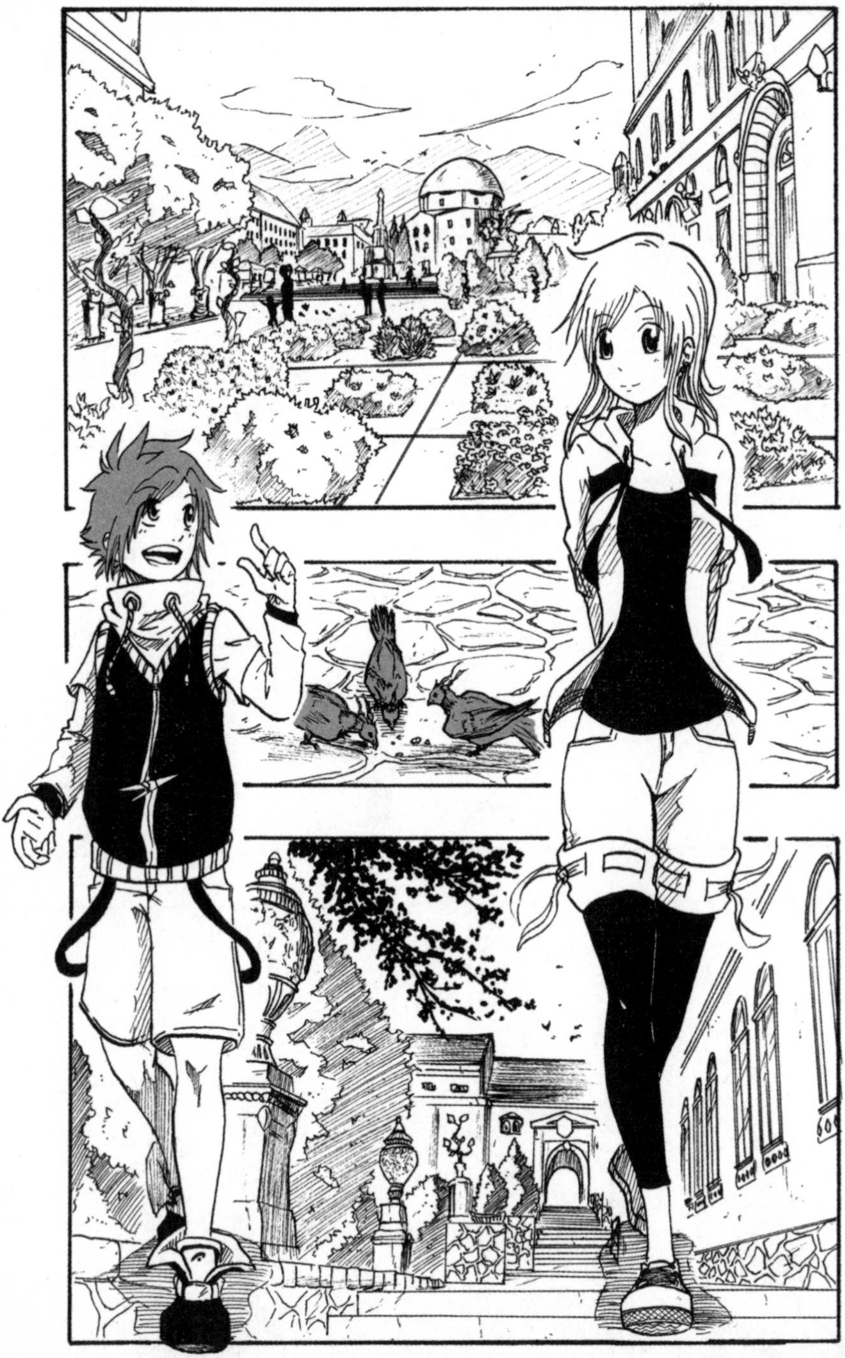

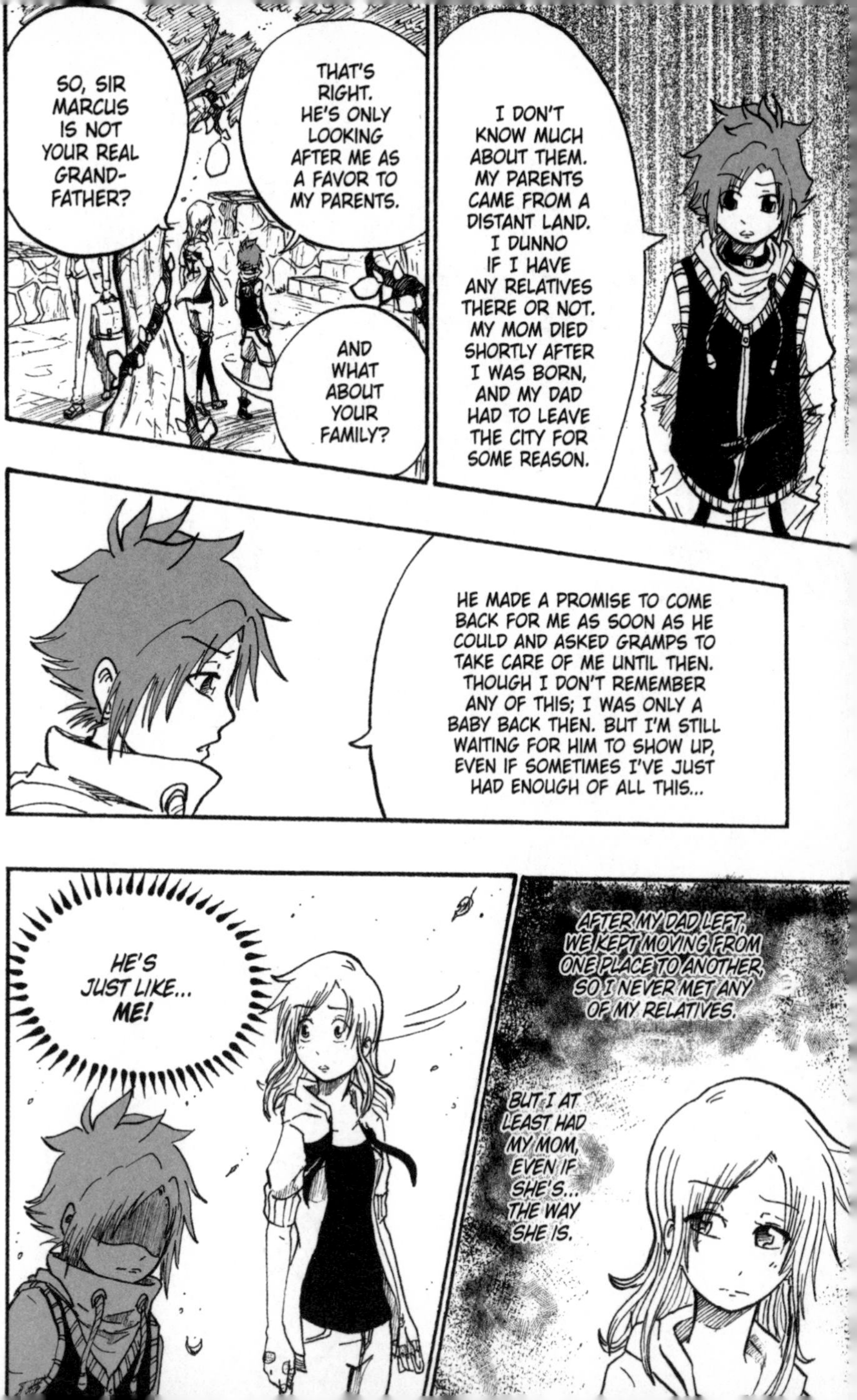
SO, SIR MARCUS IS NOT YOUR REAL GRAND-FATHER?
THAT'S RIGHT. HE'S ONLY LOOKING AFTER ME AS A FAVOR TO MY PARENTS.
AND WHAT ABOUT YOUR FAMILY?
I DON'T KNOW MUCH ABOUT THEM. MY PARENTS CAME FROM A DISTANT LAND. I DUNNO IF I HAVE ANY RELATIVES THERE OR NOT. MY MOM DIED SHORTLY AFTER I WAS BORN, AND MY DAD HAD TO LEAVE THE CITY FOR SOME REASON.
HE MADE A PROMISE TO COME BACK FOR ME AS SOON AS HE COULD AND ASKED GRAMPS TO TAKE CARE OF ME UNTIL THEN. THOUGH I DON'T REMEMBER ANY OF THIS; I WAS ONLY A BABY BACK THEN. BUT I'M STILL WAITING FOR HIM TO SHOW UP, EVEN IF SOMETIMES I'VE JUST HAD ENOUGH OF ALL THIS...
HE'S JUST LIKE... ME!
AFTER MY DAD LEFT, WE KEPT MOVING FROM ONE PLACE TO ANOTHER, SO I NEVER MET ANY OF MY RELATIVES.
BUT I AT LEAST HAD MY MOM, EVEN IF SHE'S... THE WAY SHE IS.

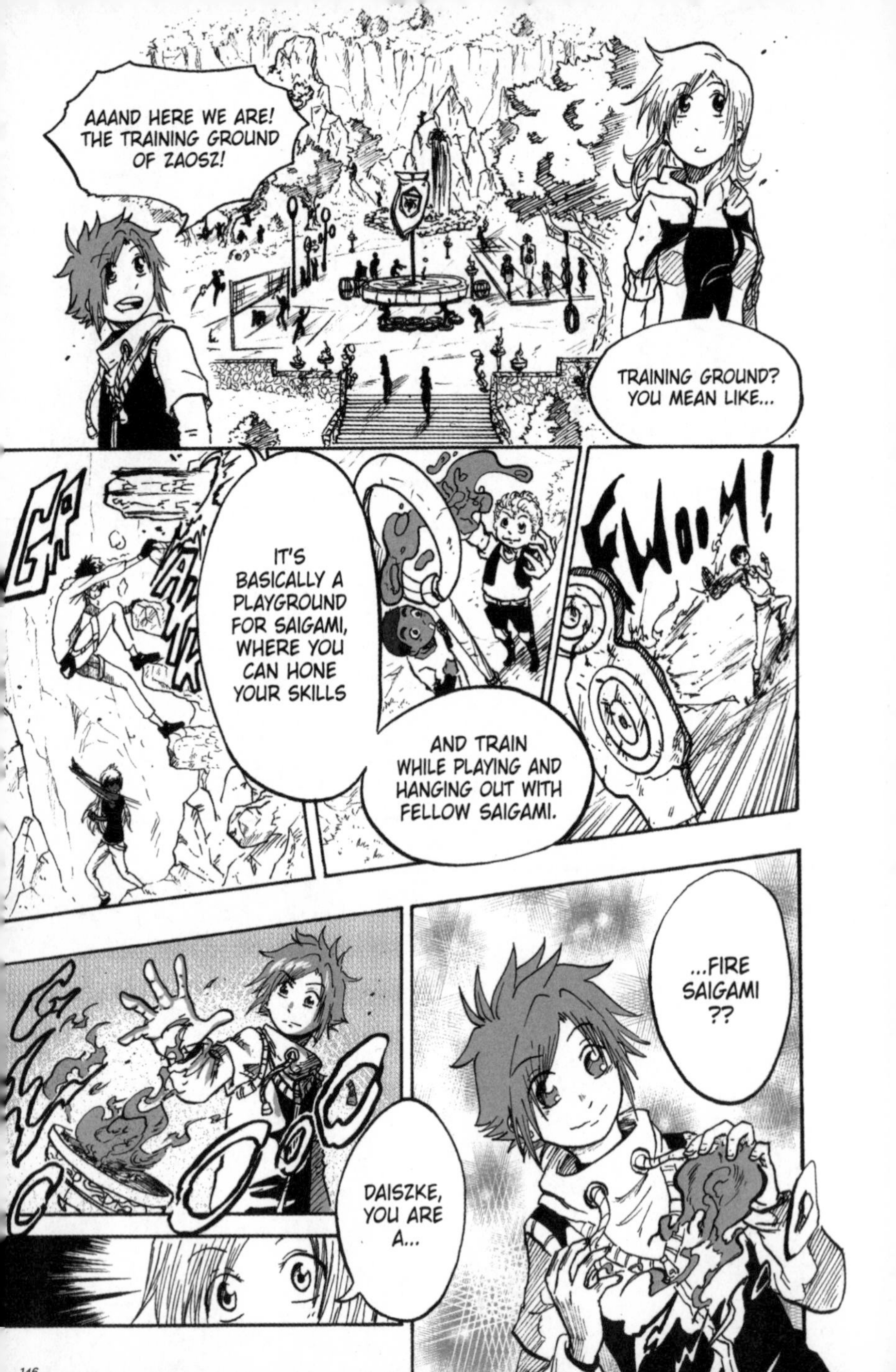
AAAND HERE WE ARE! THE TRAINING GROUND OF ZAOSZ!
TRAINING GROUND? YOU MEAN LIKE...
IT'S BASICALLY A PLAYGROUND FOR SAIGAMI, WHERE YOU CAN HONE YOUR SKILLS
AND TRAIN WHILE PLAYING AND HANGING OUT WITH FELLOW SAIGAMI.
FWOOM!
DAISZKE, YOU ARE A...
...FIRE SAIGAMI ??

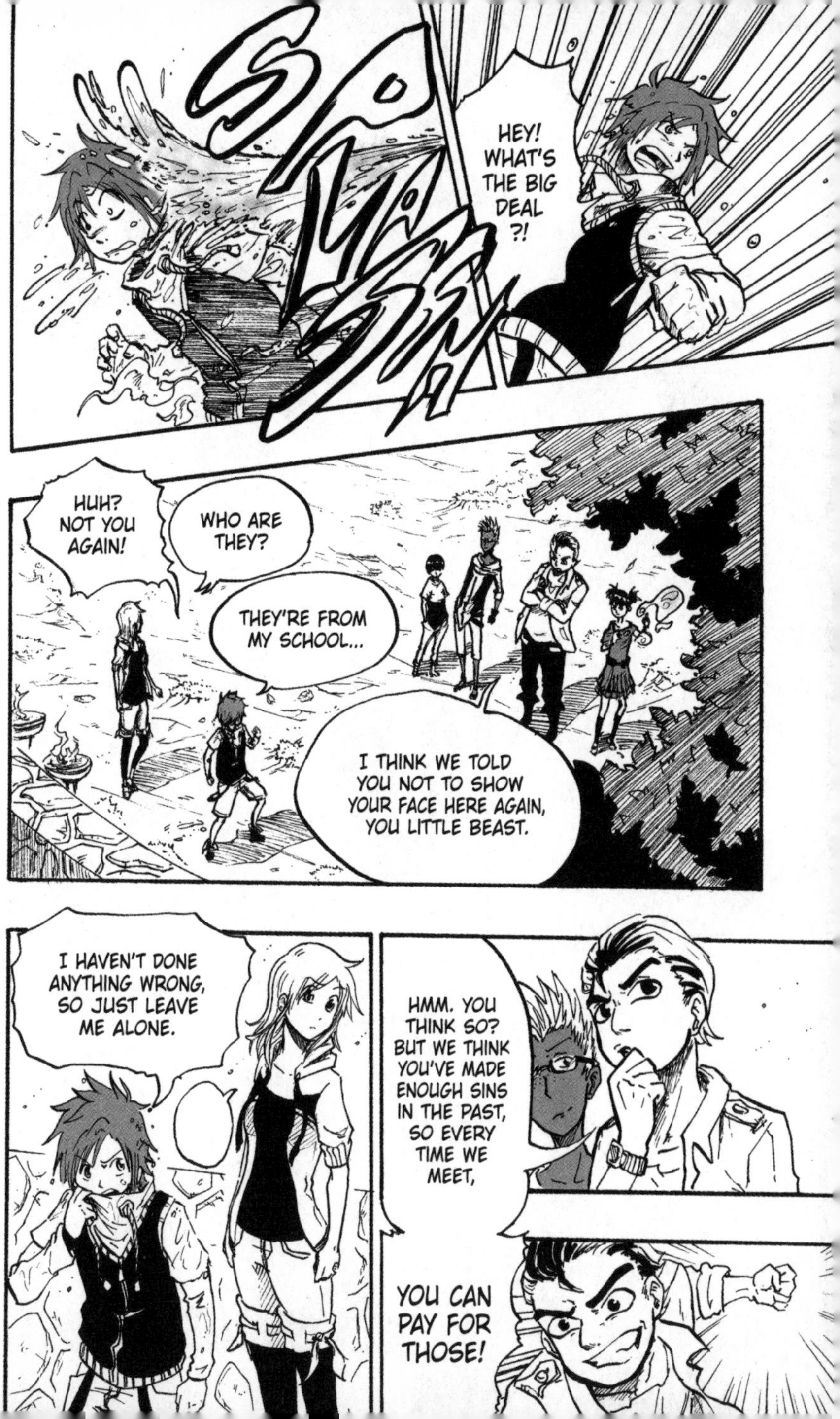
HEY! WHAT'S THE BIG DEAL ?!
HUH? NOT YOU AGAIN!
WHO ARE THEY?
THEY'RE FROM MY SCHOOL...
I THINK WE TOLD YOU NOT TO SHOW YOUR FACE HERE AGAIN, YOU LITTLE BEAST.
I HAVEN'T DONE ANYTHING WRONG, SO JUST LEAVE ME ALONE.
HMM. YOU THINK SO? BUT WE THINK YOU'VE MADE ENOUGH SINS IN THE PAST, SO EVERY TIME WE MEET,
YOU CAN PAY FOR THOSE!

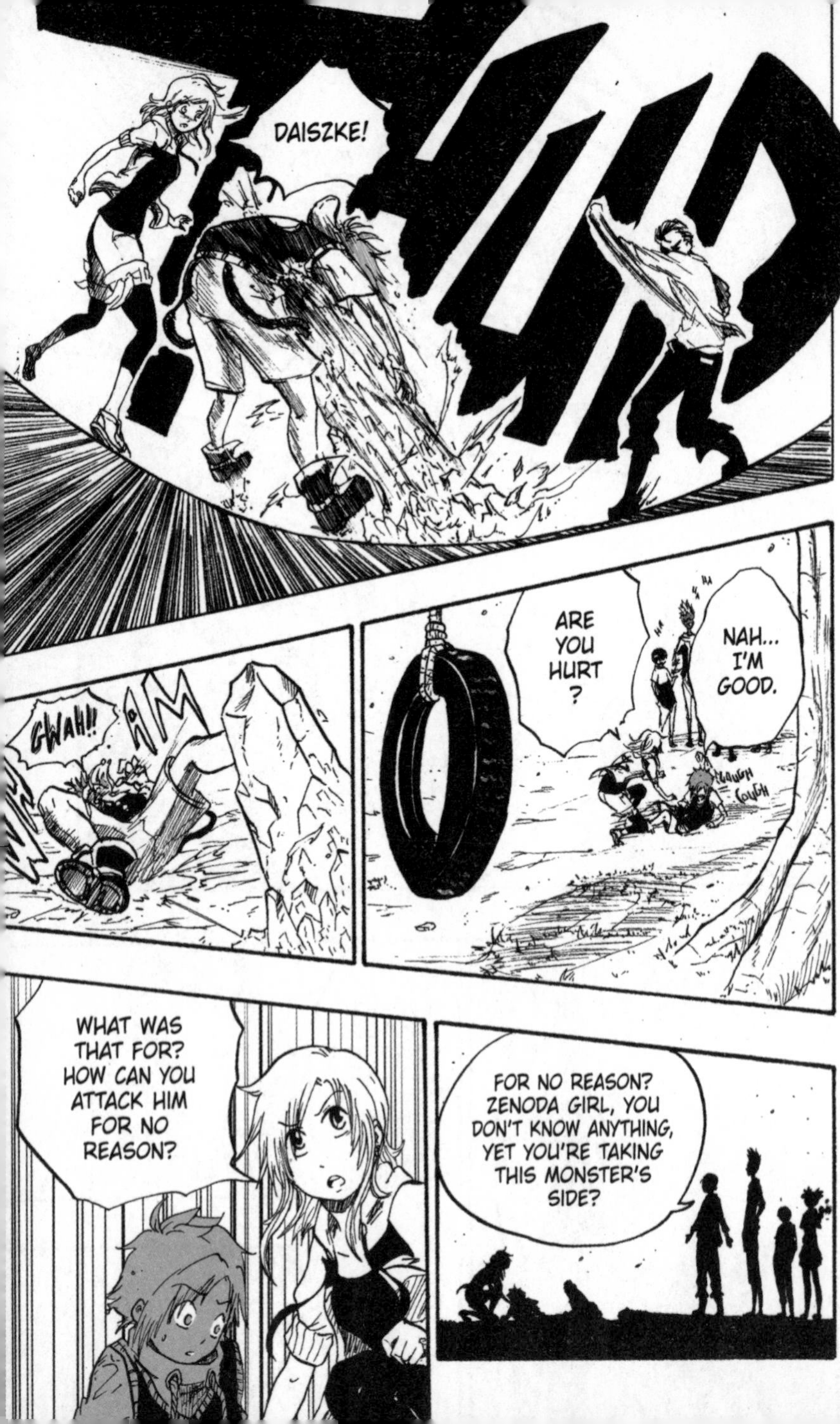
DAISZKE!
GWAH!!
ARE YOU HURT?
NAH... I'M GOOD.
COUGH COUGH
WHAT WAS THAT FOR? HOW CAN YOU ATTACK HIM FOR NO REASON?
FOR NO REASON? ZENODA GIRL, YOU DON'T KNOW ANYTHING, YET YOU'RE TAKING THIS MONSTER'S SIDE?

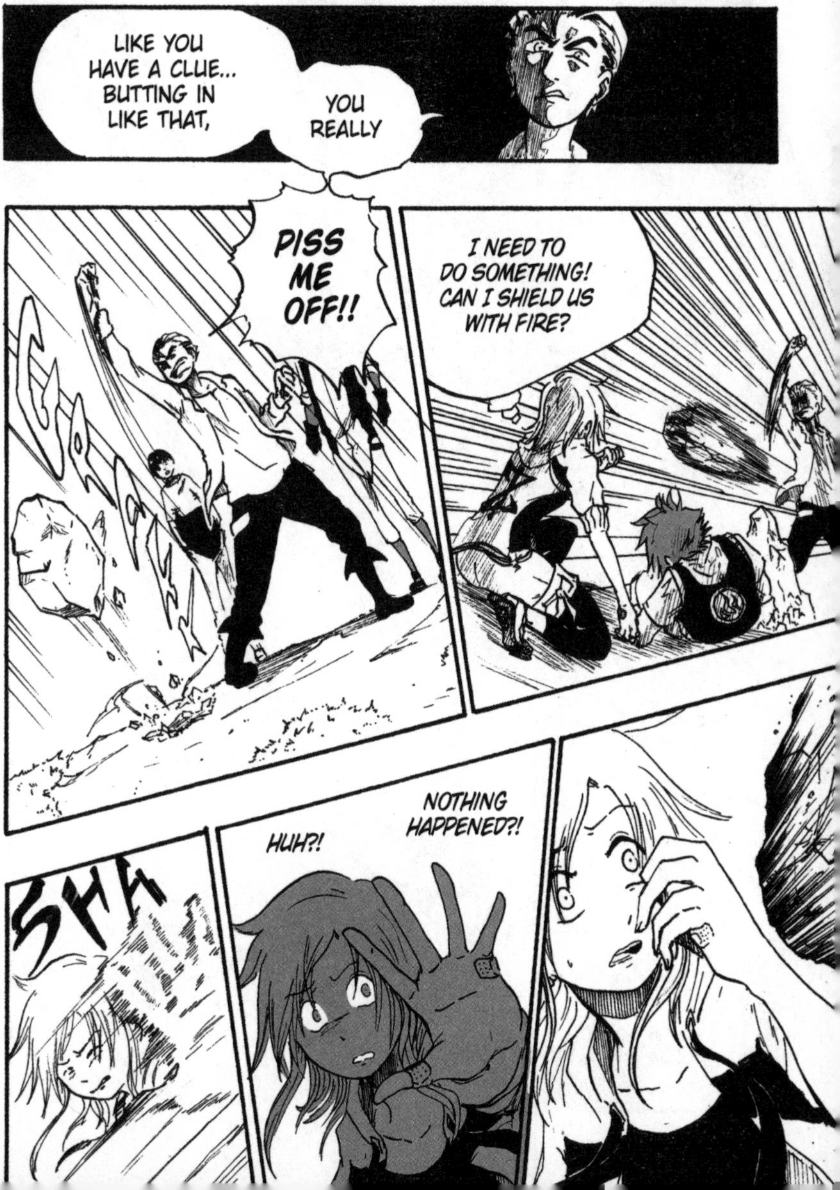
LIKE YOU HAVE A CLUE... BUTTING IN LIKE THAT,
YOU REALLY
PISS ME OFF!!
I NEED TO DO SOMETHING! CAN I SHIELD US WITH FIRE?
SHA
HUH?!
NOTHING HAPPENED?!

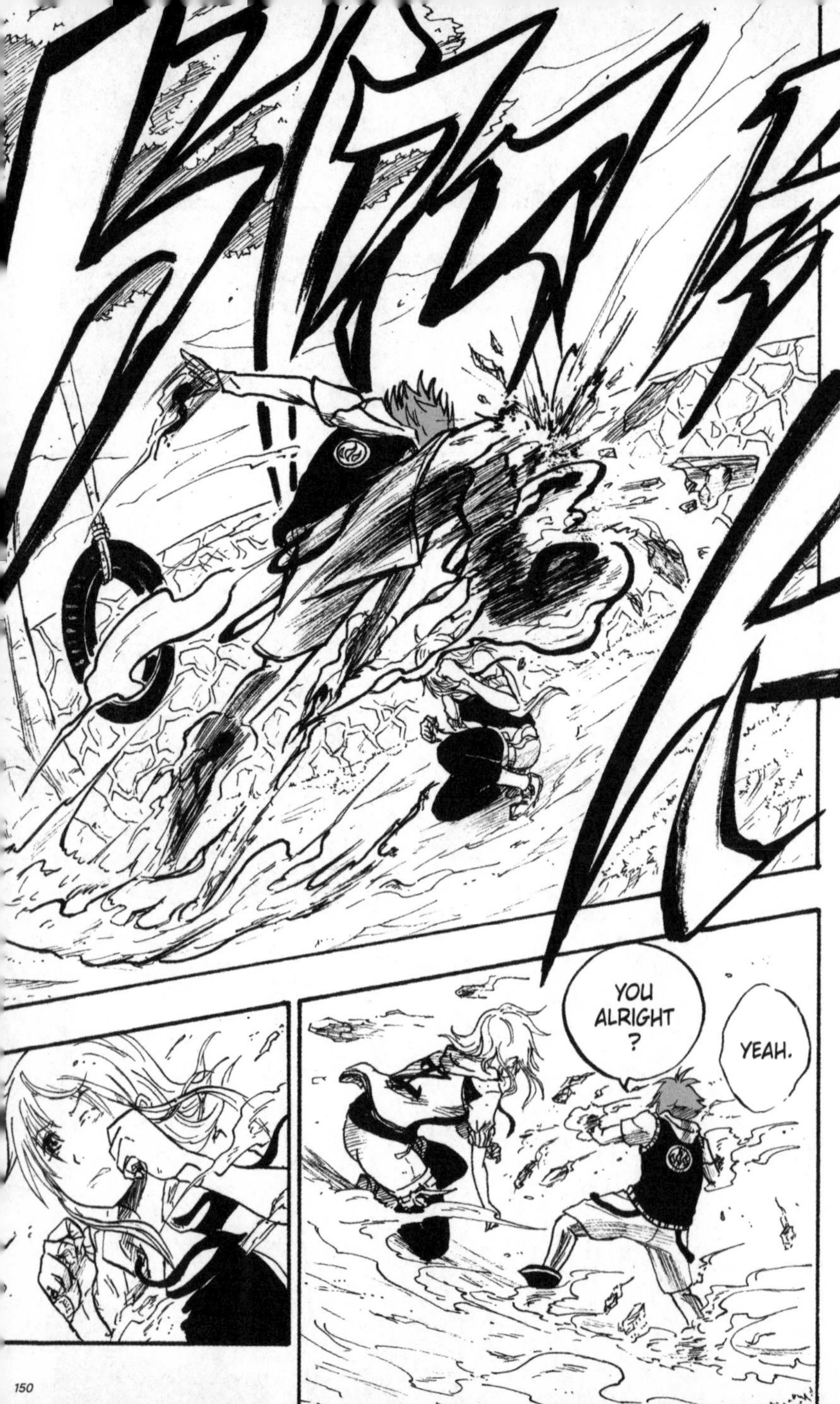
YOU ALRIGHT ?
YEAH.

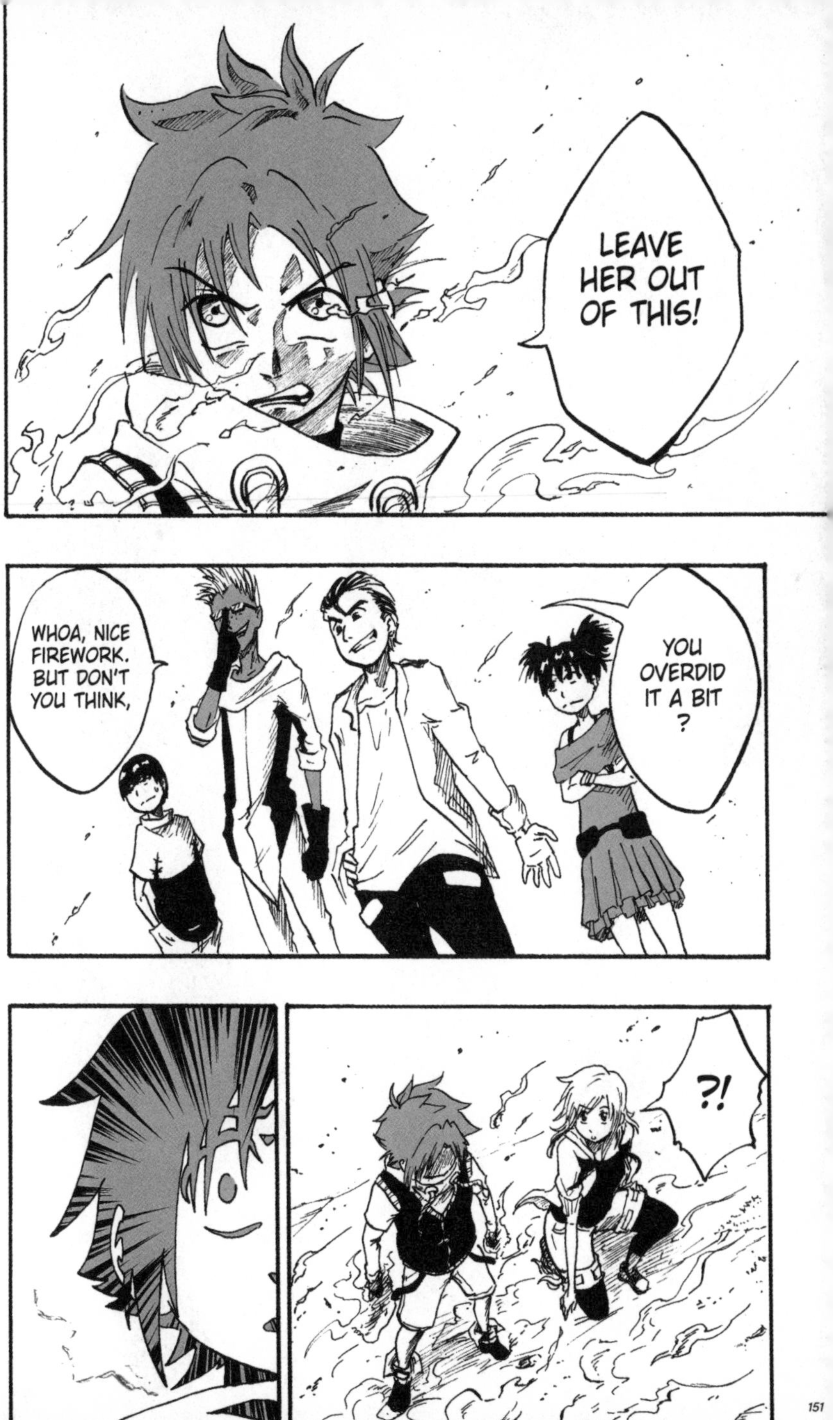
LEAVE HER OUT OF THIS!
WHOA, NICE FIREWORK. BUT DON'T YOU THINK,
YOU OVERDID IT A BIT ?
?!

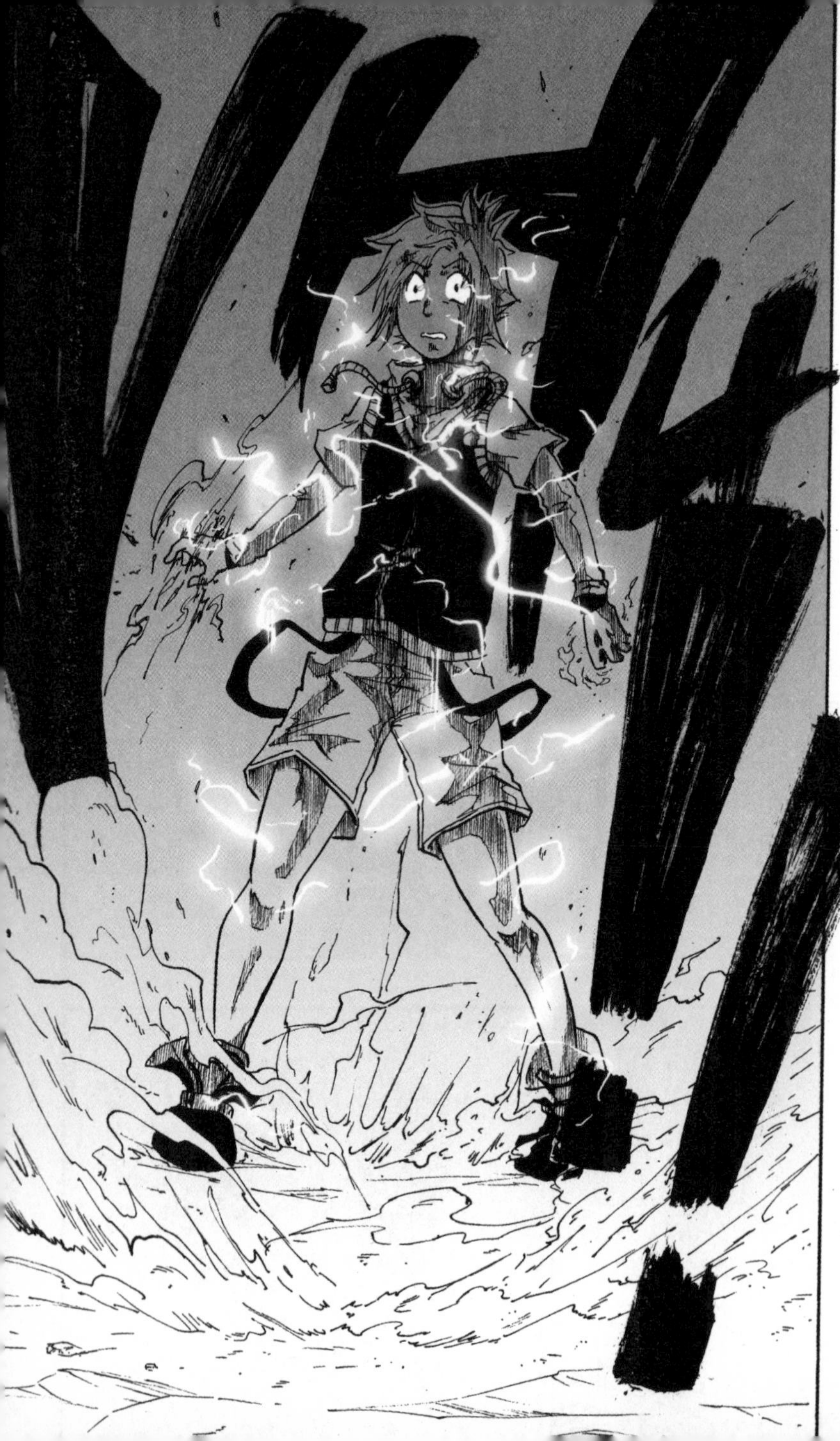

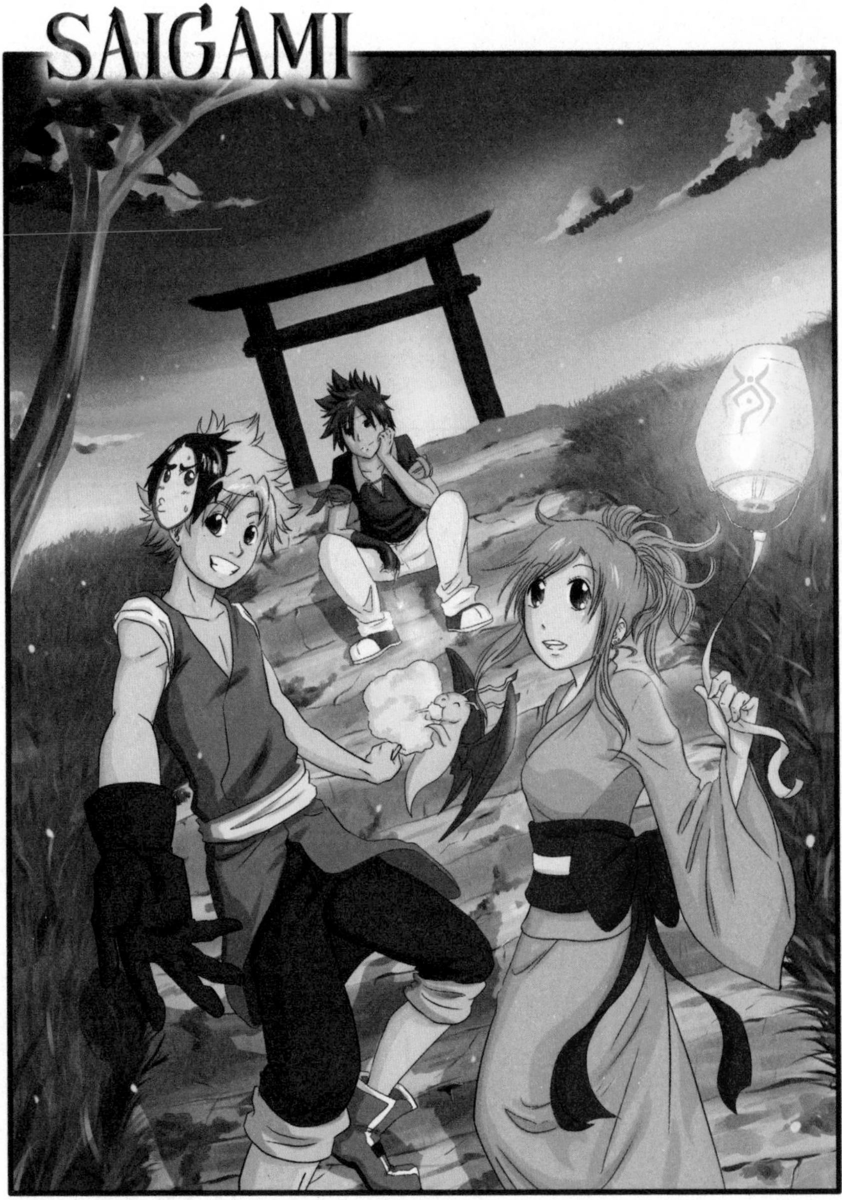
SAIGAMI

Chapter 6: Outcasts

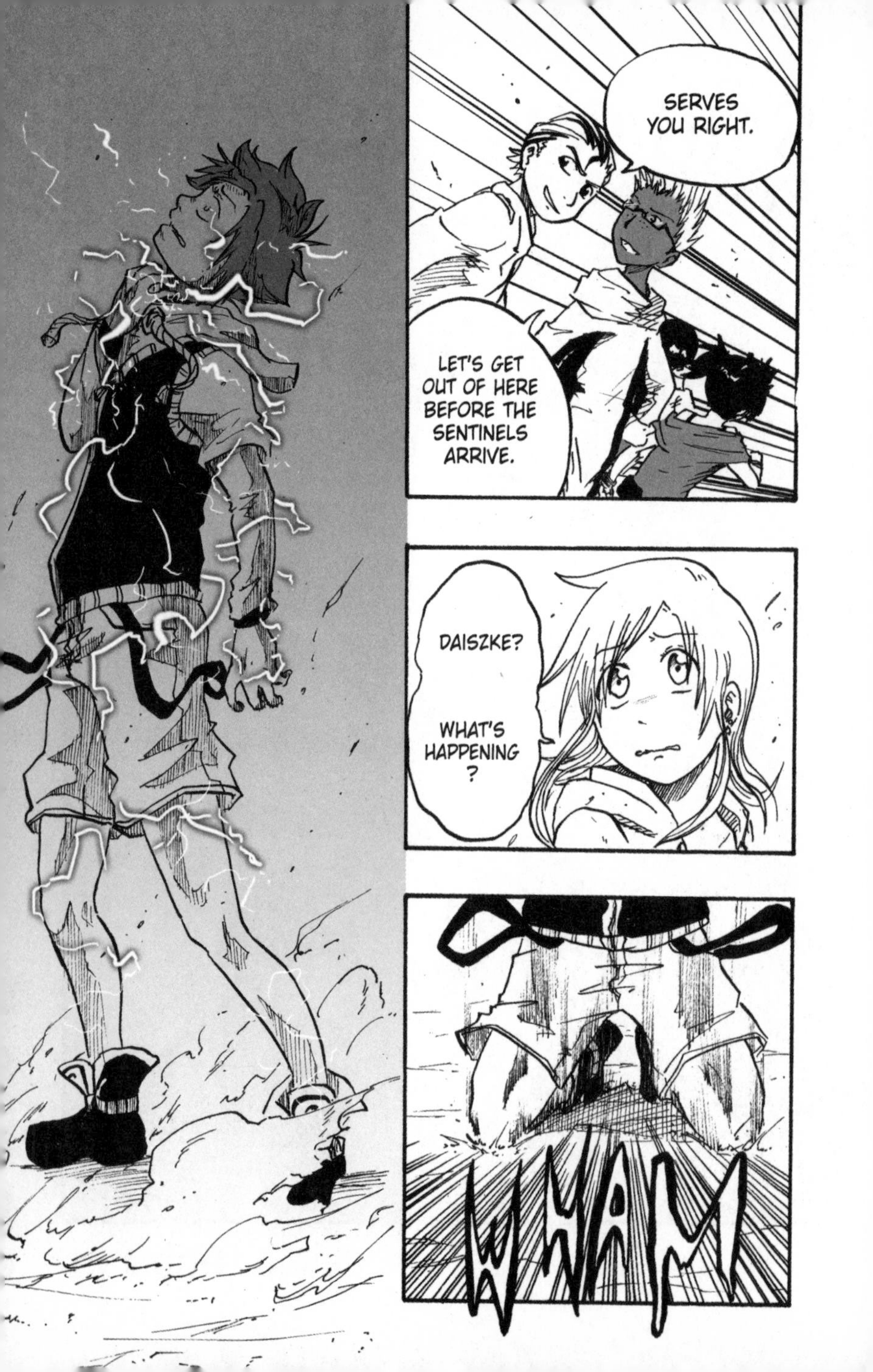
SERVES YOU RIGHT.
LET'S GET OUT OF HERE BEFORE THE SENTINELS ARRIVE.
DAISZKE?
WHAT'S HAPPENING ?
WHAM

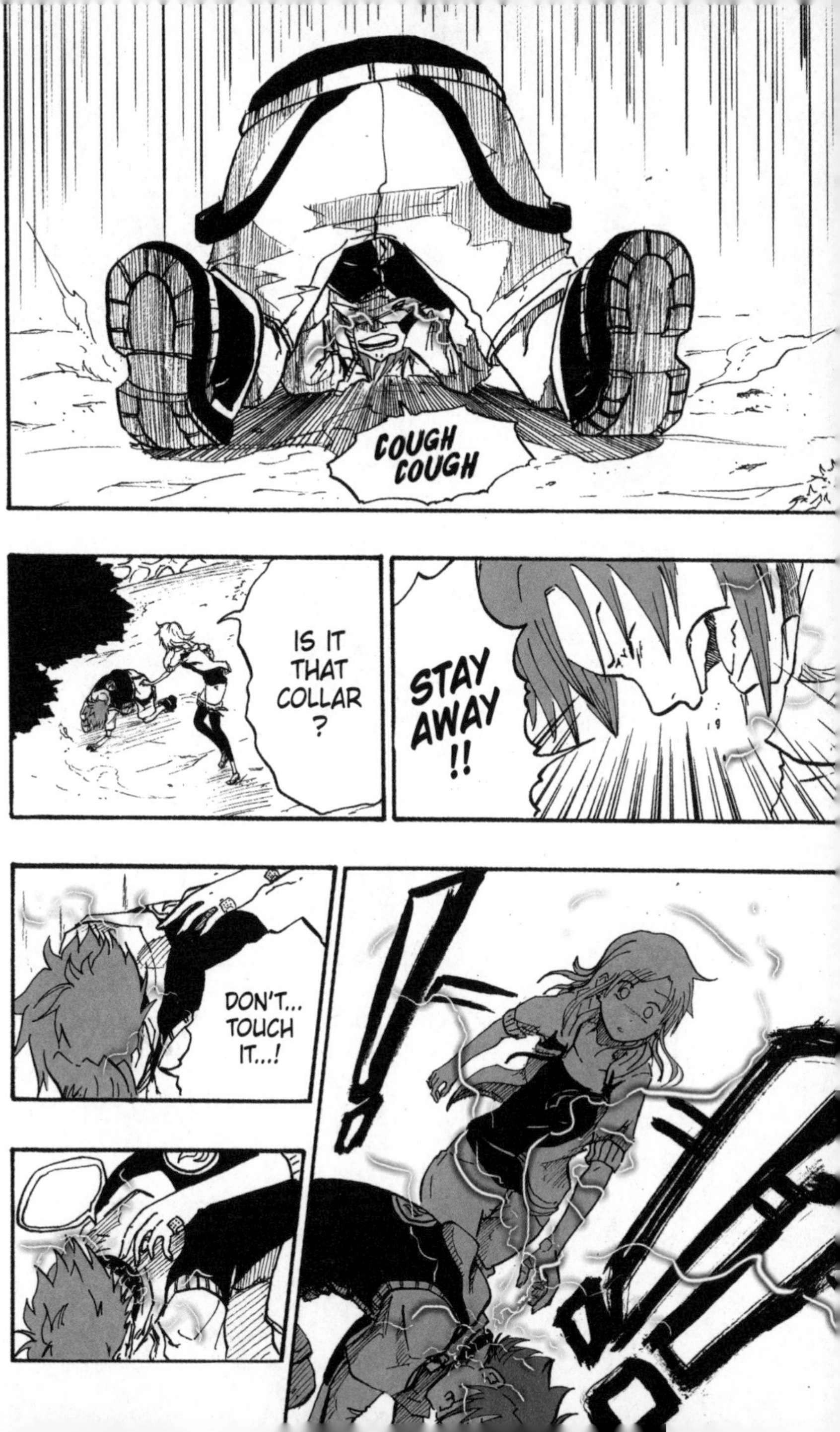
COUGH COUGH
IS IT THAT COLLAR?
STAY AWAY!!
DON'T... TOUCH IT...!

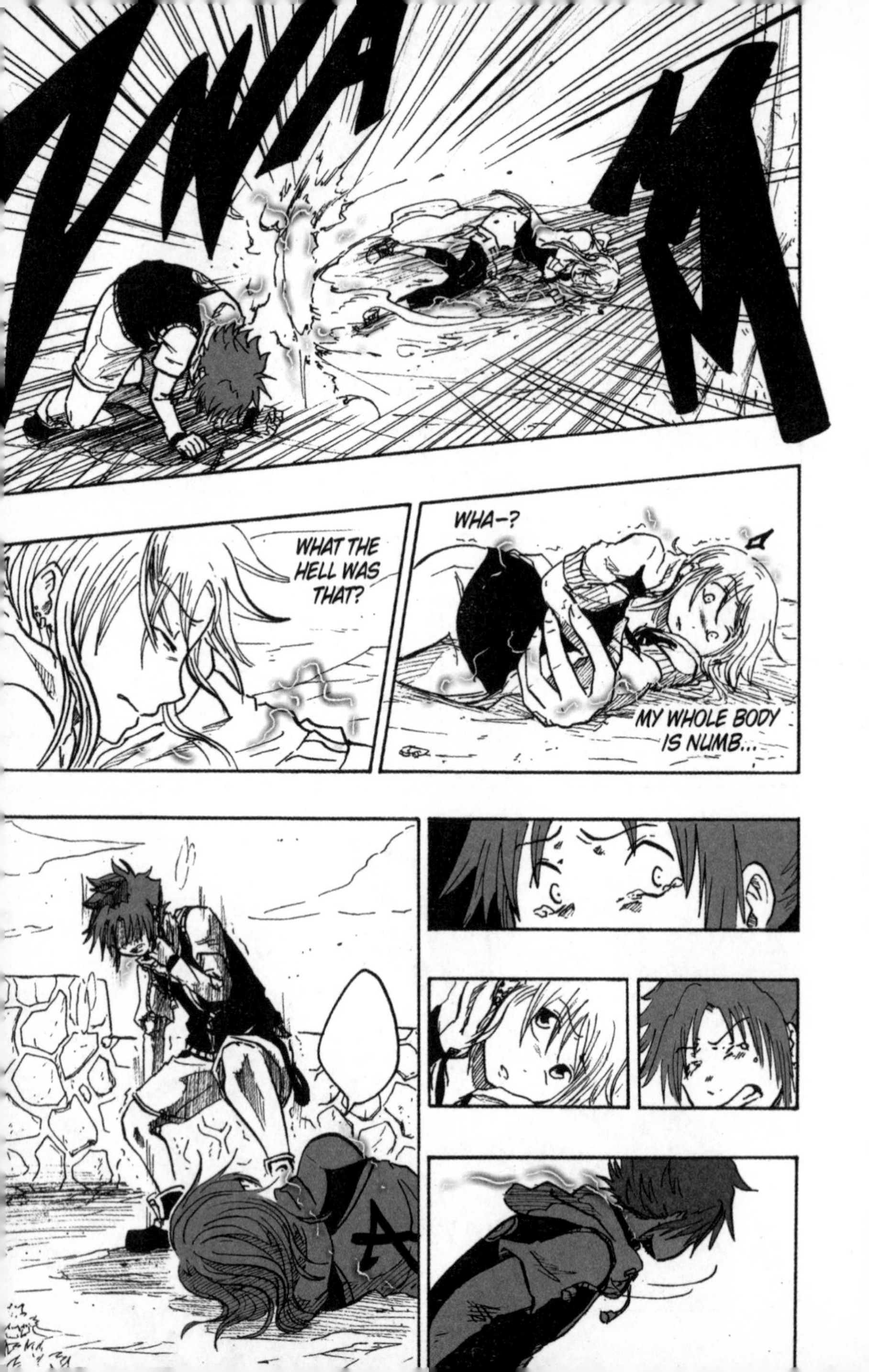
WHAT THE HELL WAS THAT?
WHA-?
MY WHOLE BODY IS NUMB...

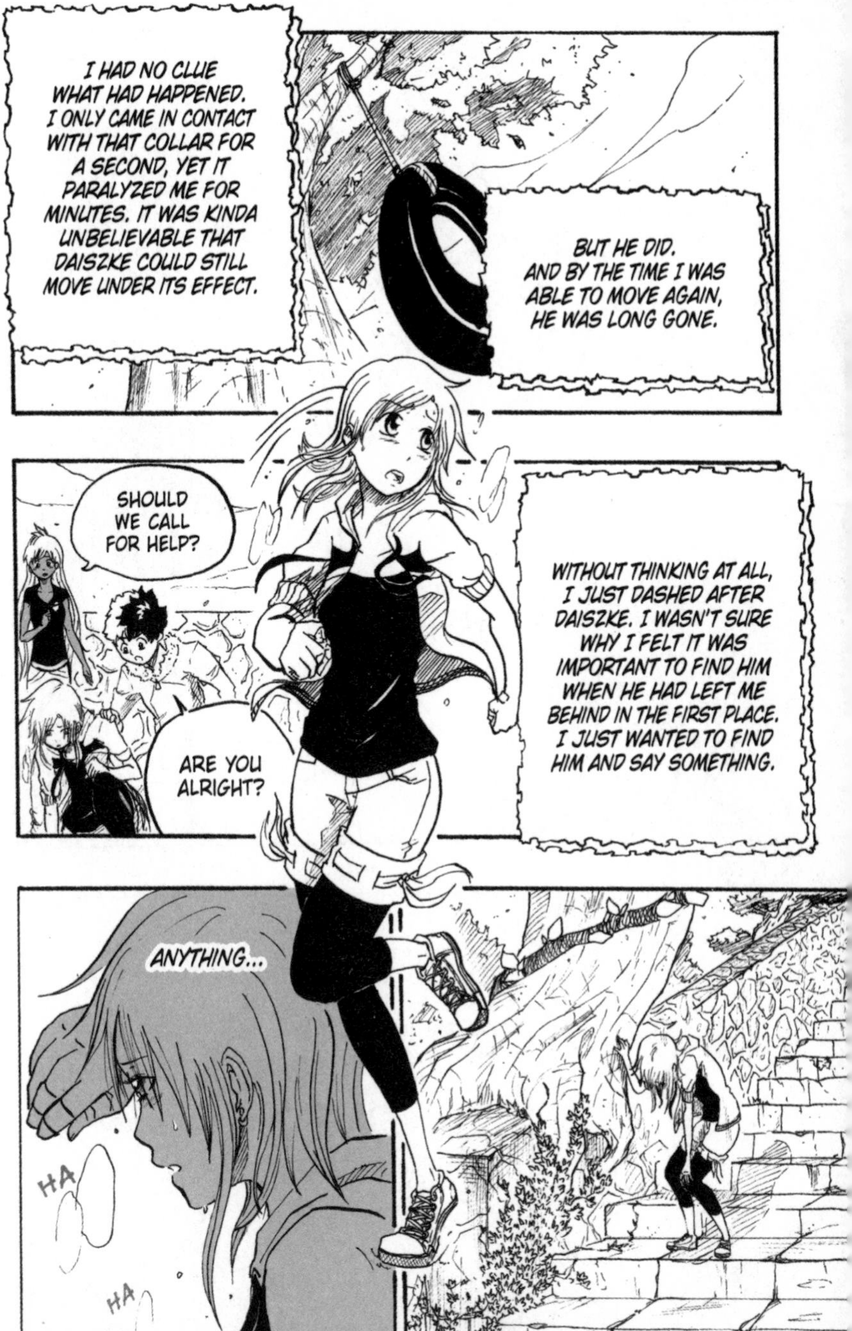

I HAD NO CLUE WHAT HAD HAPPENED. I ONLY CAME IN CONTACT WITH THAT COLLAR FOR A SECOND, YET IT PARALYZED ME FOR MINUTES. IT WAS KINDA UNBELIEVABLE THAT DAISZKE COULD STILL MOVE UNDER ITS EFFECT.
BUT HE DID. AND BY THE TIME I WAS ABLE TO MOVE AGAIN, HE WAS LONG GONE.
SHOULD WE CALL FOR HELP?
ARE YOU ALRIGHT?
WITHOUT THINKING AT ALL, I JUST DASHED AFTER DAISZKE. I WASN'T SURE WHY I FELT IT WAS IMPORTANT TO FIND HIM WHEN HE HAD LEFT ME BEHIND IN THE FIRST PLACE. I JUST WANTED TO FIND HIM AND SAY SOMETHING.
ANYTHING...
HA
HA

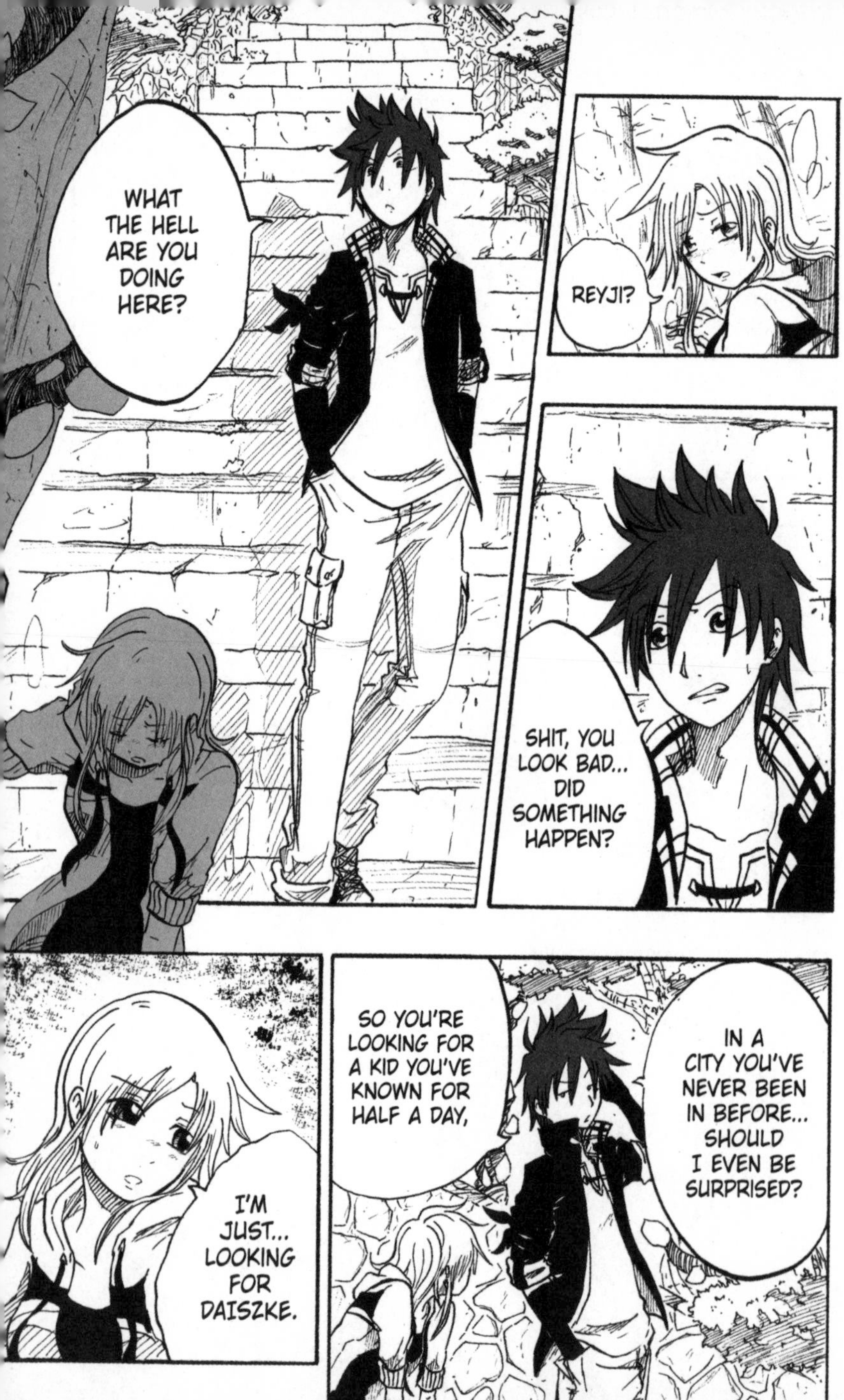
WHAT THE HELL ARE YOU DOING HERE?
REYJI?
SHIT, YOU LOOK BAD... DID SOMETHING HAPPEN?
I'M JUST... LOOKING FOR DAISZKE.
SO YOU'RE LOOKING FOR A KID YOU'VE KNOWN FOR HALF A DAY,
IN A CITY YOU'VE NEVER BEEN IN BEFORE... SHOULD I EVEN BE SURPRISED?

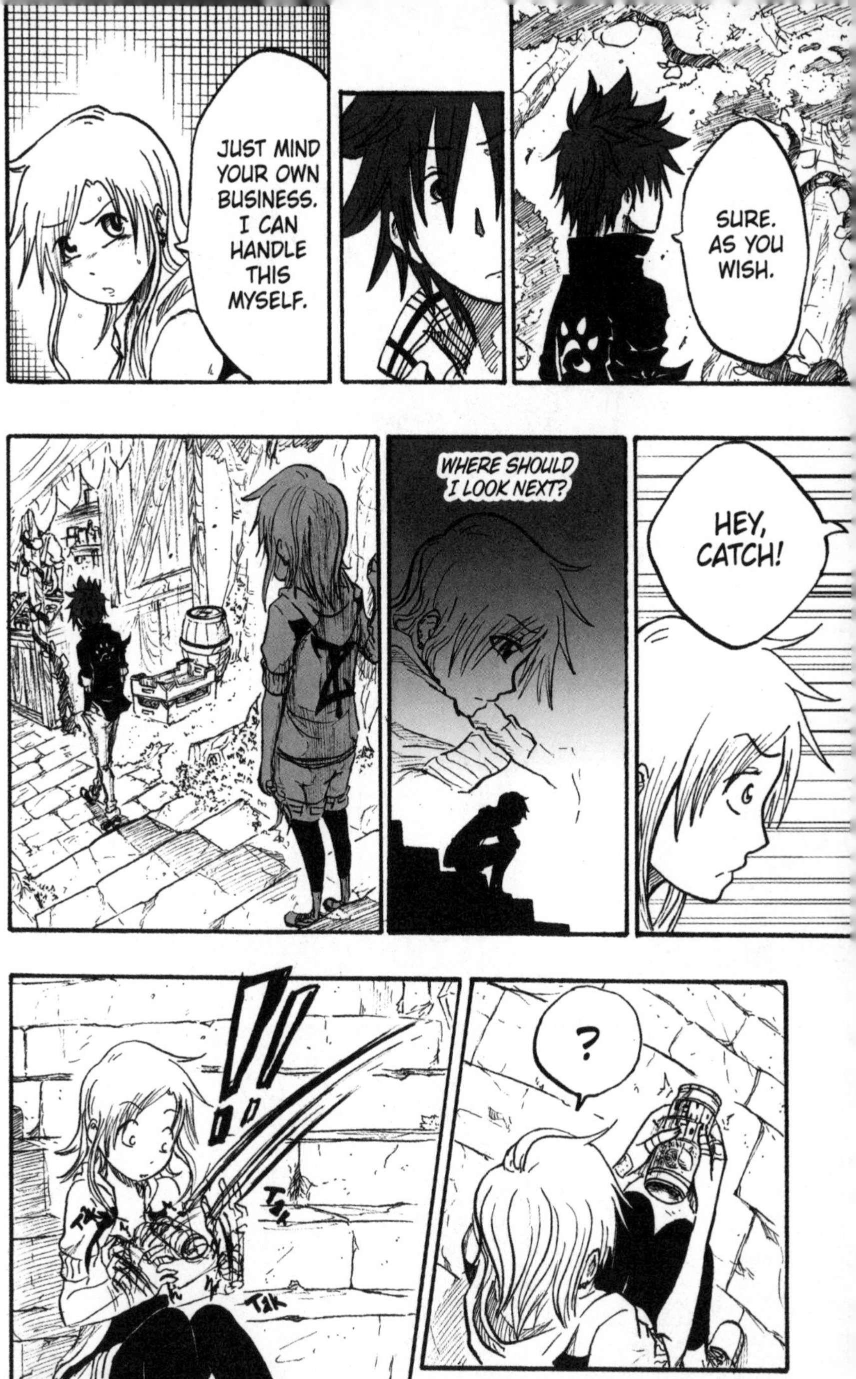
JUST MIND YOUR OWN BUSINESS. I CAN HANDLE THIS MYSELF.
SURE. AS YOU WISH.
WHERE SHOULD I LOOK NEXT?
HEY, CATCH!
!!
TAK
TAK
?

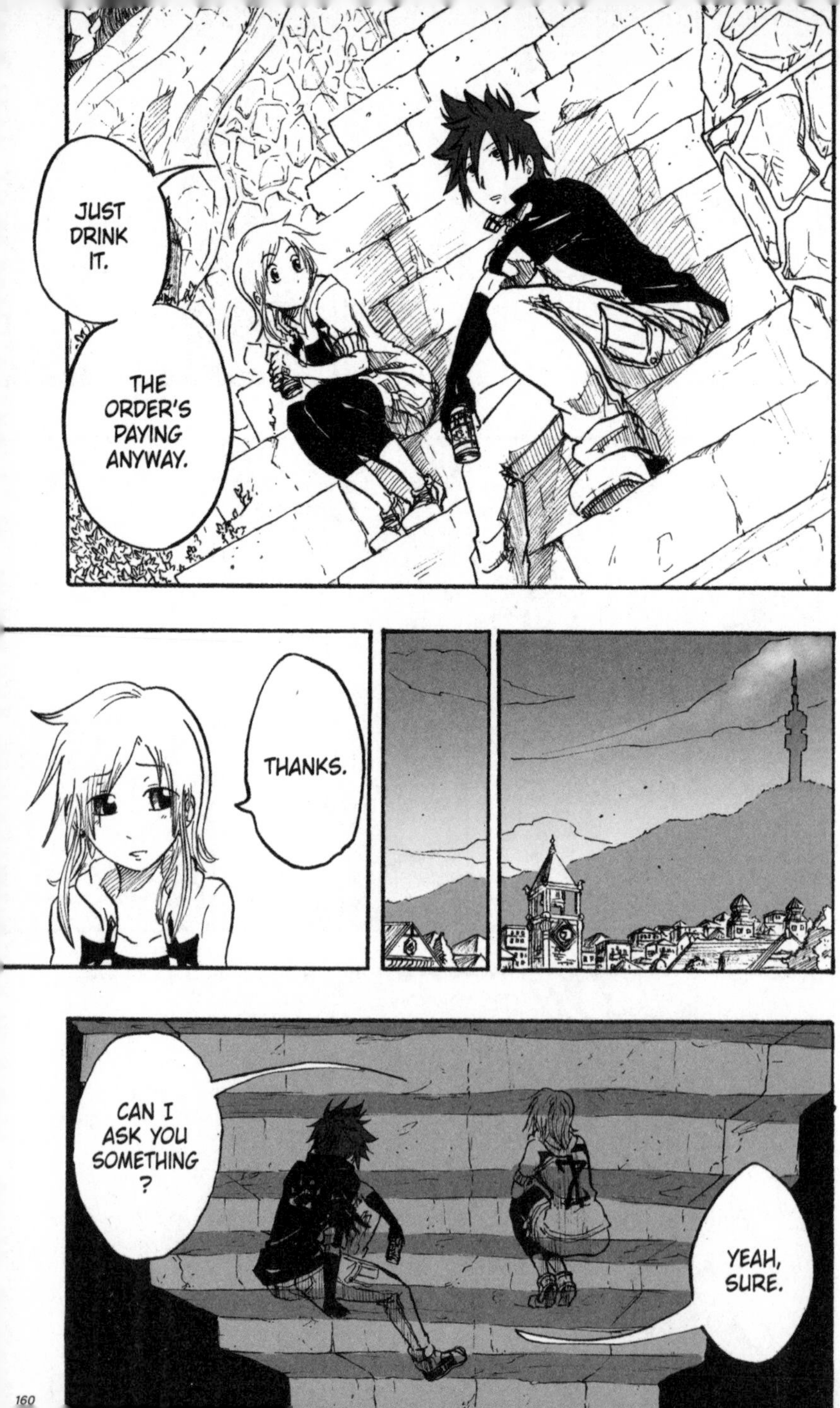
JUST DRINK IT.
THE ORDER'S PAYING ANYWAY.
THANKS.
CAN I ASK YOU SOMETHING?
YEAH, SURE.

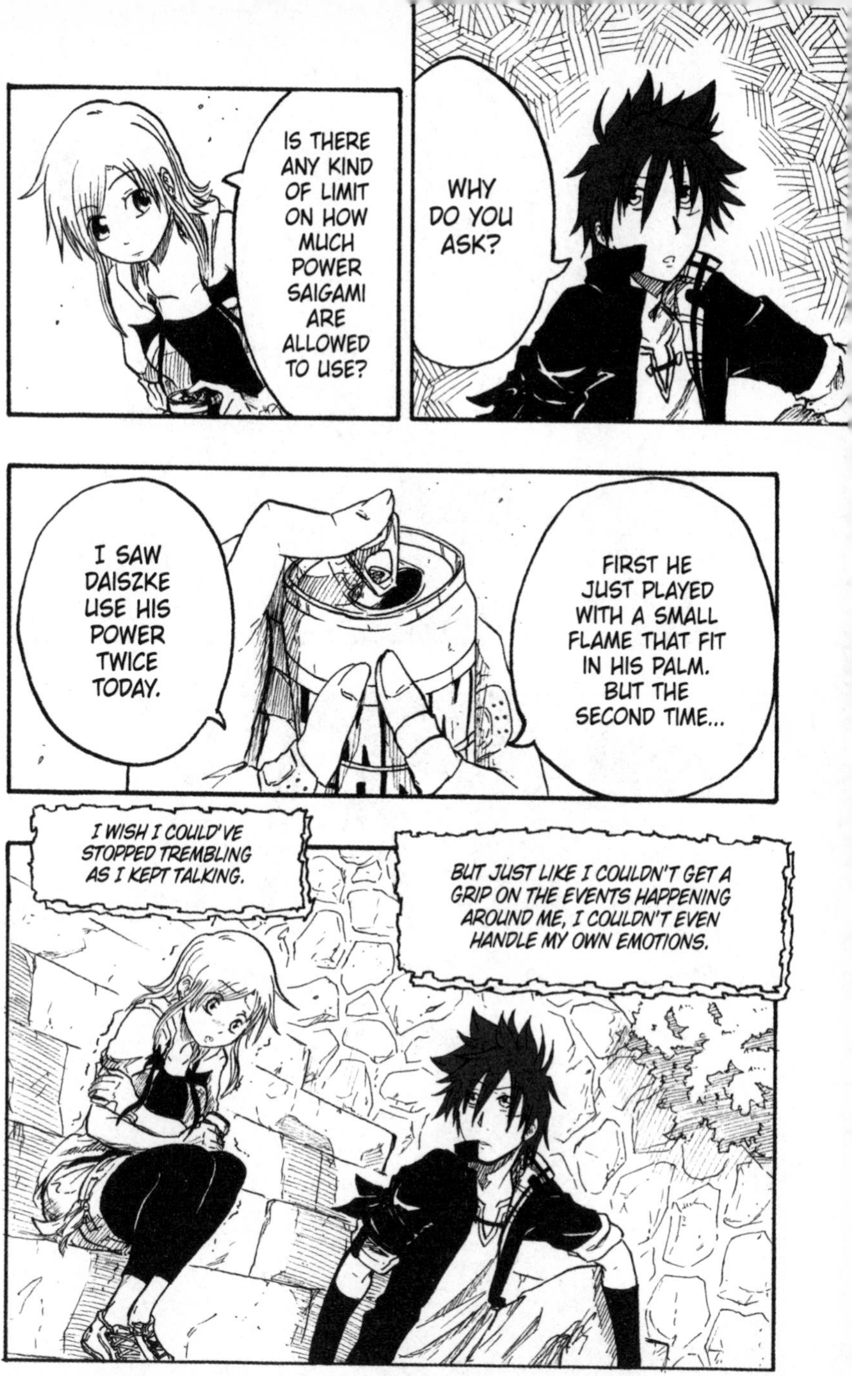
IS THERE ANY KIND OF LIMIT ON HOW MUCH POWER SAIGAMI ARE ALLOWED TO USE?
WHY DO YOU ASK?
I SAW DAISZKE USE HIS POWER TWICE TODAY.
FIRST HE JUST PLAYED WITH A SMALL FLAME THAT FIT IN HIS PALM. BUT THE SECOND TIME...
I WISH I COULD'VE STOPPED TREMBLING AS I KEPT TALKING.
BUT JUST LIKE I COULDN'T GET A GRIP ON THE EVENTS HAPPENING AROUND ME, I COULDN'T EVEN HANDLE MY OWN EMOTIONS.

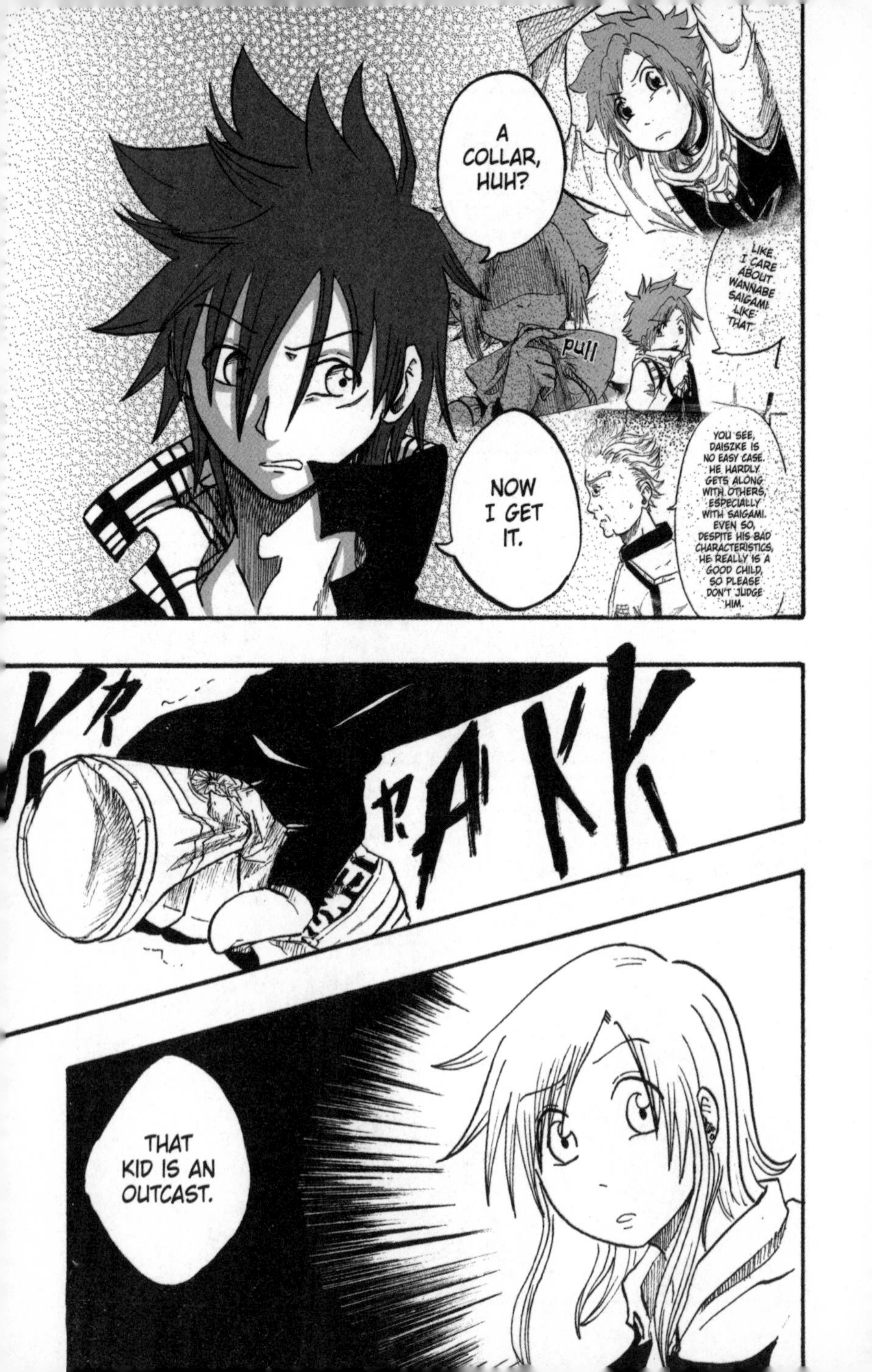
A COLLAR, HUH?
LIKE. I CARE ABOUT WANNABE SAIGAMI LIKE THAT.
pull
NOW I GET IT.
YOU SEE, DAISZKE IS NO EASY CASE. HE HARDLY GETS ALONG WITH OTHERS, ESPECIALLY WITH SAIGAMI. EVEN SO, DESPITE HIS BAD CHARACTERISTICS, HE REALLY IS A GOOD CHILD, SO PLEASE DON'T JUDGE HIM.
KRAKK
THAT KID IS AN OUTCAST.

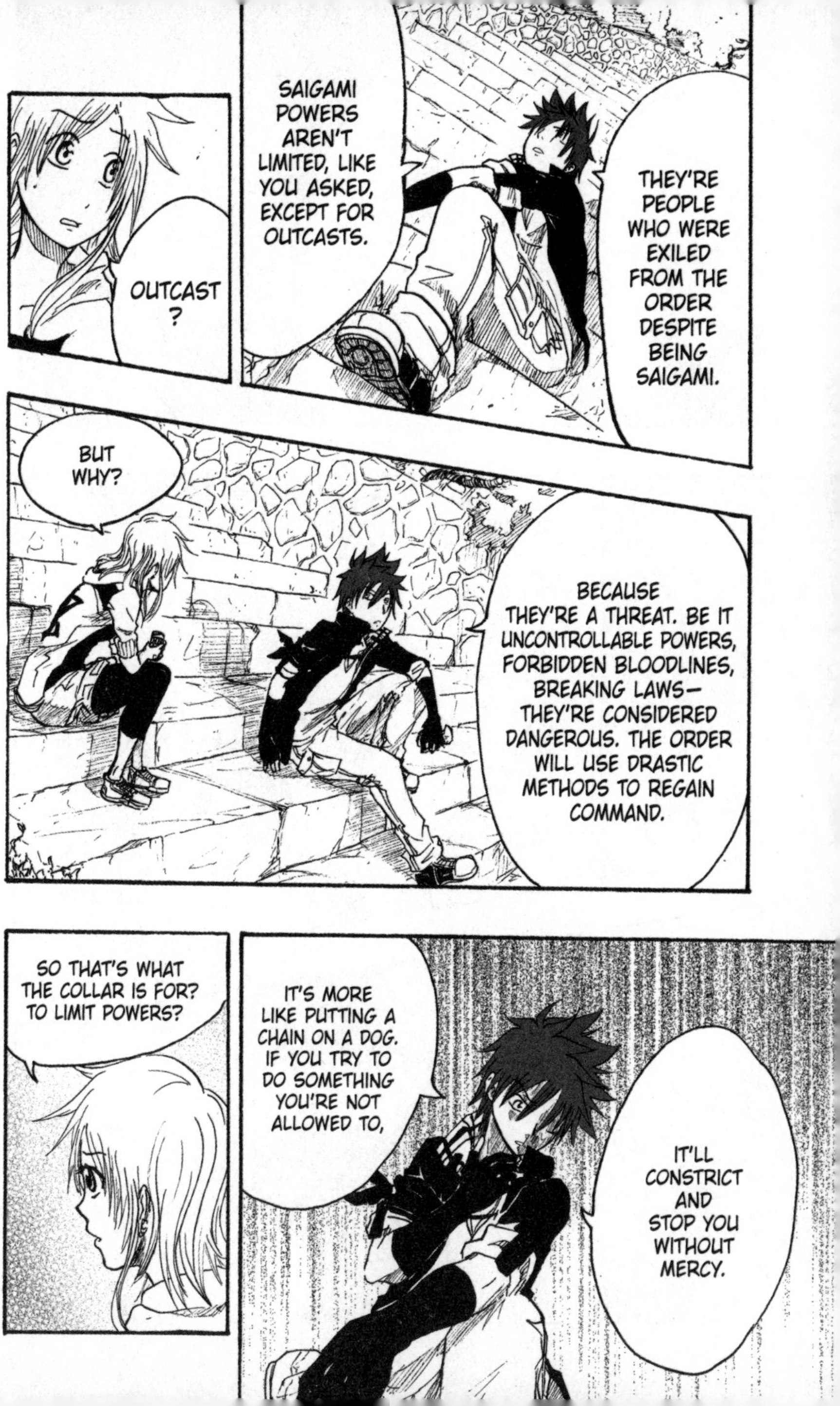
SAIGAMI POWERS AREN'T LIMITED, LIKE YOU ASKED, EXCEPT FOR OUTCASTS.
OUTCAST?
THEY'RE PEOPLE WHO WERE EXILED FROM THE ORDER DESPITE BEING SAIGAMI.
BUT WHY?
BECAUSE THEY'RE A THREAT. BE IT UNCONTROLLABLE POWERS, FORBIDDEN BLOODLINES, BREAKING LAWS— THEY'RE CONSIDERED DANGEROUS. THE ORDER WILL USE DRASTIC METHODS TO REGAIN COMMAND.
SO THAT'S WHAT THE COLLAR IS FOR? TO LIMIT POWERS?
IT'S MORE LIKE PUTTING A CHAIN ON A DOG. IF YOU TRY TO DO SOMETHING YOU'RE NOT ALLOWED TO,
IT'LL CONSTRICT AND STOP YOU WITHOUT MERCY.

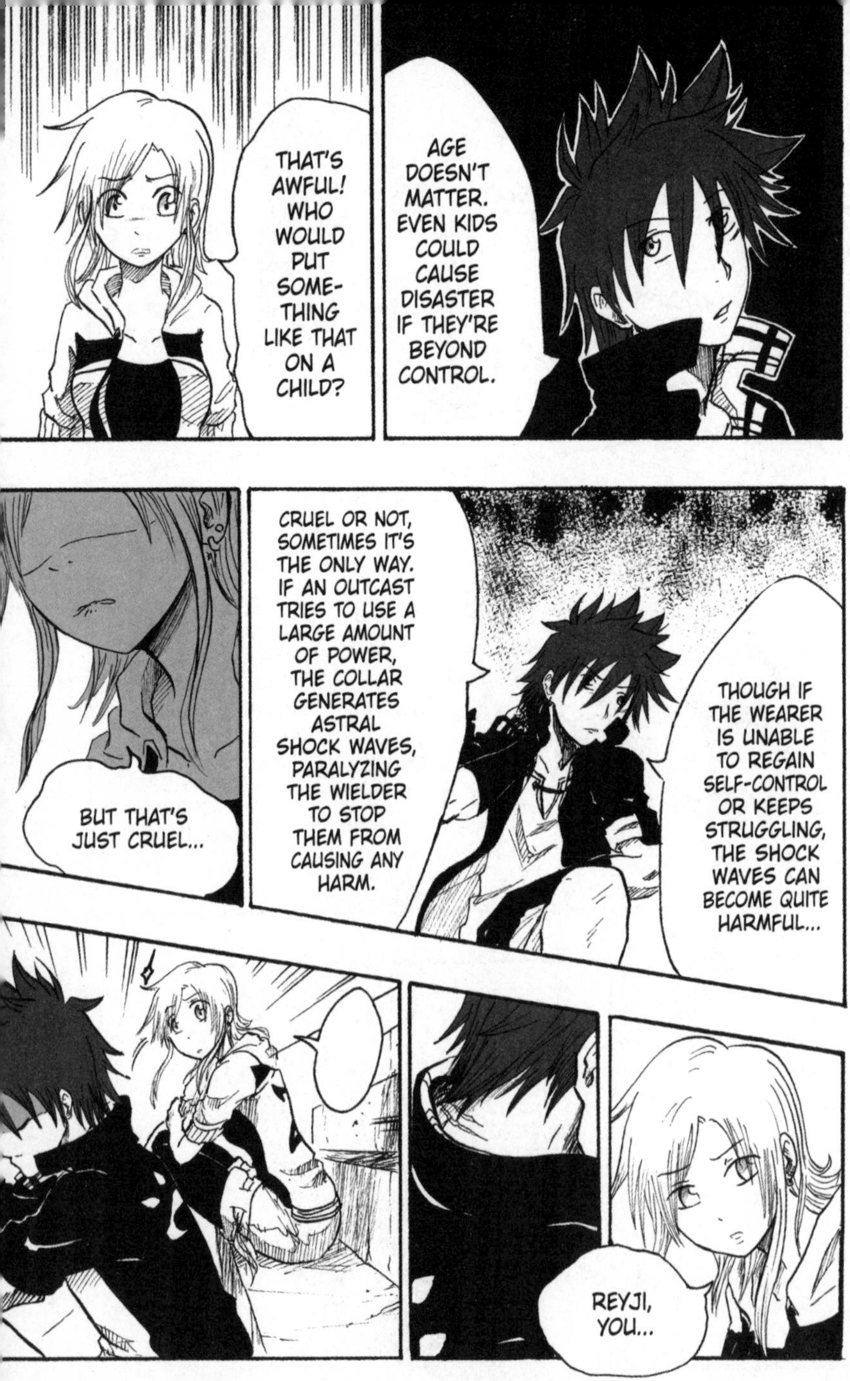
THAT'S AWFUL! WHO WOULD PUT SOME-THING LIKE THAT ON A CHILD?
AGE DOESN'T MATTER. EVEN KIDS COULD CAUSE DISASTER IF THEY'RE BEYOND CONTROL.
BUT THAT'S JUST CRUEL...
CRUEL OR NOT, SOMETIMES IT'S THE ONLY WAY. IF AN OUTCAST TRIES TO USE A LARGE AMOUNT OF POWER, THE COLLAR GENERATES ASTRAL SHOCK WAVES, PARALYZING THE WIELDER TO STOP THEM FROM CAUSING ANY HARM.
THOUGH IF THE WEARER IS UNABLE TO REGAIN SELF-CONTROL OR KEEPS STRUGGLING, THE SHOCK WAVES CAN BECOME QUITE HARMFUL...
REYJI, YOU...

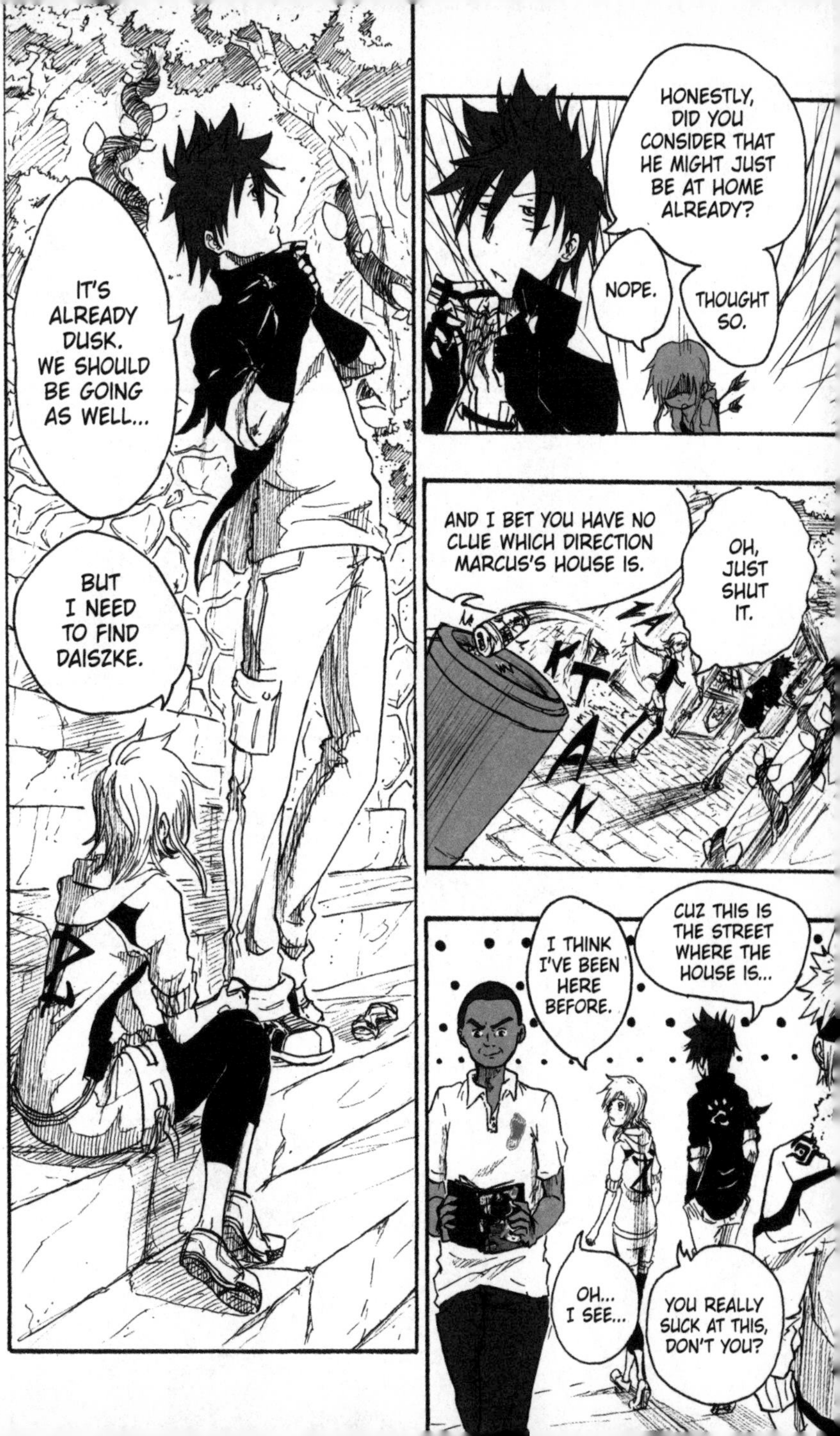
IT'S ALREADY DUSK. WE SHOULD BE GOING AS WELL...
BUT I NEED TO FIND DAISZKE.
HONESTLY, DID YOU CONSIDER THAT HE MIGHT JUST BE AT HOME ALREADY?
NOPE.
THOUGHT SO.
AND I BET YOU HAVE NO CLUE WHICH DIRECTION MARCUS'S HOUSE IS.
OH, JUST SHUT IT.
I THINK I'VE BEEN HERE BEFORE.
CUZ THIS IS THE STREET WHERE THE HOUSE IS...
OH... I SEE...
YOU REALLY SUCK AT THIS, DON'T YOU?

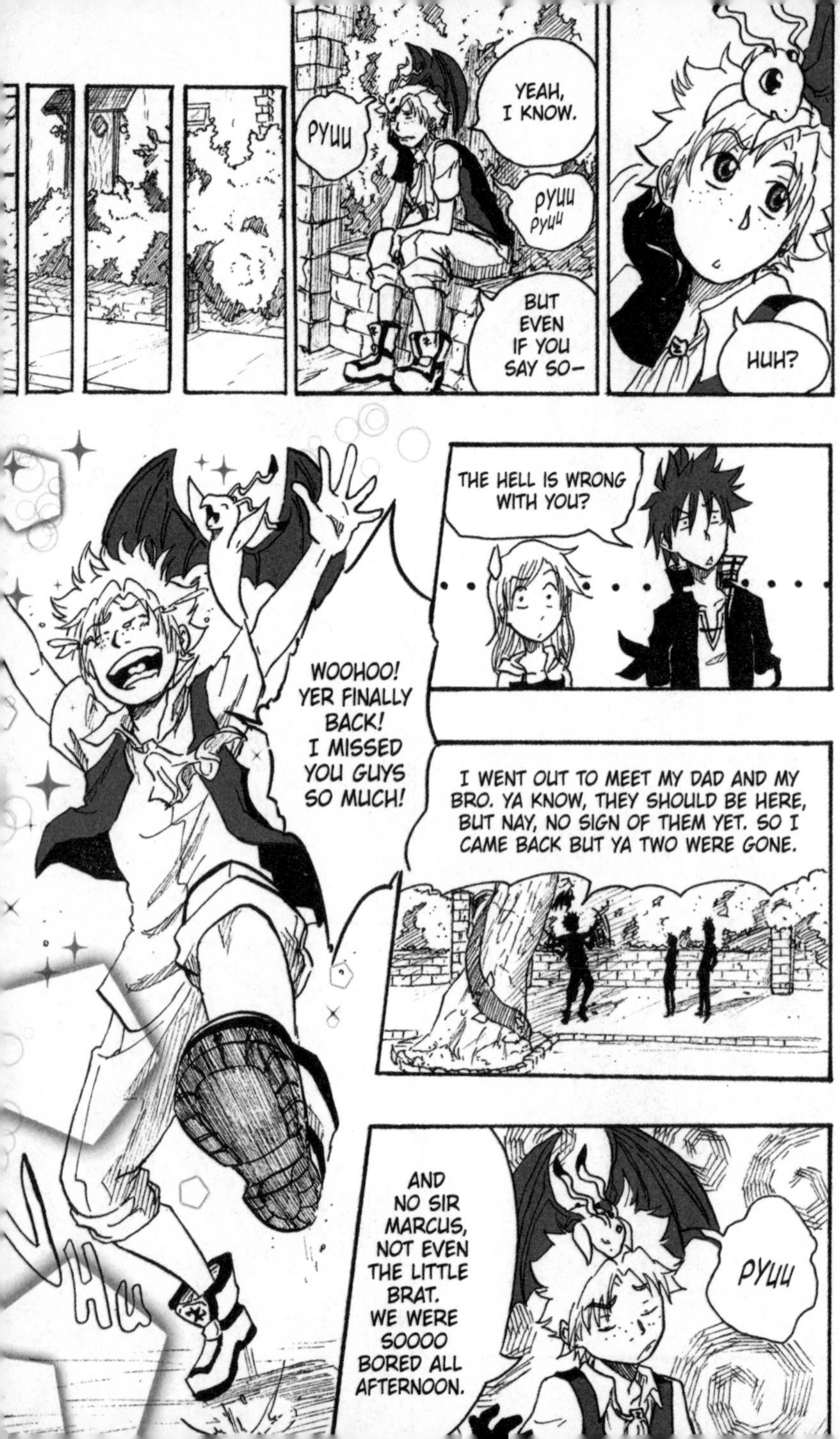

PYUU
YEAH, I KNOW.
PYUU PYUU
BUT EVEN IF YOU SAY SO—
HUH?
WOOHOO! YER FINALLY BACK! I MISSED YOU GUYS SO MUCH!
THE HELL IS WRONG WITH YOU?
I WENT OUT TO MEET MY DAD AND MY BRO. YA KNOW, THEY SHOULD BE HERE, BUT NAY, NO SIGN OF THEM YET. SO I CAME BACK BUT YA TWO WERE GONE.
AND NO SIR MARCUS, NOT EVEN THE LITTLE BRAT. WE WERE SOOOO BORED ALL AFTERNOON.
PYUU

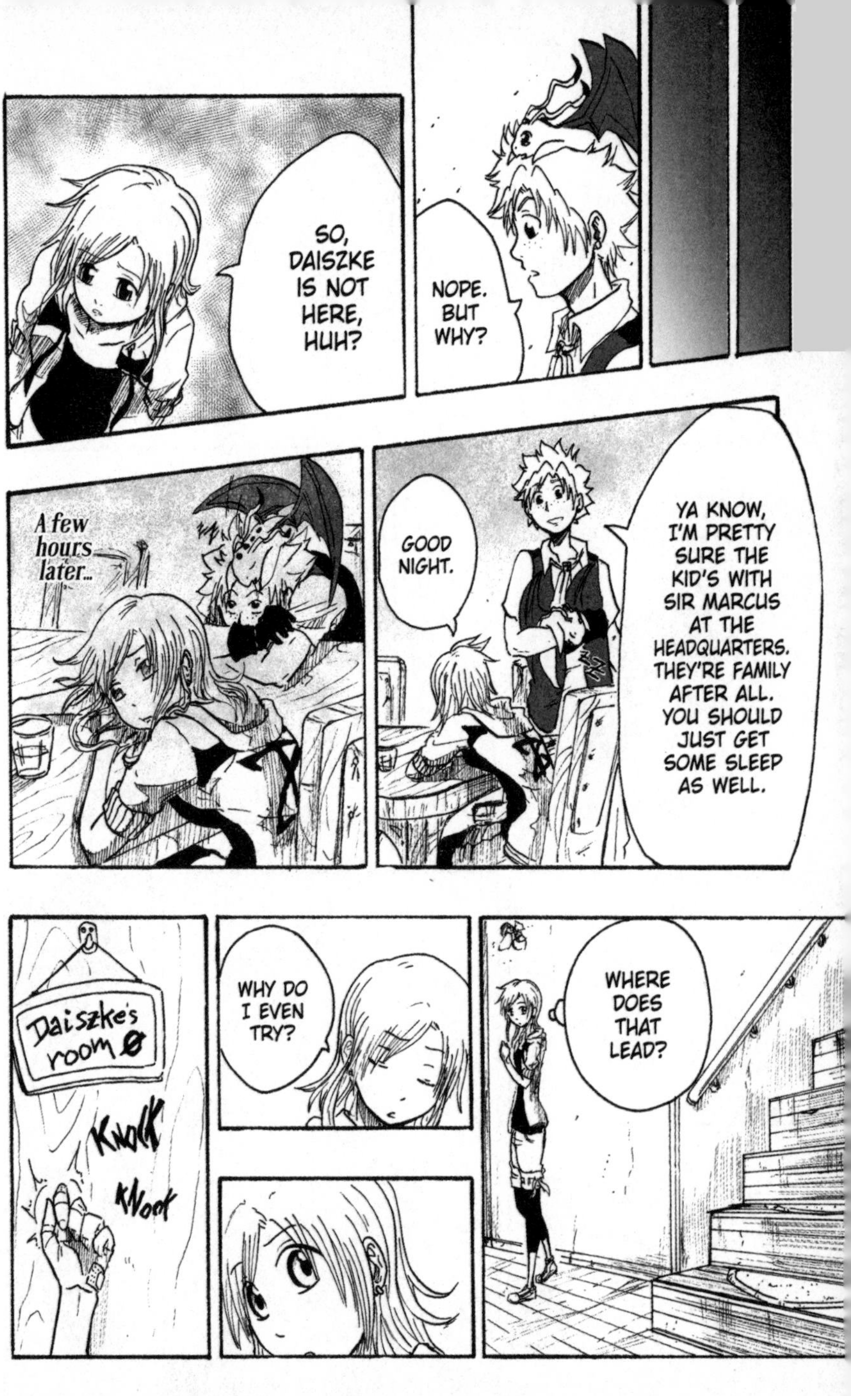
SO, DAISZKE IS NOT HERE, HUH?
NOPE. BUT WHY?
A few hours later...
GOOD NIGHT.
YA KNOW, I'M PRETTY SURE THE KID'S WITH SIR MARCUS AT THE HEADQUARTERS. THEY'RE FAMILY AFTER ALL. YOU SHOULD JUST GET SOME SLEEP AS WELL.
Daiszke's room
KNOCK
KNOCK
WHY DO I EVEN TRY?
WHERE DOES THAT LEAD?

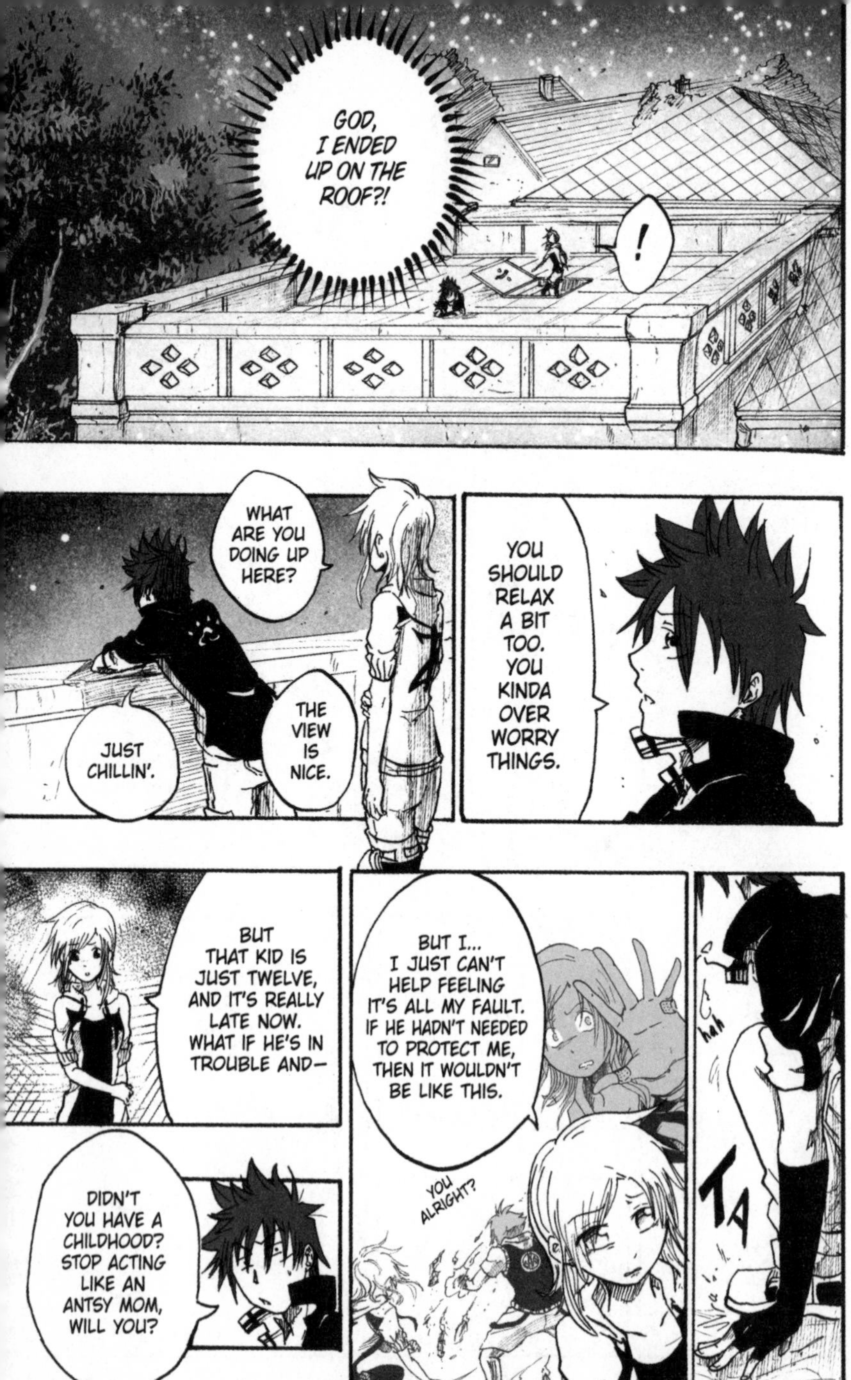
GOD, I ENDED UP ON THE ROOF?!
!
WHAT ARE YOU DOING UP HERE?
JUST CHILLIN'.
THE VIEW IS NICE.
YOU SHOULD RELAX A BIT TOO. YOU KINDA OVER WORRY THINGS.
BUT THAT KID IS JUST TWELVE, AND IT'S REALLY LATE NOW. WHAT IF HE'S IN TROUBLE AND—
DIDN'T YOU HAVE A CHILDHOOD? STOP ACTING LIKE AN ANTSY MOM, WILL YOU?
BUT I... I JUST CAN'T HELP FEELING IT'S ALL MY FAULT. IF HE HADN'T NEEDED TO PROTECT ME, THEN IT WOULDN'T BE LIKE THIS.
YOU ALRIGHT?
hah
TA

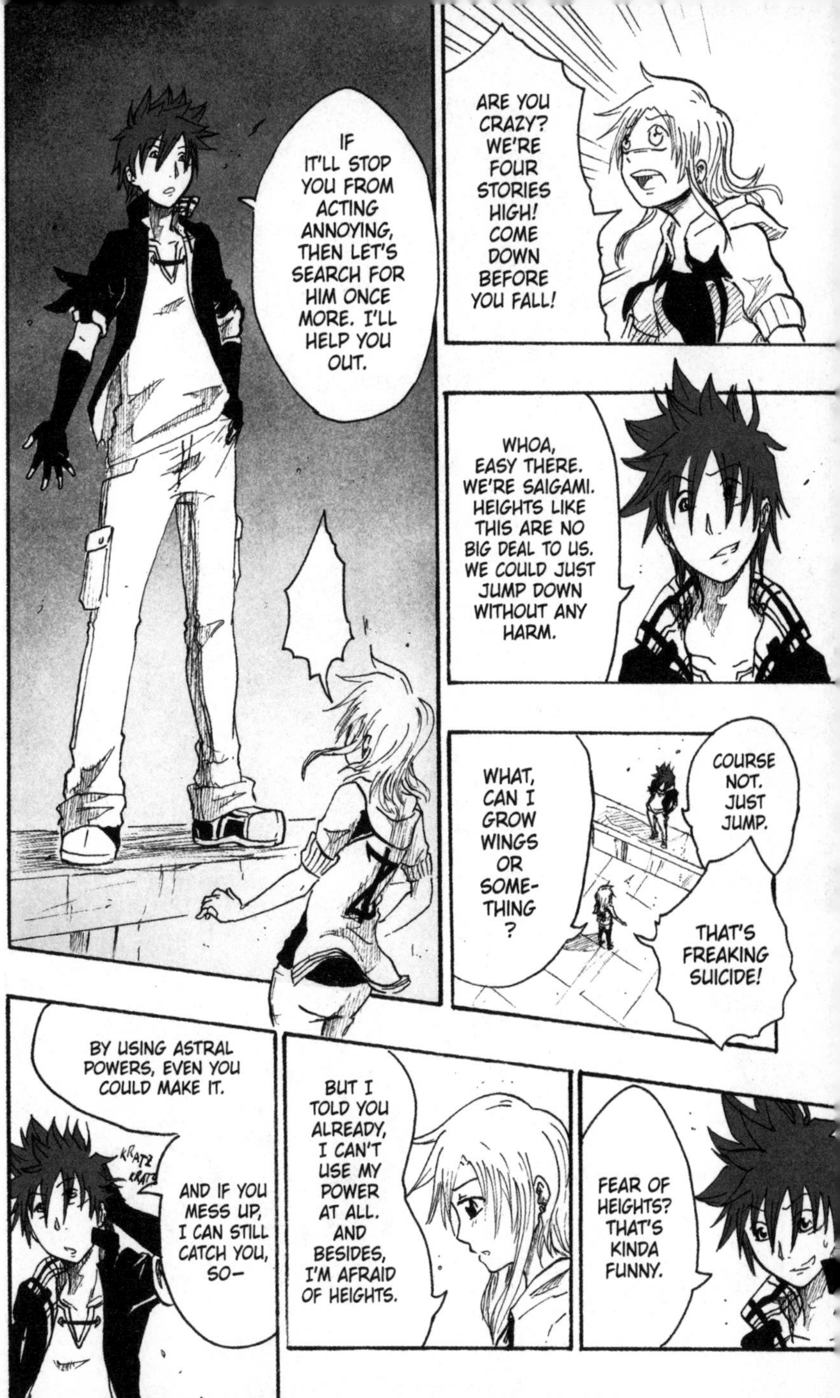
IF IT'LL STOP YOU FROM ACTING ANNOYING, THEN LET'S SEARCH FOR HIM ONCE MORE. I'LL HELP YOU OUT.
ARE YOU CRAZY? WE'RE FOUR STORIES HIGH! COME DOWN BEFORE YOU FALL!
WHOA, EASY THERE. WE'RE SAIGAMI. HEIGHTS LIKE THIS ARE NO BIG DEAL TO US. WE COULD JUST JUMP DOWN WITHOUT ANY HARM.
WHAT, CAN I GROW WINGS OR SOME-THING?
COURSE NOT. JUST JUMP.
THAT'S FREAKING SUICIDE!
BY USING ASTRAL POWERS, EVEN YOU COULD MAKE IT.
KRATZ KRATZ
AND IF YOU MESS UP, I CAN STILL CATCH YOU, SO—
BUT I TOLD YOU ALREADY, I CAN'T USE MY POWER AT ALL. AND BESIDES, I'M AFRAID OF HEIGHTS.
FEAR OF HEIGHTS? THAT'S KINDA FUNNY.

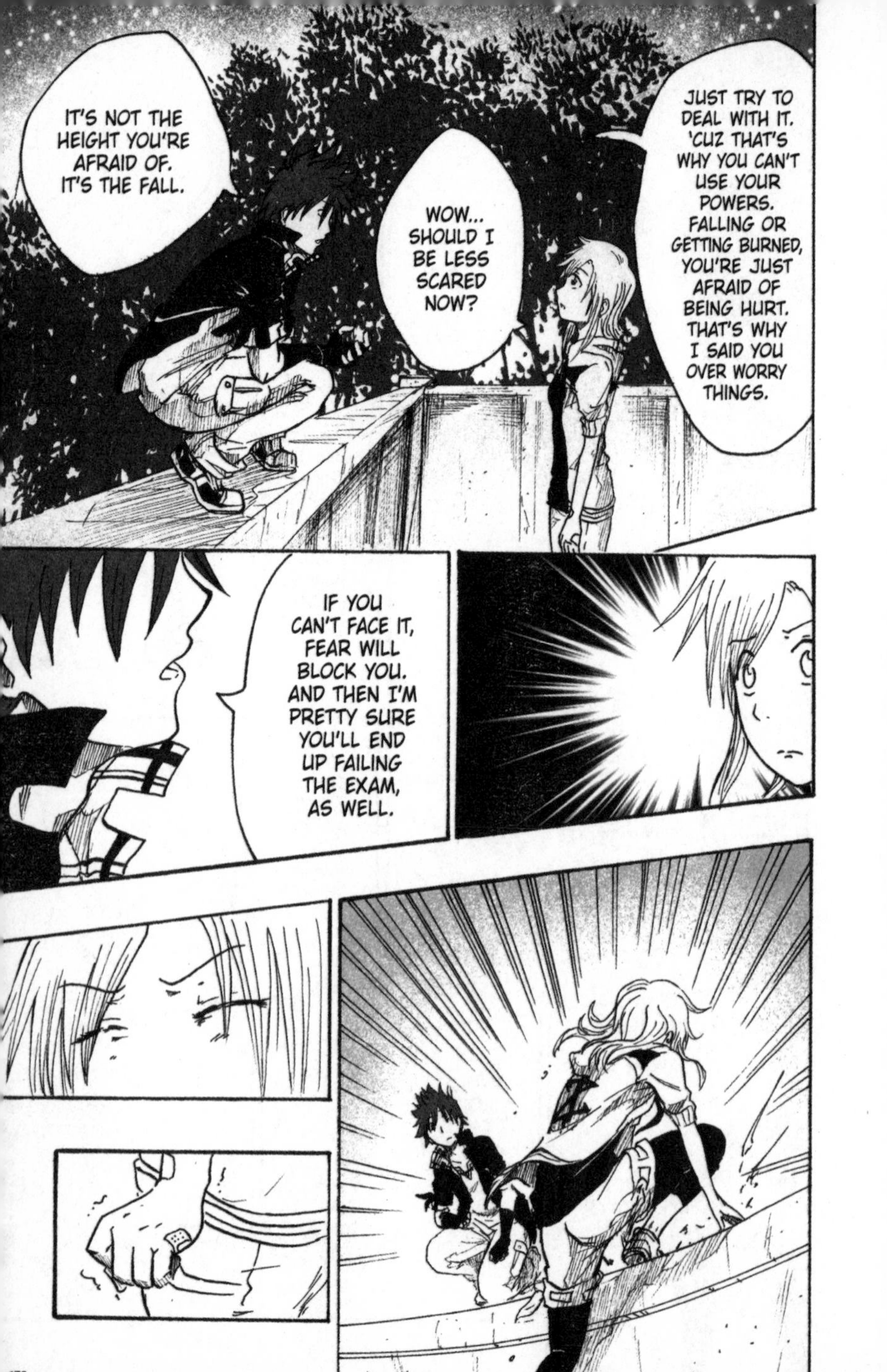
IT'S NOT THE HEIGHT YOU'RE AFRAID OF. IT'S THE FALL.
WOW... SHOULD I BE LESS SCARED NOW?
JUST TRY TO DEAL WITH IT. 'CUZ THAT'S WHY YOU CAN'T USE YOUR POWERS. FALLING OR GETTING BURNED, YOU'RE JUST AFRAID OF BEING HURT. THAT'S WHY I SAID YOU OVER WORRY THINGS.
IF YOU CAN'T FACE IT, FEAR WILL BLOCK YOU. AND THEN I'M PRETTY SURE YOU'LL END UP FAILING THE EXAM, AS WELL.

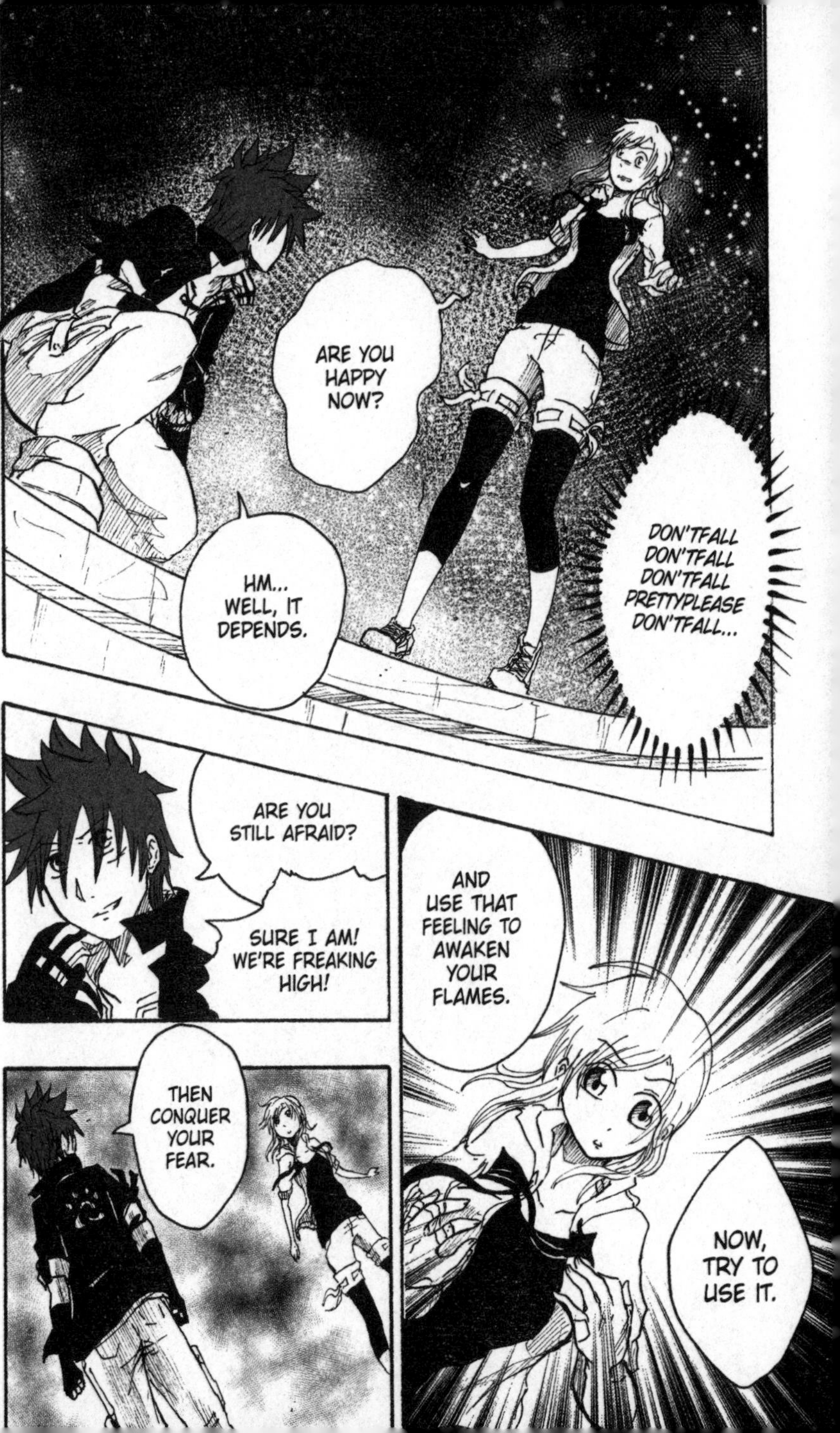
ARE YOU HAPPY NOW?
HM... WELL, IT DEPENDS.
DON'TFALL DON'TFALL DON'TFALL PRETTYPLEASE DON'TFALL...
ARE YOU STILL AFRAID?
SURE I AM! WE'RE FREAKING HIGH!
THEN CONQUER YOUR FEAR.
AND USE THAT FEELING TO AWAKEN YOUR FLAMES.
NOW, TRY TO USE IT.

SAIGAMI

SAIGAMI

Chapter 7: **Trial By Fire**

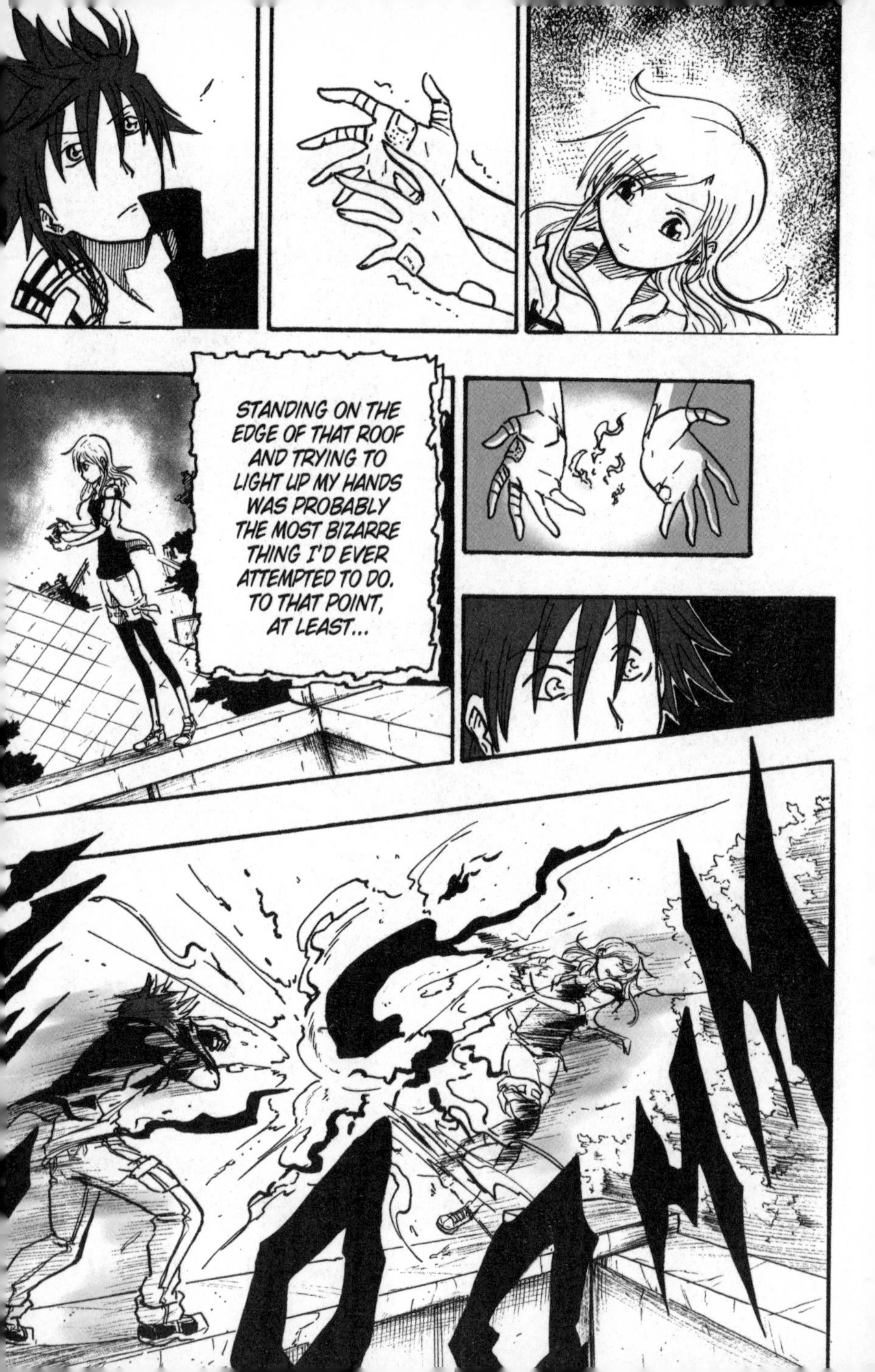
STANDING ON THE EDGE OF THAT ROOF AND TRYING TO LIGHT UP MY HANDS WAS PROBABLY THE MOST BIZARRE THING I'D EVER ATTEMPTED TO DO. TO THAT POINT, AT LEAST...

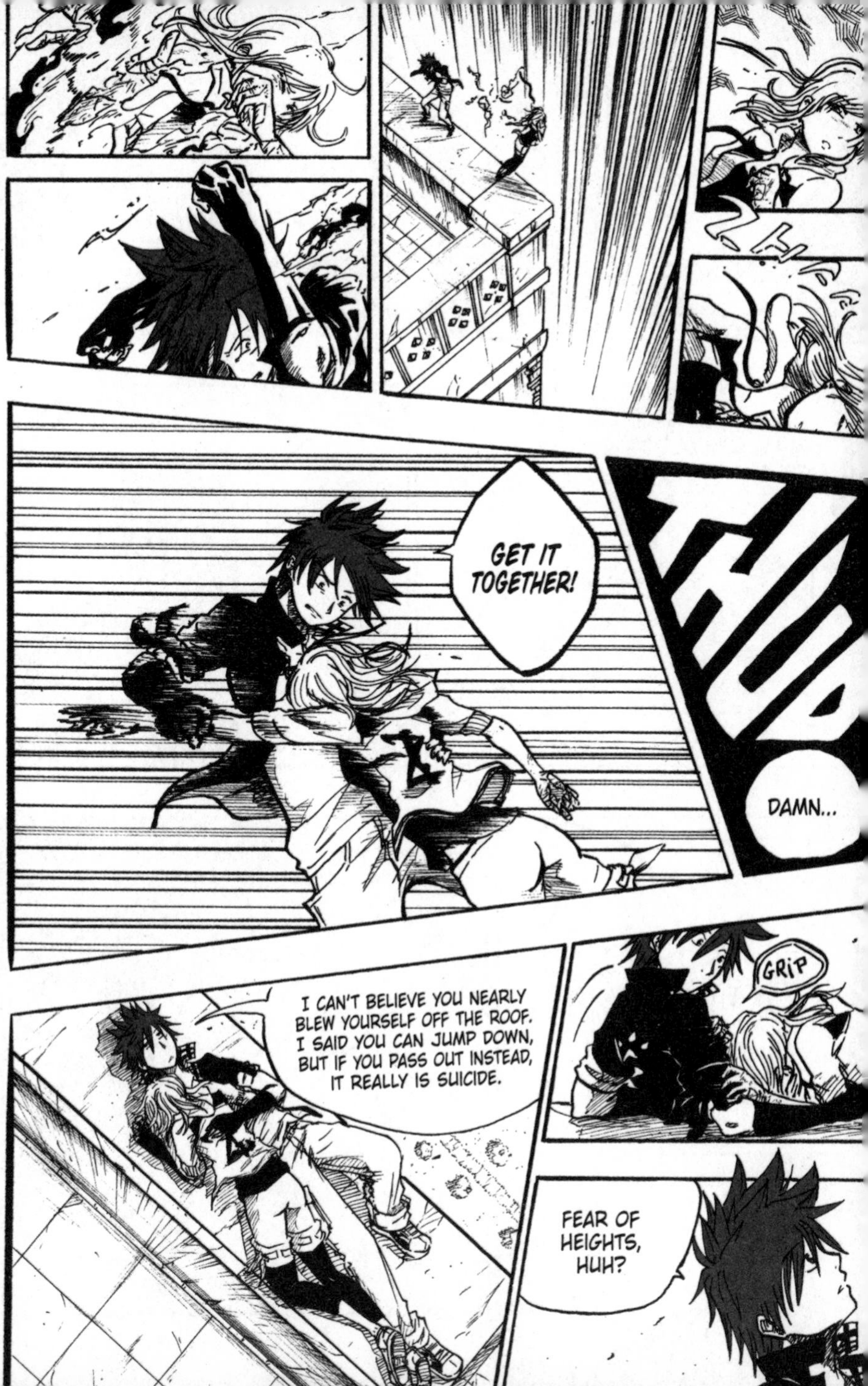
GET IT TOGETHER!
THUD
DAMN...
I CAN'T BELIEVE YOU NEARLY BLEW YOURSELF OFF THE ROOF. I SAID YOU CAN JUMP DOWN, BUT IF YOU PASS OUT INSTEAD, IT REALLY IS SUICIDE.
GRIP
FEAR OF HEIGHTS, HUH?

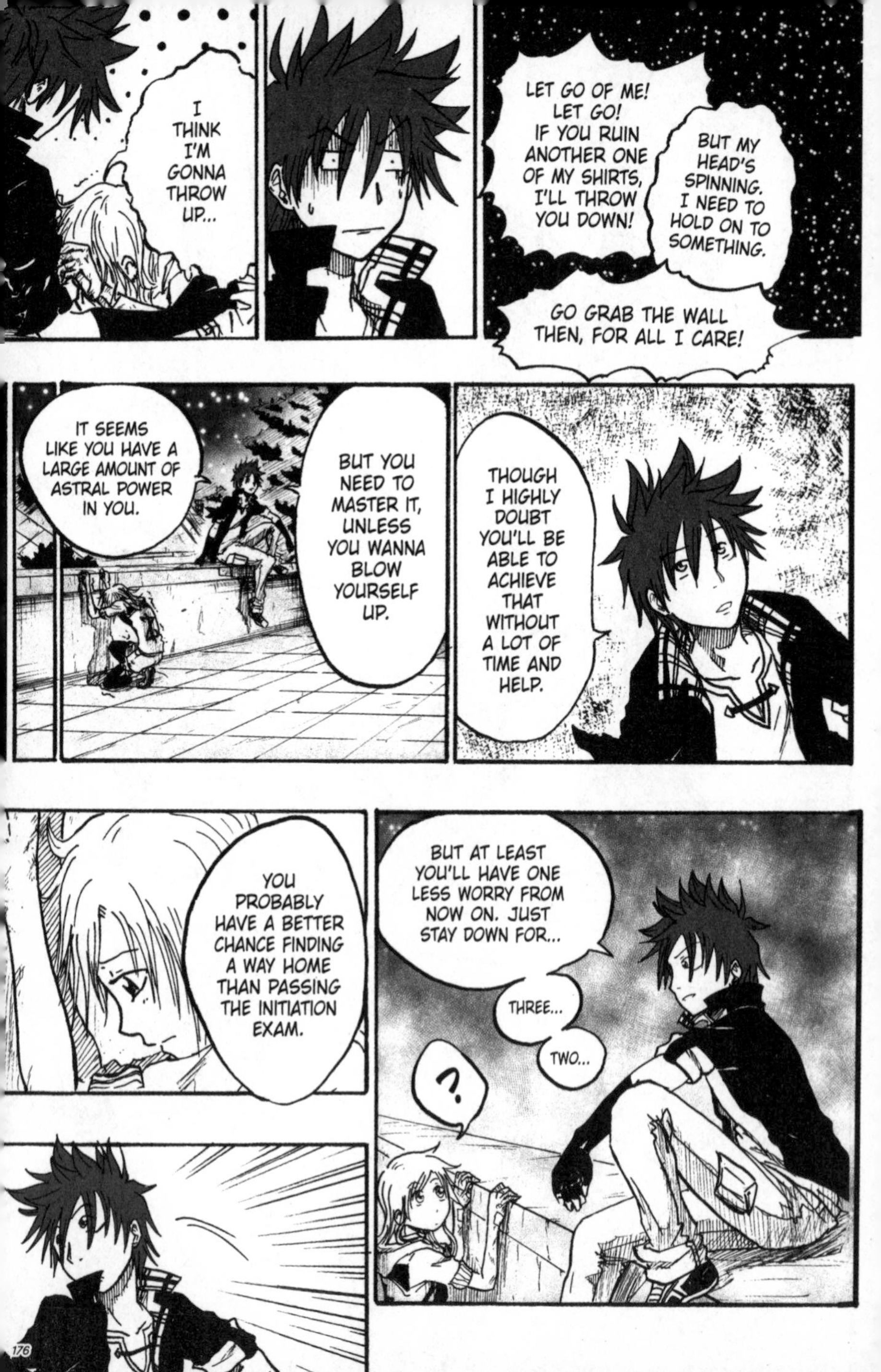
I THINK I'M GONNA THROW UP...
LET GO OF ME! LET GO! IF YOU RUIN ANOTHER ONE OF MY SHIRTS, I'LL THROW YOU DOWN!
BUT MY HEAD'S SPINNING. I NEED TO HOLD ON TO SOMETHING.
GO GRAB THE WALL THEN, FOR ALL I CARE!
IT SEEMS LIKE YOU HAVE A LARGE AMOUNT OF ASTRAL POWER IN YOU.
BUT YOU NEED TO MASTER IT, UNLESS YOU WANNA BLOW YOURSELF UP.
THOUGH I HIGHLY DOUBT YOU'LL BE ABLE TO ACHIEVE THAT WITHOUT A LOT OF TIME AND HELP.
YOU PROBABLY HAVE A BETTER CHANCE FINDING A WAY HOME THAN PASSING THE INITIATION EXAM.
BUT AT LEAST YOU'LL HAVE ONE LESS WORRY FROM NOW ON. JUST STAY DOWN FOR...
THREE...
TWO...
?

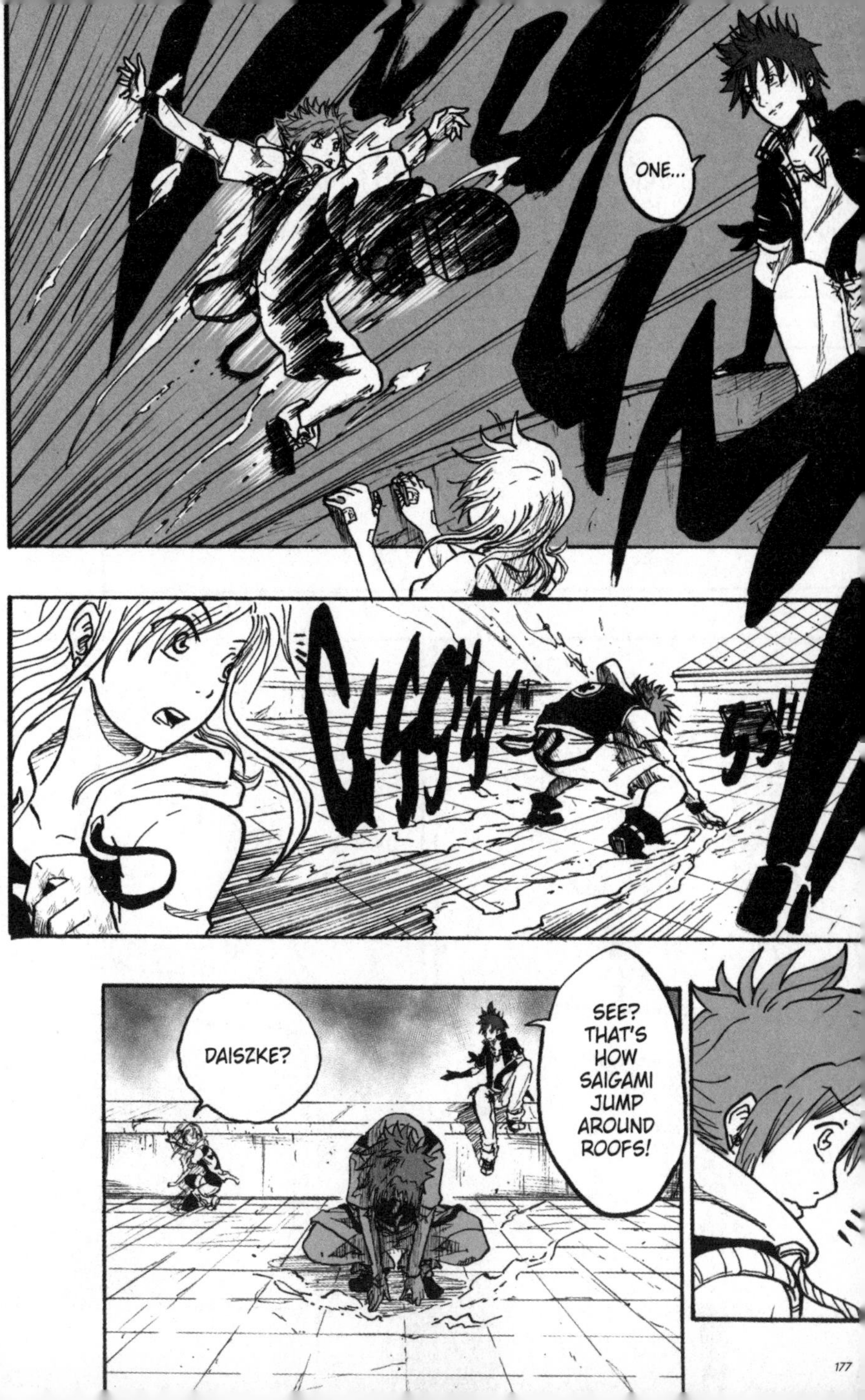

ONE...
DAISZKE?
SEE? THAT'S HOW SAIGAMI JUMP AROUND ROOFS!

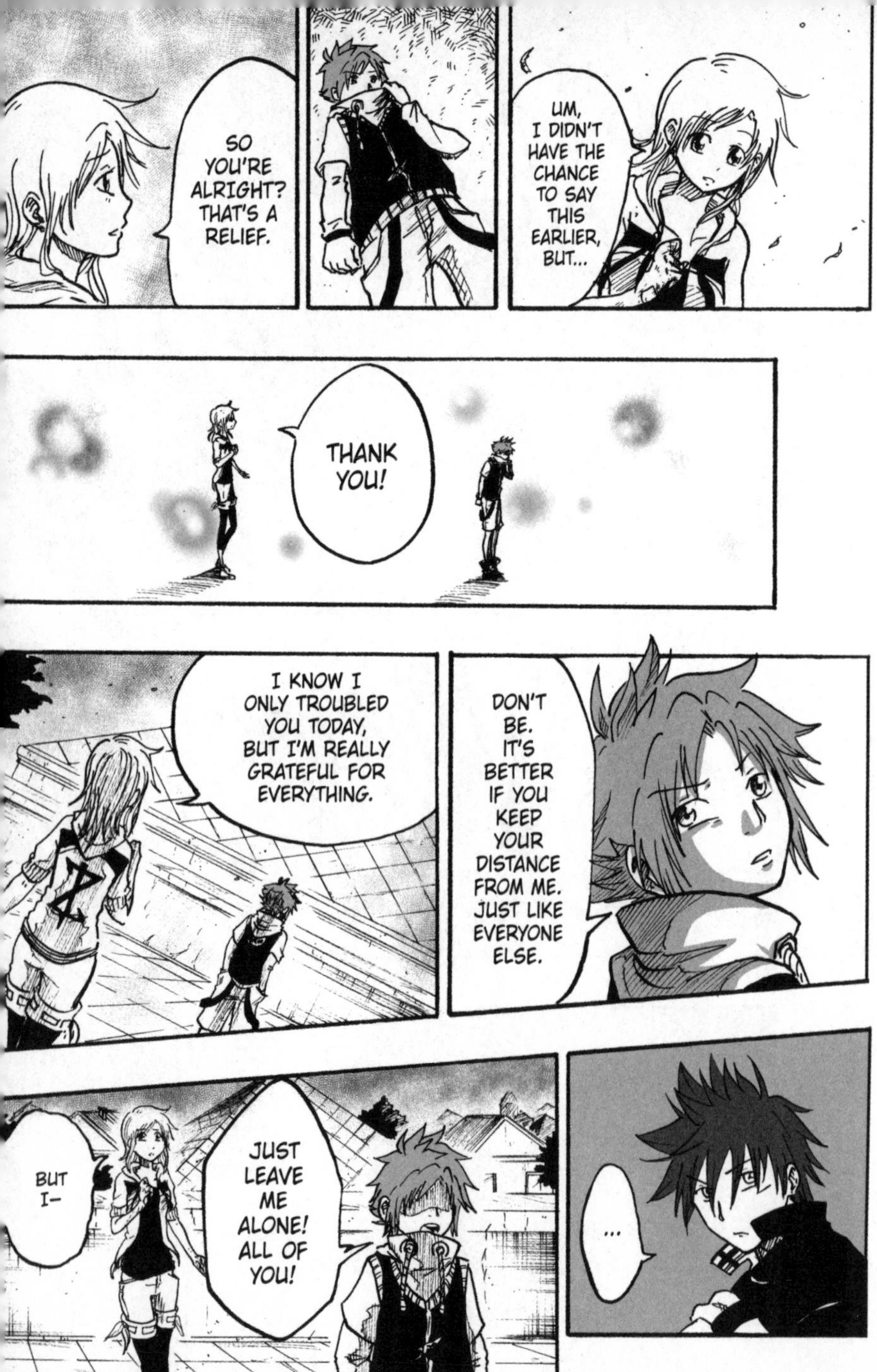
SO YOU'RE ALRIGHT? THAT'S A RELIEF.
UM, I DIDN'T HAVE THE CHANCE TO SAY THIS EARLIER, BUT...
THANK YOU!
I KNOW I ONLY TROUBLED YOU TODAY, BUT I'M REALLY GRATEFUL FOR EVERYTHING.
DON'T BE. IT'S BETTER IF YOU KEEP YOUR DISTANCE FROM ME. JUST LIKE EVERYONE ELSE.
BUT I–
JUST LEAVE ME ALONE! ALL OF YOU!
...

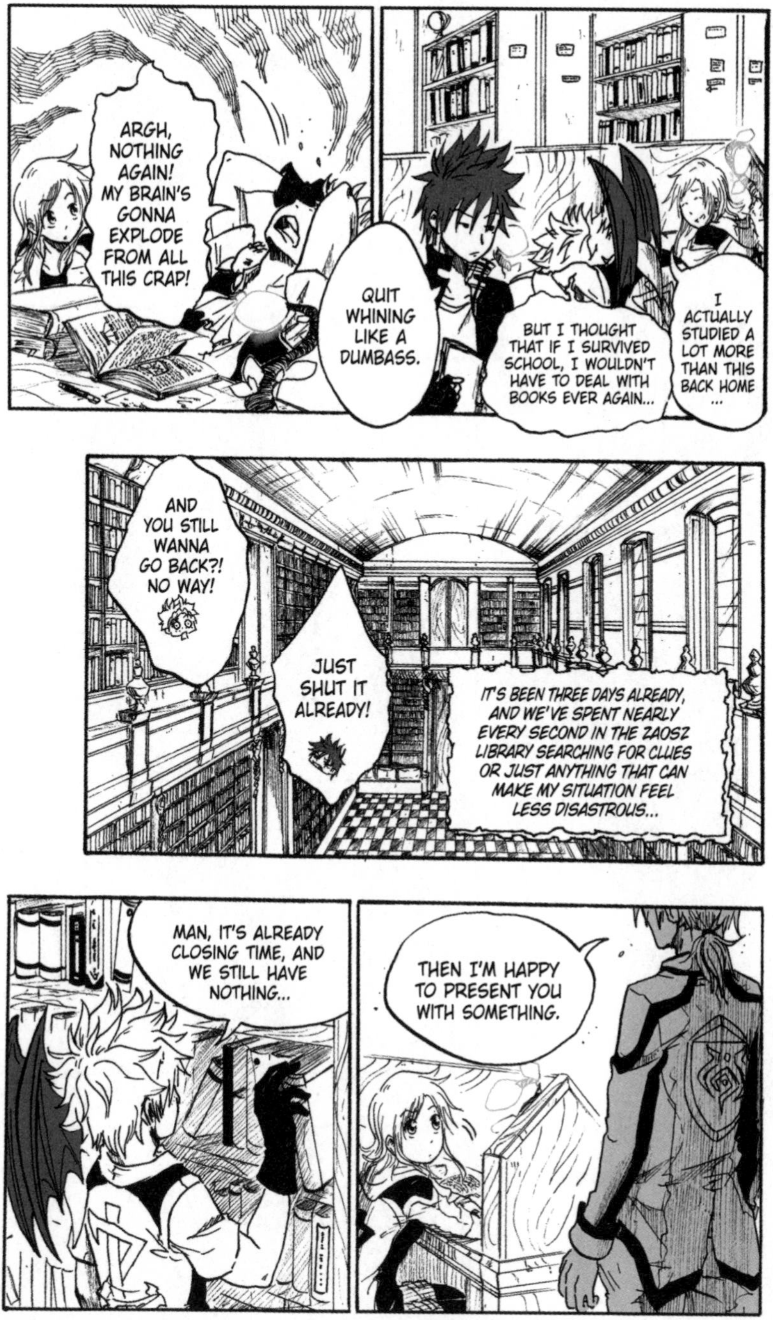
ARGH, NOTHING AGAIN! MY BRAIN'S GONNA EXPLODE FROM ALL THIS CRAP!
QUIT WHINING LIKE A DUMBASS.
BUT I THOUGHT THAT IF I SURVIVED SCHOOL, I WOULDN'T HAVE TO DEAL WITH BOOKS EVER AGAIN...
I ACTUALLY STUDIED A LOT MORE THAN THIS BACK HOME ...
AND YOU STILL WANNA GO BACK?! NO WAY!
JUST SHUT IT ALREADY!
IT'S BEEN THREE DAYS ALREADY, AND WE'VE SPENT NEARLY EVERY SECOND IN THE ZAOSZ LIBRARY SEARCHING FOR CLUES OR JUST ANYTHING THAT CAN MAKE MY SITUATION FEEL LESS DISASTROUS...
MAN, IT'S ALREADY CLOSING TIME, AND WE STILL HAVE NOTHING...
THEN I'M HAPPY TO PRESENT YOU WITH SOMETHING.

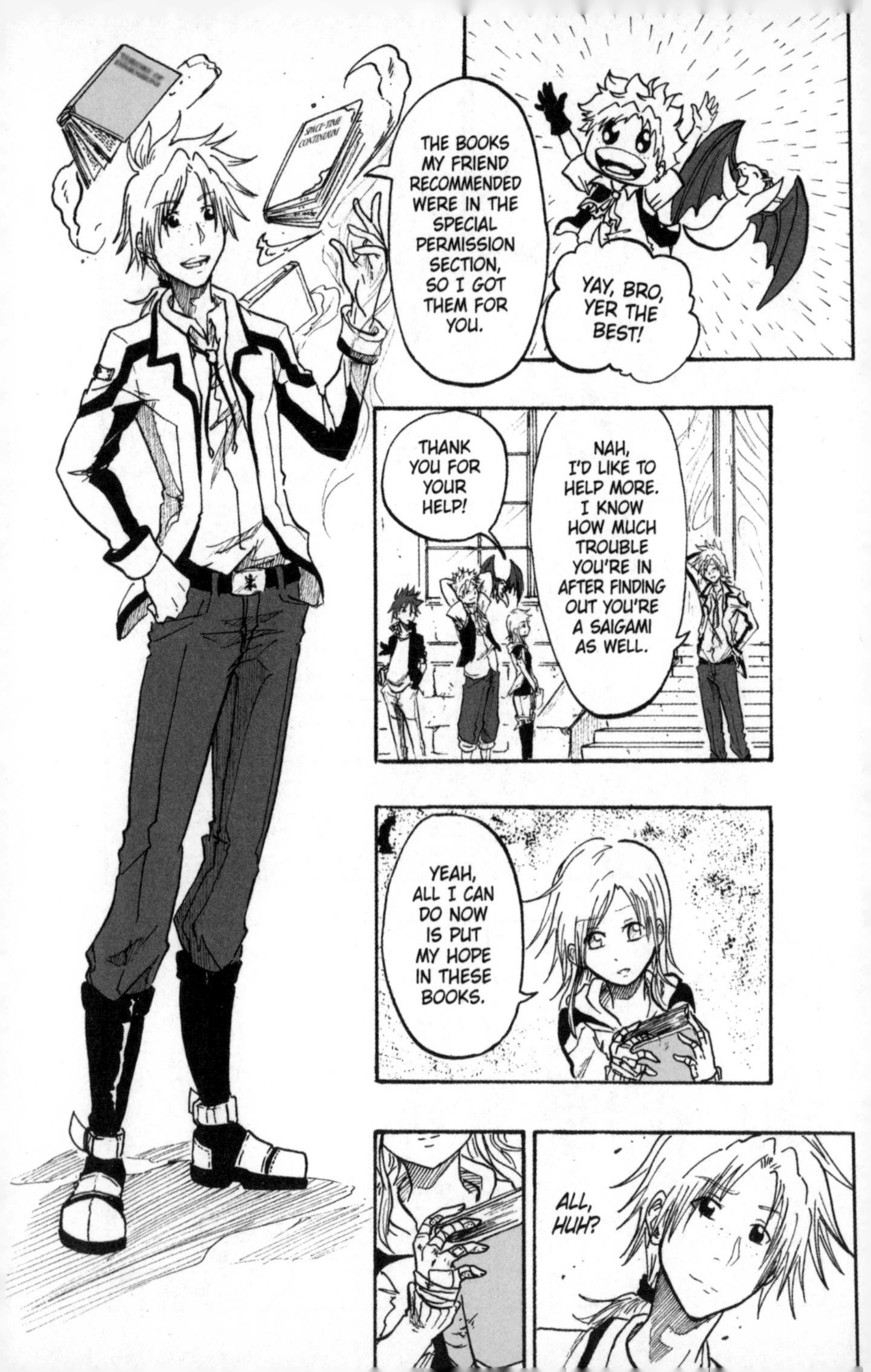
SPACE-TIME CONTINUUM
THE BOOKS MY FRIEND RECOMMENDED WERE IN THE SPECIAL PERMISSION SECTION, SO I GOT THEM FOR YOU.
YAY, BRO, YER THE BEST!
THANK YOU FOR YOUR HELP!
NAH, I'D LIKE TO HELP MORE. I KNOW HOW MUCH TROUBLE YOU'RE IN AFTER FINDING OUT YOU'RE A SAIGAMI AS WELL.
YEAH, ALL I CAN DO NOW IS PUT MY HOPE IN THESE BOOKS.
ALL, HUH?

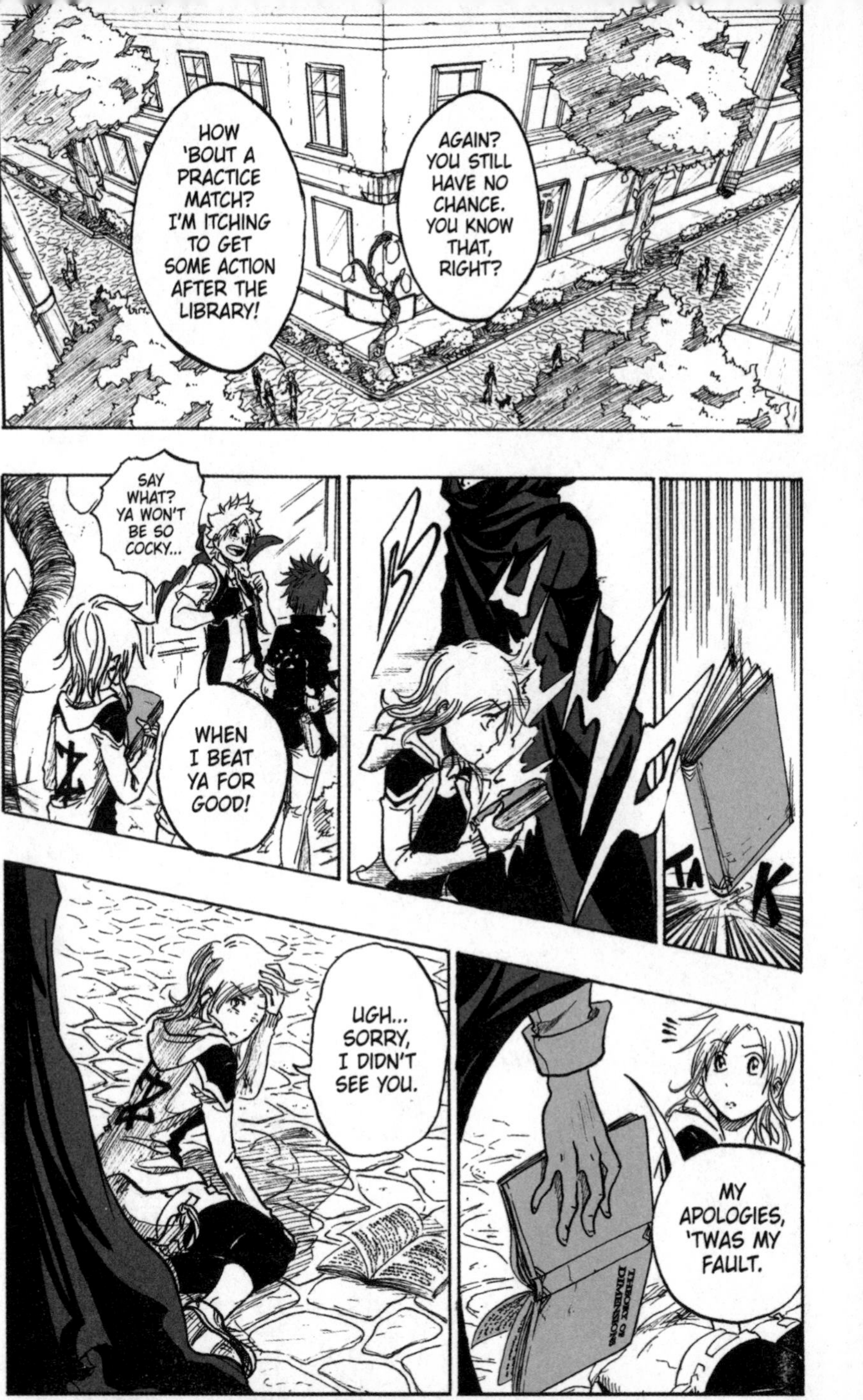
HOW 'BOUT A PRACTICE MATCH? I'M ITCHING TO GET SOME ACTION AFTER THE LIBRARY!
AGAIN? YOU STILL HAVE NO CHANCE. YOU KNOW THAT, RIGHT?
SAY WHAT? YA WON'T BE SO COCKY...
WHEN I BEAT YA FOR GOOD!
TAK
UGH... SORRY, I DIDN'T SEE YOU.
THEORY OF DIMENSIONS
MY APOLOGIES, 'TWAS MY FAULT.

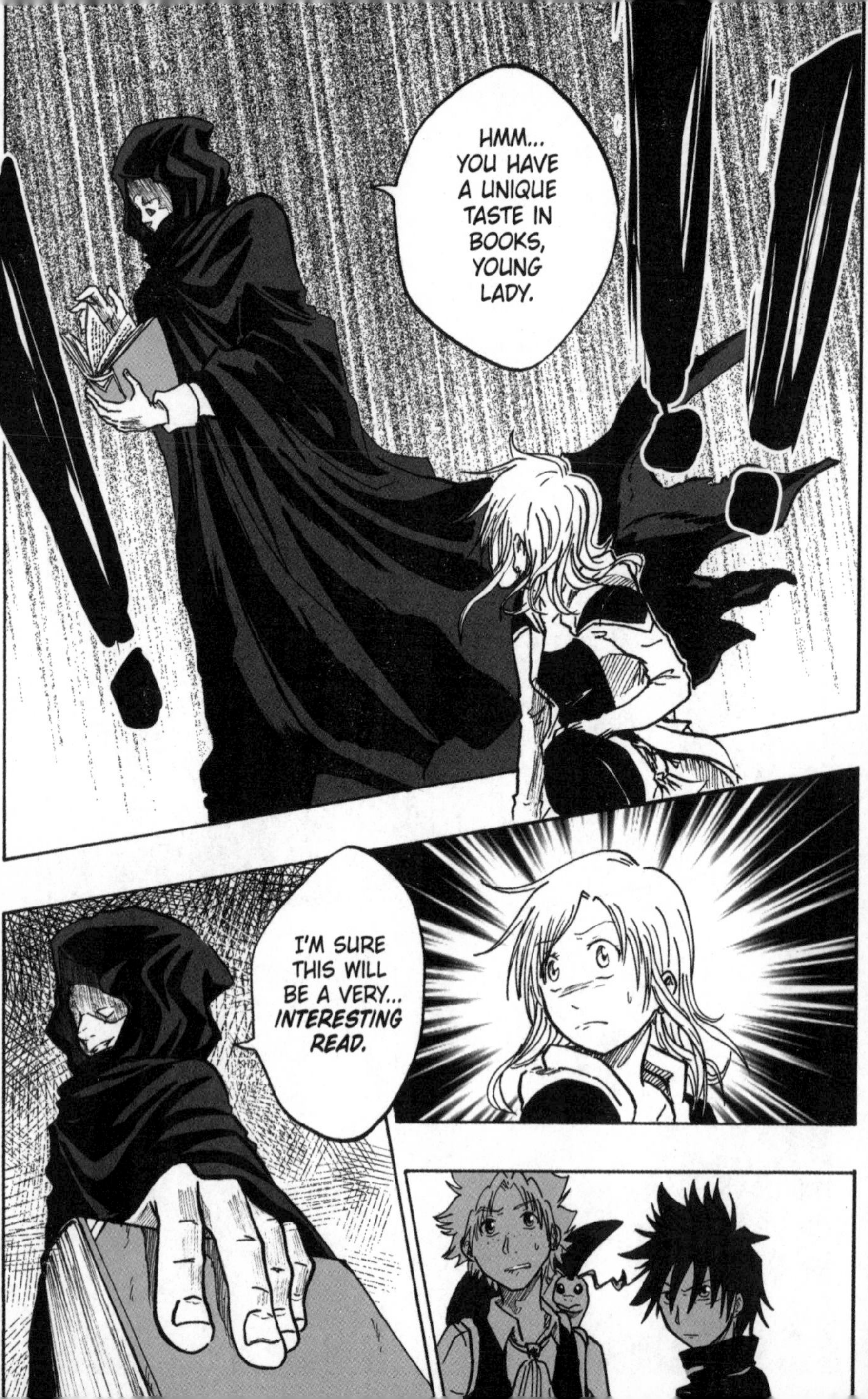
HMM... YOU HAVE A UNIQUE TASTE IN BOOKS, YOUNG LADY.
I'M SURE THIS WILL BE A VERY... *INTERESTING READ.*

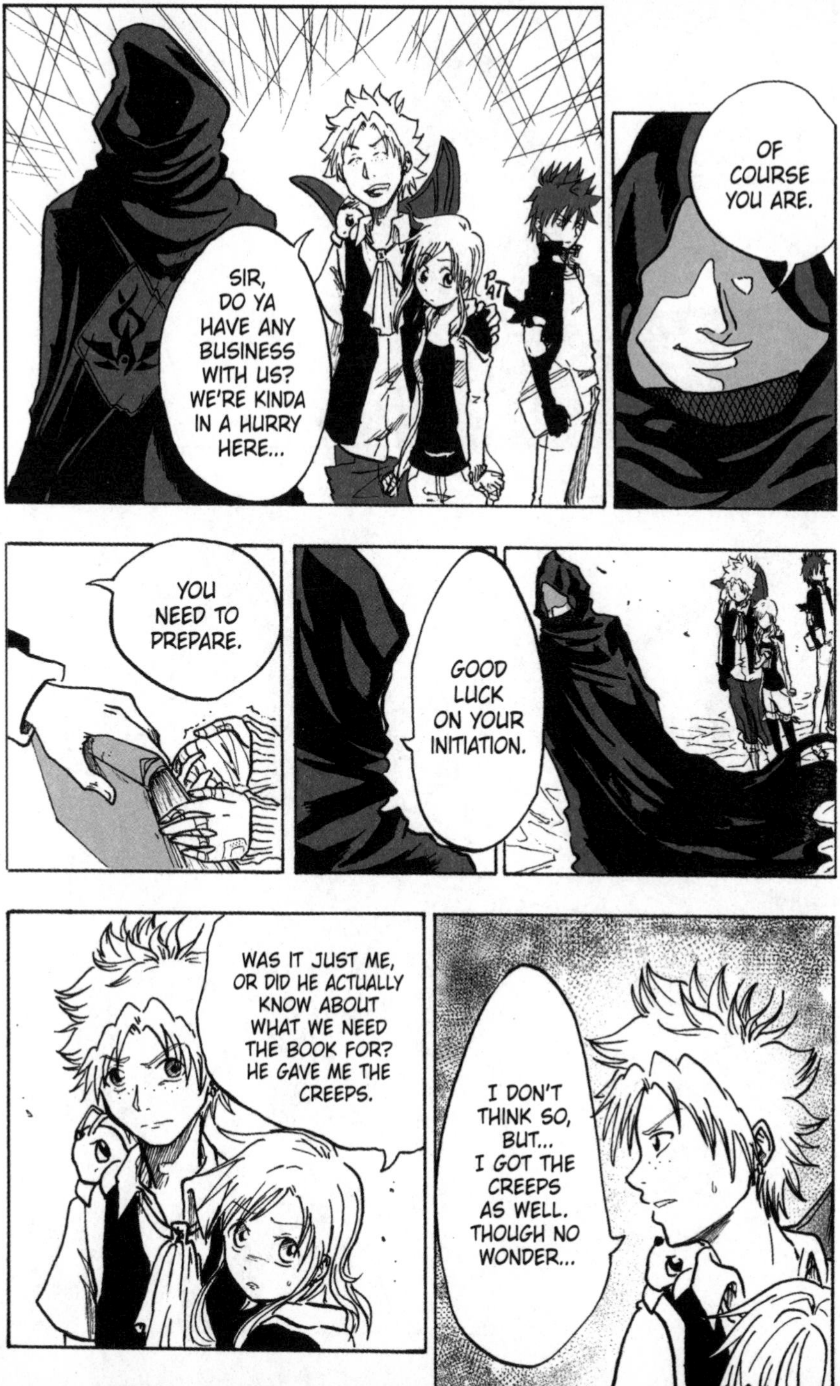
SIR, DO YA HAVE ANY BUSINESS WITH US? WE'RE KINDA IN A HURRY HERE...
PAT
OF COURSE YOU ARE.
YOU NEED TO PREPARE.
GOOD LUCK ON YOUR INITIATION.
WAS IT JUST ME, OR DID HE ACTUALLY KNOW ABOUT WHAT WE NEED THE BOOK FOR? HE GAVE ME THE CREEPS.
I DON'T THINK SO, BUT... I GOT THE CREEPS AS WELL. THOUGH NO WONDER...

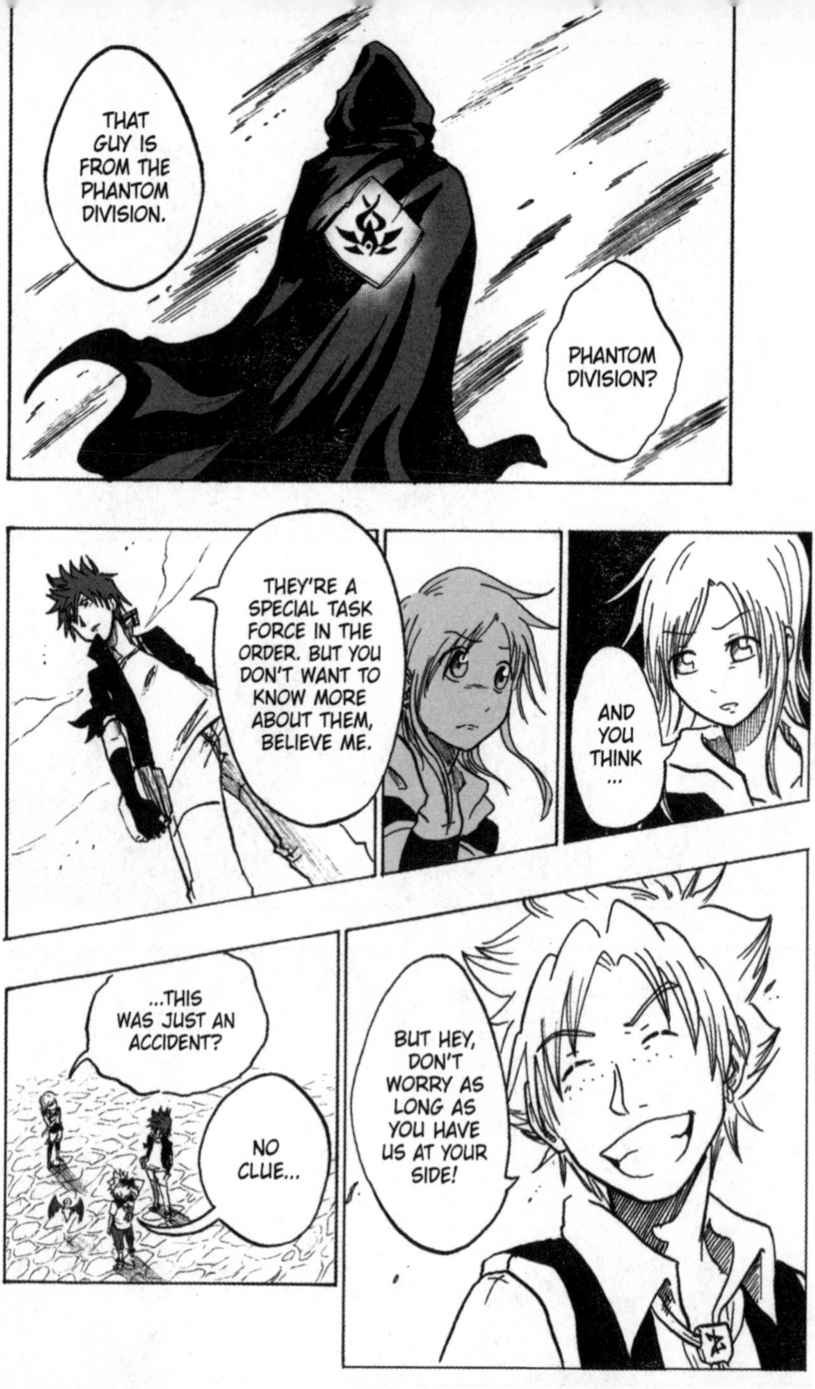
THAT GUY IS FROM THE PHANTOM DIVISION.
PHANTOM DIVISION?
THEY'RE A SPECIAL TASK FORCE IN THE ORDER. BUT YOU DON'T WANT TO KNOW MORE ABOUT THEM, BELIEVE ME.
AND YOU THINK ...
...THIS WAS JUST AN ACCIDENT?
NO CLUE...
BUT HEY, DON'T WORRY AS LONG AS YOU HAVE US AT YOUR SIDE!

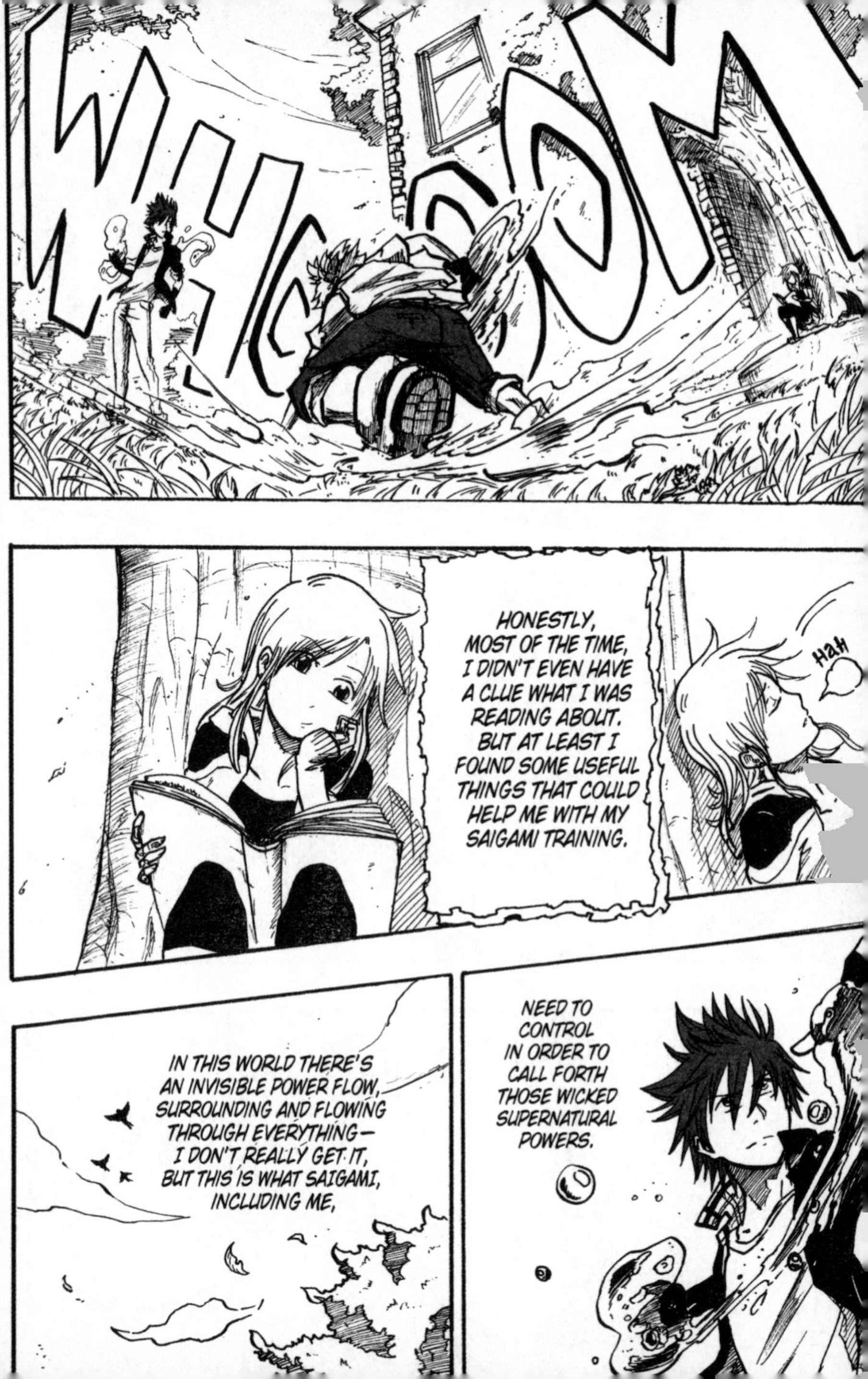
WHOOOM
HONESTLY, MOST OF THE TIME, I DIDN'T EVEN HAVE A CLUE WHAT I WAS READING ABOUT. BUT AT LEAST I FOUND SOME USEFUL THINGS THAT COULD HELP ME WITH MY SAIGAMI TRAINING.
Hah
IN THIS WORLD THERE'S AN INVISIBLE POWER FLOW, SURROUNDING AND FLOWING THROUGH EVERYTHING— I DON'T REALLY GET IT, BUT THIS IS WHAT SAIGAMI, INCLUDING ME,
NEED TO CONTROL IN ORDER TO CALL FORTH THOSE WICKED SUPERNATURAL POWERS.

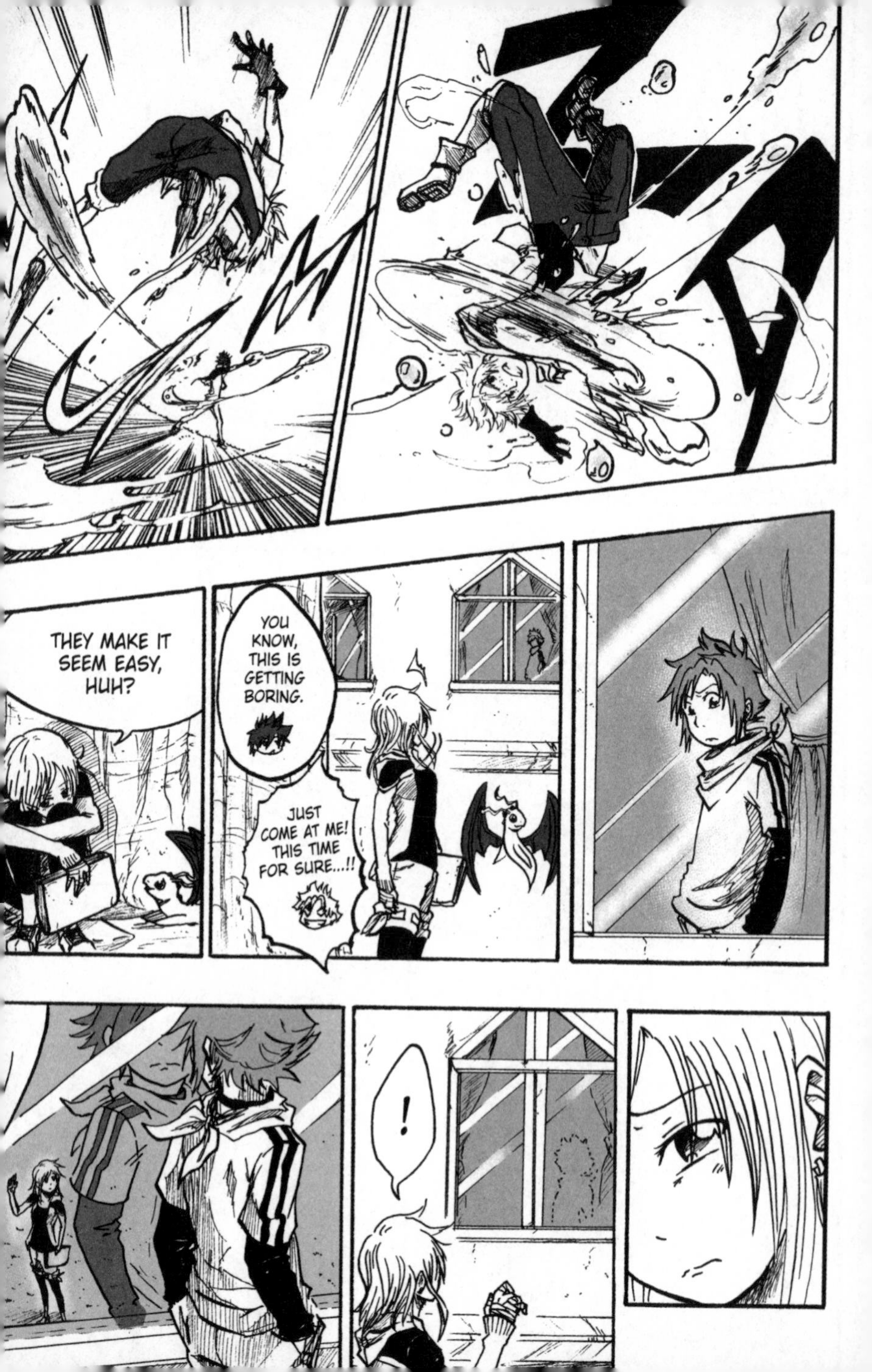
THEY MAKE IT SEEM EASY, HUH?
YOU KNOW, THIS IS GETTING BORING.
JUST COME AT ME! THIS TIME FOR SURE...!!
!

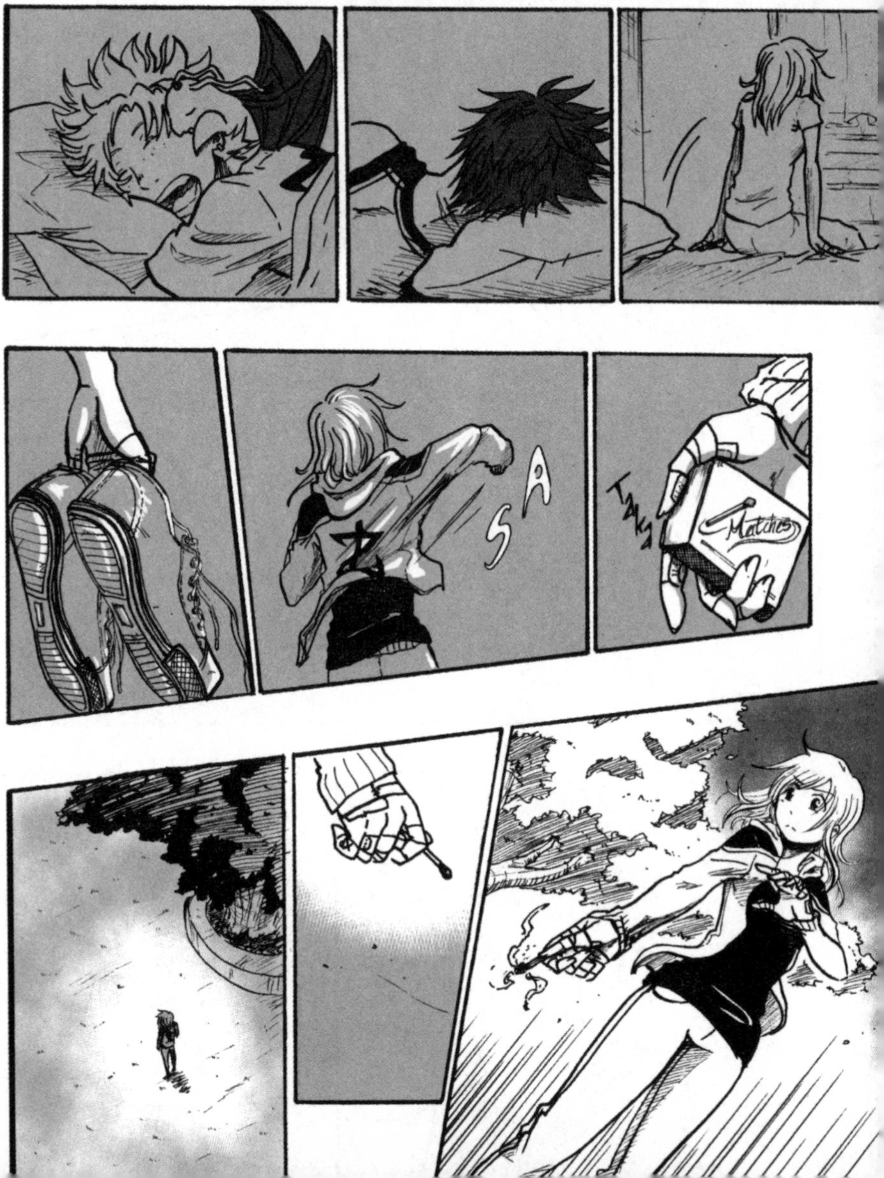
SA
TAKA
Matches

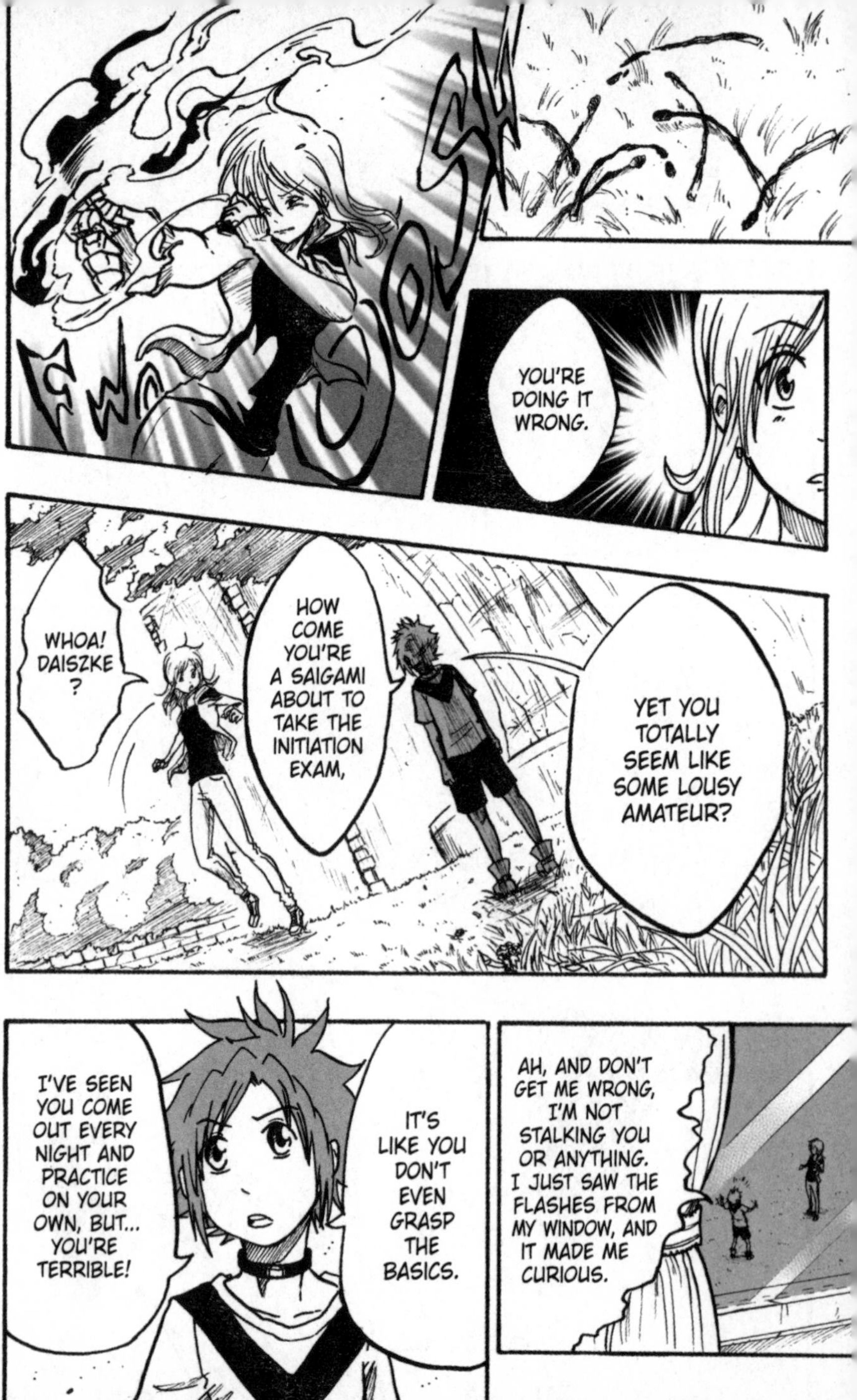
YOU'RE DOING IT WRONG.
WHOA! DAISZKE ?
HOW COME YOU'RE A SAIGAMI ABOUT TO TAKE THE INITIATION EXAM,
YET YOU TOTALLY SEEM LIKE SOME LOUSY AMATEUR?
I'VE SEEN YOU COME OUT EVERY NIGHT AND PRACTICE ON YOUR OWN, BUT... YOU'RE TERRIBLE!
IT'S LIKE YOU DON'T EVEN GRASP THE BASICS.
AH, AND DON'T GET ME WRONG, I'M NOT STALKING YOU OR ANYTHING. I JUST SAW THE FLASHES FROM MY WINDOW, AND IT MADE ME CURIOUS.

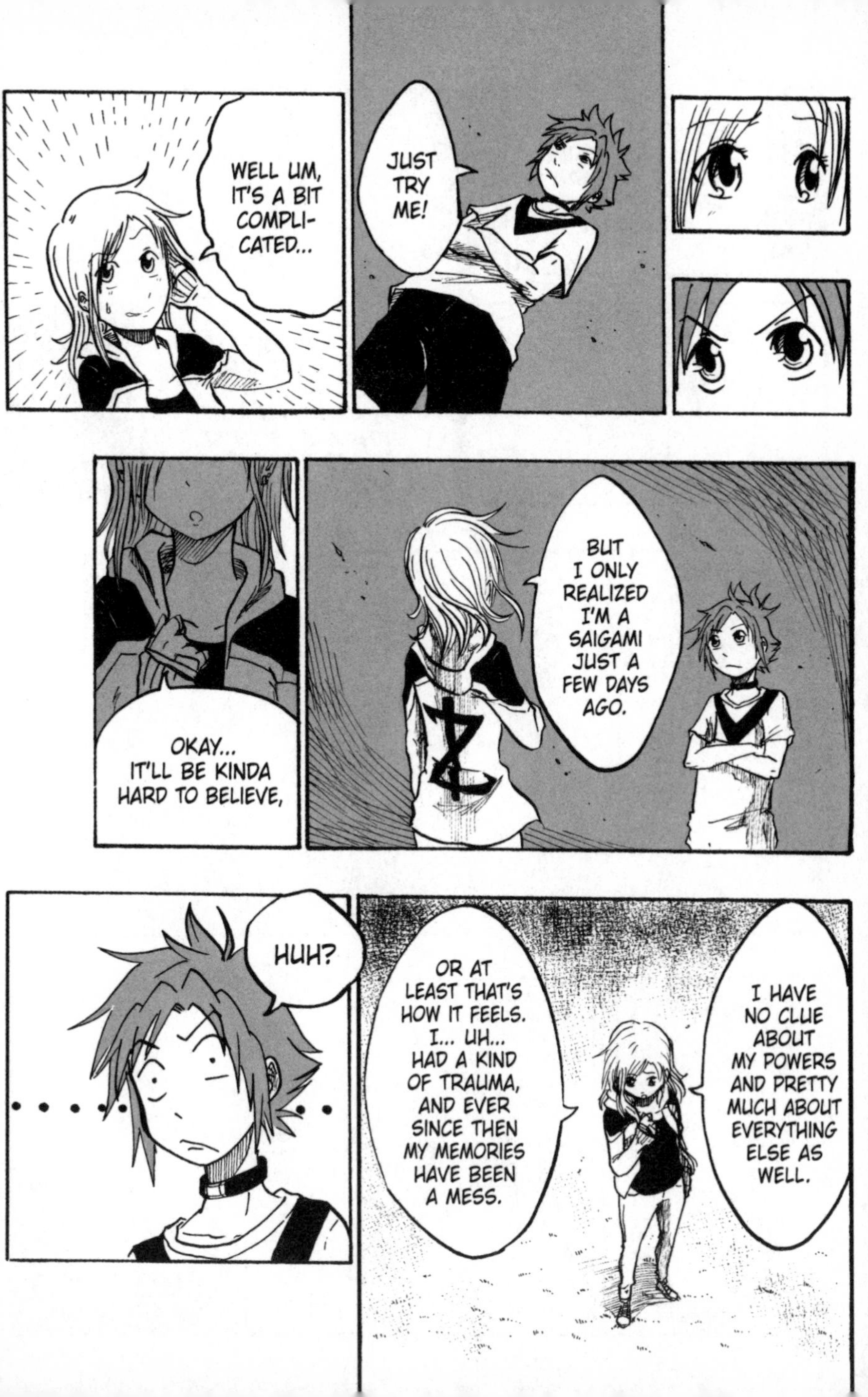
WELL UM, IT'S A BIT COMPLI-CATED...
JUST TRY ME!
OKAY... IT'LL BE KINDA HARD TO BELIEVE,
BUT I ONLY REALIZED I'M A SAIGAMI JUST A FEW DAYS AGO.
HUH?
OR AT LEAST THAT'S HOW IT FEELS. I... UH... HAD A KIND OF TRAUMA, AND EVER SINCE THEN MY MEMORIES HAVE BEEN A MESS.
I HAVE NO CLUE ABOUT MY POWERS AND PRETTY MUCH ABOUT EVERYTHING ELSE AS WELL.

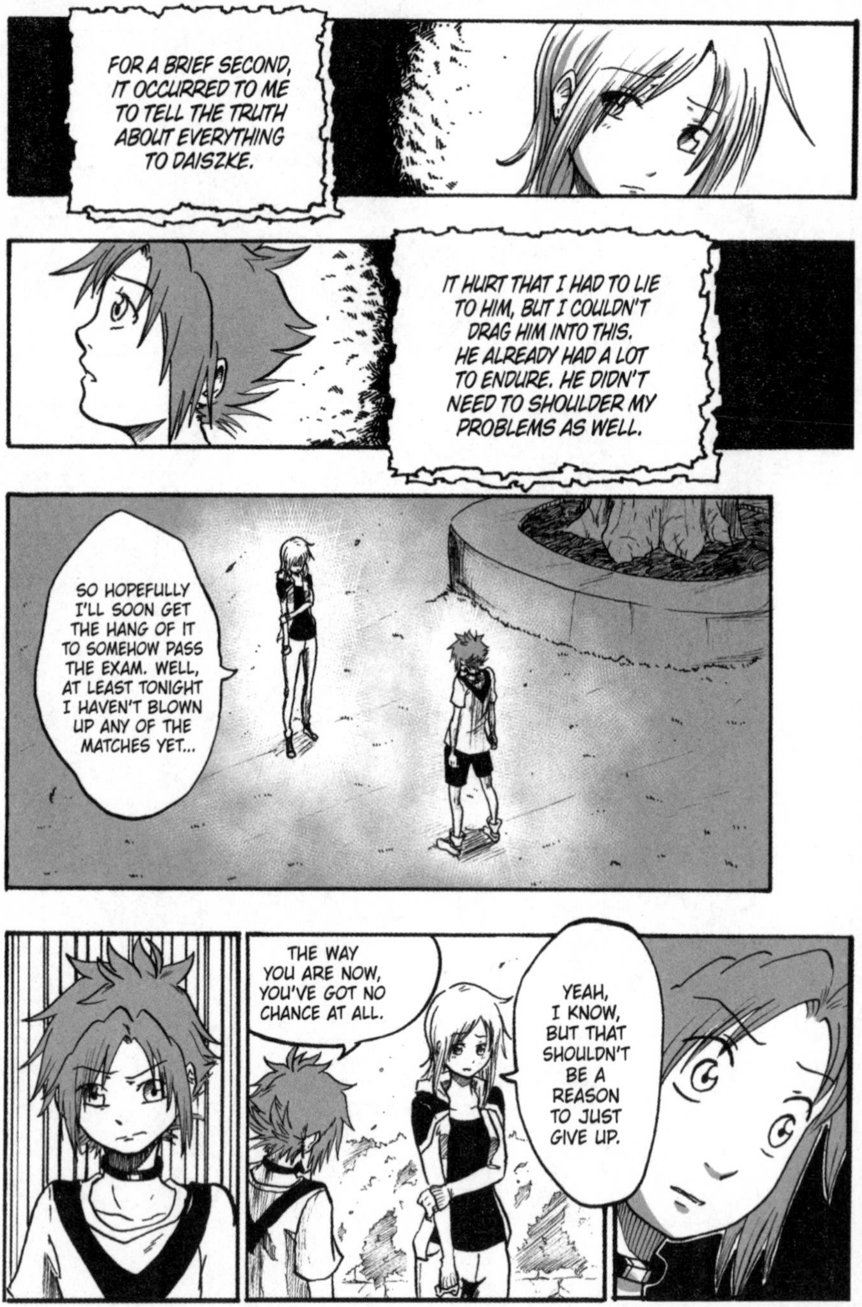
FOR A BRIEF SECOND, IT OCCURRED TO ME TO TELL THE TRUTH ABOUT EVERYTHING TO DAISZKE.
IT HURT THAT I HAD TO LIE TO HIM, BUT I COULDN'T DRAG HIM INTO THIS. HE ALREADY HAD A LOT TO ENDURE. HE DIDN'T NEED TO SHOULDER MY PROBLEMS AS WELL.
SO HOPEFULLY I'LL SOON GET THE HANG OF IT TO SOMEHOW PASS THE EXAM. WELL, AT LEAST TONIGHT I HAVEN'T BLOWN UP ANY OF THE MATCHES YET...
THE WAY YOU ARE NOW, YOU'VE GOT NO CHANCE AT ALL.
YEAH, I KNOW, BUT THAT SHOULDN'T BE A REASON TO JUST GIVE UP.

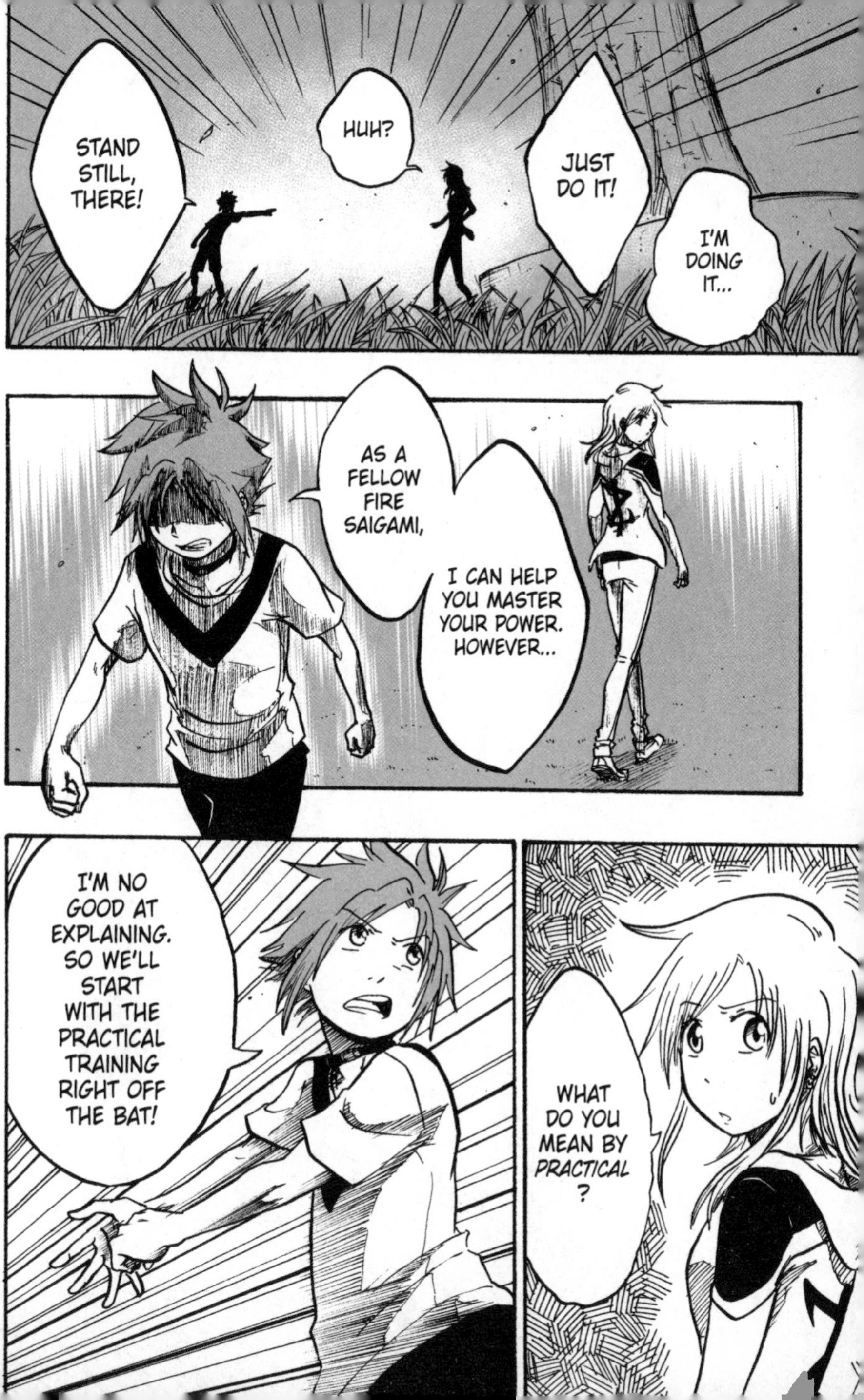
STAND STILL, THERE!
HUH?
JUST DO IT!
I'M DOING IT...
AS A FELLOW FIRE SAIGAMI,
I CAN HELP YOU MASTER YOUR POWER. HOWEVER...
I'M NO GOOD AT EXPLAINING. SO WE'LL START WITH THE PRACTICAL TRAINING RIGHT OFF THE BAT!
WHAT DO YOU MEAN BY *PRACTICAL*?

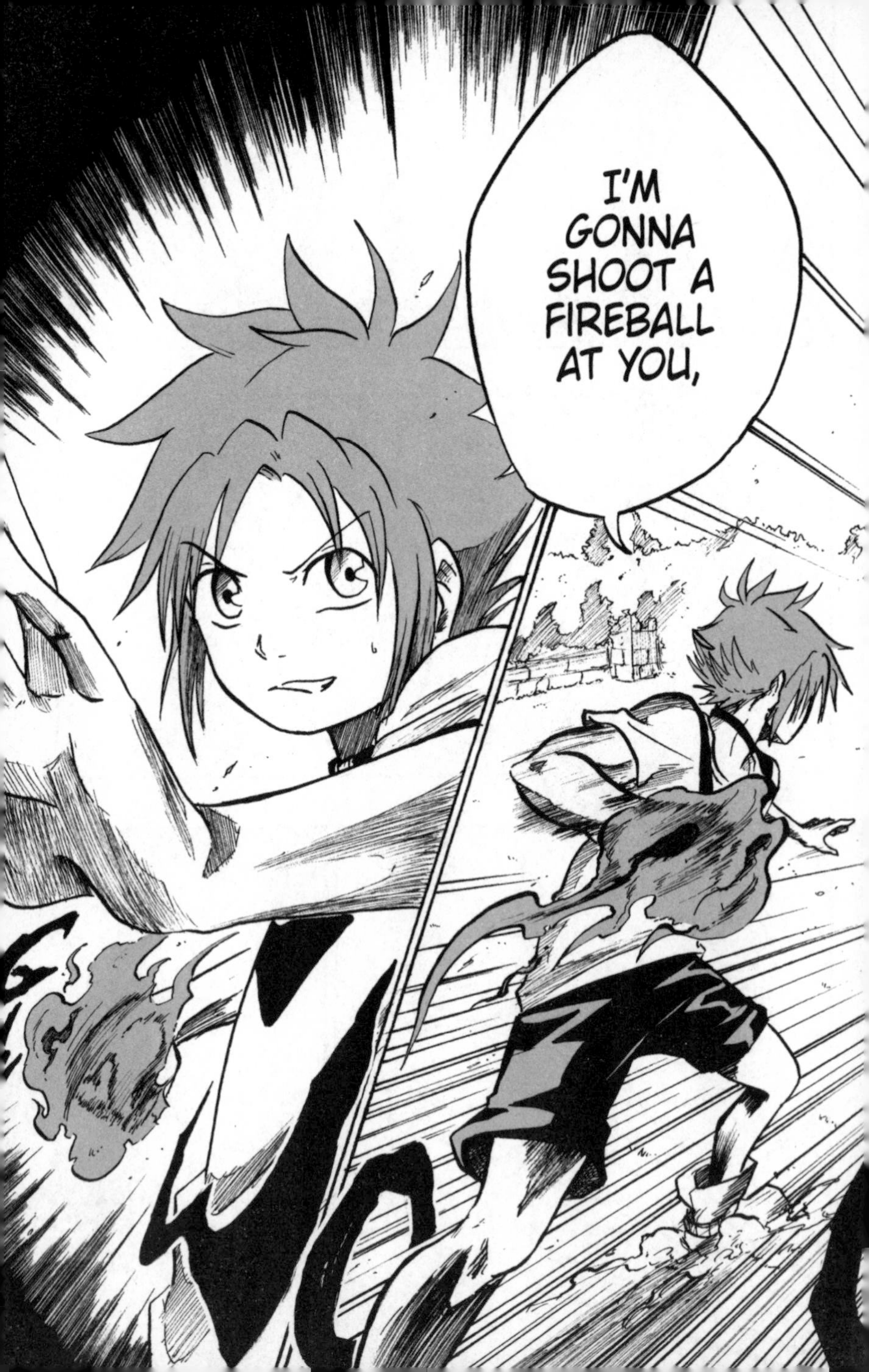
I'M GONNA SHOOT A FIREBALL AT YOU,

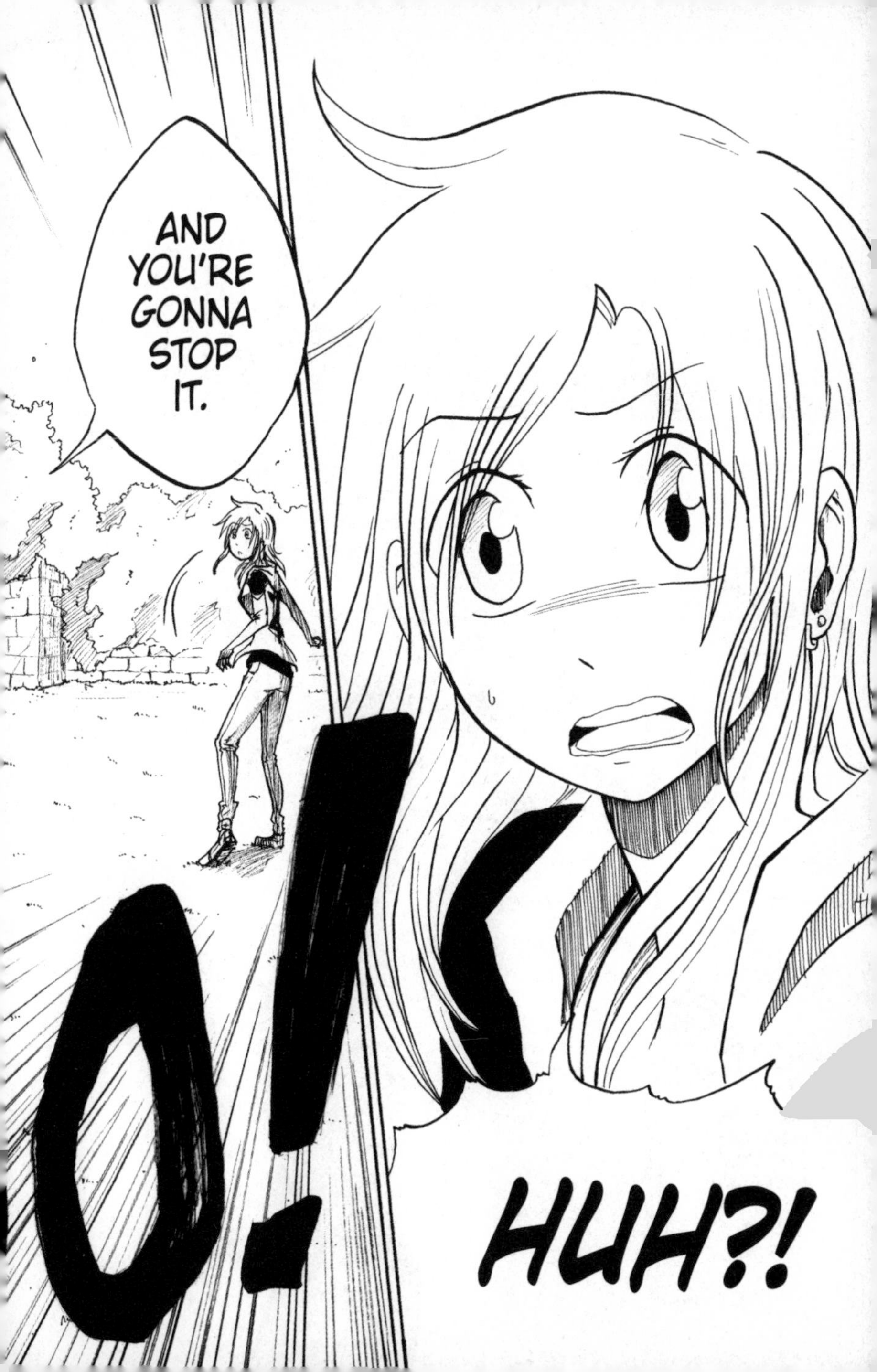
AND YOU'RE GONNA STOP IT.
O!
HUH?!

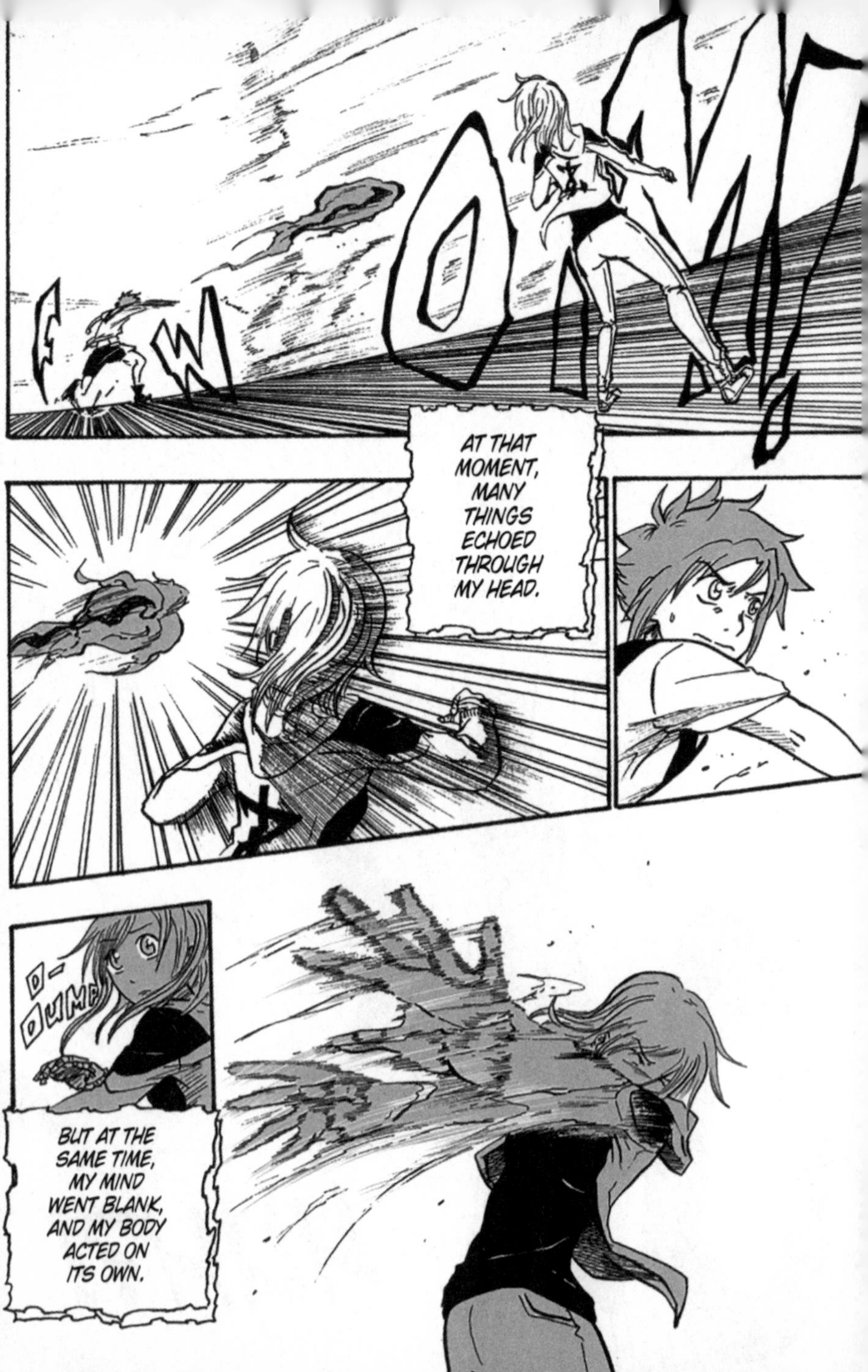
FWOOM!
AT THAT MOMENT, MANY THINGS ECHOED THROUGH MY HEAD.
D-DUMP
BUT AT THE SAME TIME, MY MIND WENT BLANK, AND MY BODY ACTED ON ITS OWN.

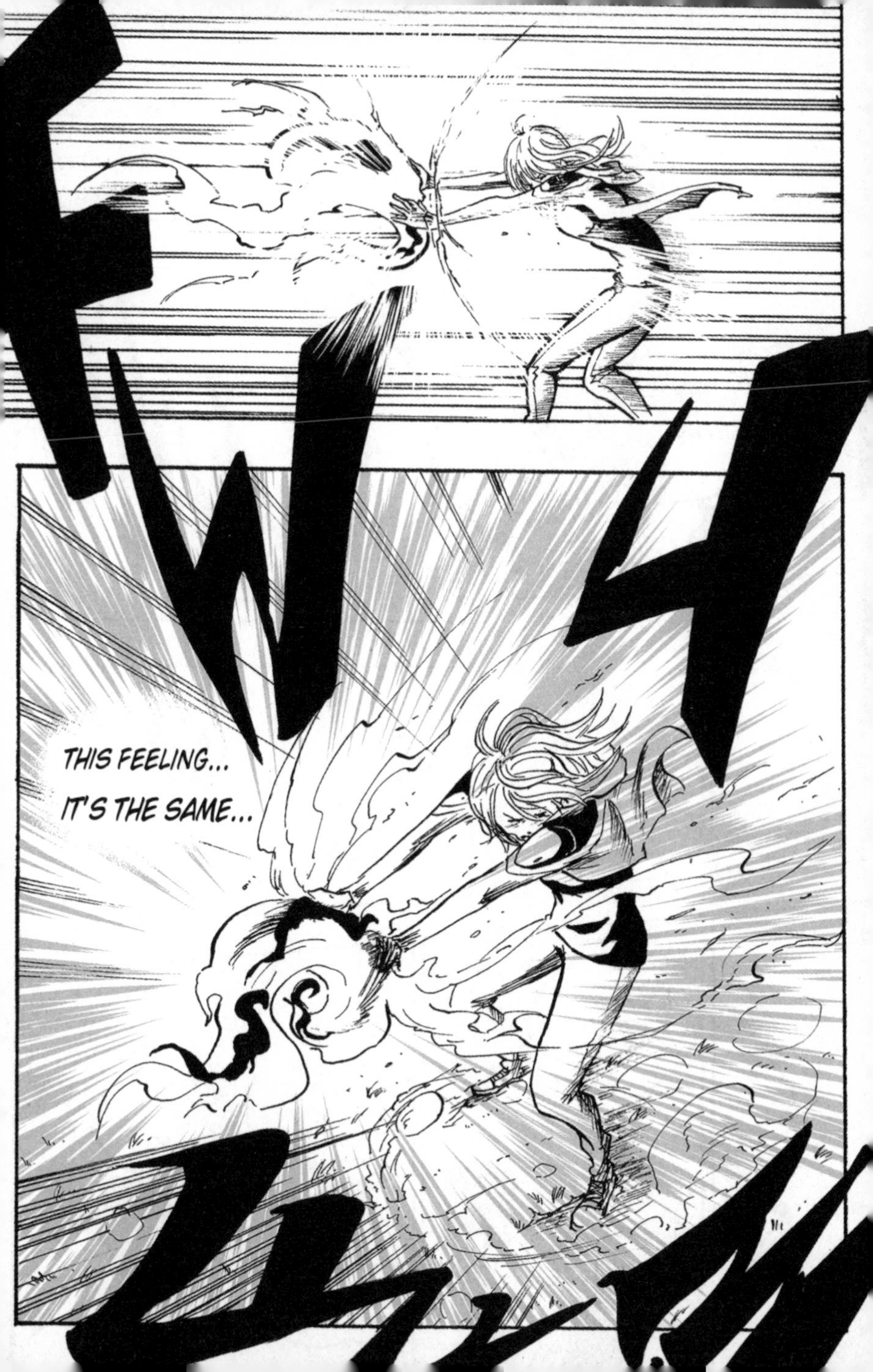
THIS FEELING...
IT'S THE SAME...

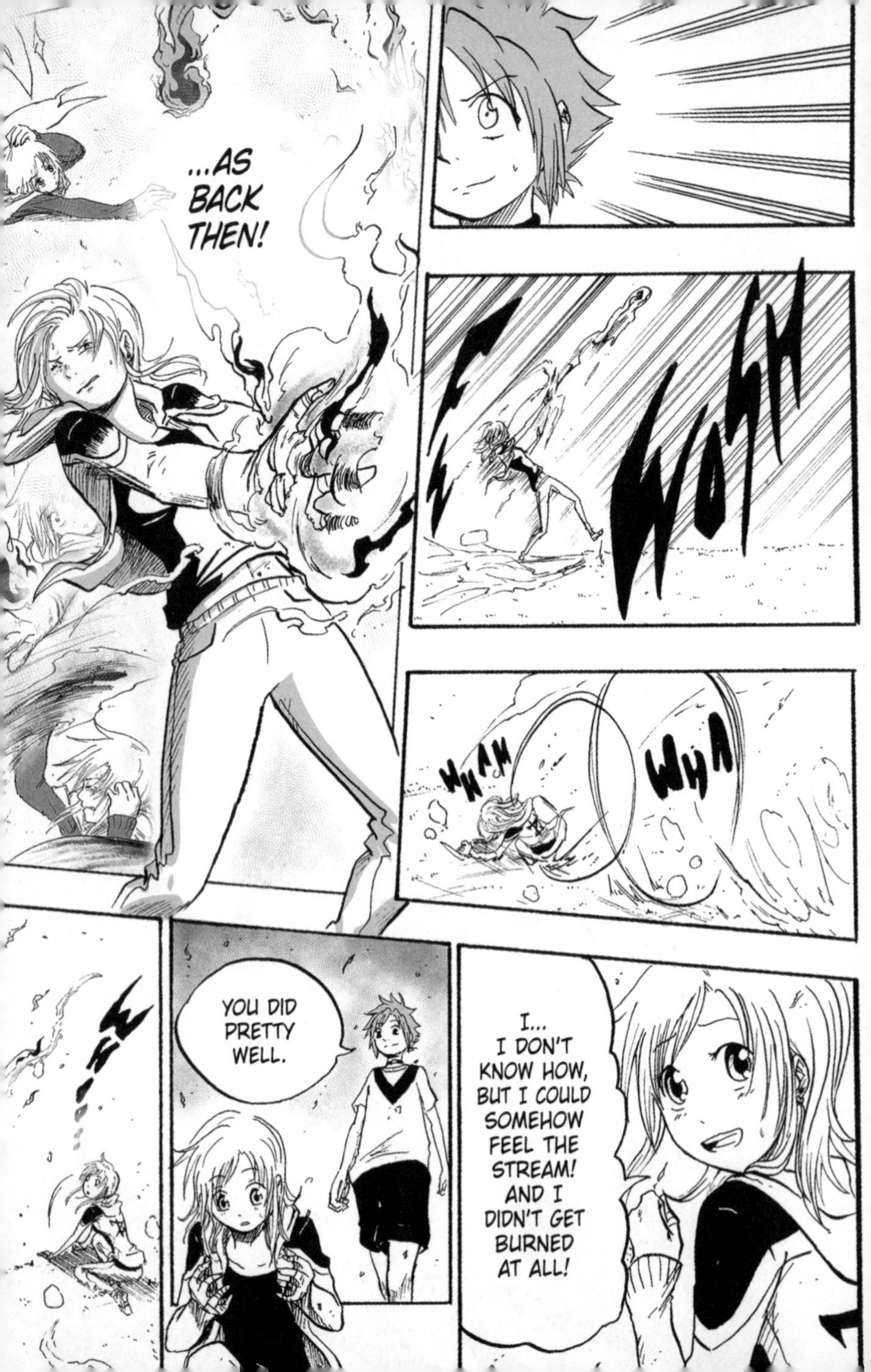
...AS BACK THEN!
YOU DID PRETTY WELL.
I... I DON'T KNOW HOW, BUT I COULD SOMEHOW FEEL THE STREAM! AND I DIDN'T GET BURNED AT ALL!

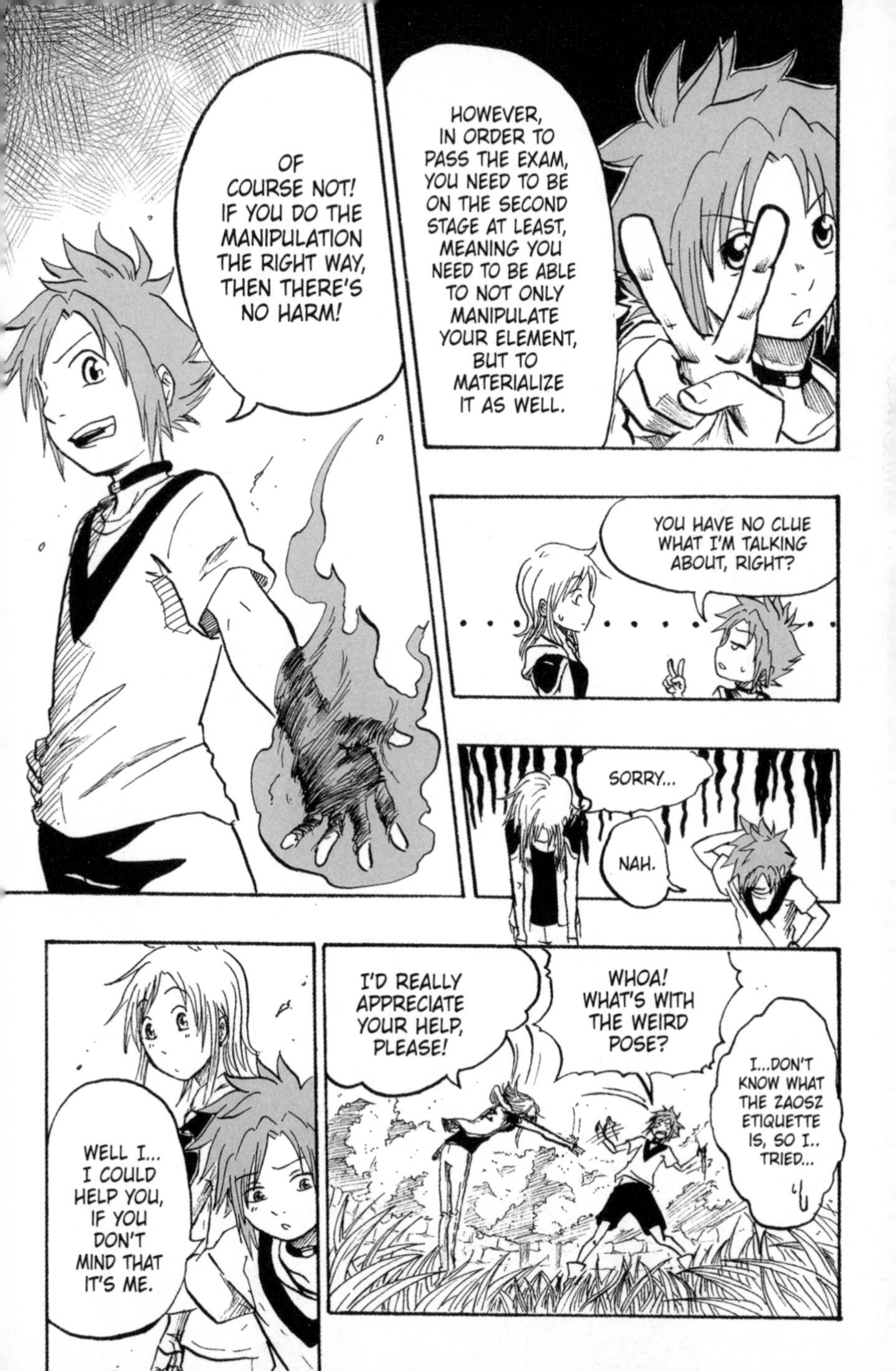
OF COURSE NOT! IF YOU DO THE MANIPULATION THE RIGHT WAY, THEN THERE'S NO HARM!
HOWEVER, IN ORDER TO PASS THE EXAM, YOU NEED TO BE ON THE SECOND STAGE AT LEAST, MEANING YOU NEED TO BE ABLE TO NOT ONLY MANIPULATE YOUR ELEMENT, BUT TO MATERIALIZE IT AS WELL.
YOU HAVE NO CLUE WHAT I'M TALKING ABOUT, RIGHT?
SORRY...
NAH.
WELL I... I COULD HELP YOU, IF YOU DON'T MIND THAT IT'S ME.
I'D REALLY APPRECIATE YOUR HELP, PLEASE!
WHOA! WHAT'S WITH THE WEIRD POSE?
I...DON'T KNOW WHAT THE ZAOSZ ETIQUETTE IS, SO I.. TRIED...

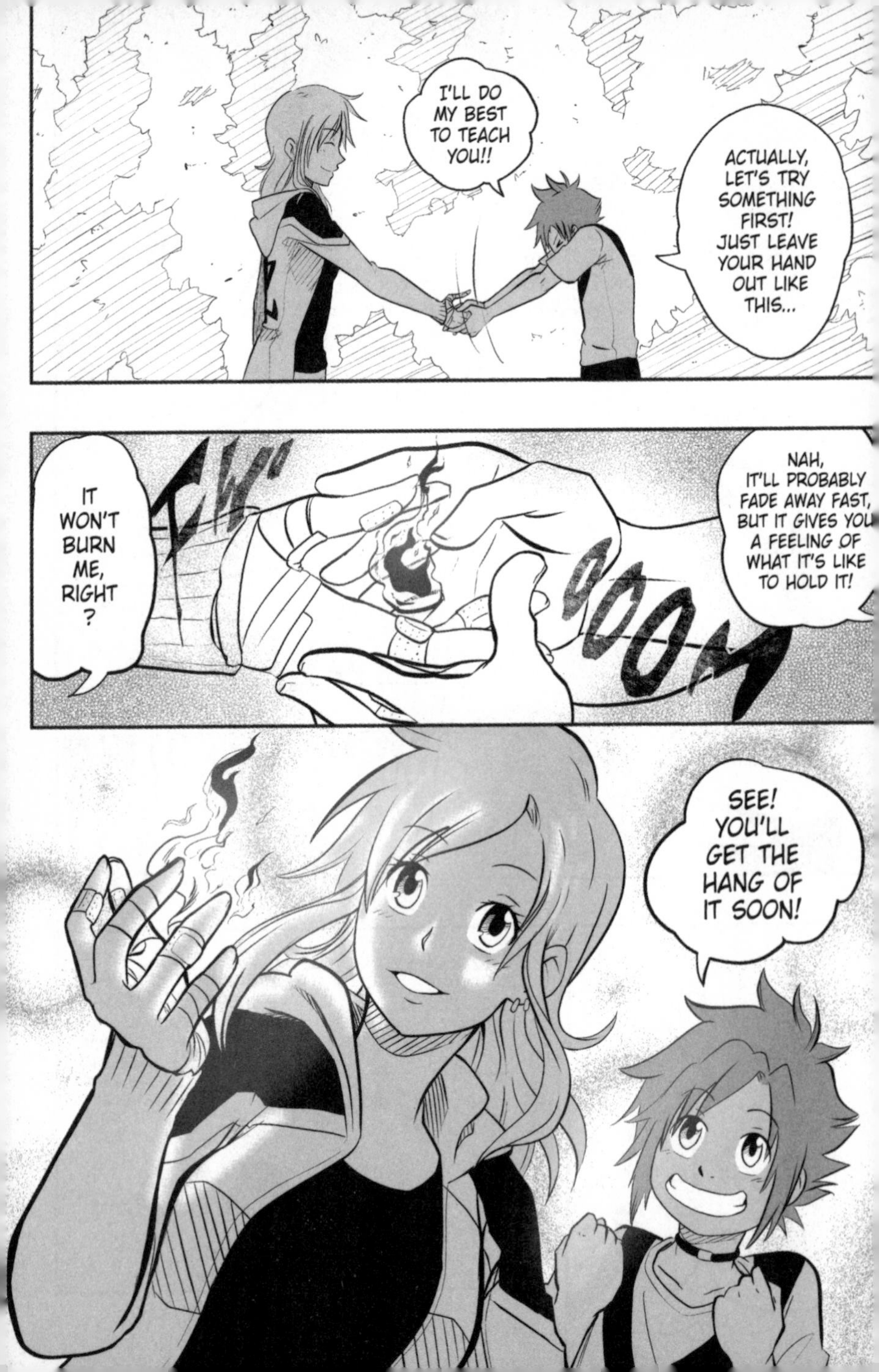
I'LL DO MY BEST TO TEACH YOU!!
ACTUALLY, LET'S TRY SOMETHING FIRST! JUST LEAVE YOUR HAND OUT LIKE THIS...
IT WON'T BURN ME, RIGHT ?
FWOOOM
NAH, IT'LL PROBABLY FADE AWAY FAST, BUT IT GIVES YOU A FEELING OF WHAT IT'S LIKE TO HOLD IT!
SEE! YOU'LL GET THE HANG OF IT SOON!

SAIGAMI

SAIGAMI

END OF VOLUME 1

ABOUT THE AUTHOR

Seny

Seny (Andrea Otília Viorál) is a European LGBTQ creator, born and raised in Pécs, Hungary. Known online as SaigamiProject, she's been active in the Western manga scene for over a decade. She aspires to create stories with proper representation of relatable, diverse characters who may be LGBTQ or strong-willed female leads who will inspire young readers. She's one of the co-founders of Saturday AM, one of the world's most diverse manga brands.

ACKNOWLEDGMENTS

IN LOVING MEMORY OF MY FATHER, WHO INTRODUCED ME
TO THE WORLD OF FANTASY BOOKS.

IT'S BEEN OVER SEVENTEEN YEARS SINCE I DREW THE
FIRST-EVER PAGE FOR SAIGAMI IN A SCHOOL NOTEBOOK.
EVER SINCE, MY LIFE HAS BEEN THROUGH SOME MAJOR
CHANGES AND UPS AND DOWNS, AND THE SAME CAN BE
SAID FOR MY PATH AS A STORYTELLER AND CREATOR.
NOW, I'M COMING BACK TO THE START OF THIS STORY
AGAIN, AND I HOPE THAT THIS BOOK CAN MEAN AN
EXCITING, FRESH BEGINNING FOR SAIGAMI AND ITS
READERS, OLD AND NEW ALIKE. THANK YOU TO EVERYONE
WHO SUPPORTED ME AND MY DREAMS FOR THESE PAST
DECADES. I TRULY APPRECIATE IT ALL!

-Seny

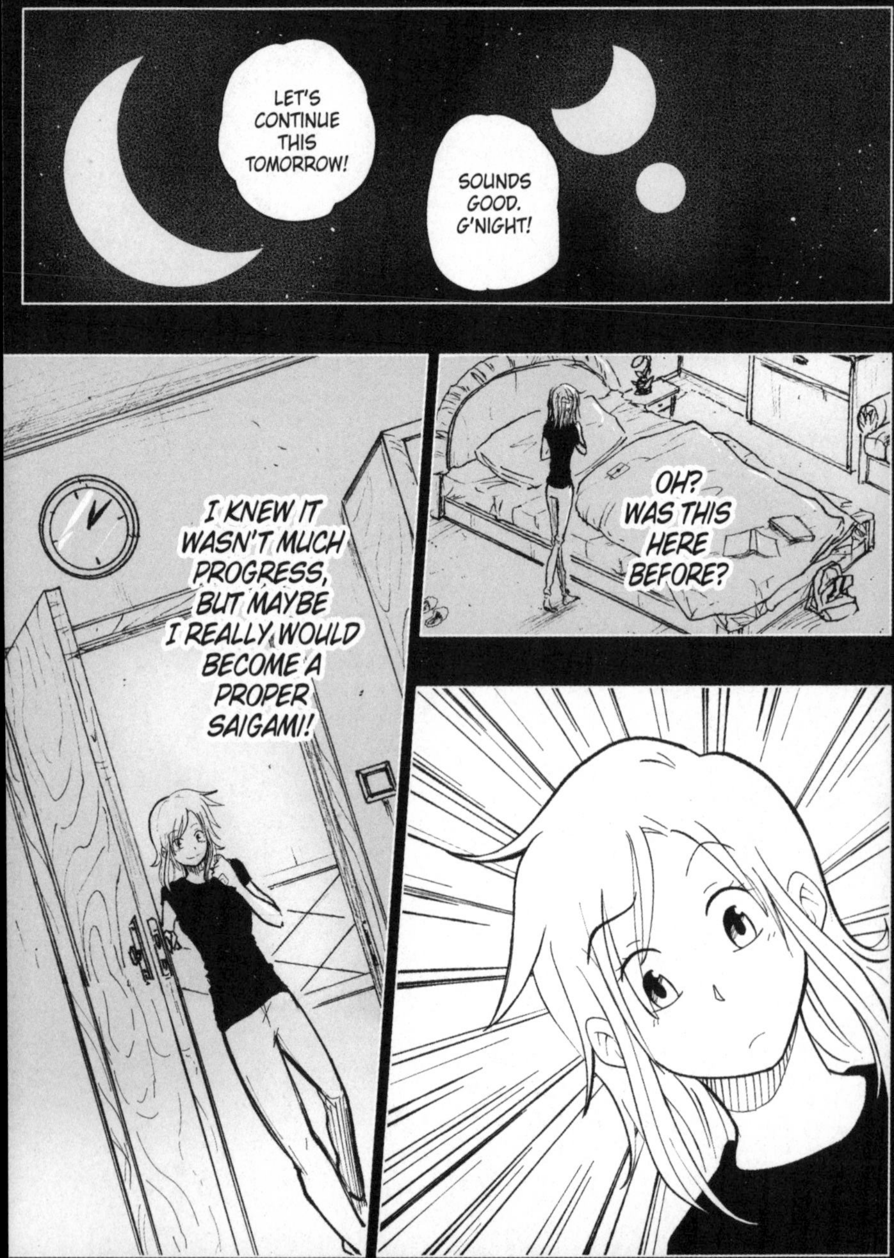
LET'S CONTINUE THIS TOMORROW!
SOUNDS GOOD. G'NIGHT!
I KNEW IT WASN'T MUCH PROGRESS, BUT MAYBE I REALLY WOULD BECOME A PROPER SAIGAMI!
OH? WAS THIS HERE BEFORE?

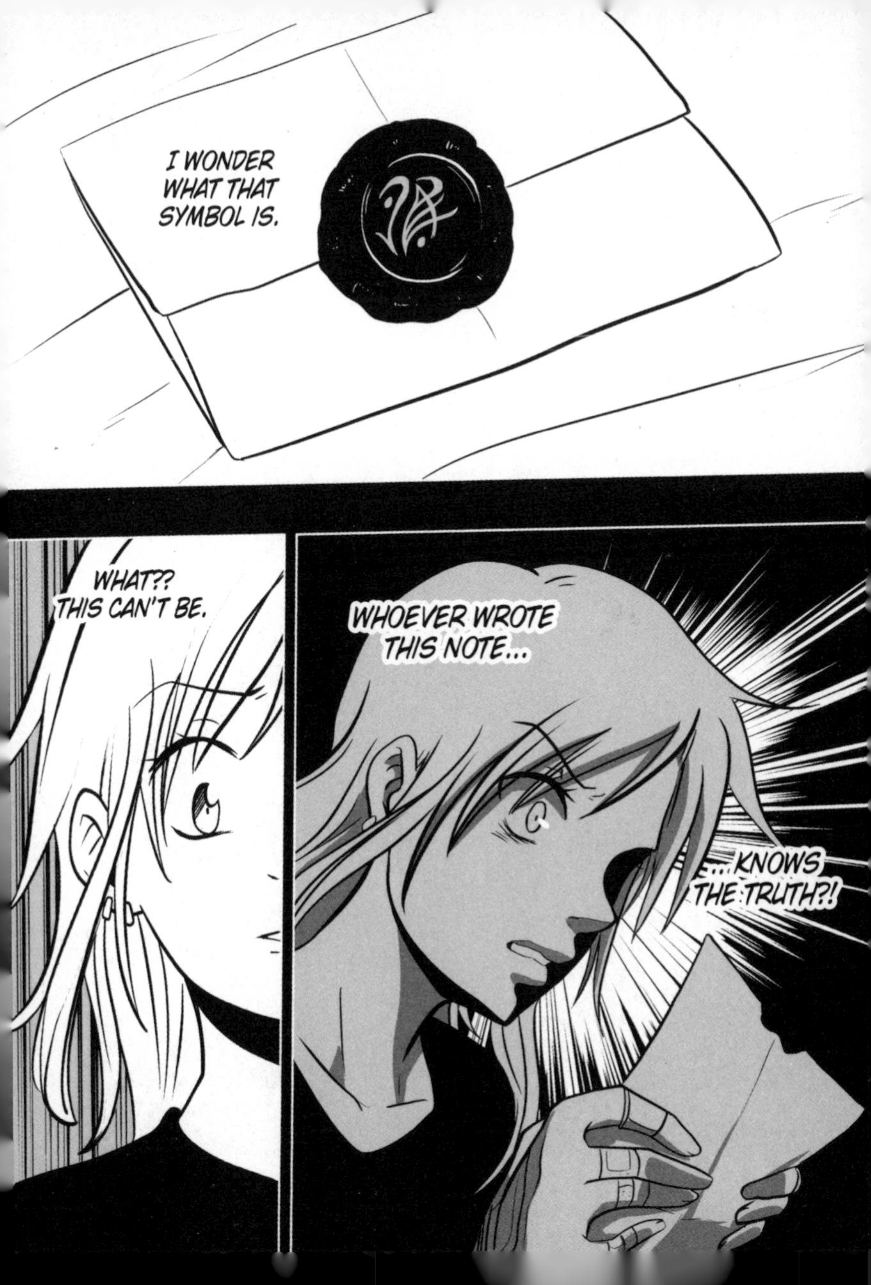
I WONDER WHAT THAT SYMBOL IS.
WHAT?? THIS CAN'T BE.
WHOEVER WROTE THIS NOTE...
...KNOWS THE TRUTH?!